China's and India's Challenge to Latin America

China's and India's Challenge to Latin America

Opportunity or Threat?

Edited by

Daniel Lederman, Marcelo Olarreaga,
and Guillermo E. Perry

THE WORLD BANK
Washington, D.C.

© 2009 The International Bank for Reconstruction and Development / The World Bank
1818 H Street NW
Washington DC 20433
Telephone: 202-473-1000
Internet: www.worldbank.org
E-mail: feedback@worldbank.org

This volume is a product of the staff of the International Bank for Reconstruction and Development / The World Bank. The findings, interpretations, and conclusions expressed in this volume do not necessarily reflect the views of the Executive Directors of The World Bank or the governments they represent.

The World Bank does not guarantee the accuracy of the data included in this work. The boundaries, colors, denominations, and other information shown on any map in this work do not imply any judgement on the part of The World Bank concerning the legal status of any territory or the endorsement or acceptance of such boundaries.

Rights and Permissions

ISBN 978-0-8213-7308-8
eISBN: 978-0-8213-7309-5
DOI: 10.1596/978-0-8213-7308-8

Library of Congress Cataloging-in-Publication Data

China's and India's challenge to Latin America : opportunity or threat? / Daniel Lederman, Marcelo Olarreaga and Guillermo Perry, editors.

    p. cm.—(Latin American Development Forum series)
  Includes bibliographical references and index.
  ISBN 978-0-8213-7308-8 (print)—ISBN 978-0-8213-7309-5 (electronic)

  1. Latin America—Foreign economic relations—China. 2. China—Foreign economic relations—Latin America. 3. Latin America—Foreign economic relations—India. 4. India—Foreign economic relations—Latin America. I. Lederman, Daniel, 1968- II. Olarreaga, M. (Marcelo). III. Perry, Guillermo.

  HF1480.5.Z4C634 2008
  337.8051—dc22

                                                                    2008024106

Cover design: ULTRAdesigns

Latin American Development Forum Series

This series was created in 2003 to promote debate, disseminate information and analysis, and convey the excitement and complexity of the most topical issues in economic and social development in Latin America and the Caribbean. It is sponsored by the Inter-American Development Bank, the United Nations Economic Commission for Latin America and the Caribbean, and the World Bank. The manuscripts chosen for publication represent the highest quality in each institution's research and activity output and have been selected for their relevance to the academic community, policy makers, researchers, and interested readers.

Advisory Committee Members

Other Titles in the Latin American Development Forum Series

Does the Investment Climate Matter? Microeconomic Foundations of Growth in Latin America (forthcoming) by Pablo Fajnzylber, José Luis Guasch, and J. Humberto López, editors

Innovative Experiences in Access to Finance: Market-Friendly Roles for the Visible Hand? (forthcoming) by Augusto de la Torre, Juan Carlos Gozzi, and Sergio L. Schmukler

Job Creation in Latin America and the Caribbean: Trends and Policy Challenges (forthcoming) by Carmen Pagés, Gaëlle Pierre, and Stefano Scarpetta

Measuring Inequality of Opportunities in Latin America and the Caribbean (forthcoming) by Ricardo Paes de Barros, Francisco H. G. Ferreira, José R. Molinas Vega, and Jaime Saavedra Chanduvi

The Promise of Early Childhood Development in Latin America (forthcoming) by Emiliana Vegas and Lucrecia Santibáñez

Fiscal Policy, Stabilization, and Growth: Prudence or Abstinence? (2008) by Guillermo E. Perry, Luis Servén, and Rodrigo Suescún, editors

The Impact of Private Sector Participation in Infrastructure: Lights, Shadows, and the Road Ahead (2008) by Luis Andres, José Luis Guasch, Thomas Haven, and Vivien Foster

Raising Student Learning in Latin America: Challenges for the 21st Century (2008) by Emiliana Vegas and Jenny Petrow

Remittances and Development: Lessons from Latin America (2008) by Pablo Fajnzylber and J. Humberto López, editors

About the Contributors

César Calderón is an economist in the World Bank's Office of the Chief Economist for Latin America and the Caribbean. Previously he worked in the research department of the Central Bank of Chile and the Central Reserve Bank of Peru. He obtained a PhD in economics from the University of Rochester. He has published in the area of open economy macroeconomics and growth.

Carlos Casacuberta is senior lecturer in the Department of Economics of the Social Sciences Faculty at the Universidad de la República, Montevideo, Uruguay. He holds an MS from the London School of Economics and Political Science. He has published various articles on international trade and productivity.

Lucio Castro is currently director of the Program on International Economics at the Centro de Implementación de Políticas Públicas para la Equidad y el Crecimiento, a leading think tank in Buenos Aires, Argentina. He is a PhD candidate in economics at the University of Sussex, England. He holds a master's degree from the Program in Economic Policy Management, Columbia University.

Javier Cravino is a PhD candidate in economics at the University of California, Los Angeles. He previously studied economics at Universidad Torcuato di Tella in Buenos Aires, Argentina. He was a consultant to the World Bank's Development Research Group when the research for this book was undertaken.

Robert C. Feenstra is the C. Bryan Cameron Distinguished Chair in International Economics at the University of California, Davis. He is also the director of the International Trade and Investment Program of the National Bureau of Economic Research and director of the Center for International Data at the University of California, Davis. He is a renowned authority in the theory and empirics of international trade.

Caroline Freund is a senior economist in the World Bank's Development Research Group. She obtained a PhD in economics from Columbia University. Before joining the World Bank, she was an economist in the

International Finance Division of the Federal Reserve Board. She has published numerous articles on international trade, regional trade agreements, and competitiveness.

Néstor Gandelman is the director of the Economics Department at Universidad ORT Uruguay. He holds an MA and a PhD in economics from the University of Rochester. He has published numerous articles on international trade, enterprise productivity, and labor markets.

Gordon H. Hanson is the director of the Center on Pacific Economies and professor of economics at the University of California, San Diego, where he holds faculty positions in the Graduate School of International Relations and Pacific Studies and the Department of Economics. Professor Hanson is coeditor of the *Journal of Development Economics*, a research associate at the National Bureau of Economic Research, a member of the Council on Foreign Relations, and a senior research fellow at the Bureau for Research and Economic Analysis of Development. He obtained his PhD in economics from the Massachusetts Institute of Technology. Professor Hanson has published extensively on topics related to international trade, foreign investment, and international migration.

Hiau Looi Kee is a senior economist with the World Bank's Development Research Group. She received her PhD in economics from the University of California, Davis. She has a master's degree in social science in economics from the National University of Singapore, and a BA from the National Taiwan University. Her published research focuses on trade, productivity, and growth.

Daniel Lederman is a senior economist in the World Bank's Development Research Group. He holds MA and PhD degrees from the Johns Hopkins University School of Advanced International Studies. He is the author of numerous books and articles on Latin American development.

Marcelo Olarreaga is professor of economics and international relations at the University of Geneva. He was a senior economist in the World Bank's Development Research Group when the research for this book was undertaken. He is also a research fellow at the Center for Economic Policy Research in London, England. He obtained an MA from the University of Sussex and a PhD from the University of Geneva. He has published extensively on trade, development, and political economy.

Çağlar Özden is a senior economist in the World Bank's Development Research Group. He received his PhD from Stanford University and BS from Cornell University. His main research area is international trade with a focus on services, preferential trade programs, and international migration.

Guillermo E. Perry was the World Bank's Chief Economist for Latin America and the Caribbean when this project was launched. He is currently a research associate in Fedesarrollo, a think tank in Bogotá, Colombia, and a nonresident fellow in the Center for Global Development in Washington, DC. He conducted graduate studies in operations research and economics at the Massachusetts Institute of Technology. He has held distinguished public service positions in Colombia, including Minister of Finance, Minister of Energy, and Budget Director. He has published on fiscal and public economics, trade, innovation, and growth.

Raymond Robertson is associate professor of economics and director of the Latin American Studies Program at Macalester College in St. Paul, Minnesota. He received his PhD in economics from the University of Texas at Austin. His publications on the effects of trade on wages in Mexico are well known around the world.

Daniel Saslavsky is an economist with the Centro de Implementación de Políticas Públicas para la Equidad y el Crecimiento in Buenos Aires, Argentina. He holds a _licenciatura_ in economics and a master's degree in international studies from Universidad Torcuato Di Tella in Argentina.

Isidro Soloaga is a researcher at El Colegio de México in Mexico City and a consultant for the United Nations Development Programme. He was previously professor of economics at Universidad de las Américas in Puebla, Mexico. He received his PhD in agricultural and resource economics from the University of Maryland, College Park. He has published widely on topics related to international trade, trade agreements, agricultural development, and poverty.

Contents

Foreword

Napoleon's prescient warning two centuries ago was not so much that the sleeping giant, China, will awaken, but that her awakening "will shake the world." China is now of course truly awake and transforming the world profoundly in multiple dimensions. The global economy is perhaps where the "shaking" produced by China is most noticeable. In a span of less than 30 years, China has gone from an inward-looking, slow-growing economy to a fast-growing and increasingly formidable presence in both the demand and the supply sides of international markets for goods, services, and capital. Along with China's colossal entry into the global marketplace, we have also witnessed a similarly impressive economic awakening of India. The obvious question is, what does the rising economic importance of China and India mean for the rest of the world in terms of pain and gain? This book asks this question from the perspective of Latin America.

When the research that led to this book began, Latin America seemed more concerned with the potential pains than with the potential gains of the China and India effect. The specter of a veritable invasion of cheap imports, especially from China, was prominent in the minds of many a policy maker and labor union leader, along with the fear that such an invasion would destroy vast sectors of the local economy, particularly in labor-intensive manufacturing activities. Arguably, such fears seem to have subsided recently, as the seemingly insatiable demand of the Chinese economy, especially for foods, fuels, and metals, has helped sustain terms-of-trade gains and output growth for a significant number of Latin American countries, particularly in the Southern Hemisphere. The concern in policy circles seems to be shifting nowadays toward the potentially adverse side effects of a respecialization of the Latin economies in primary commodity production. These swings in concerns and fears vis-à-vis the challenges that China and India pose for Latin America are, by themselves, a signal that public perceptions tend to mix myth with reality. This book, edited by Daniel Lederman, Marcelo Olarreaga, and Guillermo E. Perry, sets out to disentangle facts from illusions. It offers lucid and rigorous assessments of how the rise of China and India in international trade, foreign direct investment (FDI), non-FDI flows, and innovation have affected

Latin America, and how Latin businesses and governments have adjusted and should respond.

The authors' meticulous analyses of available data shed light on what really is going on as Latin America increasingly interacts with China and India directly and through third markets. Despite important caveats, some clear messages emerge. First, as most economists since the times of Adam Smith and Ricardo would have anticipated, the actual gains (static and dynamic) for Latin America from engaging in the global economy where these two new giants walk seem to clearly outweigh the transitional adjustment pains. In effect, the expansion of China (much more than that of India) seems to be pulling and crowding in growth in the Latin American region. Interestingly, in the trade area, this is driven only in part by the direct demand for Latin American exports; indirect effects seem to dominate, namely, demand spillovers in third markets and rising prices of natural resources where Latin America (especially South America) has a comparative advantage. Similarly, the authors find that the concerns with displacement or crowding out of Latin America in markets for FDI and innovation are not warranted. The higher involvement of China and India in FDI and patenting is found to be associated with higher involvement for Latin economies as well.

Second, adjustment pains are indeed part of the process and require an adequate policy response. The pain resulting from displacement in trade in goods (and, to a much less significant extent, in FDI flows) is focalized in some specific industries (for example, electrical machinery, electronics, furniture, textiles, and transport equipment) and subregions (particularly Mexico and to some extent Central America), where competition with China is head to head. By contrast, the fast rise in high-productivity services exports from India, although clearly outperforming Latin America, does not seem to have displaced Latin American services exports to the United States, particularly in tourism and health, where geographic proximity gives the region a clear edge.

Finally, although the rising economic importance of China and India provides potential benefits for Latin America, these are far from having been fully exploited. The authors emphasize that the main opportunities for productive expansion in Latin America that China and India open are concentrated in the areas of natural resources and knowledge-based production. Perhaps insufficiently discussed in the book is the associated corollary for Latin America's growth agenda—namely, that, given the rise of China and India, some countries can no longer count on progressing to a higher growth path by exporting manufactured products that are intensive in unskilled, low-cost labor. The future economic dynamism in the region will, therefore, largely depend on the region's capacity to transform its natural resource wealth into improvements in human capital, infrastructure, and innovation, and on its ability to enhance the knowledge content of its production. The related question is, of course, whether Latin American political and institutional processes will support economic policies consistent with such a transformation. Although this book does not address this latter question, it certainly provides us with the necessary analysis, information, and insights. The authors' sound and balanced assessment of the evidence helps us move beyond popular misperceptions and forces us to focus on the relevant issues.

Augusto de la Torre
Chief Economist for the Latin America and the Caribbean Region
The World Bank

Acknowledgments

This book summarizes and presents results from a large set of background papers commissioned for a Regional Study sponsored by the Office of the Chief Economist for the Latin America and the Caribbean Region of the World Bank. The full set of papers is referenced in the first chapter and is available at www.worldbank.org/lac.

We are grateful to Peter Drysdale, Andrea Goldstein, Gordon Hanson, Bernard Hoekman, Pravin Krishna, Rajiv Kumar, and L. Alan Winters, and participants in an authors' workshop in Washington, DC; at a SCAPE conference in Singapore; and at a conference sponsored by the Center for Global Development in Beijing for discussions and insightful comments. We presented some of the project results at the U.S. International Trade Commission's Economics Research seminar series, and we thank Judy Dean for inviting us. Maria Fernanda Rosales and Eliana Rubiano provided stellar research assistance for some of the chapters and papers commissioned for this project.

We also gratefully acknowledge the comments and suggestions written by two anonymous referees, who read the preliminary book manuscript. We have tried to address all their expressed concerns, but all remaining errors are the responsibility of the editors.

Augusto de la Torre, the World Bank's Chief Economist for the Latin America and the Caribbean Region since September 2007, provided gracious support for the completion of this project. Santiago Pombo-Bejarano and Shana Wagger steered this project through the publication and referee process. Janice Tuten patiently pushed us to complete the editorial process.

Abbreviations

ASM	asymmetries in the structures of imports
ASP	asymmetries in the structures of production
ASX	asymmetries in the structures of exports
BEA	Bureau of Economic Analysis (U.S. Department of Commerce)
BPT	business, professional, and technical services
CACM	Central America, the Caribbean, and Mexico
CEPAL	Comisión Económica para America Latina y el Caribe
CES	constant elasticity of substitution
ESI	export similarity index
EU	European Union
FCS	foreign capital stocks
FDI	foreign direct investment
FTA	free trade area
GDP	gross domestic product
GDPPC	per capita GDP
GL	Grubel-Lloyd
GLI	Grubel-Lloyd index of intra-industry trade
GMM	generalized method of moments
HS	harmonized system
IIT	intra-industry trade
INE	Instituto Nacional de Estadística
IPI	industrial production index
ISIC	International Standard Industrial Classification
IV	instrumental variables
KCM	knowledge-capital model
LAC	Latin America and the Caribbean
NAFTA	North American Free Trade Agreement
NBER	National Bureau of Economic Research
NTB	nontariff barrier

OECD	Organisation for Economic Co-operation and Development
OLS	ordinary least squares
OPS	other private services
SCM	South America, Central America, and Mexico
SITC	Standard International Trade Classification
UN	United Nations
UN Comtrade	United Nations Commodity Trade Statistics Database
UNCTAD	United Nations Conference on Trade and Development
WDI	*World Development Indicators*
WTO	World Trade Organization

Part I

Introduction

1

Latin America's Response to China and India: Overview of Research Findings and Policy Implications

Daniel Lederman, Marcelo Olarreaga, and Guillermo E. Perry[*]

Motivation and Summary of Findings

China's and India's fast economic growth since 1990 is paralleled only by their growing presence in policy discussions throughout the Latin America and the Caribbean (LAC) region. The success of these Asian countries is looked upon with admiration, but there is also concern about the effects that growing Chinese and Indian exports may have on the manufacturing and service sectors throughout LAC. Blame for the private sector's poor performance in some LAC countries often falls on the growing presence of China, and to a lesser extent India, in world markets (see box 1.1).

This overview summarizes the results of a large set of background papers commissioned for a regional study under the direction of the Office of the Chief Economist for Latin America and the Caribbean at the World Bank. The papers are listed in the references for this chapter and can be found at www.worldbank.org/lac.

* The authors are grateful to Peter Drysdale, Andrea Goldstein, Gordon Hanson, Bernard Hoekman, Rajiv Kumar, Pravin Krishna, Alan Winters, and participants at an authors' workshop in Washington, DC; at a SCAPE conference in Singapore; and at a Center for Global Development conference in Beijing for discussions and insightful comments. Maria Fernanda Rosales and Eliana Rubiano provided stellar research assistance.

Box 1.1 Public Opinion in LAC about China's Growth

"[We] must not repeat the mistakes of the nineties, when an 'invasion' of Chinese products destroyed entire sectors of our industry ...." Communiqué of CAME (Medium Enterprises Association of Argentina), April 6, 2004.

"Countries around the world are bracing for a surge of cheap imports from China, which benefits from cheap, union-free labor and rising productivity." *Taipei Times*, January 2, 2005.

"'Textiles and shoes are the sectors most harmed by the Chinese,' says Dilma Rousseff" (Brazilian President Lula's chief of staff). Bloomberg, September 29, 2005.

"I made it very clear to Minister Bo Xilai that we will take the legal steps to give Brazilian industry the right to protect itself." Luis Furlan, Brazilian Minister for Industry, Development and Commerce, after meeting with his Chinese counterpart, October 4, 2005, as reported by Yahoo!

"It is not clear whether or not China is actually competitive. Perhaps it is, but perhaps its current success is based on the fact that they do not respect a series of rules that other countries, such as Mexico, do respect." Maxico's President Fox at the October 2002 Asia-Pacific Economic Cooperation summit, as reported on October 22 by *Reforma*.

Part of the concern in LAC can be attributed to its loss of economic importance compared with the two Asian economies, despite a broad range of reforms in the region, which started in the mid- to late 1980s. In 1980, LAC's economy was twice as large as those of China and India, which jointly represented 3 percent of world gross domestic product (GDP). By 2004, LAC was 20 percent smaller than China and India. Today, China is the sixth largest economy in the world when measured according to GDP and India the tenth. Together they account for 6.4 percent of world GDP.[1]

The fast economic growth of China and India was accompanied by their rapid integration into world markets while LAC lagged behind. Today, China's and India's combined share of world exports is 50 percent larger than LAC's share, whereas in 1990 the reverse was true. In the late 1980s, LAC had a trade-to-GDP ratio roughly equal to the trade-to-GDP ratio of China, and two times larger than the trade-to-GDP ratio of India. By 2004, the trade-to-GDP ratio of China was 35 percent larger than the trade-to-GDP ratio of LAC, and India's trade-to-GDP ratio was only 14 percent smaller than LAC's. China is currently the third largest trading economy in the world (just behind the United States and Germany), while India ranks 25th.

Similar trends are observed in inward flows of foreign direct investment (FDI), trade in services, and innovation. In 1990, the stock of foreign capital in LAC from Organisation for Economic Co-operation and Development (OECD) countries was five times larger than OECD stock in China and India. By 2004, OECD's stock of foreign capital in LAC was only twice as large. China's and India's exports of services to the United States increased more than threefold during the period 1994–2004, whereas LAC exports increased twofold. Similarly, the number of patents registered in the United States by China and India was 75 percent less than the number registered by LAC in 1990. By 2004, China and India jointly registered twice as many patents as LAC, despite China's and India's lower levels of development when measured by GDP per capita.

A superficial look at these trends would suggest that China's and India's growth has been pushing LAC countries out of world markets, which is probably why defensive strategies dominate policy discussions in the region. However, China's and India's rapid growth can be seen as an opportunity that actually has been helping LAC economies, not only because of the rapid growth of the Chinese and Indian domestic markets, but also because of the opportunities their growth may offer for new production possibilities, FDI, and financial flows. The objective of this book is to disentangle these forces and assess how the overall growth of trade, FDI, finance, and innovation in China and India has affected LAC, and how LAC firms and governments have adjusted and should respond.

The main findings in this book indicate that the growth of China and India has not been a zero-sum game for LAC countries, but there is significant heterogeneity across LAC subregions. First, the growth of the two Asian economies, especially China, offers a growing opportunity for LAC exporters to these markets, although it has not yet been fully exploited. China and India also represent a growing source of financing (Chinese FDI in LAC reached US$4 billion in 2004, and the stock of Chinese FDI in Mexico in 2004 exceeded US$28 billion). As China in particular liberalizes its financial sector, the potential for becoming an important source of financing for LAC economies is large. In 2004, China was among the top 10 creditors in the world and India will soon be among them if current trends continue. With regard to innovation, the scope for bilateral cooperation is large and is exemplified by the Chinese-Brazilian agreements on satellite development, which have led to the joint production of remote sensor satellites used for space imaging. China provided 70 percent and Brazil 30 percent of the financing and technology. Bilateral agreements are also in place between Chile and China in the areas of mining and geosciences, plant quarantine, and forestry (Dominguez et al. 2006).

Moreover, there is evidence of positive net overall effects for LAC economies associated with the larger presence of China and India in third markets. For example, the rising correlation between the growth of the two Asian economies and LAC economies (with the exception of Central America and the Caribbean) seems to have been driven mainly by demand externalities and higher prices for commodities for which LAC has a comparative advantage. At the aggregate level, higher levels of Chinese and Indian trade, inward flows of FDI, and patenting are found to be generally associated with higher levels for LAC economies as well, or at least not declining levels of FDI or patenting. The growing presence of intra-industry trade, production networks, and the production opportunities facilitated by cheaper imports, lower cost of capital, and innovation are some additional channels through which trade, FDI, and innovation externalities may have positively affected LAC economies. Overall, the evidence suggests that concerns regarding China's and India's displacement of LAC from FDI, export, and innovation markets are misplaced. On the contrary, LAC has been benefiting from the two Asian economies' growing presence in world markets.

The aggregate gains have been accompanied by some pain because certain industries, firms, and subregions have been negatively affected by the rapid growth of the two Asian economies. The evidence discussed in this book supports this view, particularly in industrial and electrical machinery, electronics, furniture, textiles, and transport equipment, mainly in Mexico and to some extent in Central American countries. However, most of the deterioration in the position of LAC exports in third markets relative to China's and India's has to do more with domestic supply-side conditions than with lower demand for LAC products caused by China's and India's increase in market shares.

There is also some weak evidence of inflows of FDI into LAC's manufacturing sector being substituted for FDI into China's and India's manufacturing sectors, particularly in Central America and the Southern Cone. But these effects are not statistically robust and complementarities are the norm even in manufacturing. Furthermore, China has become a large net exporter of capital as a result of its accumulation of reserves, which has contributed to keeping international interest rates low and global liquidity ample.

In the service sector, India has outperformed Latin America in export growth since 1993. However, LAC's exports of services to the United States (its main export market) are seven times larger than China's and India's combined service exports to the United States. This partly reflects one large advantage LAC has over China and India for the delivery of services to U.S. consumers: proximity. This is particularly important in the tourism subsector, where LAC has been performing relatively well when compared with the rest of the world,[2] but also in health and retirement services. With regard to displacement of LAC service exports by Indian service exports, only one of the eight service subsectors examined (other business, professional, and technical services) exhibits robust evidence of India's export of services displacing LAC exports. For other subsectors, the impact of India's growth on LAC exports of services is not robust across specifications.[3]

Growing imports from China and India are also having an impact on manufacturing unemployment and factor adjustment costs in LAC, as expected, given the lower labor costs in the two Asian economies, but the economic significance is found to be marginal.[4] This does not mean that addressing the high unemployment levels in the manufacturing sector of some LAC countries, as well as the factor adjustment costs faced by LAC firms, is not a priority.

Moreover, the specialization pattern of LAC is changing toward natural-resource- and scientific-knowledge-intensive industries, and part of this change can be attributed to China's and India's rapid growth. Evidence also shows that China and India may be pushing some LAC manufacturing sectors in some countries toward low-wage, unskilled-labor-intensive activities (for example, the apparel sectors in Haiti and Nicaragua), because there is more scope for substitution in skilled-labor-intensive industries. In other countries and sectors, in contrast, firms are adjusting toward higher-quality and skill-intensive products (for example, apparel in Costa Rica and the Dominican Republic). Such differential effects are explained by variations in both factor endowments and the quality of policies and institutions.

The move toward natural-resource-intensive products implies a more concentrated export bundle in LAC. This raises concerns regarding the vulnerability of LAC to future (negative) terms-of-trade shocks, but more important, there is also a feeling within LAC that the gains associated with natural-resource-intensive exports are not being widely spread. The economic—and political—sustainability of this specialization in natural-resource-intensive sectors depends on the extent to which gains are shared with owners of other factors of production.

In sum, evidence suggests that at the aggregate level the effect of China's and India's growth on LAC has been positive, even though some industries in some countries may have been negatively affected. The rapid growth of China's and India's demand for LAC products (commodities, but also manufactured products), which is not being fully exploited by LAC exporters, and complementarities in trade flows, FDI, and innovation are the forces that explain why LAC countries should be rooting for more growth in China and India. But there is no gain without pain. To be able to take advantage of the opportunity offered by China's and India's growth, some industries will need to adjust to stronger competition from the two rapidly growing Asian economies. The need for adjustment varies across LAC countries depending on their factor endowments and their exposure to direct competition from China and India. For example, even though the trend changed around 2003, Mexico is the only country in LAC whose comparative advantage had been moving in the same direction as the comparative advantage of the two Asian economies. This obviously calls for larger adjustment needs than in the rest of the region.

With regard to policy implications, the evidence suggests change is needed in the policy priorities for the LAC region. To help the emerging adjustment of firms toward higher-quality and scientific-knowledge-intensive products, more emphasis should be placed on education policies that would help workers acquire the necessary skills. Support to both patentable and nonpatentable innovations should also be strengthened to help private sector firms adjust toward more scientific-knowledge-intensive sectors and products. The importance of policies to facilitate rural development and natural-resource-based industries and management should also rise to help LAC economies better respond to the higher demand and prices for commodities. Also, policies and private-sector initiatives should aim to exploit the untapped opportunities offered by the growth of the two Asian economies' internal markets through export and FDI promotion activities, as well as to help LAC firms better integrate into global production chains. In the short term, negatively affected industries and factors of production require stronger safety nets to help workers during the transition.

The rest of this introduction is organized as follows: The next section summarizes the evidence on the positive aggregate effects of China's and India's growth in world trade markets, FDI flows, and innovation activities on LAC economies, and is followed by a section presenting evidence on the effects of China's and India's growth within industries, concluding that negative effects are limited to certain manufacturing and service sectors, in particular in Mexico and to a lesser extent in Central America and the Caribbean. Next is a section that summarizes evidence of the effects of China's and India's growth on specialization patterns and factor adjustments, and actual and potential policy responses by LAC governments. The final section summarizes policy implications.

The Growth of China and India Is Not a Zero-Sum Game for LAC

As mentioned, the growth of China and India could have affected LAC economies through at least three channels: trade, FDI and financial flows, and innovation. These topics are covered in the following discussion.

Trade

Since the mid-1990s, business cycles in LAC and the two Asian economies have become increasingly correlated, with the exception of economies in Central America, where the correlation with China has been declining, especially since 1999, and Mexico, which has had a stable correlation with China, even though it has been increasing since the late 1990s (see figure 1.1). This suggests that the growth of China and India is partially mirrored by most LAC economies.

In chapter 2, Calderón builds an empirical model to disentangle the forces behind this synchronization of business cycles. The author explains 55 percent of the change in output correlation between LAC and China,

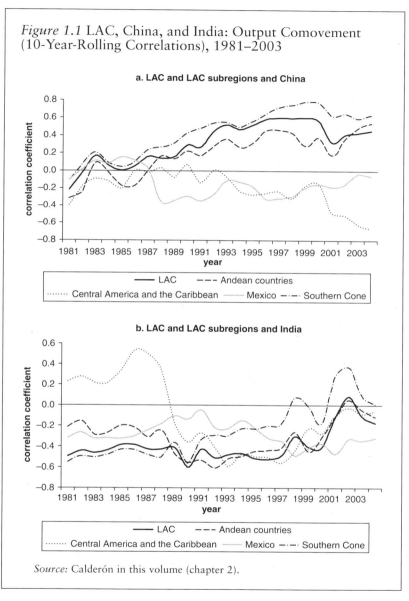

Figure 1.1 LAC, China, and India: Output Comovement (10-Year-Rolling Correlations), 1981–2003

Source: Calderón in this volume (chapter 2).

and 50 percent of the change between LAC and India, through demand spillovers, changes in production structure asymmetries, bilateral intra-industry trade, and interindustry trade.[5] As shown in figure 1.2, most of the rising correlation with China can be attributed to demand spillovers,[6] particularly in small LAC economies.[7] The same pattern is observed for India.

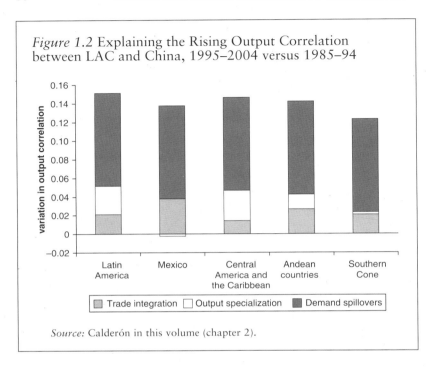

Figure 1.2 Explaining the Rising Output Correlation between LAC and China, 1995–2004 versus 1985–94

Source: Calderón in this volume (chapter 2).

Part of these demand spillovers can be explained by the rising correlation of business cycles in China and India with world commodity prices, in which LAC tends to have a natural comparative advantage (see figure 1.3).

The largest increases in correlation with China's industrial production index occurred in metals and minerals (driven by copper, and since 2004, by iron ore and zinc) and in beverages (driven by coffee); see figure 1.4. Although care must be exercised in inferring causation from these results, the coefficient of the impact of Chinese industrial output on the world price of crude oil is also large and increased from 0.81 at the beginning of 2000 to 1.88 by the end of 2005. Sugar prices also seem to have benefited from the growth of China and India, whereas the prices of soybeans and wheat showed a strong and rising correlation with the Chinese production index until late 2004, but a declining correlation thereafter. Similar patterns are observed with the correlation of Indian industrial output and world commodity prices, with the exception of minerals.

This rising correlation occurred as the share of China and India in world demand for commodities increased significantly.[8] Figure 1.5 shows the share of China and India in world markets for selected commodities in 1990 and 2004. For most commodities in figure 1.5, China's and India's share of world consumption has more than doubled over the period and is as high as 25 percent.

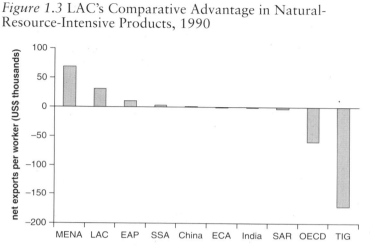

Figure 1.3 LAC's Comparative Advantage in Natural-Resource-Intensive Products, 1990

Source: Perry and Olarreaga (2007).

Note: The natural resource index is calculated as the trade balance (exports minus imports) in ores, minerals, fuel, agricultural raw materials, and food divided by the labor force. Units are US$ per worker. MENA = Middle East and North Africa; EAP = East Asia and Pacific; SSA= Sub-Saharan Africa; ECA = Europe and Central Asia; SAR = South Asia; OECD = Organisation for Economic Co-operation and Development; and TIG = the three original East Asian Tigers (Republic of Korea, Singapore, and Hong Kong [China]).

Moreover, even though the absolute level is still small in some commodities (for example, petroleum), the change in quantities consumed by China and India accounts for a larger share of world price movements observed during the period (figure 1.6).[9]

The fact that the rising correlation in business cycles seems to be better explained by demand externalities, rather than by increases in bilateral trade flows, is confirmed in chapter 3 by Lederman, Olarreaga, and Soloaga, who use a modern gravity model of trade to explain both the impact of China's and India's GDP growth on LAC's exports to these two markets, as well as the impact that the growth of China's and India's presence in world markets had on LAC exports to third markets.[10] The positive impact of the former is large but is dominated by the latter. The estimations presented in chapter 3 deal with various econometric issues, including exporter and importer time-invariant characteristics as well as systematic heteroskedasticity.[11]

The impact of China's GDP growth during the period 2000–04 on its demand for LAC goods can explain about 7 percent of LAC's exports in 2004. Despite the rapid increase in bilateral exports to China (and India)

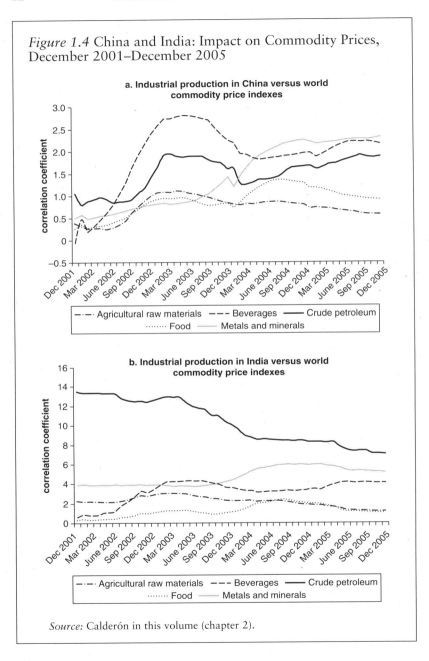

Figure 1.4 China and India: Impact on Commodity Prices, December 2001–December 2005

a. Industrial production in China versus world commodity price indexes

b. Industrial production in India versus world commodity price indexes

Source: Calderón in this volume (chapter 2).

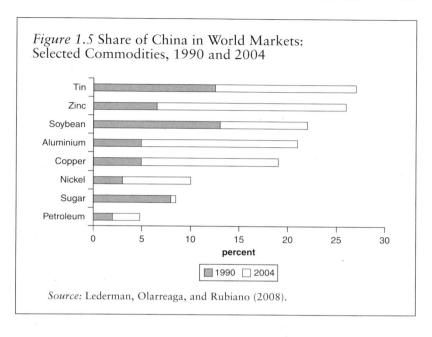

Figure 1.5 Share of China in World Markets: Selected Commodities, 1990 and 2004

Source: Lederman, Olarreaga, and Rubiano (2008).

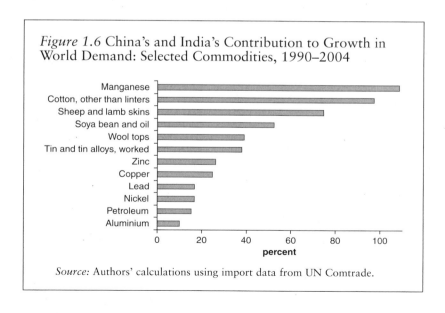

Figure 1.6 China's and India's Contribution to Growth in World Demand: Selected Commodities, 1990–2004

Source: Authors' calculations using import data from UN Comtrade.

over the period 1990–2004 (see figure 1.7), the estimated growth in China's demand for LAC exports was 28 percent higher than the observed increase in exports, signaling some missed opportunities. The growth in Chinese demand for commodities[12] was even larger, representing 10 percent of LAC exports in 2004, and accounting for 74 percent of the actual growth in LAC exports of commodities to China.[13]

The estimated growth in Chinese demand for LAC goods was quite uneven across LAC subregions. The last two columns of table 1.1 present the estimated impact of China's GDP growth on LAC exports to China by region, both as a share of total LAC exports in 2004 and as a share of LAC bilateral export growth. The largest estimated increases in Chinese demand were for Southern Cone and Andean goods (with an increase equivalent to 15 percent and 10 percent, respectively, of their total exports). The estimated growth in Chinese demand for Central American and Mexican and for Caribbean products represented only 2 percent and 1 percent, respectively, of their total exports in 2004.

Table 3.1 also gives the estimated contribution of LAC subregions' GDP growth to their exports to China. With the exception of Central America and Mexico, whose GDP growth had a marginally positive impact on its exports to China, the impact of all other subregions' GDP growth on their exports to China is not statistically different from zero.

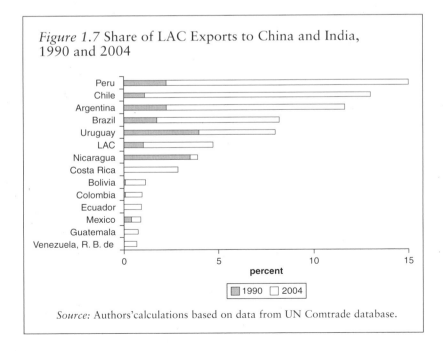

Figure 1.7 Share of LAC Exports to China and India, 1990 and 2004

Source: Authors' calculations based on data from UN Comtrade database.

Table 1.1 Impact of China's (and LAC's) GDP Growth on LAC's Non-Fuel Exports to China

Subregion and source of GDP growth	Estimated coefficient α_R (i)	p-value (ii)	$\Delta Y_{t\ or\ i}$ (iii)	(iii) × (i) (iv)	(iv) in % (v)	M_{ijt} (v) as % of total 2004 exports (vi)	(v) as % of bilateral export growth (viii)
Andean countries							
Own supply	0.38	0.19	0.20	0.00	0	0	0
China demand	4.42	0.00	0.38	1.66	427	10	203
Caribbean countries							
Own supply	−0.81	0.24	0.10	0.00	0	0	0
China demand	4.49	0.00	0.38	1.69	441	1	60
Central America and Mexico							
Own supply	−2.10	0.00	0.20	−0.42	−34	0	−11
China demand	4.25	0.00	0.38	1.60	394	2	125
Southern Cone							
Own supply	−0.09	0.58	−0.18	0.00	0	0	0
China demand	4.69	0.00	0.38	1.76	483	15	203
LAC							
Own supply						0	−1
China demand						8	135

Source: Authors' calculations based on last two columns of table 3.1 in this volume.

Note: When the p-value on the estimated coefficient α_R is larger than 0.10, the authors set column (iv) to 0, that is, the predicted change in the left-hand side variable is not different from zero. "China demand" is the impact of China's GDP growth on LAC exports. "Own supply" captures the impact of LAC's GDP growth on LAC's exports to China. The first column reports the estimated coefficient on the impact that China or LAC's GDP has on bilateral exports of each LAC subregion to China. The second column reports the p-value for the statistical significance of the estimated coefficient. For any p-value above 0.10, the authors set the estimated coefficient equal to zero in all other columns. The third column contains the in-sample change in the explanatory variable (the log of the GDP of China or LAC). The fourth column gives the product of the estimated coefficient with the change in the fourth column. The sixth column provides the change in bilateral exports as a percentage of each subregion's total exports in 2004. The last column gives the contribution to bilateral export growth over the period that can be attributed to the growth in China's demand or the LAC subregion's supply associated with their respective increases in GDP.

The estimated change in Indian demand for LAC products was also impressive. It represented 112 percent of LAC exports to India over the period, again signaling some missed opportunities. However, given that the size of bilateral trade with India is quite small, this growth in Indian demand for LAC products accounted for less than 0.5 percent of LAC exports in 2004 (driven by Andean countries and the Southern Cone). The increase in Indian demand for LAC commodities was negligible.

With regard to the impact of the growing Chinese presence in world markets on LAC exports to third markets, the evidence in chapter 3 suggests no net substitutability.[14] Rather, the growth in Chinese exports to third markets led to an increase (although not statistically significant) in LAC exports to these markets, signaling demand complementarities at the aggregate level. However, it is likely that these opportunities have not fully materialized. The authors also found a positive and statistically significant impact of Chinese exports to LAC on LAC exports to third markets, suggesting that imports of a larger variety of cheaper Chinese intermediate goods are positively affecting LAC's competitiveness in third markets. There is also evidence of "learning by exporting," because LAC exports to China have a positive and statistically significant impact on LAC exports to third markets. India, however, demonstrates some mild evidence of net substitutability between Indian trade flows and LAC exports to third markets through some channels (Indian imports from third markets), but that is partly compensated for by complementarities through other channels (exports from India to third markets, and exports from India to LAC).

Overall these results suggest that the growth of China and India in world markets has created opportunities for LAC. The growth of China's and India's demand over the period 2000–04 accounts for 8 percent of LAC exports in 2004 (mainly driven by China). However, this remains an untapped opportunity that has not been fully exploited, especially by exporters in the Southern Cone and in Andean countries. There is also no economically significant evidence of substitution between China's and India's trade flows and LAC's exports to third markets. On the contrary, LAC exporters seem to have been benefiting from the growing presence of the two Asian economies in world markets, particularly that of China.

FDI and Financial Flows

Chinese and Indian FDI in the LAC region has been growing steadily since the mid-1990s. Chinese FDI in LAC reached US$4 billion in 2004, and both Chinese and Indian FDI in the region has grown quickly in recent years. This simply reflects the emergence of China and India as exporters of capital to world markets. In 2004, China was among the top 10 countries in net foreign asset holdings, and, while India was still a net debtor, the trend was toward becoming a net creditor. As discussed by Lane and Schmukler (2006), more than 80 percent of these holdings in China and India combined were in reserve assets. However, as China and India liberalize private capital outflows, the potential for them to become major sources of portfolio investment and FDI in LAC is large.[15] More important, regardless of whether China's and India's capital flows are aimed at LAC markets, their growth, accompanied by an increase in net foreign lending, has contributed to lowering the cost of capital for LAC net debtors.

Moreover, China has become active in the region in bilateral aid, especially in Central America and the Caribbean. The Bahamas, Dominica, Grenada, Haiti, and Honduras have benefited from Chinese aid since the mid-1990s, including the construction of hospitals, schools, and roads; reconstruction after hurricanes; and so on.[16] Part of this aid could also be used to promote bilateral investment and trade relationships, which, as argued above, are below potential (at least in Central America).

China's and India's potential to displace inflows of FDI into LAC displays similar aggregate patterns to the ones observed for trade found using an empirical model based on the knowledge-capital model (KCM) of multinational enterprises, which allows for both horizontal and vertical motivations for FDI.[17] In a background paper for this study, Cravino, Lederman, and Olarreaga (forthcoming) explore the extent to which increases in OECD's aggregate FDI in China and India came at the expense of FDI in LAC. They found that China's and India's FDI inflows had a positive effect overall on the stocks of OECD capital in LAC, and in the rest of the world.[18] There are some exceptions when the authors focus on the manufacturing sector (using U.S. data), but results are not robust across specifications and will be discussed in the next section.

Regardless of whether LAC's FDI is a complement to or a substitute for growing stocks of FDI in China and India, Cravino, Lederman, and Olarreaga, in chapter 4 of this volume, assess the overall performance of LAC relative to China and India by comparing the stocks of FDI in LAC with those of the two Asian economies. Despite the rapid growth of foreign capital in China and India, OECD's stocks of FDI in LAC in 2003 were much larger than its stocks of FDI in China and India, after controlling for the relative size of the economies. Table 1.2 shows the ratio of stocks of FDI divided by GDP in some LAC countries relative to the same ratios for China, China plus Hong Kong, and India.[19] The first column in each panel provides the values of the aggregate stock of FDI from OECD, the second column provides values for U.S. stocks of FDI, and the third column provides values for U.S. stocks of FDI in the manufacturing sector. As can be seen from table 1.2, stocks of FDI in LAC were larger than stocks of FDI in China or India in most countries in 2003 after controlling for the economic size of the host-country economy. This even holds for U.S. stocks of FDI in the manufacturing sector, with the exception of Argentina and Guatemala relative to China plus Hong Kong.

Table 1.2 OECD, U.S., and U.S. Manufacturing Stocks of FDI in LAC Relative to Stock of FDI in China and India, Controlling for Host-Country Economic Size, 2003

Host economy	China			China plus Hong Kong			India		
	OECD	United States	U.S. manufacturing	OECD	United States	U.S. manufacturing	OECD	United States	U.S. manufacturing
Argentina	9.24	10.37	1.17	4.10	2.70	0.81	13.67	10.50	3.99
Brazil	4.93	7.70	3.68	2.19	2.01	2.54	7.29	7.80	12.58
Chile	10.55	15.63	2.67	4.68	4.07	1.85	15.61	15.83	9.14
Colombia	4.23	4.54	1.99	1.88	1.18	1.38	6.26	4.60	6.80
Costa Rica	2.60	6.06	3.96	1.15	1.58	2.74	3.85	6.14	13.53
El Salvador	1.47	5.30	n.a.	0.65	1.38	n.a.	2.17	5.37	n.a.
Guatemala	0.71	1.51	1.20	0.32	0.39	0.83	1.06	1.53	4.09
Mexico	4.34	11.35	3.17	1.93	2.96	2.19	6.43	11.49	10.84
Venezuela, R. B. de	4.77	13.42	4.15	2.12	3.50	2.87	7.06	13.59	14.20

Source: Cravino, Lederman, and Olarreaga in chapter 4 of this volume.
Note: n.a. = not applicable. Values represent the ratio of stocks of FDI divided by GDP in each LAC country relative to the stock of FDI divided by GDP in either China, China plus Hong Kong, or India. In the case of manufacturing FDI, we take the stocks of FDI relative to manufacturing value added. Data is from United Nations Conference on Trade and Development, OECD, U.S. Bureau of Economic Analysis, World Development Indicators, and China Statistical Yearbook 2003.

In sum, the results of Cravino, Lederman, and Olarreaga (forthcoming and chapter 4 in this volume) suggest that fears of global competition for FDI seem misplaced in light of the data. The overwhelming evidence is that growing investment opportunities for the OECD in the Chinese and Indian markets have led to more OECD FDI in LAC, as production possibilities expand for OECD's multinational firms.

With regard to FDI substitutability and complementarities within industries, table 1.2 provides some data about the relative importance of U.S. stocks of FDI in LAC's manufacturing sector relative to U.S. stocks of FDI in China and India. With the exception of Argentina and Guatemala when compared with the aggregate of China plus Hong Kong, all countries in LAC have a larger stock of U.S. manufacturing FDI. Cravino, Lederman, and Olarreaga (forthcoming) use the KCM model described above for aggregate FDI to measure the extent of substitutability with respect to U.S. FDI in the manufacturing sector. As mentioned, these authors found no robust evidence of substitution or complementarities between LAC's stocks of U.S. FDI in the manufacturing sector and China's and India's. Fears of losing foreign capital in the manufacturing sector to China and India seem unfounded. However, given that at the aggregate level they found strong complementarities, the fears may be explained by the relative performance.

The Negative Impacts of Chinese and Indian Competition on Some Industries and Countries

Even if, at the aggregate level, the rapid growth of China and India seems to be helping LAC, or at worst, is having no impact, the impact at the industry or firm level may not be so inconsequential, when positive externalities (complementarities) across industries are not taken into account. When focusing the analysis at the industry level the potential for substitutability between LAC exporters and Chinese and Indian exporters to third markets is much stronger.

Using a gravity-type empirical model for bilateral exports at the industry level, based on a monopolistic competition model of trade, and abstracting from general equilibrium effects, Hanson and Robertson in chapter 5 explore the impact of the increased supply capacity of China on manufacturing exports at the industry level in Argentina, Brazil, Chile, and Mexico. Their analysis focuses on the top manufacturing exports of these four countries, which represent at least 85 percent of their manufacturing exports (metals, machinery, electronics, transport, and industrial equipment).

More specifically, Hanson and Robertson ran a regression of bilateral sectoral exports on importer-country dummies, exporter-country dummies, and factors that affect trade costs (bilateral distance, sharing a land border, sharing a common language, belonging to a free trade area, import tariffs). When these importer and exporter dummies are allowed to vary by sector and by year, they can be interpreted as functions of structural parameters and country-specific prices and income levels that determine a country's export supply and import demand. They then decomposed manufacturing export growth for the four LAC countries into three components: (a) changes in sectoral export-supply capacity, (b) changes in import-demand conditions in a country's trading partners, and (c) trade costs and other residual factors. Changes in import-demand conditions can, in turn, be decomposed into two parts, one that captures changes in income levels in import markets and another that captures changes in sectoral import price indexes for those markets, which are themselves a function of other countries', including China's, export-supply capacities.

Results suggest that within manufacturing industries, Latin America's export capabilities tend to be relatively strong in industries in which China's export capabilities are also strong, suggesting the region is relatively vulnerable in these specific sectors to export-supply shocks from China. Although changes in Latin America's export-supply capacities have contributed to growth in exports, changes in Latin America's import-demand conditions have not made any such contribution, at least since 2000. The authors of chapter 5 examined two sources of negative import-demand shocks: China's growth in export supply, which may have lowered import prices in destination markets and diverted import demand away from Latin America; and the slowdown in the growth of the U.S. economy, which may have reduced growth in demand for LAC exports. The results suggest that had China's export-supply capacity remained constant after 1995, export growth for the four Latin American countries would have been 0.5 to 1.2 percentage points higher during the 1995–2000 period and 1.1 to 3.1 percentage points higher during the 2000–04 period. Had U.S. GDP growth been the same over the 2000–04 period as it was over the 1995–2000 period, Latin American manufacturing export growth would have been 0.2 to 1.4 percentage points higher (see table 1.3).

In chapter 6, Freund and Özden present a similar exercise covering all manufacturing and agricultural goods. They estimated a trade-gravity model in first differences, where the change in LAC exports by country at the industry level is explained by exporting-country dummies that vary by year to capture changes in export supply conditions and importing-country dummies that also vary by year to capture changes in overall demand conditions in each market, as well as product dummies that vary by year but only at the two-digit level of the International Standard Industrial Classification. The impact of China on LAC exports to third markets is captured by the change in China's exports to third markets. A negative and statistically significant coefficient on this last variable for an industry would indicate that in that industry Chinese exports are hurting LAC exporters of the same products.

Freund and Özden also found that increased exports from China are mainly hurting Mexican exporters of manufactured goods, namely textiles,

Table 1.3 Counterfactual Decomposition of Latin American Export Growth

Country and period	Actual growth in manufacturing exports	Counterfactual growth in manufacturing exports	
		Exporter coefficients in China constant over time	U.S. GDP growth 2000–04 = 1995–2000
Argentina			
1995–2000	0.081	0.085	n.a.
2000–04	–0.045	–0.034	–0.043
Brazil			
1995–2000	0.130	0.137	n.a.
2000–04	0.111	0.125	0.119
Chile			
1995–2000	0.071	0.079	n.a.
2000–04	0.053	0.076	0.060
Mexico			
1995–2000	0.165	0.177	n.a.
2000–04	0.024	0.055	0.038

Source: Hanson and Robertson in chapter 5 of this volume.

Note: n.a. = not applicable. This table reports actual and counterfactual export growth in Latin American countries based on two scenarios: U.S. GDP growth over 2000–04 equals that for 1995–2000, and China's export-supply capacity remains constant over the sample period (1995–2004) at levels equal to 1995 values.

electronics and electrical appliances, and telecommunications equipment. Despite the differences in specification and estimation techniques, the results obtained by Freund and Özden are qualitatively similar to those of Hanson and Robertson. Freund and Özden found large impacts for Mexico in electronics and telecommunications equipment. In other industries, such as textiles, they found smaller numbers that indicate that Mexico's exports are 1 percentage point lower in the absence of China's export growth to third markets. Freund and Özden do report some negative impacts for other LAC regions (Central America), and again for manufacturing exports only, but the impacts are not economically meaningful. When focusing on the impact by industry (two digits of the Harmonized System), they found that of the 97 two-digit industries, only 16 experienced a statistically significant decline in exports to third markets caused by growing exports of those same products by China to these same markets. Overall, the results of Hanson and Robertson and those of Freund and Özden suggest that there is some evidence of substitutability between

LAC exports and Chinese exports to third markets within industries, but these effects are limited to a few countries (mainly Mexico and, to a minor extent, those in Central America) and a few manufacturing sectors.

Services is a sector in which India, in particular, has outperformed LAC in export growth. However, LAC's exports of services to the United States are still seven times larger than exports of services by China and India combined (see figure 1.8). This partly reflects the importance of proximity for the delivery of services, for example, tourism, which is particularly important for the Caribbean region, and where Indian and Chinese competition may not be very strong.

Using a similar approach to that of Freund and Özden described above, chapter 7 by Freund explores the extent of substitutability between LAC and Indian exports of services to the United States. Using panel data on business, professional, and technical services, she finds no evidence that Indian exports have significantly displaced LAC exports of services. When the analysis is undertaken by service industry, she finds robust evidence of displacement in only one subsector—other business, professional, and technical services—where a 1 percent increase in growth from India has been associated with a 0.3 percent decline in growth from LAC. However, this is a "catch-all" subsector, so it is difficult to pinpoint the true economic importance.

The other eight service subsectors considered exhibit either no impact or a positive and statistically significant impact on LAC exports to the United States, again suggesting some complementarities. Nonetheless, when India's export growth is weighted by the importance of India in each

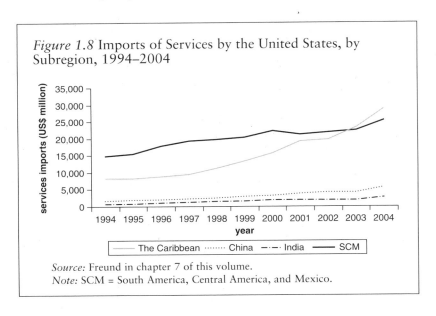

Figure 1.8 Imports of Services by the United States, by Subregion, 1994–2004

Source: Freund in chapter 7 of this volume.
Note: SCM = South America, Central America, and Mexico.

market, Freund finds a negative and statistically significant impact in four subsectors (legal services; research and development and testing services; industrial engineering; and other business, professional, and technical services), and a positive and statistically significant impact in one subsector (construction and engineering services). In the other four subsectors, there is no statistically significant effect.

China's export growth to third markets may be hurting not only existing LAC exporters (the so-called intensive margin), but also exporters of goods and services that have not yet been exported (the so-called extensive margin). In chapter 8, Feenstra and Kee focus on the extent to which the growing export variety from China to the U.S. market decreased the extent of export variety from Mexico. They found that every 1 percentage point increase in export variety from China (China's export variety has been growing at an average of 3 percent per year) has led to a half percentage point reduction in export variety growth from Mexico.[20] However, this reduction has been more than compensated for by Mexico's preferential access to the U.S. market, which has led to a 2 percent to 4 percent increase in export variety from Mexico for every percentage point reduction in preferential tariffs. In fact, the semi-elasticity between tariff cuts and export variety estimated by Feenstra and Kee is *higher* when the competition from Chinese exports is taken into account. This result has long-term implications because increases in export variety have been shown to positively affect total factor productivity and growth in a sample of developing countries (Feenstra and Kee 2006).

Factor Adjustments and Specialization Patterns

Positive impacts of China's and India's growth at the aggregate level in LAC, together with some negative impacts at the industry level, suggest the need for within- and across-industry adjustments, as well as some potential policy responses by LAC's governments.

Freund and Özden found evidence of quality downgrading in Central America using a price equation that explains changes in LAC unit export prices to third markets as a result of changes in the size of the export market and changes in prices and imports from China. For the other subregions, there is no statistically significant evidence one way or the other, except on overall exports of LAC to the OECD where there is weak evidence of quality upgrading as competition from China intensifies.

Focusing on the apparel industry, which has been hard hit by competition from China and India after the removal of the General Agreement on Tariffs and Trade's Textiles and Clothing Agreement quotas under the Multifibre Arrangement (MFA), Özden (2006) observes that different countries have shown different adjustment patterns. Costa Rica, the Dominican Republic, and Mexico took advantage of the Caribbean Basin

Initiative preferences and North American Free Trade Agreement to initially increase their export volume. However, with the removal of MFA quotas, they moved to higher-priced, higher-quality exports (see figure 1.9).[21] El Salvador, Guatemala, and Honduras did not seem to implement any structural changes in their apparel industries but simply increased their production and exports at the same quality and price level. Nicaragua and Haiti were new entrants to the apparel markets and their exports increased dramatically, but under competition from Asian countries they moved down the quality ladder to lower-priced, lower-quality exports.[22]

Using an index of potential industry wages—measured by the export-weighted sum of GDP per capita—Freund and Özden in chapter 6 observe that LAC is moving toward higher-wage products, though at a slow rate, especially when compared with China. Some evidence also indicates that China is depressing LAC's upward movement because China is displacing LAC in some relatively high-wage industries.

This observation is also confirmed by Lederman, Olarreaga, and Rubiano (2008), who found that LAC and China's specialization patterns exhibit some substitutability for skilled-labor-intensive industries but appear unrelated in unskilled-labor-intensive industries. India, however, shows signs of strong substitutability in both unskilled- and skilled-labor-intensive industries, suggesting that India is putting pressure on labor at both ends of the skill spectrum. Lederman, Olarreaga, and Rubiano (2008) also

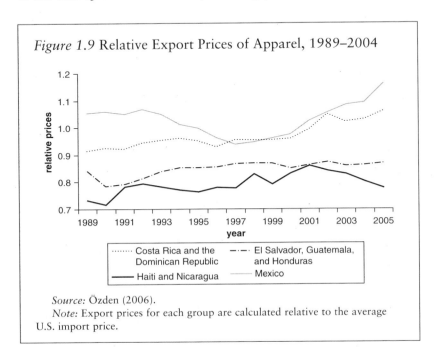

Figure 1.9 Relative Export Prices of Apparel, 1989–2004

Source: Özden (2006).
Note: Export prices for each group are calculated relative to the average U.S. import price.

found evidence of strong complementarities between LAC's and China's and India's specialization patterns in natural-resource-intensive industries and, to some extent, in industries intensive in scientific knowledge. Without China's and India's growth, and the induced increase in their demand for commodities since the mid-1990s, LAC's revealed comparative advantage in natural resources would have been 30 percent smaller, and the revealed comparative advantage in scientific-knowledge-intensive industries would have been 17 percent smaller. This suggests that the growth of China and India may be pushing LAC toward sectors intensive in these two factors and away from both skilled- and unskilled-labor-intensive industries. Indeed, the authors found that there may have been some scope for substitutability in the trade specialization patterns of LAC, and of China and India in the early 1990s, but with the exception of Mexico, LAC and the two Asian economies have been moving apart in their trade specialization patterns.

Figure 1.10 also shows the evolution of an export concentration Herfindahl index (higher values indicate a more concentrated export bundle), where the vertical axis on the right provides the scale and the line labeled "Herfindahl LAC" shows the evolution of the index. The evidence suggests that LAC as a whole has been moving toward higher concentration of its export bundle since the mid-1990s.[23] During the same period, China has moved toward a more concentrated export bundle, whereas India has shown some diversification. Overall, this suggests that the explanation behind the falling correlation between LAC and China is that LAC and China are moving toward specialization in a different set of products. In the case of India, the trend would also be explained by the diversification of India's export bundle.

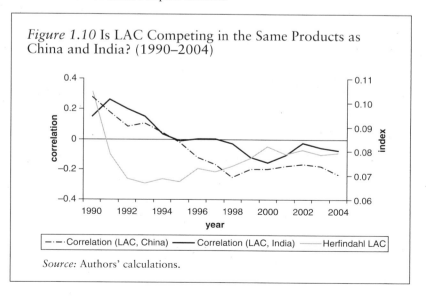

Figure 1.10 Is LAC Competing in the Same Products as China and India? (1990–2004)

Source: Authors' calculations.

Finally, some literature suggesting that dependence on natural resource exports might hinder long-term growth, and thus the observed patterns of specialization in LAC, could be interpreted as bad news. However, new econometric and case-study evidence seems to suggest that there is no such resource curse (see Lederman and Maloney 2007). Furthermore, to the extent that export-revenue concentration can hurt long-term growth prospects, the data suggest that despite recent increases in the level of concentration (as shown in figure 1.10), the region remains below the levels of concentration of 1990–92.[24]

Concerns about the potential adjustment costs faced by Latin American firms subject to increased import competition from China and India in their domestic markets led Casacuberta and Gandelman (see chapter 10) to examine whether firms that were exposed to competition from the two Asian economies were subject to higher adjustment costs for unskilled labor, skilled labor, and capital. They measured the impact of adjustment costs on firms' behavior by looking at the extent to which firms adjust to their factor shortages from one period to the next. Factor shortages are defined as the difference between actual levels of factor employment and desired levels of factor employment; the latter are given by optimal factor demands derived from a Cobb-Douglas production framework in a frictionless world.[25]

Casacuberta and Gandelman found that only a small share of factor shortages or surpluses are addressed by firms from one period to another, which they interpret as a signal of large adjustment costs in a sample of Uruguayan manufacturing firms. However, increasing competition from China and India only marginally changes the extent of the adjustment, even though adjustment costs seem to be marginally higher for both skilled and unskilled labor in the presence of factor surpluses (that is, when firms would like to reduce their level of factor employment) when competition from China and India is strong. Conversely, adjustment costs seem to be marginally lower for skilled and unskilled labor in the presence of factor shortages (that is, when firms would like to hire).

A potential explanation for this asymmetry lies in the perceived volatility of Chinese and Indian imports. If these imports are perceived to be more volatile than imports from other regions (because they are new players in world markets, are relatively more distant trading partners, and have widely different cultural and business practices), then one would expect firms to be more reluctant to fire workers and more willing to hire workers when exposed to more import competition from China or India rather than from more established and better-understood trading partners. The data confirm this with a coefficient of variation for imports from China and India that is twice the coefficient of variation of imports from the rest of the world. Addressing the causes of this volatility (which can sometimes be policy induced, for example, through antidumping duties, nontariff barriers, and the like) is likely to help reduce adjustment costs in the presence of surpluses.

An important concern for policy makers associated with the growing presence of China and India in LAC markets (see figure 1.11) is the impact this competition may have on employment, particularly labor-intensive manufacturing employment, for which China and India have a comparative advantage. Manufacturing employment significantly declined in LAC while imports from China and India were growing. A quick analysis would suggest that the two Asian economies carry the blame for the loss of employment opportunities in manufacturing activities in LAC.

A more careful analysis suggests otherwise. Castro, Olarreaga, and Saslavsky, in chapter 9, explore the impact that growing imports from China and India had on manufacturing employment in Argentina, which is among the countries in the region that experienced the largest declines in manufacturing employment during the 1990s (31 percent), while experiencing an important increase in import penetration from China (see figure 1.11). These authors built a dynamic econometric model in which labor demand in each industry is a function of wages, capital stock, prices, and productivity. Prices and productivity are functions of import and export penetration and allow the authors to identify the impact that trade with China and India is having—through these two channels—on labor demand in Argentina's manufacturing sector.[26]

Results suggest that increased trade with China can explain just a negligible share of the decline in Argentina's manufacturing labor demand. Moreover, the increase in overall import penetration during the period

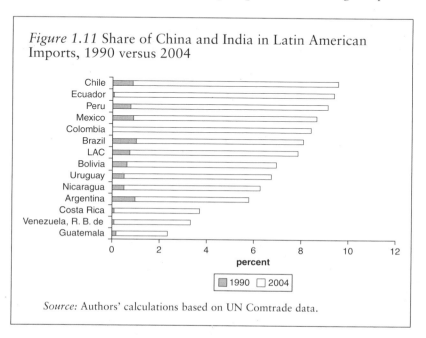

Figure 1.11 Share of China and India in Latin American Imports, 1990 versus 2004

Source: Authors' calculations based on UN Comtrade data.

could explain only a relatively small share of the decline in manufacturing employment.[27] To be more precise, a 1 percent increase in import penetration leads to a 0.07 percent decline in labor demand. Given that import penetration increased by 79 percent over the sample period (1991–2003), the decline in labor demand that can be attributed to the increase in import penetration is around 6 percent. Because manufacturing employment declined by 31 percent over the sample period, the increase in import penetration can at most explain 20 percent of the observed loss in manufacturing employment. The other 80 percent had other causes (labor legislation, privatization, technological change, and the like). Moreover, the increased importance of China as a source of imports had an almost negligible marginal impact on the decline in labor demand associated with the increase in overall imports. An increase in the share of imports from China of 1 percentage point led to an additional 0.02 percent decline in the growth of Argentina's labor demand. Thus, the sixfold increase in the share of imports from China over the period (from 1 percent to 6 percent) could only explain an additional 0.1 percent to 0.2 percent of the observed decline in labor demand. Results for India suggest that the increase in its share of Argentina's imports has had no impact on labor demand (beyond the overall impact of import penetration on labor demand).

Perhaps surprisingly, export penetration does not seem to affect labor demand in Argentina's manufacturing industry. The reason could be that exports do increase output and therefore labor demand, but they are also often accompanied by export-induced technological change that is labor saving. The evidence suggests that in Argentina these two forces cancel out, with no large impact on employment. This implies that Chinese and Indian competition in third markets may not be having much of an impact on Argentina's manufacturing employment either. This result, however, may not carry over to countries subject to a higher degree of competition in third markets, such as Mexico.

With regard to LAC governments' responses to the growth of imports from China and India into the region, Facchini et al. (2007) found that tariffs tended to be higher on products heavily imported from China, but lower on goods imported from India. The evidence they provide is not limited to tariffs, however: nontariff barriers have become a predominant form of protectionism and Chinese exporters have been particularly hit by LAC countries, while Indian exporters enjoyed below-average levels of protection in LAC. For example, Brazil initiated 15 antidumping cases against China as notified to the World Trade Organization; Argentina initiated 40 cases; and in the early 1990s, Mexico imposed antidumping duties of more than 1,000 percent on imports of shoes, toys, and textiles from China (Dominguez et al. 2006). Together, LAC governments have initiated more cases against China than the European Union, the United States, or Canada.[28]

Facchini et al. (2007) explained the differences in protection levels in relation to China and India using a lobbying model with imperfect substitution between domestically produced goods and imported goods. They found that incentives to lobby were higher when products were close substitutes for the ones domestically produced, resulting in higher tariffs in equilibrium. After bringing the model to the data, they found that this was a reasonable explanation for the higher tariffs observed on goods imported from China because estimates suggest that they are closer substitutes for domestically produced goods than goods imported from the rest of the world. Similarly, the lobbying model can also explain the lower levels of protection on goods imported from India because estimates suggest that goods imported from India are more distant substitutes for domestically produced goods than goods imported from the rest of the world. However, the fact that production-efficiency losses are likely to be higher in goods with higher substitution suggests that the protectionist response is occurring in sectors where import competition hurts the most.

Protectionist responses can also occur behind the border. Baroncelli, Krivonos, and Olarreaga (2007) measured the degree of discrimination imposed on foreign applicants in the trademark registration processes in China, India, and Latin America using the differences in the rate of registration of foreign and domestic applicants. They found some significant differences in the rate of registration of LAC trademarks in China with respect to domestic applicants, as well as between the rates of registration of Chinese and domestic trademarks in LAC's trademark registration offices.

Baroncelli, Krivonos, and Olarreaga (2007) explain this pattern using a model with vertically differentiated goods, and show that incentives to discriminate against relatively close substitutes are larger because they lead to larger increases in profits for domestic producers and smaller declines in consumer welfare. Conversely, incentives to discriminate against products at opposite ends of the quality spectrum are small because any discrimination would be captured by other producers in the middle of the quality spectrum. They then test the model empirically and find some evidence that discrimination in the trademark registration process tends to be higher against applicants from countries that produce goods of similar quality.[29] The high substitutability between Chinese goods and LAC's goods estimated by Facchini et al. (2007) would then explain why there may be higher trademark protectionism between LAC and China.

Policy Implications

In general, the evidence discussed in this book suggests that LAC countries should reshuffle their development-policy priorities in response to the emergence of China and India in global markets. The higher correlation between the business cycles of LAC and the two Asian economies is mainly driven by demand spillovers, largely explained by the high correlation between China's and India's industrial output and world commodity prices. This finding suggests that the current commodity boom that is benefiting LAC is largely dependent on the continuing growth of the two Asian economies. Fragilities in China's and India's economies, or changes in consumer preferences, should therefore be tracked with particular attention by those LAC economies with strong attachments to natural-resource-intensive products.

As indicated, partly under pressure from China and India, LAC's specialization patterns have been shifting toward higher natural-resource- and knowledge-intensive activities and products. To facilitate this shift and increase the potential benefits from it, LAC countries should improve their natural resource management and rural development policies, while at the same time strengthening policies and institutions for the promotion of skills and innovation (patentable or not).

Trade policies, both at the border and behind the border, show evidence of a protectionist response on the part of LAC governments to the growth of imports from China in particular, partly because of the larger vertical and horizontal product substitutability between domestically produced goods and goods imported from China. This is inefficient as well as costly for users of imported intermediate goods, who cannot take full advantage of cheaper inputs to improve their competitiveness in world markets. Giving more weight to consumers and users of imported intermediate goods in the trade policy formation process may yield better outcomes.

One area in which some LAC countries seem to have been underperforming is bilateral exports to the two Asian economies. Negotiating free trade agreements (as some countries are already doing) and export promotion activities focused on these two markets may help reverse this trend.[30] Also, special attention should be given to integration into global production networks that involve Chinese and Indian firms.

For FDI promotion through specialized agencies, it seems that there is no need for a change of course because LAC has benefited from growing FDI to China and India. LAC has been quite successful in attracting FDI and should continue to improve the overall investment climate and the role of specialized promotion agencies to maintain their lead.[31] It is unfortunate that a couple of countries have been backtracking recently from the generally open environment in the region toward FDI.

In services, there may be a need for enhancing the relative competitiveness of LAC in relation to India in the business, professional, and technical services sector (as well as legal and industrial engineering services). The literature suggests that this could be achieved by developing Internet penetration through investment in telecommunication infrastructure and reforms that expand Internet access, but also by aligning exchange rates to correct, in particular, for overvalued exchange rates (see Freund and Weinhold 2002).

Also, to exploit the evidence of synergies in innovation patterns between LAC and India, governments may want to consider scaling up scientific exchange programs and cooperation in research and development programs. The same may eventually be useful in some areas with China, too.

Because some industries are negatively affected by the growth of China and India, and these tend to be labor-intensive industries, adjustment assistance for workers may need to be considered. For those countries adjusting toward skilled-labor-intensive and scientific-knowledge-intensive industries, short-term adjustment policies should concentrate on helping unskilled labor in the transition, while focusing on skill improvements and innovation policies in the long term. For the few countries adjusting toward unskilled-labor-intensive industries, short-term adjustment policies should probably focus on the higher end of the skill spectrum while also trying to improve the overall endowment of skilled labor and scientific knowledge in the long term.

Notes

1. All calculations are based on GDP data measured at market prices.

2. This may be explained by proximity, but endowments and entrepreneurship also play a role. There are 116 United Nations Educational, Scientific, and Cultural Organization Heritage sites in LAC, compared with 33 in China and 26 in India.

3. In an alternative specification in which exports from China are weighted by the lagged share of Indian exports, Freund (chapter 7 in this volume) found a negative and statistically significant impact in four service subsectors, a positive and statistically significant impact in one service subsector, and no statistically significant impact in three service subsectors.

4. In the early 2000s, according to statistics provided by UNIDO's INDSTAT database, the average monthly salary in manufacturing in China and India oscillated between US$120 and US$150. The equivalent figure in Argentina was US$1,112; in Uruguay, US$1,010; in Chile, US$882; in Brazil, US$860; in Mexico, US$670; in Costa Rica, US$495; in Colombia, US$350; in Bolivia, US$262; and in Guatemala, US$120.

5. The degree of business cycle synchronization between countries is measured by the correlation between the cyclical components of real output. The cyclical component of real output is obtained using the band-pass filter proposed by Baxter and King (1999). Once the business cycle is computed for each country, Calderón (chapter 2) calculates the correlation between de-trended output in countries i and j over the following non-overlapping 10-year periods: 1965–74, 1975–84, 1985–94, and 1995–2004. He then regresses these correlations on variables that measure the degree of trade integration, output specialization, and demand spillovers, controlling for other factors.

6. A word of caution is warranted here because demand spillovers are identified using time dummies in a regression explaining the correlation of output. Other factors (common supply shifts, for example) could be captured by time dummies.

7. For Central America, demand spillovers also explain a large share of the declining output correlation. This signals that the relative demand in China for goods produced in Central America has been declining, especially since the late 1990s.

8. The statistical significance of the correlation coefficients increases more sharply and the coefficients are statistically different from zero from 2002 onward.

9. China and India have contributed, on average, 12 percent of the increase in demand in world markets over the period 1990–2004.

10. The gravity model of trade explains bilateral trade flows using economic size (GDP) of importers and exporters, the bilateral distance between trading partners, and other control variables. To capture the impact of China's and India's growth on LAC exports to the two Asian economies' markets in a sample composed of Latin American exporters to and importers from the world, Lederman, Olarreaga, and Soloaga (chapter 3 in this volume) isolate the impact of China's and India's GDP growth on LAC's bilateral exports by estimating subregion-specific effects that vary by exporting and importing country or subregion. To control for the correlation between the expected value of bilateral trade flows among country pairs and the variance of their regression errors, which itself may be increasing with trade flows, thus biasing estimates from linear regressions, they use a negative binomial estimator (see Santos Silva and Tenreyro 2006).

11. We acknowledge that the estimation of the gravity model by Lederman, Olarreaga, and Soloaga (chapter 3), as well as the estimations by Freund and Özden (chapter 6), and Hanson and Robertson (chapter 5) in this volume might suffer from an endogeneity bias. Eichengreen, Rhee, and Tong (2007) used geographic (time invariant) variables as instrumental variables to control for unobserved omitted variables that could be correlated with East Asian exports and Chinese exports to common markets. The gravity model estimations in this volume do not use instrumental variables, but they do control for time-period effects that capture any such unobserved common effects. Nonetheless, there might be some remaining bias from reverse causality, especially for LAC economies that are large exporters of certain commodities. In this case, however, the bias would yield coefficient estimates that *underestimate* the positive effects of Chinese and Indian exports to third markets, because export expansions of large commodity exporters would reduce the prices of those commodities, thus reducing the positive estimated partial correlation between LAC exports and Chinese and Indian exports to a common market.

12. Commodities are here defined as goods falling in the Harmonized System (HS) classification of HS 01 to HS 24.

13. Thus, there is less evidence of missed opportunities in commodity exports.

14. The growing Chinese or Indian presence is captured by exports from China or India to the same third market.

15. A 2002 Chinese pilot scheme to promote outward FDI was extended nationally in 2006, and in 2007 the government launched a qualified domestic institutional investor program aimed at increasing the ability of domestic residents to invest in foreign securities, including stocks and bonds. Restrictions on outflows of FDI in India are also being removed (Lane and Schmukler 2006).

16. Part of the motivation behind this bilateral aid is associated with the recognition of Taiwan: of the 26 countries in the world that recognize Taiwan, 11 are in Central America and the Caribbean (Dominguez et al. 2006).

17. See Carr, Markusen, and Maskus (2001). In the KCM, bilateral FDI stocks are explained by variables that capture horizontal and vertical motives for FDI. Horizontal motives are captured by the sum of source-country and host-country GDPs as a measure of total market size, and the squared GDP differences. According to the KCM, the coefficient on the sum of GDP should be positive because larger markets should attract multinational enterprises. The KCM predicts that, controlling for the sum of GDP, differences in country size discourage horizontal FDI. The intuition is that when one of the countries is small, multinational firms would open production facilities mostly in large economies. Vertical motives are captured by the absolute value of differences in skilled labor abundance between the source and the host country. The model also includes other control variables to capture investment and trade costs.

18. Cravino, Lederman, and Olarreaga (2008) use various estimators: ordinary least squares, Poisson to correct for the correlation between the expected value of bilateral capital stocks and the variance of their regression errors, and negative binomial to control for over-dispersion (the increasing correlation between the expected capital stocks and the variance of their regression errors).

19. Hong Kong has been a part of China since 1997 and therefore should be considered part of the Chinese economy. Moreover, some observers have argued that China's and Hong Kong's trade data should be combined to approximate the trade flows coming from China mainland as a result of transshipments of merchandise through Hong Kong.

20. Causality is derived using Chinese tariffs as instruments for Chinese export variety.

21. Part of the higher price of Mexico, Costa Rica, and the Dominican Republic in figure 1.9 is explained by their increasing preferential access to the U.S. market, but results regarding quality upgrading for Costa Rica and Nicaragua hold after controlling for tariff preferences.

22. Caution must be exercised in attributing these changes to the removal of the MFA quotas and the growing presence of China and India in these markets. Other factors, such as preferences to the U.S. markets (which Özden controls for in his econometric framework) may be partly driving these results.

23. There was a move toward export diversification at the beginning of the 1990s, probably prompted by LAC's trade reforms in the late 1980s and early 1990s, as also shown in De Ferranti et al. (2002), but this was followed by a move toward specialization as trade theory would predict, also partly explained by the commodity boom. The trends in figure 1.10 are dominated by the large LAC economies of Brazil and Mexico.

24. We also acknowledge that the rise of the Herfindahl index since the late 1990s could be due to the rise of commodity prices and not necessarily be due to increases in the quantities of commodity exports.

25. This assumes that production and adjustment costs are separable. But without this assumption, it is impossible to estimate factor shortages without having a measure of adjustment costs.

26. Wages, capital stock, and import and export penetration are instrumented using lagged values, the share of unskilled labor in the industry, and a proxy for transport costs.

27. Hoekman and Winters (2005) in their recent survey of the evidence on the links between trade and employment conclude that there is no robust evidence either way, particularly in the manufacturing sectors of developing countries.

28. The use of antidumping duties by LAC on imports from China will be limited by most LAC countries' recognition of China as a "market economy" in 2006. This affects the flexibility LAC enjoyed earlier under World Trade Organization rules to set high and discretionary duties, even though Article VI of the General Agreement on Tariffs and Trade, which regulates antidumping duties, is quite flexible and subject to abuse.

29. Quality proximity is proxied by the absolute value of the difference in the share of industry-level exports to the TRIAD.

30. As shown by Lederman, Olarreaga, and Payton (2006) in a background paper for a regional study on *Enhancing Firm Capabilities*, export promotion agencies in Latin America have been particularly successful at promoting exports in recent years. However, their focus has been almost exclusively on the western hemisphere, and to some extent, Europe. Addressing the Asia deficit would help them take advantage of the growing opportunity that China and India represent.

31. For a recent study on the role of FDI promotion agencies in attracting FDI, see Harding, Javorcik, and Sawada (2006).

References

Baroncelli, Eugenia, Ekaterina Krivonos, and Marcelo Olarreaga. 2007. "Trademark Protection or Protectionism?" *Review of International Economics* 15 (1): 126–45.

Baxter, M., and R. G. King. 1999. "Measuring Business Cycles: Approximate Band-Pass Filters for Economic Time Series." *The Review of Economics and Statistics* 81 (4): 575–93.

Carr, David L., James R. Markusen, and Keith E. Maskus. 2001. "Estimating the Knowledge-Capital Model of the Multinational Enterprise." *American Economic Review* 91 (3): 693–708.

Cravino, Javier, Daniel Lederman, and Marcelo Olarreaga. Forthcoming. "Substitution between Foreign Capital in China, India, and the Rest of the World: Much Ado about Nothing?" *Journal of Economic Integration.*

De Ferranti, D., G. Perry, D. Lederman, and W. Maloney. 2002. *From Natural Resources to the Knowledge Economy: Trade and Job Quality.* Washington, DC: World Bank.

Dominguez, Jorge, with Amy Catalinac, Sergio Cesarin, Javier Corrales, Stephanie R. Golob, Andrew Kennedy, Alexander Liebman, Marusia Musacchio-Farias, João Resende-Santos, Roberto Russell, and Yongwook Ryu. 2006. "China's Relations with Latin America: Shared Gains, Asymmetric Hopes." Working Paper, Inter-American Dialogue, Washington, DC.

Eichengreen, B., Y. Rhee, and H. Tong. 2007. "China and the Exports of Other Asian Countries." *Review of World Economics/Weltwirtschaftliches Archiv* 143 (2): 201–26.

Facchini, Giovanni, Marcelo Olarreaga, Peri Silva, and Gerald Willmann. 2007. "Substitutability and Protectionism: Latin America's Trade Policy and Imports from China and India." Policy Research Working Paper 4188, World Bank, Washington, DC.

Feenstra, R. C., and H. L. Kee. 2006. "Export Variety and Country Productivity: Estimating the Monopolistic Competition Model with Endogenous Productivity." World Bank Policy Research Group, Washington, DC, and University of California, Davis.

Freund, Caroline, and Diana Weinhold. 2002. "The Internet and International Trade in Services." *American Economic Review* 92 (2): 236–40.

Harding, Torfinn, Beata Javorcik, and Naotaka Sawada. 2006. "Investment Promotion: Why, What and How Lessons for Latin America and the Caribbean." Background paper for the Office of the Chief Economist for Latin American and the Caribbean Regional Study, *Enhancing Firm Capabilities*, World Bank, Washington, DC.

Hoekman, Bernard, and L. Alan Winters. 2005. "Trade and Employment: Stylized Facts and Research Findings." Policy Research Working Paper 3676, World Bank, Washington, DC.

Lane, Philip R., and Sergio L. Schmukler. 2006. "The International Financial Integration of China and India." Unpublished, World Bank, Washington, DC.

Lederman, Daniel, and William F. Maloney, eds. 2007. *Natural Resources, Neither Curse nor Destiny.* Washington, DC: Stanford University Press and World Bank.

Lederman, Daniel, Marcelo Olarreaga, and Lucy Payton. 2006. "Export Promotion Agencies: What Works and What Doesn't." Policy Research Working Paper 4044, World Bank, Washington, DC.

Lederman, Daniel, Marcelo Olarreaga, and Eliana Rubiano. 2008. "Trade Specialization in Latin America: The Impact of China and India." *Review of World Economics/Weltwirtschaftliches Archiv* 144 (2): 248–71.

Özden, Çağlar. 2006. "Caribbean Basin Initiative Beneficiary Countries and the Apparel Sector: Same Preferences, Different Responses." Background paper for the Office of the Chief Economist for Latin American and the Caribbean Regional Study, *Latin America and the Caribbean's Response to the Growth of China and India*. World Bank, Washington, DC.

Perry, Guillermo, and Marcelo Olarreaga. 2007. "Trade Liberalization, Inequality and Poverty Reduction in Latin America." In *Annual World Bank Conference on Development Economics, Regional: Beyond Transition*, ed. François Bourguignon and Boris Pleskovic. Washington, DC: World Bank.

Santos Silva, J. M. C., and Silvana Tenreyro. 2006. "The Log of Gravity." *The Review of Economics and Statistics* 88 (4): 641–58.

Part II

The Growth of China and India Is Not a Zero-Sum Game for Latin America and the Caribbean: Short- and Long-Term Effects

2

Trade, Specialization, and Cycle Synchronization: Explaining Output Comovement between Latin America, China, and India

César Calderón*

Introduction

Since 1980, world trade has grown twice as fast as world output (6 percent versus 3 percent), thus deepening economic integration (IMF 2001; Kouparitsas 2001). To the extent that countries are becoming more integrated into the world economy, their macroeconomic fluctuations have become increasingly affected by external disturbances—which include output fluctuations in other economies. Shocks occurring in one country can be transmitted to another country through three basic channels: international trade in goods and services, international trade of financial assets, and direct links between sectors of production across countries. The role of international trade in transmitting business cycle fluctuations across countries has been widely recognized and analyzed (Canova and Dellas 1993; Baxter 1995). Trade links have proved to be important in the literature of

*The author would like to thank Daniel Lederman, Marcelo Olarreaga, Guillermo Perry, and Claudio Raddatz for comments and suggestions. He also thanks Ileana Jalile for superb research assistance.

optimum currency areas, which argues that countries are more likely to benefit from a currency union if they have higher trade integration and more synchronized business cycles (Frankel and Rose 1998; Mundell 1961). Recent empirical research has found that country pairs with stronger international trade links tend to have more highly correlated business cycles, not only among industrial countries (Clark and van Wincoop 2001; Rose and Engel 2002) but also among developing countries, although to a weaker degree (Calderón, Chong, and Stein 2007).

However, China's and India's faster growth and deeper integration into the world economy may be affecting the business cycles of other economies. This chapter is concerned with whether developments in China and India are affecting output prospects in the Latin America and the Caribbean (LAC) region. Rising correlations for LAC countries with China and India (figure 2.1) are accompanied by increasing world demand for some of LAC's commodities (figure 2.2) and a sharp increase in bilateral trade between LAC and China and India (figure 2.3). The largest LAC economies have increased their shares of trade with China in total trade from less than 2 percent in the 1980s to 6 percent in 2000–04, with Chile and Peru having trade shares with China higher than 10 percent of total trade in the 2000s. Trade between LAC and India has also increased, although this growth has been modest compared with trade with China. The largest LAC economies have raised their trade shares with India from 0.44 percent to 0.73 percent of their total trade.

This chapter's main goal is to analyze whether higher trade integration between the LAC region and China and India is driving higher output correlations. According to the literature, the impact of trade integration on business cycle correlation could go either way (Frankel and Rose 1998): First, trade integration may increase output correlation if the demand channel is the dominant force driving business cycles. For instance, positive output shocks in a country might increase its demand for foreign goods, and the impact on the output of the country's trading partner will depend on the depth of their trade links. Second, if industry-specific shocks are the dominant force explaining cyclical output, the relationship would be negative if increasing specialization in production leads to interindustry trade (as usually observed in developing countries). In this case, trade integration leads to specialization in different industries, which in turn leads to asymmetric effects of industry-specific shocks. Finally, if intra-industry trade prevails (as observed in industrial countries), specialization does not necessarily lead to asymmetric effects of industry-specific shocks because the pattern of specialization occurs mainly within industries.

Using a sample of 147 countries (23 industrial economies and 124 developing countries) with annual information for the period 1965–2004, this analysis updates and extends the results in Calderón, Chong, and

Figure 2.1 Output Comovement: 10-Year-Window Rolling Correlations

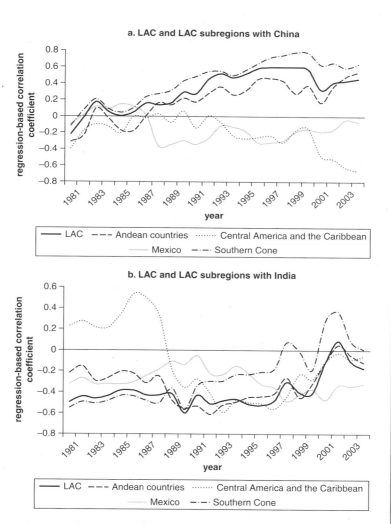

Source: Author's calculations using data on real gross domestic product from World Bank World Development Indicators.

Note: Ten-year rolling regression of output growth in LAC on output growth in China. Year on *x*-axis is end year of the 10-year regression.

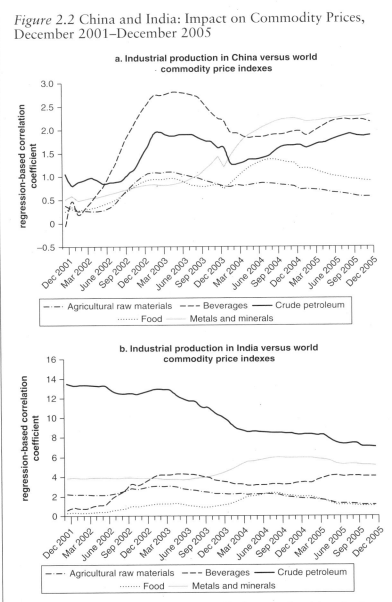

Figure 2.2 China and India: Impact on Commodity Prices,
December 2001–December 2005

a. Industrial production in China versus world commodity price indexes

regression-based correlation coefficient

--- Agricultural raw materials   – – Beverages   —— Crude petroleum
········· Food   —— Metals and minerals

b. Industrial production in India versus world commodity price indexes

regression-based correlation coefficient

--- Agricultural raw materials   – – Beverages   —— Crude petroleum
········· Food   —— Metals and minerals

Source: Author's calculations using monthly data on industrial production
index of India from Haver Analytics database.

Note: Figure 2.2(b) shows 5-year (60-month) rolling regression of the percentage
variation in the international price of a selected commodity group on India. Year on
x-axis is end year of the 5-year regression.

Figure 2.3 Trade Integration of LAC with China and India, 1985–2004

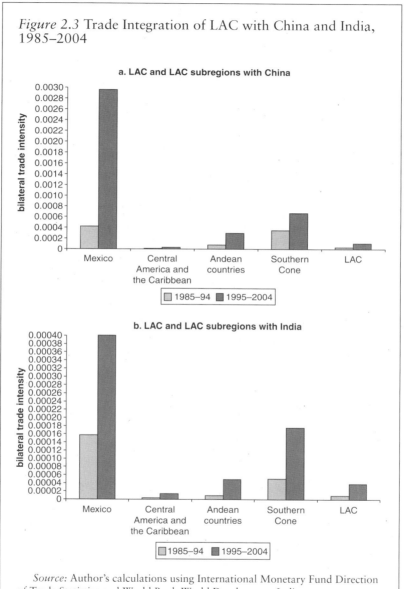

Source: Author's calculations using International Monetary Fund Direction of Trade Statistics and World Bank World Development Indicators.

Note: Bilateral trade intensity is the ratio of bilateral exports and imports between the LAC (country or group) and India to the total output of the LAC (country or group) and India.

Stein (2007) for the sample of LAC countries compared with the rest of the world. The regression analysis reveals the following:

- Countries with more extensive trade links display higher output comovement. The evidence indicates that a higher degree of intra-industry trade among country pairs may generate a higher degree of business cycle synchronization.
- Output specialization, as proxied by the degree of asymmetry in the structure of production among countries, may lead to more-asynchronous business cycles. The same result holds for asymmetries in export and import baskets, although the analysis fails to find a significant effect for asymmetries in structure of imports.
- Output specialization—as well as specialization in exports and imports—may reduce the sensitivity of cycle synchronization to changes in bilateral trade. That is, the impact of trade intensity on output comovement is higher for countries with more symmetric structures of production and trade.

Using the results of this regression analysis, the study evaluates how well the model tracks the changes in output comovement for the LAC region, as well as selected LAC countries, with China and India in 1995–2004 relative to 1985–94:

- On average, the model does a fairly good job predicting changes in output correlation for the region in relation to China and India. However, the country-by-country analysis shows wide heterogeneity in performance.
- For the LAC region as a whole, the model explains 54 percent of the actual change in output correlation with China; the predicted change is mostly attributable to demand spillovers (65 percent), while bilateral trade and asymmetries in production structures explain the remaining 35 percent.
- Demand spillovers explain most (70 percent) of the increase in predicted correlation with India, with the remaining 30 percent attributable to trade integration and output specialization.
- As mentioned, the ability of the model to track changes in output correlation of LAC countries with China and India varies signifi-cantly. However, its performance in tracking changes in correlation seems to fit the evolution of the correlation with China better than the evolution of the correlation with India.

This chapter is organized as follows: The next section provides theo-retical insights about the relationship between trade integration and the synchronization of business cycles. It is followed by a section that discusses the data and presents the econometric methodology used in the empirical evaluation. The subsequent section discusses the main results of the regression analysis and is followed by a section that uses the regression results to explain changes in output correlation for Latin American countries with China and India. The final section offers conclusions.

Theoretical Insights

This section presents a simple theoretical framework for understanding the different channels through which trade intensity may affect the degree of synchronization of business cycles. It first defines the cyclical component of real output $\tilde{y}_{it} = y_{it} - \bar{y}_{it}$ as the deviation of (the log of) real output from its trend component, $\bar{y}_{it}$. Following Stockman (1988), it can be argued that the cyclical component of real output in country i at time t, $\tilde{y}_{it}$, can be decomposed as the weighted average of the cyclical components of all the k sectors in the economy, $\tilde{y}_{kit}$ (where $k = 1, \ldots, n$), with weights s_{ki} being approximated by the share of sector k's output in total output ($\Sigma_k s_{ki} = 1$),

$$\tilde{y}_{it} = \sum_k s_{ki} \tilde{y}_{kit}. \tag{2.1}$$

Next, the cyclical component of real output in sector k at time t can be expressed as deviations from the country's average fluctuation across sectors at time t, $\bar{y}_{it}$. Equation 2.1 can be rewritten as

$$\tilde{y}_{it} = \sum_k s_{ki} \eta_{kit} + \zeta_{it}, \tag{2.2}$$

where the cyclical component of real output for country i at time t consists of the weighted average of k sectoral output shocks at time t, $\eta_{it} = \tilde{y}_{kit} - \tilde{y}_{it}$, and the aggregate shock to output of country i at time t, ζ_{it}. Analogously, the cyclical component of real output for the foreign country—that is, country j—can be defined as

$$\tilde{y}_{jt} = \sum_k s_{kj} \eta_{kjt} + \zeta_{jt} \tag{2.2*}$$

The following assumptions (Stockman 1988) are used:

(1) $\{\eta_{kit}\}$ are distributed independently of each other across both sectors k and time t, with sectoral variance σ_k^2;
(2) industry shocks are similar across countries, $\eta_{kit} = \eta_{kjt}$, and have the same variance σ_k^2;
(3) $\{\zeta_{it}\}$ is distributed independently over time; and
(4) $\{\eta_{kit}\}$ and $\{\zeta_{it}\}$ are independent of each other.

Using assumptions (1) through (4), the covariance between the cyclical component of real output in countries i and j can be computed as follows:

$$\sigma(\tilde{y}_i, \tilde{y}_j) = \sigma_k^2 \sum_K s_{Ki} s_{Kj} + \sigma(\zeta_i, \zeta_j) \qquad\qquad (2.3)$$

where σ_k^2 is the variance of real output in sector k, and $\sigma(\zeta_i, \zeta_j)$ is the covariance between country-specific aggregate shocks.

Theoretically, the impact of rising trade integration on business cycle synchronization is ambiguous. Assuming that business cycles are dominated by *industry-specific shocks*, η_{kit}, the Heckscher-Ohlin paradigm predicts that rising trade integration between countries i and j may lead to deeper specialization in both countries and to declining output correlation between countries i and j. Given that sectoral variance is always positive, that is, $\sigma_k^2 > 0$, rising trade will lead to negative comovement between s_{ki} and s_{kj} (because of specialization in production) and, all other things equal, to declining output correlation between countries i and j. Recent research has found another mechanism that yields a negative association between trade integration and business cycle synchronization (Kalemli-Ozcan, Sorensen, and Yosha 2001): higher integration in both international goods and financial markets allows countries to ensure against asymmetric shocks through diversification of ownership; thus, they can afford to have a specialized production structure. Hence, enhanced opportunities for income diversification induce higher specialization in production and more asymmetric business cycles.

Conversely, if patterns of specialization in production and international trade are dominated by *intra-industry trade*, deeper trade links will not necessarily result in deeper specialization along industry lines as predicted by the Heckscher-Ohlin paradigm. In this case, industry-specific shocks, η_{kit}, will not necessarily affect different countries more asymmetrically as they become more integrated (Krugman 1993). Here, deeper trade integration does not necessarily lead to a negative correlation between s_{ki} and s_{kj}. Hummels, Ishii, and Yi (2001) find that countries are increasingly specializing in particular stages of a good's production sequence rather than producing the entire good (vertical specialization).[1] In addition, Kose and Yi (2001) have argued that a rising trend in this "back and forth" trade might lead to greater response of business cycle correlations to higher trade integration.

Finally, higher trade integration may have an impact on the correlation between country-specific aggregate shocks, $\rho(\zeta_i, \zeta_j)$ through different channels. First, aggregate demand shocks may lead to spillover effects. Favorable income shocks in one country might lead to higher demand for both foreign and domestic goods. The effect on $\rho(\zeta_i, \zeta_j)$ might be stronger if trade integration leads to coordinated policy shocks (Frankel and Rose 1998).[2] Second, rising trade integration might lead to a more rapid spread of productivity shocks through more rapid diffusion of knowledge and technology (Coe and Helpman 1995) or through inward foreign direct investment and technology sourcing (Lichtenberg and van Pottelsberghe 1998).

In sum, the relationship between trade integration and business cycle correlation is theoretically ambiguous. Although the impact is positive if country-specific aggregate shocks dominate business cycles, the effect of trade integration is not clear if industry-specific shocks are the main source of business cycles. In the latter case, the nature of the relationship between trade integration and cyclical output correlations depend on the patterns of specialization in production once the economy is open to international markets.

Data and Methodology

This section describes the data used in the statistical analysis of the relationship between trade integration and cycle correlation between Latin America and China and India, and it outlines the econometric methodology undertaken to accomplish the task.

The Data

The dependent variable is the *degree of business cycle synchronization between* countries i and j at period τ (of length T). To measure this variable, the correlation between the cyclical components of output for countries i and j is computed as

$$\rho(\tilde{y}_i, \tilde{y}_j)_\tau = \frac{\text{cov}(\tilde{y}_i, \tilde{y}_j)_\tau}{\sqrt{\text{var}(\tilde{y}_i) \cdot \text{var}(\tilde{y}_j)}}, \tag{2.4}$$

where $\tilde{y}_i$ is the cyclical component of real output (y) in country i. The measure of real output is the real gross domestic product (GDP), in local currency at constant prices (in logs), taken from the World Bank's *World Development Indicators*. The cyclical component of output in country i is obtained using the band-pass filter proposed by Baxter and King (1999). Unlike other trend-cycle decomposition techniques, this filter takes into account the statistical features of the business cycle.[3] In accordance with these statistical properties, Baxter and King showed that the desired filter is a band-pass filter, that is, a filter that passes through components of the time series with periodic fluctuations between 6 and 32 quarters, while removing components at higher and lower frequencies.[4] Specifically, the cyclical component of real output is computed here by applying the band-pass filter on the series over the period 1960–2004. Once the business cycle is computed for each country, the correlation between detrended output in countries i and j is calculated over the following non-overlapping 10-year periods: 1965–74, 1975–84, 1985–94, and 1995–2004. According to this measure, higher output correlation between countries i and j implies a higher degree of business cycle synchronization.

The *bilateral intensity of international trade* between countries i and j in period τ (of length N) is approximated with the following measures:

$$T^F_{i,j,\tau} = \ln\left(\frac{1}{N}\sum_t \frac{1+f_{i,j,t}}{F_{i,t}+F_{j,t}}\right) \text{ and } T^Y_{i,j,\tau} = \ln\left(\frac{1}{N}\sum_t \frac{1+f_{i,j,t}}{Y_{i,t}+Y_{j,t}}\right), \quad (2.5)$$

where $f_{i,j,t}$ denotes the amount of bilateral trade flows (exports and imports) between countries i and j, while F_{kt} represents total (multilateral) trade— exports and imports—of country c (with $c = i, j$) in period t. Note that the numerator of the explanatory variables is $(1 + f_{i,j,\tau})$ to deal with the observations with zero trade flows, which would otherwise be dropped by taking logs. This is not a problem in studies that focus on industrial countries, because bilateral trade flows are nonzero. In the present case, approximately 23 to 25 percent of the observations in the panel data set, which includes 147 countries, have zero trade flows. To prevent the loss of these observations, which may contain important information, 1 is added to the bilateral trade flows, which is a standard way to deal with this problem in the context of gravity models of bilateral trade.[5] Equation (2.5) computes $T^F_{i,j,\tau}$ as the ratio of bilateral trade flows between countries i and j divided by the sum total trade flows (exports and imports) of countries i and j, and $T^F_{i,j,\tau}$ as the ratio of bilateral trade flows between countries i and j to output in both countries ($Y_{i,t}$ and $Y_{j,t}$, respectively).[6]

The bilateral trade data are taken from the International Monetary Fund's Direction of Trade Statistics, whereas nominal and real GDP data are taken from the World Bank's *World Development Indicators*. Annual data for 1965–2004 were gathered on bilateral trade flows for the 147 countries in the sample (see the annex for the list of countries), and only imports CIF (cost, insurance, and freight) data are used to construct the measures specified in equation (2.5).[7] Following Feenstra et al. (2005), importers' reports are preferable whenever they are available, given that these are more accurate than reports by the exporter.[8] Next, averages are computed over the annual data for the non-overlapping 10-year periods spanning 1965–2004. The discussion of the results mainly focuses on the bilateral trade figures normalized by output because they capture with more accuracy the effective degree of integration between two countries.[9]

The impact of *intra-industry trade intensity* on business cycle synchronization is also evaluated. To accomplish this task, the Grubel-Lloyd (1975) measure of intra-industry trade between countries i and j, $GLI_{i,j}$, is constructed:

$$GLI_{i,j} = 1 - \frac{\sum_s \left|x^s_{i,j} - m^s_{i,j}\right|}{\sum_s \left(x^s_{i,j} + m^s_{i,j}\right)}, \quad (2.6)$$

where $x_{i,j}^s$ and $m_{i,j}^s$ are exports from country i to country j and imports from country i to country j, respectively, and s represents an index over industries. This measure of intra-industry trade between countries i and j, $GLI_{i,j}$, represents the proportion of intra-industry trade in the total trade of these two countries. The data on intra-industry trade was obtained from the National Bureau of Economic Research–United Nations world trade data as collected by Feenstra et al. (2005). The Standard Industrial Trade Classification (SITC Rev. 2) two-digit-level bilateral exports and imports between countries i and j were used here. Annual data on bilateral trade across industries are available for the period 1962–2000 and the corresponding 10-year period averages are computed over this annual data set. For a more detailed description of the data, see Feenstra et al. (2005).

Another possible determinant of business cycle correlation is the extent of the similarities or differences between the structures of production or trade among countries. A measure of the *similarities in the structure of production* are considered first. Evidence shows that industry-specific shocks will generate higher degrees of business cycle synchronization among regions with similar production structures than among regions with asymmetric structures (Imbs 2001, 2004; Loayza, López, and Ubide 2001; Kalemli-Ozcan, Sorensen, and Yosha 2001). This variable is approximated using the absolute value index suggested by Krugman (1993). Letting $\theta_{s,i}$ and $\theta_{s,j}$ denote the GDP shares for industry s in countries i and j ($s = 1, 2, \ldots, S$ industries), an index of asymmetries in structures of production (or industry specialization) is computed as

$$ASP_{i,j,\tau} = \frac{1}{N} \sum_t \sum_{s=1}^{S} \left| \theta_{si} - \theta_{sj} \right|, \tag{2.7}$$

where $ASP_{i,j,\tau}$ is the index of asymmetries in structures of production between countries i and j averaged over period τ (of length T). The higher the value of $ASP_{i,j,\tau}$, the greater the difference in industry shares between countries i and j and, therefore, the greater the differences in structures of production.[10] Given that industry specialization may affect business cycle synchronization through different mechanisms, specialization is measured using the nine-sector classification from the one-digit-level International Standard Industrial Classification (SIC) code.[11] Data for the construction of these indexes was obtained from the World Bank's *World Development Indicators* and United Nations Industrial Development Organization. Finally, the index of *asymmetries in the structures of exports* between countries i and j over period τ, $ASX_{i,j,\tau}$, was constructed using the export shares for industry k in countries i and j at the two-digit-level SITC categories. Again, the higher the values of $ASX_{i,j,\tau}$, the greater the differences in export structures between countries i and j. Analogously, the index of *asymmetries in the structures of imports* between countries i and j over period τ, $ASM_{i,j,\tau}$, was constructed.

Empirical Strategy

To test the impact of trade integration (approximated by coefficients of bilateral trade intensity) on business cycle synchronization (measured by the correlation between cyclical outputs), the following baseline regression was run using the panel data[12]:

$$\rho(\tilde{y}_i, \tilde{y}_j)_\tau = \alpha_{i,j} + \beta_\tau + \gamma T_{i,j,\tau}^K + \phi GLI_{i,j,\tau} + \delta ASP_{i,j,\tau} + u_{i,j,\tau}, \qquad (2.8)$$

where $\rho(\tilde{y}_i, \tilde{y}_j)$ denotes the business cycle correlation between countries i and j over time period τ (of length $T = 10$ years); $T_{i,j,\tau}^Y$ is the average bilateral trade intensity between countries i and j over time period τ, either normalized by trade ($K = F$) or output ($K = Y$); $GLI_{i,j,\tau}$ is the Grubel-Lloyd index of intra-industry trade; and $ASP_{i,j,\tau}$ is the measure of industry specialization. In addition, $\alpha_{i,j}$ represent country-pair-specific effects, while β_τ are time effects that are proxied by decade dummies. Note that other specifications are also run that include asymmetries in the structure of exports or imports instead of asymmetries in structures of production.

The inclusion of country-pair fixed effects allows the analysis to control for all the time-invariant, country-pair-specific variables that may have an impact on output correlation.[13] More important, including the country-pair fixed effects leads to a focus on the time-series dimension and, thus, on the right policy question: what happens to the output correlation in Latin America with respect to China and India when bilateral trade intensity among them increases? This is not exactly the same as asking whether country pairs with higher bilateral trade intensity have higher output correlation than other country pairs, which is the question answered by the cross-section regressions. As Glick and Rose (2002) have argued convincingly in their analysis of the impact of monetary unions on trade, the former—and not the latter—is the right policy question.[14]

The main interest here lies on the sign and the magnitude of the slope coefficient γ. If industry shocks are the dominant source of business cycles and openness to trade leads to complete specialization (as Heckscher-Ohlin would predict), γ would be expected to be negative. However, if openness to trade leads to vertical specialization (and, therefore, more intra-industry trade), or if global shocks dominate economic fluctuations, then γ would be expected to be positive.

A problem with equation (2.8) is that, as discussed earlier, trade intensity itself may be endogenous. Higher output correlation could encourage countries to become members of a currency union, which, in turn, could lead to increased trade intensity (Frankel and Rose 1998, 2002; Rose and Engel 2002). Alternatively, both variables of interest—output correlation and trade intensity—could be explained by a third variable, such as currency union, which at the same time reduces transaction costs in trade flows and links the macroeconomic policies of their members. Hence, countries joining a currency union might exhibit a positive correlation between trade integration and business cycle synchronization. In this context, running an ordinary least squares (OLS) regression for equation (2.8) would yield biased and inconsistent estimates of γ. Given the problems mentioned above, instruments for bilateral trade intensity are needed to estimate γ consistently. This analysis uses the gravity model of bilateral trade to motivate the choice of instrumental variables.

Following Wei (1996) and Deardorff (1998), bilateral trade flows between country i and country j, $T_{i,j}^K$—normalized by either trade ($K = F$) or output ($K = Y$)—are regressed on the following determinants: the (log of the) distance between countries i and j, (d_{ij}); a dummy variable for countries sharing a common border, (B_{ij}); and indicators of geographical remoteness for countries i and j that measure how far each country lies from alternative trading partners, REM_i and REM_j, respectively.[15] A dummy for the presence of a free trade agreement in the country-pair (FTA_{ij}) is included, as are the population densities of countries i and j; dummy variables for countries sharing common language, colonial origin, main trading partner, and geographic region; and dummies for islands, landlocked countries, and legal origin.[16]

Empirical Evaluation

This section describes some stylized facts about the patterns of output comovement and international trade between Latin America and China as well as between Latin America and India, and conducts the regression analysis that links patterns of inter- and intra-industry trade as well as output specialization with the comovement of business cycles.

Descriptive Statistics

The following describes the main statistics (averages and standard deviations) for business cycle synchronization, bilateral trade intensity, the extent of intra-industry trade, asymmetries in structures of production, and trade for the sample of countries over the period 1965–2004. In addition, it highlights the evolution of these variables for LAC in comparison with China and India. Table 2.1 presents summary statistics for 1965–2004 for all the variables involved in the analysis.

Business cycle synchronization. Figures 2.1a and 2.1b, respectively, present the 10-year-window rolling correlation of real output fluctuations for LAC and LAC subregions with respect to China and India over the 1981–2004 period.

The first point to observe is that the output correlation between LAC and China rises sharply over time, from –0.22 in 1981 to 0.46 in 2004.

Table 2.1 Basic Statistics
(10-year non-overlapping periods)

| | Output correlation[a] | Bilateral trade intensity[b] | | Intra-industry trade[c] | Structural asymmetries | | |
		Normalized by trade	Normalized by output		In production	In exports	In imports
LAC							
(LAC, IND)	0.117	−9.31	−10.02	0.0418	0.280	1.412	0.756
	[0.39]	[2.73]	[2.55]	[0.07]	[0.14]	[0.22]	[0.18]
(LAC, DEV)	0.035	−13.41	−13.98	0.0110	0.438	1.281	0.840
	[0.37]	[4.82]	[4.73]	[0.04]	[0.24]	[0.32]	[0.20]
(LAC, LAC)	0.095	−9.10	−9.88	0.0511	0.288	1.294	0.805
	[0.38]	[3.63]	[3.52]	[0.09]	[0.15]	[0.29]	[0.23]
China							
(China, IND)	−0.066	−6.33	−7.48	0.1177	0.988	1.192	0.632
	[0.39]	[1.58]	[1.92]	[0.09]	[0.20]	[0.20]	[0.10]
(China, DEV)	−0.013	−8.44	−9.70	0.0182	1.022	1.320	0.481
	[0.37]	[2.72]	[2.58]	[0.04]	[0.20]	[0.24]	[0.17]
(China, LAC)	0.058	−10.34	−11.89	0.0146	1.053	1.339	0.532
	[0.36]	[3.72]	[3.90]	[0.03]	[0.23]	[0.20]	[0.16]

(continued)

Table 2.1 Basic Statistics *(continued)*
(10-year non-overlapping periods)

	Output correlation[a]	Bilateral trade intensity[b]		Intra-industry trade[c]	Structural asymmetries		
		Normalized by trade	Normalized by output		In production	In exports	In imports
(China, East Asia)	0.112	−8.34	−9.56	0.0958	0.994	1.221	0.493
	[0.38]	[4.67]	[5.12]	[0.15]	[0.24]	[0.26]	[0.23]
India							
(India, IND)	−0.033	−6.50	−7.76	0.1079	0.915	1.286	0.589
	[0.40]	[1.22]	[1.43]	[0.09]	[0.08]	[0.18]	[0.14]
(India, DEV)	0.044	−8.51	−10.10	0.0344	0.992	1.331	0.385
	[0.38]	[3.24]	[3.50]	[0.08]	[0.14]	[0.24]	[0.20]
(India, LAC)	−0.035	−10.20	−11.96	0.0144	0.971	1.319	0.425
	[0.35]	[2.16]	[2.14]	[0.03]	[0.14]	[0.18]	[0.18]
(India, South Asia)	0.107	−5.90	−7.48	0.0938	0.901	1.112	0.220
	[0.36]	[1.17]	[0.80]	[0.07]	[0.17]	[0.16]	[0.14]

Source: Author.

Note: IND = industrial countries; DEV = developing countries. The figures in brackets below the averages are the standard deviations of the series.

a. The correlation of the (band-pass filtered) cyclical component of real output in countries *j* and *k*.
b. Bilateral trade intensity, as a share of total trade of the country-pair as well as the output in both countries, is expressed in logs.
c. The Grubel-Lloyd index of intra-industry trade.

This upward trend is mainly attributable to the rising output correlation between (a) China and the Andean countries, which increases from −0.31 in 1981 to 0.54 in 2004, and (b) China and the Southern Cone, which increases from −0.11 to 0.63 over the same time period. Conversely, Mexico displays a declining output correlation with China that becomes negative beginning in 1988. Finally, output fluctuations in Central America and the Caribbean are negatively associated with the business cycle in China for most of the period. This correlation is increasingly negative from the beginning of the 1980s, reaching −0.67 in 2004 (see figure 2.1a).

Second, output fluctuations for Latin America with respect to India are negatively associated with cyclical fluctuations in India's real output for most of the period, although showing an upward trend. Specifically, the correlation increased from −0.49 in 1981 to −0.17 in 2004. An analogous pattern of comovement is displayed by all subregions except Central America and the Caribbean. In the latter case, the cycle synchronization with India shows a declining trend up to 1993, and afterward increases from −0.59 to −0.06 in 2004 (see figure 2.1b).

Finally, the upward trend in the output correlation of LAC with both countries might be attributable to the increasing demand for commodities from China and India. In particular, Chinese demand for commodities increased approximately 50 percent between 2000 and 2003, with China representing approximately 28 percent of world consumption of steel in 2003, 27 percent of world consumption of iron ore, 21 percent of aluminum, 21 percent of zinc, 19 percent of copper, and 11 percent of nickel (Fiess 2005). Hence, the analysis investigates the impact of year-over-year percentage changes of the monthly industrial production index (IPI) in China and India on the year-over-year variation of the monthly IPI in Latin American countries.[17] To investigate whether the relationship has changed over time, a recursive OLS is applied, using 36 observations as a base period and adding one observation at a time until the sample end (December 2005) is reached. To distinguish the impact of China and India from global trends, U.S. industrial production is included as a control variable and only the portion of Chinese industrial production that is orthogonal to U.S. industrial production is included as a regressor (see more details in Fiess 2005).

Figure 2.2a shows that 2002–03 may represent the turning point in the relationship between Chinese industrial production and world commodity prices. China not only seems to have a positive and significant impact on world commodity prices but its effect has also increased over time. In particular, metals and minerals and beverages (especially coffee) seem to be most affected by the rapid growth in China. Analogous behavior is exhibited by the correlation between Chinese IPI and the world price of crude oil, where the coefficient estimate for industrial production in China grew from 0.81 at the beginning of 2002 to 1.88 by the end of 2005. Figure 2.2b reports the relationship between Indian IPI and world commodity prices. This relationship shows an upward trend and became significant beginning in 2003, with the exception of crude oil prices.

Trade integration. Figure 2.3 shows the evolution of bilateral trade intensity (normalized by output) of LAC and LAC subregions with respect to China and India.[18] Trade links have grown deeper between all LAC subregions and China and all LAC subregions and India over the past 20 years. On average, the bilateral trade coefficient between LAC and China tripled in 1995–2004 relative to 1985–94, while the coefficient with India is now four times larger than it was for 1985–94. In particular, Mexico and the Andean countries show the largest increases in trade intensity with China (see figure 2.3a), while trade integration with India was more dynamic among Andean countries (see figure 2.3b).

In addition, figure 2.4 depicts the evolution of the Grubel-Lloyd index of intra-industry trade (IIT) of LAC and LAC subregions with China and India. IIT between LAC and China almost doubled in 1995–2004 relative to 1985–94, and almost tripled with India. While the former is mainly explained by primary sectors and machinery and transport equipment, the latter is attributable to an increasing trade share in chemicals (of which LAC is a net importer). For Mexico, IIT with China grew more than 50 percent while its IIT with India more than tripled. Finally, IIT between Andean countries and China increased significantly over the past 20 years.

Specialization in production and foreign trade. Figure 2.5 presents the evolution of asymmetries in the structure of production ($ASP_{i,j}$) for LAC with respect to China and India. Asymmetries in structures of production of LAC with both China and India have decreased in the past 20 years, although at a faster pace with India. For Mexico, although asymmetries in structures of production with China have remained almost invariant in 1995–2004 relative to 1985–94, asymmetries in the baskets of exports and imports with China have declined (see figures 2.5 through 2.7). However, asymmetries in export structures with China have increased over time for all other LAC subregions (figure 2.6a).

In addition, the analysis evaluates whether LAC countries compete with either China or India in LAC's relevant export markets by constructing an *export similarity index* (ESI). The study uses export flows by partner and commodity code using the UN Comtrade Harmonized System database. Following Finger and Kreinin (1979), the ESI is

$$ESI_{i,j;p} = \left\{ \sum_k \min\left[X_{g,i;p}, X_{g,j;p} \right] \right\} \times 100, \tag{2.9}$$

where $ESI_{i,j;p}$ measures the extent of similarity of the export patterns of countries i and j to market p, with $X_{g,i;p}$ being the share of commodity g in country i's exports to trading partner p. The index ranges from 0 to 100;

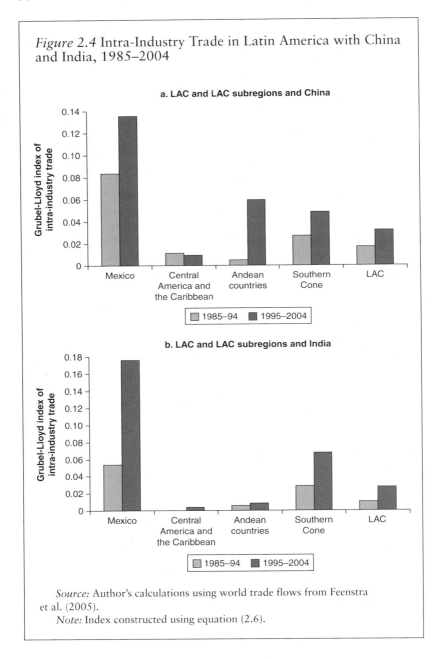

Figure 2.4 Intra-Industry Trade in Latin America with China and India, 1985–2004

a. LAC and LAC subregions and China

b. LAC and LAC subregions and India

Source: Author's calculations using world trade flows from Feenstra et al. (2005).

Note: Index constructed using equation (2.6).

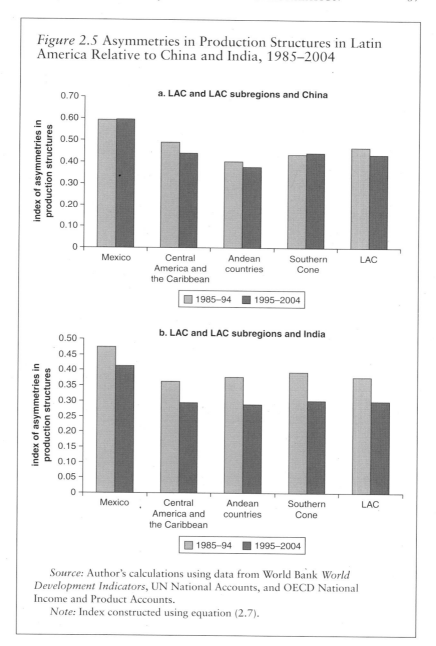

Figure 2.5 Asymmetries in Production Structures in Latin America Relative to China and India, 1985–2004

Source: Author's calculations using data from World Bank *World Development Indicators*, UN National Accounts, and OECD National Income and Product Accounts.

Note: Index constructed using equation (2.7).

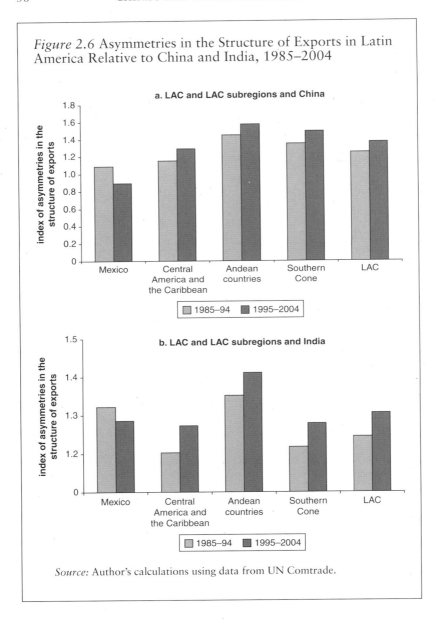

Figure 2.6 Asymmetries in the Structure of Exports in Latin America Relative to China and India, 1985–2004

Source: Author's calculations using data from UN Comtrade.

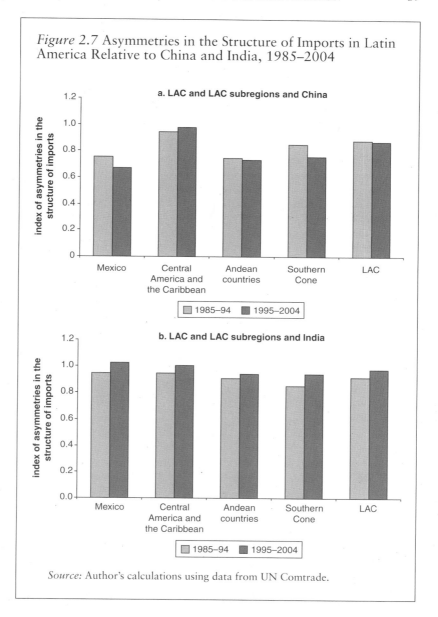

Figure 2.7 Asymmetries in the Structure of Imports in Latin America Relative to China and India, 1985–2004

a. LAC and LAC subregions and China

index of asymmetries in the structure of imports

■ 1985–94   ■ 1995–2004

b. LAC and LAC subregions and India

index of asymmetries in the structure of imports

■ 1985–94   ■ 1995–2004

Source: Author's calculations using data from UN Comtrade.

it takes the value of 0 if the baskets of exports of countries i and j to trading partner p are completely different—that is, they do not compete in p's market. It takes the value of 100 if their baskets of exports to trading partner p are the same. Here, the analysis is especially interested in evaluating the similarity of the LAC export basket to those of China and India in the U.S. market.

Figure 2.8 shows the ESI between LAC and China and between LAC and India with respect to the U.S. market for 1985–94 and 1995–2004.[19] Mexico's export basket most resembles the Chinese basket of exports to the United States. In addition, the ESI between other LAC subregions and China has declined over time—especially for Andean countries and the Southern Cone. This decline implies a reduction in the degree of competition with China in the U.S. market for these subregions (see figure 2.8a). Finally, the ESI between LAC and India has increased slightly, as in Mexico. The other subregions show only a slight reduction in competition with India in the U.S. markets.

Correlation Analysis

Before discussing the regression analysis, some basic correlations are presented between the measure of output synchronization; bilateral trade intensity; intra-industry trade; and asymmetries in the structures of production, exports, and imports for the panel data of country pairs during the period 1965–2004. The results are reported in table 2.2.

First, the correlation between LAC and industrial countries is negative (–0.040). However, the output correlations among LAC countries and between LAC and other developing countries are positive (0.034 and 0.029, respectively). This result may suggest the prevalence of interindustry trade when considering LAC and industrial country pairs. Furthermore, although the correlation between output comovement and trade intensity between LAC economies and China is positive (0.138), it is negative between LAC countries and India (–0.126).

Second, output correlation and the degree of intra-industry trade are positively related for the samples of LAC-industrial countries (0.070), LAC-LAC countries (0.092), and LAC-developing country pairs (0.026). Again, higher intra-industry trade is associated with higher output comovement for (LAC, China) country pairs, while the converse is true for (LAC, India) country pairs (0.071 and –0.075, respectively).

Finally, a weak positive relationship is found between asymmetries in production between LAC-industrial country pairs, while the association is negative among LAC countries and for LAC-developing country pairs. This implies that higher asymmetries in production structures may lead to more asynchronous business cycles. This result holds for (LAC, China) and (LAC, India) country pairs.

Figure 2.8 Export Similarity Index between Latin America, India, and China with Respect to the U.S. Market, 1985–2004

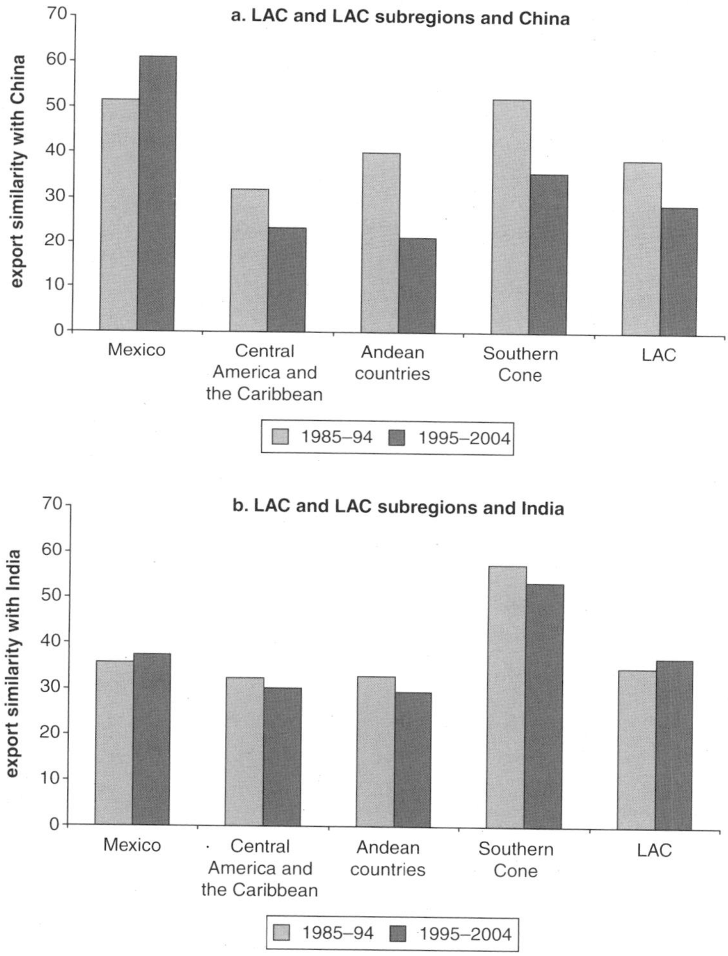

a. LAC and LAC subregions and China

1985–94   1995–2004

b. LAC and LAC subregions and India

1985–94   1995–2004

Source: Author's calculations using data from UN Comtrade.
Note: Similarity indexes computed using equation (2.9).

Table 2.2 Correlation Analysis
(10-year non-overlapping periods)

	Bilateral trade intensity			Structural asymmetries		
	Normalized by trade	Normalized by output	Intra-industry trade	In production	In exports	In imports
LAC						
(LAC, IND)	-0.0445	-0.0401	0.0703**	0.0033	0.0087	0.0610*
(LAC, DEV)	0.0184	0.0286	0.0263	-0.0179	0.0037	-0.0144
(LAC, LAC)	0.0471	0.0341	0.0926*	-0.0314	-0.0235	-0.0536
China						
(China, IND)	-0.1006	-0.1921	-0.1911	0.1399	0.3537**	0.3755**
(China, DEV)	0.0942	0.0851	0.1616	-0.0679	0.0490	-0.0127
(China, LAC)	0.1200	0.1386	0.0709	-0.1071	0.2233*	-0.2722*
(China, East Asia)	-0.0352	-0.0542	0.1564	0.0815	-0.0839	0.0008
India						
(India, IND)	0.1292	0.0998	0.0825	-0.1294	-0.0447	-0.2610
(India, DEV)	0.0009	-0.0005	-0.0490	-0.0898	-0.1120	-0.0970
(India, LAC)	-0.1642	-0.1256	-0.0749	-0.0692	0.1633	-0.0097
(India, South Asia)	-0.1894	-0.1431	-0.1657	-0.0903	0.0421	-0.3415

Source: Author.
Note: IND = industrial countries; DEV = developing countries.
*Statistically significant at the 10 percent level.
**Statistically significant at the 5 percent level.

Regression Analysis

Estimates for the baseline regression. To evaluate the impact of trade integration and specialization on business cycle synchronization of LAC countries with China and India, the analysis first presents OLS estimates of the baseline regression, equation (2.8). The present regression analysis uses the *LAC Sample*, which consists of country pairs that include Latin American countries—LAC-industrial, LAC-developing, and LAC-LAC country pairs.

Table 2.3 presents the least squares estimates of the baseline regression that includes country-pair dummies, country-group dummies (LAC-developing and LAC-LAC country pairs), time-period dummies (for 1975–84, 1985–94, and 1995–2004). In addition, the regression includes time dummies specific to (LAC, China) and (LAC, India) country pairs, which allows the computation of the impact of demand spillovers from China and India to LAC economies. From now on, the discussion focuses on the results obtained with bilateral trade intensity normalized by total output.

The first finding is that countries with higher bilateral trade intensity, normalized by either total trade or total output, usually display higher business cycle synchronization. All the coefficient estimates of trade integration are positive and significant regardless of their normalization factors and the control variables included in the regression. The coefficient estimates in columns (4)–(6) of table 2.3 illustrate the economic significance of the regression analysis. For instance, if trade integration with China for the median country in the region (Paraguay, with an average log of trade intensity of –8.9 in 1995–2004) rises sharply, to the levels observed by the leader of the region (Mexico, at –5.85), Paraguay's output correlation with China will increase by 0.011. However, an analogous shift in trade integration with China for the worst trade performer (Haiti) would imply, on average, an increase in output correlation of 0.023. Analogous exercises are performed regarding trade integration with India. If trade integration between the median LAC country and India (Guatemala, –10.4 in 1995–2004) increases sharply, to the levels of the leading country (Argentina, –7.3), Guatemala's output correlation will rise by 0.011. For the country with the lowest trade share with India (Nicaragua, –13.25 in 1995–2004), reaching the levels of trade intensity displayed by Argentina implies an output correlation with India that is 0.021 higher. Finally, if the average country in Central America (excluding Mexico) increases its trade integration with either China or India to the levels displayed by South America, its output correlation with those countries will increase by 0.01.

Second, countries with higher levels of intra-industry trade tend to show larger cyclical output correlations. All coefficient estimates associated with the Grubel-Lloyd index of intra-industry trade are positive and significant regardless of the specification used. Again, the estimates in columns (4)–(6) of table 2.3, using trade intensity normalized by total output,

Table 2.3 Baseline Regression: Least Squares
Dependent variable: Output correlation for countries j and k
LAC sample, 1965–2004 (10-year period observations)

	Bilateral trade intensity (normalized by total trade)			Bilateral trade intensity (normalized by total output)		
	(1)	(2)	(3)	(4)	(5)	(6)
Trade integration	0.003** [0.00]	0.004** [0.00]	0.003** [0.00]	0.003** [0.00]	0.004** [0.00]	0.004** [0.00]
Grubel-Lloyd index of intra-industry trade	0.302** [0.08]	0.305** [0.08]	0.320** [0.08]	0.287** [0.08]	0.292** [0.08]	0.311** [0.08]
Structural asymmetries						
In production (ASP)	-0.178 [0.14]			-0.234* [0.14]		
In exports (ASX)		-0.025 [0.02]			-0.029* [0.02]	
In imports (ASM)			-0.015 [0.03]			-0.012 [0.02]

(continued)

Table 2.3 Baseline Regression: Least Squares *(continued)*
Dependent variable: Output correlation for countries j *and* k
LAC sample, 1965–2004 (10-year period observations)

	Bilateral trade intensity (normalized by total trade)			Bilateral trade intensity (normalized by total output)		
	(1)	*(2)*	*(3)*	*(4)*	*(5)*	*(6)*
Dummies						
Period[a]	Yes	Yes	Yes	Yes	Yes	Yes
Period × (China and India)[a]	Yes	Yes	Yes	Yes	Yes	Yes
Country group[b]	Yes	Yes	Yes	Yes	Yes	Yes
Country pairs	Yes	Yes	Yes	Yes	Yes	Yes

Source: Author.

Note: ASM = asymmetries in the structures of imports; ASP = asymmetries in the structures of exports. Numbers in brackets represent robust standard errors (White 1980).

a. Dummies are included for the periods 1975–84, 1985–94, and 1995–2004. Time dummies are also included, multiplied by (LAC, China) and (LAC, India) country-pairs. They are separately included in the regressions and are intended to capture demand spillovers in LAC from China and India.

b. The regression analysis includes dummies for (LAC, DEV) and (LAC, LAC) country pairs.

*Statistically significant at the 10 percent level.

**Statistically significant at the 5 percent level.

suggest that an increase in the extent of intra-industry trade between Central America and the Caribbean with China to the levels displayed by the average Andean country would lead to a higher output correlation by 0.015, and by 0.037 if the increasing intra-industry trade reaches the levels displayed by Mexico. However, the output correlation between India and the average country in Central America and the Caribbean would increase by 0.019 if that country's intra-industry trade goes up to the levels displayed by the average Southern Cone country. In addition, the correlation for the average Central American country would increase by 0.051 if its intra-industry trade with India rises to the level of Mexico.

Finally, countries with similar patterns of specialization in either production or trade tend to display more symmetric business cycles. However, the results are not robust: the coefficients of *ASP* and *ASX* are negative and significant only when using trade intensity normalized by output. Economically speaking, a reduction in the asymmetries of export structures between the average Central American country and China to the ones displayed by China and Mexico would be associated with an increase in output correlation of 0.012, while an analogous reduction for the average Andean country would enhance the cycle correlation by 0.02.

Controlling for endogeneity in trade intensity. The association between trade intensity and cycle correlation could be attributed to reverse causality or to both variables being explained by a third variable omitted from the model (a monetary union, for example). In this context, the OLS estimates presented above would be biased and inconsistent. Hence, instruments for bilateral trade are needed to estimate the coefficient of interest more consistently. The analysis takes advantage of the vast literature on the gravity model of international trade to choose a set of instruments for bilateral trade intensity (Frankel and Romer 1999; Rose 2000). Following this literature, bilateral trade intensity between countries i and j is instrumented with the distance between countries i and j; remoteness of countries i and j; population density in both countries; dummy variables for common border, common language, colonial heritage, geographic region, legal origin, common main trading partner, islands, and landlocked countries; and a dummy for a regional free trade agreement. Except for the dummy variables, the determinants are expressed in logs.

The results for the gravity model of bilateral trade (that is, first-stage regressions) are presented in table 2.4. In general, trade intensity rises among countries that (a) are closer together, share a common border, have trading partners that are farther away from the rest of the world, and are members of the same region; (b) have greater population density; (c) have engaged in a free trade agreement or have the same main trading partner; and (d) speak the same language.

Instrumental variables (IV) estimation. Based on the first-stage results, the baseline regression is reestimated using instrumental variables (IV). The IV

Table 2.4 First-Stage Regressions: Gravity Model of
Bilateral Trade
Dependent variable: Bilateral trade intensity between countries
j *and* k
LAC sample, 1965–2004 (10-year period observations)

Variable	Normalized by total trade (1)	Normalized by outputs (2)
Border (j, k)	1.578**	1.156**
	[0.42]	[0.40]
Distance (j, k) (in logs)	–2.069**	–2.088**
	[0.15]	[0.14]
Remoteness of country j	11.273**	9.865**
	[0.81]	[0.75]
Remoteness of country k	10.148**	8.395**
	[0.79]	[0.72]
Free trade agreement dummy	0.552*	0.982**
	[0.34]	[0.32]
Population density of j	0.474**	0.477**
	[0.03]	[0.03]
Population density of k	0.272**	0.243**
	[0.03]	[0.03]
Common language dummy	1.865**	1.501**
	[0.22]	[0.19]
Colonial origin dummy	–0.742**	–0.123
	[0.22]	[0.19]
Common trading partner dummy	2.058**	1.873**
	[0.47]	[0.43]
Common region dummy	1.330**	0.906**
	[0.21]	[0.19]
Common legal origin dummy	–0.743**	–0.871**
	[0.10]	[0.10]

(continued)

Table 2.4 First-Stage Regressions: Gravity Model of
Bilateral Trade *(continued)*
Dependent variable: Bilateral trade intensity between countries
j *and* k
LAC sample, 1965–2004 (10-year period observations)

Variable	Normalized by total trade (1)	Normalized by outputs (2)
Islands	−1.502**	−1.306**
	[0.09]	[0.09]
Landlocked countries	−1.532**	−1.455**
	[0.11]	[0.11]
Constant	−10.581**	−8.707**
	[1.10]	[1.00]
Observations	9,535	10,479
R squared	0.154	0.153
Adjusted R squared	0.153	0.152

Source: Author.
Note: Numbers in brackets represent robust standard errors.
**Statistically significant at the 5 percent level.

estimates, presented in table 2.5, confirm the results: higher business cycle synchronization between countries could be explained by rising trade intensity—especially along the lines of intra-industry trade—and increased similarities in the patterns of specialization in production and foreign trade (in particular, exports). Note that these results are robust to changes in the specification of the model and to the use of different measures of bilateral trade intensity.

Based on the coefficient estimates of columns (4)–(6) in table 2.5, which use bilateral trade intensity normalized by total output, the following economic interpretations are provided:

- *Trade integration.* The analysis first simulates the impact on output correlation of an increase in trade intensity for a selected LAC country to the maximum level of trade integration with China (Mexico, with a log of trade intensity normalized by output of −5.85 in 1995–2004). The increase in output correlation for the least integrated country with China (Belize) would lie between 0.06 and 0.081, while the output correlation for the median country with China (Paraguay) would increase between 0.029 and 0.039. Second, if the

Table 2.5 Baseline Regression: Instrumental Variables (IV) Estimation
Dependent variable: Output correlation for countries j and k
LAC sample, 1965–2004 (10-year period observations)

	Bilateral trade intensity (normalized by total trade)			Bilateral trade intensity (normalized by total output)		
	(1)	(2)	(3)	(4)	(5)	(6)
Trade integration	0.009**	0.013**	0.013**	0.009**	0.013**	0.013**
	[0.00]	[0.00]	[0.00]	[0.00]	[0.00]	[0.00]
Grubel-Lloyd index of intra-industry trade	0.253**	0.239**	0.255**	0.248**	0.240**	0.255**
	[0.08]	[0.08]	[0.08]	[0.08]	[0.08]	[0.08]
Structural asymmetries						
In production (ASP)	-0.597**			-0.626**		
	[0.17]			[0.17]		
In exports (ASX)		-0.034*			-0.034*	
		[0.02]			[0.02]	
In imports (ASM)			-0.011			-0.013
			[0.02]			[0.02]

(continued)

Table 2.5 Baseline Regression: Instrumental Variables (IV) Estimation *(continued)*
Dependent variable: Output correlation for countries j and k
LAC sample, 1965–2004 (10-year period observations)

	Bilateral trade intensity (normalized by total trade)			Bilateral trade intensity (normalized by total output)		
	(1)	*(2)*	*(3)*	*(4)*	*(5)*	*(6)*
Dummies						
Period[a]	Yes	Yes	Yes	Yes	Yes	Yes
Period × (China and India)[a]	Yes	Yes	Yes	Yes	Yes	Yes
Country group[b]	Yes	Yes	Yes	Yes	Yes	Yes
Country pairs	Yes	Yes	Yes	Yes	Yes	Yes

Source: Author.

Note: ASM = asymmetries in the structures of imports; ASP = asymmetries in the structures of production; ASX = asymmetries in the structures of exports. Numbers in brackets represent robust standard errors.

a. Dummies are included for the periods 1975–84, 1985–94, and 1995–2004.

b. Dummies are included for (LAC, DEV) and (LAC, LAC) country pairs.

*Statistically significant at the 10 percent level.

**Statistically significant at the 5 percent level.

average levels of trade integration with China for Central America and the Caribbean (excluding Mexico) rise to the levels displayed by the Southern Cone, the output correlation with China of Central America would go up between 0.028 and 0.039. Analogously, an increase in the average trade intensity with China of the Andean countries to Southern Cone standards would raise the Andean countries' output correlation with China, although to a lesser extent—output correlation between Andean countries and China would increase between 0.007 and 0.010.

A similar exercise is carried out for trade integration of LAC countries with India. Argentina and Brazil show the largest trade integration with India (with an average of –7.35 in 1995–2004). Increasing trade integration for Nicaragua (the country with the minimum value in trade intensity for 1995–2004) would raise its output correlation between 0.055 and 0.075, whereas it would increase between 0.028 and 0.039 for the median country in the LAC sample (Ecuador). If trade integration between Central America and the Caribbean and India rises to the levels of the Southern Cone and India, that subregion's output correlation would increase between 0.024 and 0.032, while the impact for the Andean countries would be between 0.012 and 0.016.

- *Degree of intra-industry trade.* Among LAC countries, Mexico and República Bolivariana de Venezuela show the largest Grubel-Lloyd index of intra-industry trade with China (at an average of 0.15 for the 1995–2004 period). If the median country in the LAC sample (Ecuador) were to raise its degree of intra-industry trade to Mexico's level, Ecuador's output correlation would increase by 0.037, while for countries in the 75th percentile of the LAC sample (Argentina and Uruguay), the increase in output correlation would be 0.025.

  Analogously, Brazil shows the largest degree of intra-industry trade with India (with an average of 0.22 for the period 1995–2004), followed by Mexico (with 0.18). Again, the analysis simulates the impact on output correlation of higher intra-industry trade for the median countries (Ecuador and Colombia) and the 75th percentile (Paraguay) of intra-industry trade in the LAC sample of country pairs with India. Higher intra-industry trade for the median country would lead to an increase in output correlation between 0.051 and 0.055, while for Paraguay, the cycle synchronization with India would increase between 0.049 and 0.052.

- *Asymmetries in the structures of production (ASP).* Column (4) of table 2.5 reports the regression results using the asymmetries in economic structures. Of interest is that for the period 1995–2004, República Bolivariana de Venezuela has the lowest value in the ASP index with China (with an average of 0.22) while Panama exhibits the largest value (at 0.73). Here the analysis will simulate the impact on output correlation of reaching the levels of ASP displayed by República Bolivariana de Venezuela (the country with the lowest value of ASP) for selected LAC countries. In this case, for the country with the median ASP with China (Paraguay), a further reduction in the ASP (to Venezuelan levels) raises its output correlation by 0.12, while the increase in output correlation for Argentina (75th percentile) associated with a reduction in ASP is 0.17. However, Paraguay shows the lowest degree of ASP with India (0.046) while Panama shows the largest ASP (0.536) over the period 1995–2004. A reduction in ASP to the minimum levels by countries such as Costa Rica (median) and Argentina (75th percentile) would lead to increases in output correlation of 0.077 and 0.099, respectively.

- *Asymmetries in foreign trade structure.* The regression analysis uses measures of asymmetries in the structure of exports and imports for LAC countries with respect to China and India. Here, the analysis evaluates the economic impact of changes in asymmetries in the structure of exports (ASX) using the coefficients in column (5) of table 2.5. Mexico is the LAC country with the lowest value of the ASX index with China—that is, among LAC economies, Mexico's export basket most resembles China's export basket (with an average of 0.89 for the period 1995–2004). Chile, Ecuador, and República Bolivariana de Venezuela show the largest ASX index for the period 1995–2004, with values ranging between 1.64 and 1.70. The analysis again simulates the gains in output correlation for selected LAC countries with a decline in the degree of asymmetries in the export baskets with China. For República Bolivariana de Venezuela (the country with the largest degree of ASX), the output correlation with China may increase by 0.027, whereas for the median country (Uruguay), the output correlation with China goes up by 0.016.

  Finally, the analysis evaluates the reduction of asymmetries in export baskets of LAC countries with respect to India. The countries with the lowest degree of asymmetries in export structures with India are Uruguay and Brazil (with average indexes of 1.07 and 1.13, respectively, for 1995–2004). A simulation of the impact on output correlation of reducing the degree of ASX relative to India for some LAC countries to the levels displayed by Uruguay and Brazil finds that for Ecuador and República Bolivariana de Venezuela (the countries with the largest ASX with India), output correlation increases by 0.02. In addition, the increase in output correlation with India for the median country pairs (Mexico and Peru) is approximately 0.01.

Trade intensity and cycle synchronization: The role of structural asymmetries and intra-industry trade. Evidence suggests that the link between trade intensity and cycle correlation is stronger among industrial countries than among developing countries or mixed industrial-developing country pairs (Calderón, Chong, and Stein 2007). These differences in the responsiveness of cycle synchronization to trade intensity are broadly explained by patterns of specialization and international trade in the country pair. It has been argued that industrial country pairs are more likely to have more symmetric structures of production and foreign trade as well as a higher degree of intra-industry trade compared with developing and mixed industrial-developing country pairs. Note that this conjecture is corroborated by Calderón, Chong, and Stein (2007). Regarding the country pairs of interest in this analysis, LAC-China and LAC-India (that is, developing country pairs), increased trade intensity may lead, on average, to increased specialization in different industries, which would lead to asymmetric effects of industry-specific shocks.

Complementing the evidence presented in Calderón, Chong, and Stein (2007), this analysis explores the role of structural asymmetries (in production and foreign trade) and intra-industry trade in determining the sensitivity of cyclical output correlation to higher trade integration among country pairs. In particular, the following regression is run:

$$\rho(\tilde{y}_i, \tilde{y}_j)_\tau = \alpha_{i,j} + \beta_\tau + \gamma_0 T^K_{i,j,\tau} + \phi GLI_{i,j,\tau} + \delta ASP_{i,j,\tau} + \gamma_1 T^K_{i,j,\tau} \times ASP_{i,j,\tau}$$
$$+ \gamma_2 T^K_{i,j,\tau} \times GLI_{i,j,\tau} + u_{i,j,\tau}. \tag{2.10}$$

The regression includes two interaction terms that capture complementarities between bilateral trade intensity and (a) similarities in the structure of production (as well as in foreign trade), and (b) the pattern of intra-industry trade. It has been argued that similarities in the structure of production as well as in the structure of foreign trade may affect the responsiveness of cycle correlation to trade integration because similar economies are more prone to show a pattern of intra-industry specialization. Hence, the coefficient for the interaction term γ_1 is expected to be negative and significant. That is, the impact of trade integration on cycle correlation should be weaker for countries with more asymmetries in structures of production or trade. However, including the interaction between the Grubel-Lloyd index of intra-industry trade and the ratio of bilateral trade intensity allows the analysis to distinguish the impact on business cycle synchronization of interindustry trade from the effects of intra-industry trade. According to the literature, the coefficient of γ_2 is expected to be positive and significant.

Table 2.6 reports the full specification of the regression analysis that includes not only the interaction term between trade intensity and the degree of intra-industry trade but also the interaction between trade intensity and structural asymmetries in production or foreign trade. Adjusting this regression for the LAC sample yields a positive and robust estimate for the coefficients of bilateral trade intensity normalized by output $\left(T^Y_{i,j,\tau}\right)$

Table 2.6 Augmented Regression: Instrumental Variables (IV) Estimation
Dependent variable: Output correlation for countries j and k
LAC sample, 1965–2004 (10-year period observations)

	(1)	(2)	(3)	(4)	(5)	(6)
Bilateral trade intensity (normalized by total output)						
Trade integration (TI)	0.008**	0.011**	0.011**	0.011**	0.027**	0.057*
	[0.00]	[0.00]	[0.00]	[0.00]	[0.01]	[0.03]
Grubel-Lloyd index of intra-industry trade (GLI)	0.516** (0.19)	0.521** [0.19]	0.528** [0.19]	0.361* [0.22]	0.517** [0.19]	0.472** [0.20]
GLI(j, k) × TI(j, k)	0.031	0.032	0.032	0.018	0.031	0.027
	[0.02]	[0.02]	[0.02]	[0.02]	[0.02]	[0.02]
Structural asymmetries						
In production (ASP)	−0.612**	n.a.	n.a.	−0.654**	n.a.	n.a.
	[0.17]			[0.19]		
In exports (ASX)	n.a.	−0.015	n.a.	n.a.	−0.017	n.a.
	[0.02]	[0.02]				
In imports (ASM)	n.a.	n.a.	−0.007	n.a.	n.a.	−0.692
			[0.03]			[0.48]

(continued)

Table 2.6 Augmented Regression: Instrumental Variables (IV) Estimation *(continued)*
Dependent variable: Output correlation for countries j and k
LAC sample, 1965–2004 (10-year period observations)

	(1)	(2)	(3)	(4)	(5)	(6)
Interaction: Trade intensity and structural asymmetries						
TI1(j, k) × ASP (j, k)	n.a.	n.a.	n.a.	−9.17E−04 [0.00]	n.a.	n.a.
TI1(j, k) × ASX (j, k)	n.a.	n.a.	n.a.	n.a.	−1.13E−02 [0.01]	n.a.
TI1(j, k) × ASM (j, k)	n.a.	n.a.	n.a.	n.a.	n.a.	−5.83E−02 [0.04]
Period-specific dummies						
D(75–84)	0.092**	0.091**	0.092**	0.077**	0.091**	0.092**
D(85–94)	−0.073**	−0.072**	−0.068**	−0.086**	−0.074**	−0.068**
D(95–04)	0.054**	0.058**	0.060**	0.050**	0.055**	0.061**
D(LAC, China) × D(75–84)	−0.102*	−0.084	−0.081	−0.116*	−0.097*	−0.081

(continued)

Table 2.6 Augmented Regression: Instrumental Variables (IV) Estimation *(continued)*
Dependent variable: Output correlation for countries j and k
LAC sample, 1965–2004 (10-year period observations)

	(1)	(2)	(3)	(4)	(5)	(6)
D(LAC, China) × D(85–94)	0.106	0.119	0.120	0.104	0.109	0.120
D(LAC, China) × D(95–04)	0.050	0.065	0.066	0.067	0.056	0.066
D(LAC, India) × D(75–84)	−0.221**	−0.205**	−0.203**	−0.187**	−0.214**	−0.202**
D(LAC, India) × D(85–94)	−0.050	−0.035	−0.035	−0.082	−0.044	−0.034
D(LAC, India) × D(95–04)	−0.051	−0.037	−0.035	−0.055	−0.045	−0.036
	[0.06]	[0.06]	[0.06]	[0.06]	[0.06]	[0.06]
Country-pair dummies	Yes	Yes	Yes	Yes	Yes	Yes
Country-group dummies	Yes	Yes	Yes	Yes	Yes	Yes

Source: Author.
Note: ASM = asymmetries in the structure of imports; n.a. = not available. Numbers in brackets represent robust standard errors (White 1980). The regressions include (a) dummies for the periods 1975–84, 1985–94, and 1995–2004; and (b) period dummies for the (LAC, China) and (LAC, India) country pairs. The period dummies are included to capture the effects of demand spillovers on LAC of China and India, respectively.
* Statistically significant at the 10 percent level.
** Statistically significant at the 5 percent level.

and of the Grubel-Lloyd index of intra-industry trade (GLI). However, the coefficient estimate for the interaction between trade integration (TI) and the GLI is positive although not statistically significant. Finally, the asymmetries in structures of production and foreign trade have the expected negative signs. The same holds when they are each interacted with $T_{i,j,\tau}^{Y}$. However, no statistically significant relationship is found for any of these coefficient estimates with the exception of ASP—see columns (1) and (4) in table 2.6.[20]

To give an economic interpretation to the coefficient estimates, the following simulation exercise is performed: the analysis evaluates the gains in output correlation for country l in the LAC region in relation to China and India caused by an increase in trade intensity to the levels exhibited by the countries more integrated with China and India—that is, Mexico for trade with China, and Argentina and Brazil for trade with India. For this exercise, the degree of asymmetries in the structure of production or foreign trade of LAC countries with China and India is kept constant. The results are reported in table 2.7.

- *Effects of higher integration with China.* The analysis assesses the potential gains in output correlation with China of higher integration in a group of selected LAC countries (and subregions) if the country's bilateral trade intensity with China were to increase to the levels displayed by Mexico, the country with the highest degree of trade integration with China. To compute this effect, the analysis takes into account not only the direct impact of trade integration on cycle correlation but also its effects through intra-industry trade and through the interaction between asymmetries in structures of output and foreign trade and trade integration. This exercise keeps constant the degree of structural symmetries (either on output or foreign trade) of LAC countries with China. For more details on the results, see columns (1)–(3) in table 2.7.

  According to the simulations presented in table 2.7, the countries with higher potential increases in output correlation with China are those with the lowest degree of trade integration with China. For instance, higher trade integration with China would raise the output correlation for Belize (the country with the lowest degree of trade integration with China) between 0.103 and 0.143. We also find that if the levels of trade intensity for Mexico and China are reached, the output correlation for Central America and the Caribbean and China will increase between 0.082 and 0.116. In addition, the output correlation with China of the Andean countries will rise between 0.047 and 0.072, whereas the cycle correlation for countries in the Southern Cone will increase on average between 0.039 and 0.058.

- *Effects of trade integration with India.* Columns (4)–(6) of table 2.7 present the simulations for (LAC, India) country pairs. Again, the

Table 2.7 Effects on Business Cycle Synchronization of Higher Integration with China and India

| Economy | Level of improved trade intensity | | | | | |
| | (LAC, China) leader | | | (LAC, India) leader | | |
	(1)	(2)	(3)	(4)	(5)	(6)
Argentina	0.025	0.031	0.037	0.042	0.054	0.054
Belize	0.103	0.118	0.143	—	—	—
Bolivia	—	—	—	0.097	0.114	0.129
Brazil	0.013	0.017	0.018	n.a.	n.a.	n.a
Chile	0.036	0.044	0.050	0.055	0.068	0.073
Colombia	0.049	0.057	0.077	0.065	0.081	0.088
Costa Rica	0.049	0.065	0.078	0.086	0.105	0.116
Dominican Republic	0.074	0.094	0.106	0.087	0.107	0.115
Ecuador	0.061	0.064	0.092	0.082	0.090	0.113
El Salvador	0.081	0.098	0.122	0.097	0.120	0.132
Guatemala	0.066	0.081	0.100	0.084	0.100	0.114
Guyana	0.095	0.132	0.136	0.095	0.127	0.127
Haiti	0.096	0.130	0.119	—	—	—
Honduras	0.086	0.101	0.119	0.094	0.113	0.120
Jamaica	0.073	0.085	0.097	0.095	0.114	0.130
Mexico	n.a.	n.a.	n.a.	0.015	0.020	0.021
Nicaragua	0.093	0.114	0.136	0.116	0.142	0.166
Panama	0.084	0.102	0.099	0.078	0.095	0.093
Paraguay	0.067	0.072	0.094	0.082	0.093	0.106
Peru	0.044	0.053	0.065	0.068	0.085	0.092
Suriname	0.083	0.097	0.119	0.096	0.119	0.136
Trinidad and Tobago	0.078	0.081	0.115	0.082	0.093	0.117
Uruguay	0.053	0.064	0.083	0.069	0.092	0.095
Venezuela, R. B. de	0.033	0.028	0.056	0.072	0.081	0.097
Central America and the Caribbean	0.082	0.100	0.116	0.092	0.112	0.124
Andean countries	0.047	0.051	0.072	0.077	0.091	0.104
Southern Cone	0.039	0.046	0.058	0.050	0.063	0.068
Latin America	0.064	0.076	0.094	0.076	0.093	0.103

Source: Author.

Note: — = Complete data not available; n.a. = not applicable.

Columns (1) and (4) use the coefficient estimates of column (4) in table 2.6, columns (2) and (5) use the estimates of column (5) in table 2.6, and columns (3) and (6) use the estimates of column (6) in table 2.6. The (LAC, China) leader in trade integration is Mexico, and the (LAC, India) leader in trade integration is Brazil.

analysis computes the potential increase in output correlation if trade integration for selected countries and subregions in Latin America surges to the level of the leader in trade intensity with India, Brazil. The subregion that shows the smallest degree of trade integration, Central America and the Caribbean, registers the largest potential increase in output correlation with India, between 0.092 and 0.124. Higher trade integration with India for the Andean countries may raise the output correlation with India between 0.077 and 0.104, while the output correlation for countries in the Southern Cone increases between 0.050 and 0.068.

Explaining Changes in Output Correlation of LAC Countries with China and India

This section evaluates the ability of the regression model to track changes in the cyclical correlation of LAC with China and India and to what extent those changes are attributable to the evolution over time of trade integration and patterns of specialization in production and foreign trade.

In addition to trade integration and specialization, the analysis computes the contribution of demand spillovers to explaining the changes in business cycle synchronization in LAC with China and India. The time dummies in the regression analysis of table 2.6 capture the impact of global shocks on LAC countries with respect to the rest of the world. However, to capture the impact of global shocks specific to (LAC, China) and (LAC, India) country pairs, the specification includes not only time dummies but also time dummies interacted with (LAC, China) and (LAC, India) country pairs. These parameters will allow the computation of the impact of demand spillovers on cycle correlation specific to those country pairs.

Business Cycle Synchronization between LAC and China

Table 2.8 reports the actual and predicted changes in cyclical output correlation in the period 1995–2004 relative to 1985–94 for LAC countries and subregions in relation to China. The analysis calculates the contribution of foreign trade, output specialization, and demand spillovers using IV regressions (4) through (6) reported in table 2.6. According to those regressions, business cycles among countries become more synchronized if structures of production are more symmetric and there is a higher degree of intra-industry trade among countries.

Panel I of table 2.8 reports the changes in output synchronization predicted by the model for selected LAC subregions with China. On average, the model does a reasonable job predicting the changes in output correlation for the LAC region with China. Using the coefficient

Table 2.8 Explaining Changes in Output Correlation for Latin America and the Caribbean with Respect to China (Changes in the period 1995–2004 relative to the period 1985–94)

	Actual correlation change	ASP model: Equation (4) of table 2.6				ASX model: Equation (5) of table 2.6				ASM model: Equation (6) of table 2.6			
		Predicted change in correlation	Trade inte-gration	Output speciali-zation	Demand spillovers	Predicted change in correlation	Trade inte-gration	Export speciali-zation	Demand spillovers	Predicted change in correlation	Trade inte-gration	Import speciali-zation	Demand spillovers
I. Latin America and the Caribbean													
Latin America and the Caribbean	0.280	0.151	0.021	0.031	0.099	0.112	0.050	−0.014	0.076	0.157	0.105	−0.022	0.074
Central America and the Caribbean	−0.042	0.146	0.014	0.033	0.099	0.107	0.034	−0.003	0.076	0.080	0.071	−0.065	0.074
South America	0.297	0.123	0.019	0.005	0.099	0.106	0.036	−0.006	0.076	0.113	0.064	−0.025	0.074
Andean countries	0.491	0.142	0.027	0.016	0.099	0.114	0.051	−0.013	0.076	0.112	0.090	−0.052	0.074
Southern Cone	0.160	0.123	0.021	0.003	0.099	0.120	0.037	0.007	0.076	0.115	0.043	−0.003	0.074
II. Selected LAC countries													
Argentina	−0.202	0.122	0.013	0.010	0.099	0.099	0.024	−0.001	0.076	0.118	0.041	0.002	0.074
Belize	−0.171	0.085	0.001	−0.015	0.099	0.120	0.002	0.042	0.076	0.075	0.005	−0.004	0.074
Brazil	0.147	0.084	0.019	−0.034	0.099	0.103	0.031	−0.004	0.076	0.201	0.047	0.080	0.074
Chile	0.483	0.143	0.011	0.033	0.099	0.088	0.026	−0.015	0.076	0.100	0.052	−0.026	0.074

(continued)

Table 2.8 Explaining Changes in Output Correlation for Latin America and the Caribbean with Respect to China *(continued)*
(Changes in the period 1995–2004 relative to the period 1985–94)

| | Actual correlation change | ASP model: Equation (4) of table 2.6 | | | | ASX model: Equation (5) of table 2.6 | | | | ASM model: Equation (6) of table 2.6 | | | |
| | | Predicted change in correlation | Contribution to predicted changes | | | Predicted change in correlation | Contribution to predicted changes | | | Predicted change in correlation | Contribution to predicted changes | | |
			Trade inte-gration	Output speciali-zation	Demand spillovers		Trade inte-gration	Export speciali-zation	Demand spillovers		Trade inte-gration	Import speciali-zation	Demand spillovers
Colombia	1.039	0.074	0.031	−0.056	0.099	0.116	0.064	−0.024	0.076	0.122	0.122	−0.074	0.074
Costa Rica	−0.575	0.125	0.042	−0.017	0.099	0.130	0.089	−0.036	0.076	0.124	0.172	−0.122	0.074
Dominican Rep.	−1.221	0.224	0.016	0.108	0.099	0.113	0.038	0.000	0.076	0.082	0.077	−0.069	0.074
Ecuador	0.488	0.070	0.030	−0.059	0.099	0.115	0.068	−0.030	0.076	0.104	0.139	−0.109	0.074
El Salvador	−0.265	0.186	0.038	0.049	0.099	0.134	0.092	−0.034	0.076	0.105	0.193	−0.163	0.074
Guatemala	−0.154	0.096	0.031	−0.034	0.099	0.118	0.072	−0.031	0.076	0.108	0.152	−0.118	0.074
Guyana	−0.414	0.053	0.006	−0.053	0.099	0.067	0.015	−0.024	0.076	0.075	0.032	−0.030	0.074
Haiti	−0.015	0.111	0.000	0.011	0.099	0.107	0.001	0.030	0.076	0.073	0.002	−0.003	0.074
Honduras	−0.161	0.187	0.018	0.070	0.099	0.111	0.039	−0.004	0.076	0.076	0.079	−0.076	0.074
Jamaica	0.983	0.109	0.013	−0.003	0.099	0.107	0.033	−0.003	0.076	0.053	0.073	−0.095	0.074
Mexico	−0.349	0.135	0.038	−0.002	0.099	0.118	0.075	−0.033	0.076	0.148	0.130	−0.056	0.074
Nicaragua	0.025	0.138	−0.015	0.053	0.099	0.075	−0.028	0.027	0.076	0.068	−0.052	0.046	0.074
Panama	−0.050	0.184	0.012	0.073	0.099	0.095	0.027	−0.009	0.076	0.051	0.057	−0.080	0.074

(continued)

Table 2.8 Explaining Changes in Output Correlation for Latin America and the Caribbean with Respect to China *(continued)*
(Changes in the period 1995–2004 relative to the period 1985–94)

	Actual correlation change	ASP model: Equation (4) of table 2.6				ASX model: Equation (5) of table 2.6				ASM model: Equation (6) of table 2.6			
		Predicted change in correlation	Contribution to predicted changes			Predicted change in correlation	Contribution to predicted changes			Predicted change in correlation	Contribution to predicted changes		
			Trade integration	Output specialization	Demand spillovers		Trade integration	Export specialization	Demand spillovers		Trade integration	Import specialization	Demand spillovers
Paraguay	0.740	0.108	0.015	-0.007	0.099	0.104	0.040	-0.012	0.076	0.072	0.087	-0.089	0.074
Peru	0.391	0.191	0.008	0.083	0.099	0.099	0.014	0.008	0.076	0.113	0.023	0.015	0.074
Suriname	0.581	0.209	0.017	0.093	0.099	0.117	0.050	-0.009	0.076	0.069	0.111	-0.117	0.074
Trinidad and Tobago	0.892	0.194	0.005	0.089	0.099	0.102	0.011	0.015	0.076	0.078	0.020	-0.016	0.074
Uruguay	-0.090	0.081	0.005	-0.023	0.099	0.106	0.001	0.029	0.076	0.082	-0.012	0.019	0.074
Venezuela, R. B. de	0.046	0.232	0.038	0.095	0.099	0.125	0.055	-0.007	0.076	0.109	0.074	-0.039	0.074

Source: Author.
Note: ASM = asymmetries in the structures of imports.

estimates of equation (4) in table 2.6, which includes the ASP index, we find that trade integration, output specialization, and demand spillovers predicted an increase in output correlation between LAC and China of 0.151—that is, these variables explain 54 percent of the actual change in cycle correlation. Of the 0.151 increase in business cycle synchronization explained by the model, almost two-thirds is explained by demand spillovers from China and India (0.099), 20 percent is attributable to output specialization (0.031), and the remaining 14 percent (0.021) is attributable to higher trade intensity with China. In addition, using the coefficient estimates of equations (5) and (6)—that is, including the index of structural asymmetries in exports and imports, respectively, instead of ASP—yields similar results. Specifically, the model predicts between 40 percent and 56 percent of the predicted changes in output synchronization between the LAC region and China.

When the LAC region is broken down into subregions, the model does a poor job explaining the evolution of output correlation for Central America and the Caribbean with China. While this output correlation actually declines over time (−0.042), the model predicts an increase in output correlation (0.146). Conversely, the model predicts an increase in the output correlation with China of the Andean countries and the Southern Cone, with a better fit for the latter group. In particular, the model predicts more than three-quarters of the change in business cycle synchronization of the Southern Cone with China (0.123 of the actual 0.160).

When the ability of the model to predict output correlation changes with respect to China for the sample of LAC economies is analyzed, the performance of the model varies across countries and usually cannot track declines in output correlation. Regarding the major LAC countries, the output correlation between Brazil and China increased 0.147 in 1995–2004 relative to 1985–94. The model predicts an increase in output correlation between 0.084 (model with ASP) and 0.201 (model with ASM), with trade integration with China explaining between 25 and 30 percent of the predicted changes in correlation.

The cycle synchronization between Chile and China increased 0.483, and the model predicted an increase between 0.100 and 0.143 (that is, between 20 and 30 percent of actual variation). In this case, the increase in output correlation is mostly explained by demand spillovers (between 70 and 87 percent). An analogous result holds for the correlation between Peru and China. That is, the output synchronization between Peru and China grew by 0.391 in 1995–2004 relative to 1985–94 and the model predicted an increase between 0.099 and 0.191 for the same period, mostly attributable to demand spillovers (between 52 and 77 percent of the predicted increase in correlation). For Chile and Peru, the important role of demand spillovers is explained by the increasing demand for metals and minerals—in particular, copper from Chile, and copper, gold, and platinum from Peru. China had a 19 percent share of world copper ore imports in 2004 (second largest importer in the world after Japan) and this share increases to 25 percent if copper waste and scrap are included (Trinh and Voss 2006). Of interest, in República Bolivariana de Venezuela the model over-predicts the increase in output correlation with China. While the output correlation between these two countries actually increased by 0.046 in 1995–2004 relative to 1985–94, the model predicts an increase between 0.109 and 0.232, with trade integration and output specialization explaining between 35 and 60 percent of the predicted increase in correlation. In this case, República Bolivariana de Venezuela has benefited from the increasing Chinese demand for oil. In 2005, China was the world's third largest importer of oil, accounting for approximately 6.8 percent of world imports and 8.5 percent of world consumption (British Petroleum 2006).

Conversely, the output correlation between Argentina and China actually declined in 1995–2004 relative to 1985–94 (–0.202), but the model suggests that the evolution of trade and production specialization would have caused an increase ins their output correlation of between 0.099 and 0.122. Finally, for Mexico, the model predicts an increase in the output correlation between Mexico and China of between 0.118 and 0.148 while the actual correlation declined 0.349 in 1995–2004 relative to 1985–94. In this case, structural asymmetries in foreign trade help explain a decline in correlation, while the contribution of trade integration explains between 30 and 50 percent of the predicted increase in correlation.

Business Cycle Synchronization between LAC and India

Table 2.9 presents the actual and predicted changes in cyclical output correlation in the period 1995–2004 relative to 1985–94 for LAC countries and subregions with respect to India.

On average, the output correlation of the LAC region with India increased 0.134 in 1995–2004 relative to 1985–94 and the model predicts an increase that ranges between 0.126 (model with ASM) and 0.232 (model with ASP). Almost 70 percent of the predicted increase in correlation is attributable to demand spillovers in the ASP model. For Central America and the Caribbean, the model does a better job of tracking changes in output correlation than when analyzing Central America and China; that is, the model predicts an increase in output correlation between Central America and India of 0.123 (ASM model), 0.155 (ASX model), and 0.223 (ASP model), whereas the actual correlation increased 0.175. For the Andean countries, the model predicts an increase in correlation (between 0.128 and 0.238), which is significantly higher than the actual increase (0.015). Finally, the model performs fairly well in predicting changes in output correlation between India and the Southern Cone. While the actual correlation increased by 0.213, the ASM and ASX model predict that the correlation grows between 0.127 and 0.161,

Table 2.9 Explaining Changes in Output Correlation for Latin America and the Caribbean with Respect to India (Changes in the period 1995–2004 relative to the period 1985–94)

	Actual correlation change	ASP model: Equation (4) of table 2.6				ASX model: Equation (5) of table 2.6				ASM model: Equation (6) of table 2.6			
		Predicted change in correlation	Contribution to predicted changes			Predicted change in correlation	Contribution to predicted changes			Predicted change in correlation	Contribution to predicted changes		
			Trade integration	Output specialization	Demand spillovers		Trade integration	Export specialization	Demand spillovers		Trade integration	Import specialization	Demand spillovers
I. Latin America and the Caribbean													
Latin America and the Caribbean	0.134	0.232	0.019	0.050	0.163	0.157	0.042	−0.013	0.128	0.126	0.084	−0.085	0.127
Central America and the Caribbean	0.175	0.223	0.016	0.044	0.163	0.155	0.038	−0.011	0.128	0.123	0.079	−0.083	0.127
South America	0.114	0.242	0.021	0.058	0.163	0.157	0.045	−0.016	0.128	0.127	0.087	−0.088	0.127
Andean countries	0.015	0.238	0.019	0.056	0.163	0.153	0.045	−0.019	0.128	0.128	0.094	−0.093	0.127
Southern Cone	0.213	0.246	0.023	0.059	0.163	0.161	0.045	−0.012	0.128	0.127	0.081	−0.082	0.127
II. Selected LAC countries													
Argentina	1.156	0.256	0.018	0.075	0.163	0.146	0.043	−0.025	0.128	0.114	0.092	−0.105	0.127
Belize	−0.099	0.234	0.014	0.058	0.163	0.166	0.033	0.006	0.128	0.125	0.068	−0.071	0.127
Brazil	−0.246	0.273	0.038	0.072	0.163	0.179	0.053	−0.002	0.128	0.140	0.061	−0.048	0.127
Chile	−0.076	0.214	0.018	0.032	0.163	0.146	0.044	−0.026	0.128	0.126	0.092	−0.094	0.127

(continued)

Table 2.9 Explaining Changes in Output Correlation for Latin America and the Caribbean with Respect to India *(continued)*

(Changes in the period 1995–2004 relative to the period 1985–94)

| | Actual correlation change | ASP model: Equation (4) of table 2.6 | | | | ASX model: Equation (5) of table 2.6 | | | | ASM model: Equation (6) of table 2.6 | | | |
| | | Predicted change in correlation | Contribution to predicted changes | | | Predicted change in correlation | Contribution to predicted changes | | | Predicted change in correlation | Contribution to predicted changes | | |
			Trade integration	Output specialization	Demand spillovers		Trade integration	Export specialization	Demand spillovers		Trade integration	Import specialization	Demand spillovers
Colombia	-0.203	0.206	0.008	0.034	0.163	0.138	0.019	-0.009	0.128	0.115	0.040	-0.052	0.127
Costa Rica	0.416	0.177	0.023	-0.010	0.163	0.165	0.056	-0.019	0.128	0.130	0.117	-0.115	0.127
Dominican Rep.	-0.736	0.223	0.007	0.053	0.163	0.153	0.017	0.008	0.128	0.122	0.035	-0.040	0.127
Ecuador	-0.584	0.258	0.059	0.036	0.163	0.187	0.138	-0.079	0.128	0.143	0.289	-0.273	0.127
El Salvador	0.393	0.212	0.025	0.024	0.163	0.166	0.059	-0.020	0.128	0.147	0.123	-0.103	0.127
Guatemala	-0.419	0.229	0.019	0.046	0.163	0.153	0.045	-0.019	0.128	0.132	0.095	-0.090	0.127
Guyana	0.545	0.096	0.017	-0.084	0.163	0.129	0.040	-0.039	0.128	0.122	0.084	-0.089	0.127
Honduras	-0.348	0.225	0.024	0.038	0.163	0.172	0.056	-0.012	0.128	0.123	0.119	-0.123	0.127
Jamaica	0.069	0.308	0.011	0.134	0.163	0.153	0.026	-0.001	0.128	0.131	0.055	-0.052	0.127
Mexico	-0.106	0.241	0.039	0.039	0.163	0.173	0.063	-0.018	0.128	0.143	0.092	-0.077	0.127
Nicaragua	0.905	0.211	-0.001	0.049	0.163	0.151	-0.003	0.026	0.128	0.123	-0.005	0.001	0.127
Panama	0.709	0.268	0.033	0.071	0.163	0.166	0.076	-0.038	0.128	0.063	0.158	-0.222	0.127

(continued)

Table 2.9 Explaining Changes in Output Correlation for Latin America and the Caribbean with Respect to India (continued)
(Changes in the period 1995–2004 relative to the period 1985–94)

| | Actual correlation change | ASP model: Equation (4) of table 2.6 | | | | ASX model: Equation (5) of table 2.6 | | | | ASM model: Equation (6) of table 2.6 | | | |
| | | Predicted change in correlation | Contribution to predicted changes | | | Predicted change in correlation | Contribution to predicted changes | | | Predicted change in correlation | Contribution to predicted changes | | |
			Trade integration	Output specialization	Demand spillovers		Trade integration	Export specialization	Demand spillovers		Trade integration	Import specialization	Demand spillovers
Paraguay	−0.454	0.249	0.019	0.066	0.163	0.162	0.042	−0.007	0.128	0.120	0.084	−0.091	0.127
Peru	0.548	0.263	0.014	0.086	0.163	0.152	0.034	−0.010	0.128	0.133	0.073	−0.068	0.127
Suriname	−0.512	0.274	0.019	0.092	0.163	0.160	0.039	−0.008	0.128	0.134	0.078	−0.071	0.127
Trinidad and Tobago	0.906	0.233	0.003	0.067	0.163	0.137	0.007	0.002	0.128	0.129	0.014	−0.012	0.127
Uruguay	0.683	0.236	0.022	0.051	0.163	0.171	0.042	0.001	0.128	0.133	0.078	−0.073	0.127
Venezuela, R. B. de	0.412	0.228	0.001	0.064	0.163	0.123	0.000	−0.004	0.128	0.123	−0.002	−0.003	0.127

Source: Author.

respectively, while the ASP model predicts an increase of 0.246. Again, demand spillovers seem to be the most influential factor in explaining predicted changes in correlation in the ASP model, while trade integration has an increasing role in the other models.

For most LAC countries, the model predicts an increase in correlation with India, although the actual output correlation declined in 11 out of 22 countries in the LAC region. Argentina had the largest increase in output correlation with India, from −0.712 in 1985–94 to 0.445 in 1995–2004 (an increase of 1.156). The model only explains an increase of 0.256 with the ASP model (that is, 22 percent of the actual variation) and only between 0.114 and 0.146 with the other models. And for Peru and República Bolivariana de Venezuela, the ASP model explains about 50 percent of the actual increase in output correlation with India. In both cases, a reduction in output asymmetries contributes to explaining more than one-third of the increase in output correlation. Finally, the decline in output correlation with India for some LAC countries may be attributable to an increase in structural asymmetries in exports and imports.

Conclusion

Using a sample of 147 countries for the period 1965–2004, this chapter updates and extends the findings of Calderón, Chong, and Stein (2007) on the link between output comovement, trade intensity, and specialization with specific attention to LAC countries. The regression results confirm and complement the results of Calderón, Chong, and Stein (2007) along the following dimensions: First, countries with increasing trade links will display more synchronous business cycles. Second, countries with increasing specialization in either output or foreign trade structures will display more asynchronous output fluctuations. To the extent that asymmetries in production and trade decline in LAC with respect to China and India, rising output correlations will be observed. Finally, the chapter argues that the sensitivity of business cycle synchronization to changes in bilateral trade is affected by patterns of output and trade specialization among countries. This result is found for the full sample of country pairs, and the study fails to find a robust result for the LAC–Rest of the World sample of countries.[21]

The regression results are used to evaluate the ability of the model to track changes in the degree of business cycle synchronization for LAC countries with respect to China and India for the period 1995–2004 relative to 1985–94. The objective is to assess to what extent changes in trade and specialization patterns, as well as demand spillovers, can explain the evolution of output correlation for LAC countries. In general, the performance of the regression model is fairly good when explaining the changes in output correlation for LAC as a region. However, the country-by-country performance of the model varies significantly.

On average, the model predicts more than half of the variation in output comovement for LAC with China. The model may over-predict the changes in cycle synchronization for LAC and India. The analysis also finds the following:

First, demand spillovers and declining structural asymmetries in output seem to explain the predicted increases in output correlation for Central America and the Andean countries, while trade integration and demand spillovers seem to be the best explanation for Mexico and the Southern Cone (see figure 2.9a). When structural asymmetries in exports are considered, trade integration and demand spillovers explain most of the increase in output correlation with China for Mexico and all subregions of LAC. However, the evolution of asymmetries in export structures predicts a decline in output correlation with China and Central America and the Caribbean (see figure 2.10a).

Second, trade integration seems to have a larger role in explaining increases in output correlation in Southern Cone countries than among Andean countries. In particular, for Brazil, Paraguay, and Uruguay, trade integration predicts an increase in output correlation with China while output specialization signals a decline in this correlation (figure 2.11a). Conversely, for the Andean countries, output specialization plays a larger role in explaining movements in output comovement with China than trade integration in Peru and República Bolivariana de Venezuela, whereas changes in output specialization in Colombia and Ecuador in relation to China predict a decline in this correlation (figure 2.11a).

Third, increasing demand spillovers and less asymmetric structures of production are the factors that explain most of the predicted increase in cycle synchronization for LAC and India. The same result holds for Mexico and all other LAC subregions. While trade integration seems to explain 10 percent of the predicted increase in comovement, output specialization explains between 20 and 25 percent of this predicted increase (see figure 2.9b). However, if asymmetries in the structure of exports (ASX) are incorporated, changes in ASX predict a decline in the output comovement of Mexico and LAC subregions with India. Approximately one-third of the predicted surge in output correlation is explained by higher trade integration with India (see figure 2.10b).

Finally, when evaluating the performance of the model across countries for evolution of trade intensity and specialization patterns of LAC countries with China and India, the model predicts, in most cases, an increase in output correlation. However, this is not the case for some LAC countries in the sample, especially in the case of output correlation with India. The results are consistent to some extent with existing evidence in the literature. For instance, Blázquez-Lidoy, Rodríguez, and Santiso (2005) found that the impact of Chinese trade on the LAC region is generally positive, although this may imply a greater specialization in LAC toward commodities. However, further improvements could still be undertaken

Figure 2.9 Contribution of Trade Integration, Output Specialization, and Demand Spillovers to Predicted Changes in Output Correlation, 1995–2004 Compared with 1985–94

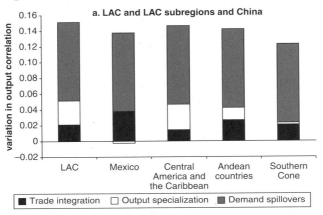

Source: Author's calculations.

Note: Contribution of the determinants of output correlation between LAC (country or group) and China computed by multiplying the regression coefficient of the different determinants (trade, output specialization, and demand spillovers) on changes in those determinants in 1995–2004 relative to 1985–94. Computation uses the regression coefficient of regression (4) of table 2.6. The estimated contributions are presented in table 2.8 for China.

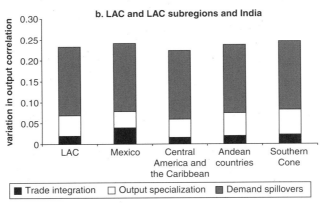

Source: Author's calculations.

Note: Contribution of the determinants of output correlation between LAC (country or group) and India computed by multiplying the regression coefficient of the different determinants (trade, output specialization, and demand spillovers) on changes in those determinants in 1995–2004 relative to 1985–94. Computation uses the regression coefficient of regression (4) of table 2.6. The estimated contributions are presented in table 2.9 for India.

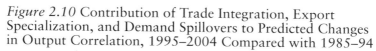

Figure 2.10 Contribution of Trade Integration, Export Specialization, and Demand Spillovers to Predicted Changes in Output Correlation, 1995–2004 Compared with 1985–94

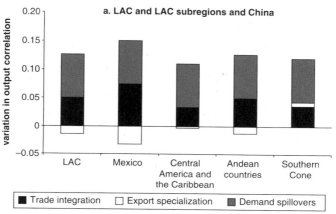

Source: Author's calculations.

Note: Contribution of the determinants of output correlation between LAC (country or group) and China computed by multiplying the regression coefficient of the different determinants (trade, export specialization, and demand spillovers) on changes in those determinants in 1995–2004 relative to 1985–94. Computation uses the regression coefficient of regression (4) of table 2.6. The estimated contributions are presented in table 2.8 for China.

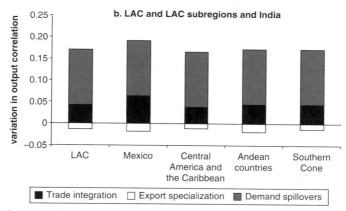

Source: Author's calculations.

Note: Contribution of the determinants of output correlation between LAC (country or group) and India computed by multiplying the regression coefficient of the different determinants (trade, export specialization, and demand spillovers) on changes in those determinants in 1995–2004 relative to 1985–94. Computation uses the regression coefficient of regression (4) of table 2.6. The estimated contributions are presented in table 2.9 for India.

in the analysis of the determinants of output comovement for LAC countries with China and India. For instance, the failure of the model to explain the variation in the output correlation of Mexico with China could be attributed to the omission of bilateral foreign direct investment (FDI). According to García-Herrero and Santabárbara (2005), there is evidence of FDI diversion from LAC recipients to China, mainly attributable to the negative impact on FDI flows to Mexico and Colombia. Other factors to evaluate are the impact on cycle correlation of increasing financial integration (Imbs 2004) and macroeconomic policy convergence (Clark and van Wincoop 2001). These extensions go beyond the scope of this chapter, and some of them are difficult to undertake because of data availability problems.

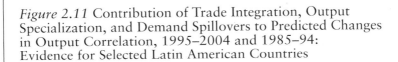

Figure 2.11 Contribution of Trade Integration, Output Specialization, and Demand Spillovers to Predicted Changes in Output Correlation, 1995–2004 and 1985–94: Evidence for Selected Latin American Countries

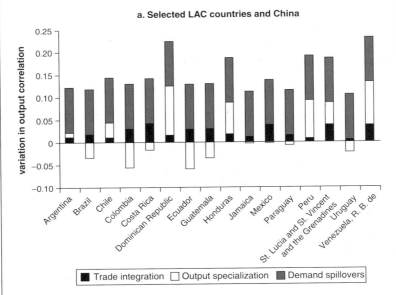

Source: Author's calculations.

Note: Contribution of the determinants of output correlation between LAC (country or group) and China computed by multiplying the regression coefficient of the different determinants (trade, output specialization, and demand spillovers) on changes in those determinants in 1995–2004 relative to 1985–94. Computation uses the regression coefficient of regression (4) of table 2.6. The estimated contributions are presented in table 2.8 for China.

Figure 2.11 Contribution of Trade Integration, Output Specialization, and Demand Spillovers to Predicted Changes in Output Correlation, 1995–2004 and 1985–94: Evidence for Selected Latin American Countries (*continued*)

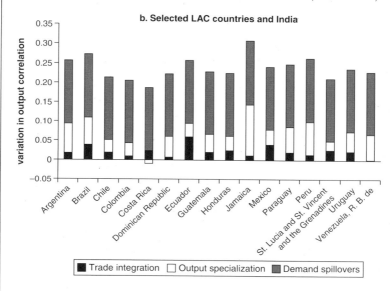

Source: Author's calculations.

Note: Contribution of the determinants of output correlation between LAC (country or group) and India computed by multiplying the regression coefficient of the different determinants (trade, output specialization, and demand spillovers) on changes in those determinants in 1995–2004 relative to 1985–94. Computation uses the regression coefficient of regression (4) of table 2.6. The estimated contributions are presented in table 2.9 for India.

Annex

Table 2A.1 Economies Included in Regression Analysis

Economy	Region	Economy	Region
Albania	ECA	Congo,	SSA
Algeria	MENA	Rep. of	
Angola	SSA	Costa Rica	LAC
Antigua and	LAC	Côte d'Ivoire	SSA
Barbuda		Cyprus	MENA
Australia	IND	Czech	ECA
Austria	IND	Republic	
Bahamas, The	LAC	Denmark	IND
Bangladesh	SA	Dominica	LAC
Barbados	LAC	Dominican	LAC
Belgium	IND	Republic	
Belize	LAC	Ecuador	LAC
Benin	SSA	Egypt, Arab	MENA
Bermuda	LAC	Rep. of	
Bolivia	LAC	El Salvador	LAC
Botswana	SSA	Estonia	ECA
Brazil	LAC	Ethiopia	SSA
Brunei	EAP	Fiji	EAP
Bulgaria	ECA	Finland	IND
Burkina Faso	SSA	France	IND
Burundi	SSA	Gabon	SSA
Cameroon	SSA	Gambia, The	SSA
Canada	IND	Germany	IND
Central African	SSA	Ghana	SSA
Republic		Greece	IND
Chad	SSA	Grenada	LAC
Chile	LAC	Guatemala	LAC
China	EAP	Guinea	SSA
Colombia	LAC	Bissau	
Comoros	EAP	Guyana	LAC
Congo, Dem.	SSA	Haiti	LAC
Rep. of		Honduras	LAC

(continued)

Table 2A.1 Economies Included in Regression Analysis
(*continued*)

Economy	Region	Economy	Region
Hong Kong, China	EAP	Morocco	MENA
		Mozambique	SSA
Hungary	ECA	Myanmar	EAP
Iceland	IND	Namibia	SSA
India	SA	Nepal	SA
Indonesia	EAP	Netherlands	IND
Iran, Islamic Rep. of	MENA	New Caledonia	EAP
		New Zealand	IND
Iraq	MENA	Nicaragua	LAC
Ireland	IND	Niger	SSA
Israel	MENA	Nigeria	SSA
Italy	IND	Norway	IND
Jamaica	LAC	Oman	MENA
Japan	IND	Pakistan	SA
Jordan	MENA	Panama	LAC
Kenya	SSA	Papua New Guinea	EAP
Kiribati	EAP	Paraguay	LAC
Korea, Rep. of	EAP	Peru	LAC
Kuwait	MENA	Philippines	EAP
Latvia	ECA	Poland	ECA
Lesotho	SSA	Portugal	IND
Liberia	SSA	Puerto Rico	LAC
Libya	MENA	Romania	ECA
Luxembourg	IND	Russian Federation	ECA
Madagascar	SSA	Rwanda	SSA
Malawi	SSA	Samoa	EAP
Malaysia	EAP	Saudi Arabia	MENA
Mali	SSA	Senegal	SSA
Malta	MENA	Seychelles	SSA
Mauritania	SSA	Sierra Leone	SSA
Mauritius	SSA	Singapore	EAP
Mexico	LAC	Slovak Republic	ECA

(*continued*)

Table 2A.1 Economies Included in Regression Analysis
(*continued*)

Economy	Region	Economy	Region
Solomon Islands	EAP	Thailand	EAP
Somalia	SSA	Togo	SSA
South Africa	SSA	Trinidad and	LAC
Spain	IND	Tobago	
Sri Lanka	SA	Tunisia	MENA
St. Lucia	LAC	Turkey	MENA
St. Vincent and	LAC	United Arab	MENA
the Grenadines		Emirates	
Sudan	SSA	United Kingdom	IND
Suriname	LAC	United States	IND
Swaziland	SSA	Uruguay	LAC
Sweden	IND	Vanuatu	EAP
Switzerland	IND	Venezuela, R. B. de	LAC
Syrian Arab Rep.	MENA	Zambia	SSA
Taiwan, China	EAP	Zimbabwe	SSA

Source: Author.
Note: EAP = East Asia and Pacific; ECA = Europe and Central Asia;
IND = Industrial economies; LAC = Latin America and the Caribbean;
MENA = Middle East and North Africa; SA = South Asia; SSA = Sub-Saharan Africa.

Notes

1. Yi (2003) showed that models of international trade with vertical specialization can explain about 70 percent of growth in world trade.
2. In the presence of fiscal consolidation or more coordinated monetary policies, the impact of spillovers from aggregate demand is even larger.
3. The National Bureau of Economic Research chronology lists 30 complete cycles since 1858. The shortest full cycle (peak to peak) was 6 quarters, and the longest 39 quarters, with 90 percent of these cycles being no longer than 32 quarters (Stock and Watson 1999).
4. Baxter and King (1999) argue that the ideal band-pass filter is a moving average process with infinite order. For practical reasons, we must approximate this filter with finite moving averages. Baxter and King specifically recommend the use of a seven-year centered moving average when working with both quarterly and annual time series data. Finally, note that although we used the band-pass filter as the preferred detrending technique, the results presented in later sections are robust to any of the four trend-cycle decomposition techniques used in this chapter.
5. See, for example, Eichengreen and Irwin (1998). We should note, however, that dropping the zero observations (that is, not adding unity to the bilateral trade flow) does not change the results in any significant way.

6. In addition to these two measures of trade intensity, we also used a theoretical measure of bilateral trade intensity derived by Deardorff (1998), in which the bilateral trade is divided by the product of the GDPs, and multiplied by world GDP. For reasons of space, we have not included these results in the present version. They are qualitatively similar to the results using our other measures, and are available upon request.

7. Although there was data for imports FOB (free on board) in the International Monetary Fund's Direction of Trade Statistics, the data availability was more limited. That is, it represents at most 20 percent of the coverage available with imports CIF.

8. A problem typical of bilateral trade data is that export flows from country i to country j are not necessarily equal to import flows of country j from country i.

9. For example, the share of bilateral trade to total trade between countries i and j could be very high (say, for a pair of remote countries). However, both could have a small external sector and, therefore, the share of bilateral trade to their outputs could be very small.

10. Although there is no standard measure of industry specialization in the literature, the index specified in equation (2.7) is used by Krugman (1993), Clark and van Wincoop (2001), and Imbs (2004). However, Imbs (2001) uses the correlation between sectoral shares in total output and employment.

11. Our index comprises the following one-digit-level ISIC code activities: (i) Agriculture, Hunting, Forestry, and Fishing; (ii) Mining and Quarrying; (iii) Manufacturing; (iv) Electricity, Gas, and Water; (v) Construction; (vi) Wholesale and Retail Trade; (vii) Transport, Storage, and Communication; (viii) Finance, Insurance, Real Estate, and Business Services; and (ix) Community, Social, and Personal Services.

12. We address the issue of nonnormality of the error process due to the censored dependent variable by applying a logistic transformation to the output correlation, $\tilde{\rho} = \ln\left(\dfrac{1+\rho}{1-\rho}\right)$. The results remain qualitatively invariant.

13. For example, a pair of countries may be very proximate and subject to common natural disasters such as hurricanes or floods. Alternatively, both countries in the pair may have a very high degree of trade intensity with the same third country, and through this channel their outputs may be highly correlated. These factors, as well as other omitted variables, will be captured by the country-pair fixed effect.

14. Our panel regressions include time dummies for the 1975–84, 1985–94, and 1995–2004 periods, with the constant representing the period 1965–74 (*Base* category). Although the estimates for the time dummies are not reported, they are jointly significant in the majority of cases.

15. Presumably, trade intensity would increase the farther the countries in the pair are from alternative markets. Following Wei (1996) and Deardorff (1998), we construct a formula for the remoteness of country i as the weighted average of that country's distances to all of its trading partners (except for country j involved in a determined country pair), using as weights the share of the partner's output in world GDP. That is, for a determined (i,j) country pair, the remoteness of country i is defined as $REM_i = \sum\limits_{m \neq j}\left(\dfrac{y_m}{y^W}\right)d_{im}$. Stein and Weinhold (1998) argue that this measure complies with several desirable properties for a measure of remoteness.

16. The specification of our gravity equation model follows Rose and Engel (2002).

17. We specifically use monthly data on the IPI for China, India, and the major LAC countries from January 1997 to December 2005. Note that for Central American and Caribbean nations, we use monthly indexes of economic

activity because of the lack of information on IPIs for these countries. The sources of data are the World Bank's Development Prospects Group (DECPG) and Haver Analytics database, and the *Secretaria Ejecutiva del Consejo Monetario Centroamericano*.

18. Here we report the anti-log of the expressions reported in equation (2.5)—that is, we graph the ratio of bilateral trade between the country pairs relative to their total trade flows or their total outputs. From now on, we will discuss the bilateral trade figures normalized by total output in the country pair.

19. When comparing the export similarity of LAC, India, and China with the OECD–European market, we find the following: First, Indian exports are more oriented toward the OECD-European markets; on average, 25 percent of the value of India's exports goes to this region. Second, the U.S. market becomes increasingly important for LAC countries. It represents 60 percent of its exports in 2002, while the OECD-European market declined in importance—from 30 percent of its exports in 1978 to 12 percent in 2002. Third, before 1992, the value of Chinese exports to OECD-Europe was larger than the value of Chinese exports oriented to the U.S. market. However, this trend reversed in 1992 and the United States has become the main destination for Chinese exports.

20. For the full sample of country pairs—that is, including non-LAC country pairs—we find the interaction terms to be negative and statistically significant. The results are not reported here but are available from the author upon request.

21. Specifically, we show that this sensitivity is higher for country pairs with more symmetric structures of production (as well as foreign trade). The results for the full sample of country pairs are not reported here but are available from the authors upon request.

References

Baxter, M. 1995. "International Trade and Business Cycles." In *Handbook of International Economics*, vol. 3, ed. G. Grossman and K. Rogoff. Amsterdam: North-Holland.

Baxter, M., and R. G. King. 1999. "Measuring Business Cycles: Approximate Band-Pass Filters for Economic Time Series." *The Review of Economics and Statistics* 81 (4): 575–93.

Blázquez-Lidoy, J., J. Rodríguez, and J. Santiso. 2005. "Angel or Devil? Chinese Trade Impact on Latin American Emerging Markets." Paper prepared for the Annual Bank Conference on Development Economics, Amsterdam, May.

British Petroleum. 2006. "Quantifying Energy: BP Statistical Review of World Energy 2006." London.

Calderón, C., A. Chong, and E. Stein. 2007. "Trade Intensity and Business Cycle Synchronization: Are Developing Countries Any Different?" *Journal of International Economics* 71 (1): 1–21.

Canova, F., and H. Dellas. 1993. "Trade Interdependence and the International Business Cycle." *Journal of International Economics* 34 (1–2): 23–47.

Clark, T. E., and E. van Wincoop. 2001. "Borders and Business Cycles." *Journal of International Economics* 55 (1): 59–85.

Coe, D. T., and E. Helpman. 1995. "International R&D Spillovers." *European Economic Review* 39 (5): 859–87.

Deardorff, A. V. 1998. "Determinants of Bilateral Trade: Does Gravity Work in a Neoclassical World?" In *The Regionalization of the World Economy*, ed. J. A. Frankel, 7–22. Chicago, IL: University of Chicago Press.

Eichengreen, B., and D. A. Irwin. 1998. "The Role of History in Bilateral Trade Flows." In *The Regionalization of the World Economy*, ed. J. A. Frankel, 33–57. Chicago, IL: University of Chicago Press.

Feenstra, R. C., R. E. Lipsey, H. Deng, A. C. Ma, and H. Mo. 2005. "World Trade Flows: 1962–2000." NBER Working Paper 11040, National Bureau of Economic Research, Cambridge, MA.

Fiess, N. 2005. "China and Latin America: Opportunities and Challenges." Unpublished, World Bank, Washington, DC.

Finger, J. M., and M. E. Kreinin. 1979. "A Measure of Export Similarity and Its Possible Uses." *The Economic Journal* 89 (356): 905–12.

Frankel, Jeffrey A., and Andrew K. Rose. 1998. "The Endogeneity of the Optimum Currency Area Criteria." *The Economic Journal* 108 (449): 1009–25.

———. 2002. "An Estimate of the Effect of Common Currencies on Trade and Income." *Quarterly Journal of Economics* 117 (2): 437–66.

Frankel, J., and D. Romer. 1999. "Does Trade Cause Growth?" *American Economic Review* 89 (3): 379–99.

García-Herrero, A., and D. Santabárbara. 2005. "Does China Have an Impact on Foreign Direct Investment to Latin America?" Banco de España, Documentos de Trabajo No. 0517.

Glick, R., and A. K. Rose. 2002. "Does a Currency Union Affect Trade? The Time-Series Evidence." *European Economic Review* 46 (6): 1125–51.

Grubel, H. G., and P. J. Lloyd. 1975. *Intra-Industry Trade: The Theory and Measurement of International Trade in Differentiated Products*. London: John Wiley & Sons.

Hummels, D., J. Ishii, and K.-M. Yi. 2001. "The Nature and Growth of Vertical Specialization in World Trade." *Journal of International Economics* 54 (1): 75–96.

Imbs, Jean. 2001. "Co-Fluctuations." CEPR Discussion Paper 2267, Centre for Economic Policy Research, London.

———. 2004. "Trade, Finance, Specialization, and Synchronization." *Review of Economics and Statistics* 86 (3): 723–34.

IMF (International Monetary Fund). 2001. *World Economic Outlook: The Information Technology Revolution*. Washington, DC: IMF.

———. Various years. *Direction of Trade Statistics*. Washington, DC: IMF.

Kalemli-Ozcan, S., B. E. Sorensen, and O. Yosha. 2001. "Economic Integration, Industrial Specialization, and the Asymmetry of Macroeconomic Fluctuations." *Journal of International Economics* 55 (1): 107–37.

Kose, M. A., and K.-M. Yi. 2001. "International Trade and Business Cycles: Is Vertical Specialization the Missing Link." *American Economic Review* 91 (2): 371–75.

Kouparitsas, M. A. 2001. "Evidence of the North-South Business Cycle." Federal Reserve Bank of Chicago. *Economic Perspectives* 1Q: 46–59.

Krugman, P. 1993. "Lessons of Massachusetts for EMU." In *The Transition to Economic and Monetary Union in Europe*, ed. F. Giavazzi and F. Torres, 241–61. New York: Cambridge University Press.

Lichtenberg, F., and B. van Pottelsberghe. 1998. "International R&D Spillovers: A Comment." *European Economic Review* 42 (8): 1483–91.

Loayza, N., H. Lopez, and A. Ubide. 2001. "Comovements and Sectoral Dependence: Evidence for Latin America, East Asia, and Europe." *IMF Staff Papers* 48 (2): 367–96.

Mundell, R. 1961. "A Theory of Optimum Currency Areas." *American Economic Review* 51 (4): 509–17.

Rose, A. K. 2000. "One Money, One Market: The Effect of Common Currencies on Trade." *Economic Policy* 15 (30): 9–45.

Rose, A. K., and C. Engel. 2002. "Currency Unions and International Integration." *Journal of Money, Credit, and Banking* 34 (3): 804–25.

Stein, E., and D. Weinhold. 1998. "Canadian-U.S. Border Effects and the Gravity Equation Model of Trade." Unpublished, Inter-American Development Bank, Washington, DC.

Stock, J. H., and M. W. Watson. 1999. "Business Cycle Fluctuations in U.S. Macroeconomic Time Series." In *Handbook of Macroeconomics*, ed. J. B. Taylor and M. Woodford, 3–64. Amsterdam: Elsevier.

Stockman, A. C. 1988. "Sectoral and National Aggregate Disturbances to Industrial Output in Seven European Countries." *Journal of Monetary Economics* 21 (2–3): 387–410.

Trinh, Tamara, and Silja Voss. 2006. "China's Commodity Hunger: Implications for Africa and Latin America." Deutsche Bank Research, Frankfurt am Mein, Germany.

Wei, S.-J. 1996. "Intra-National versus International Trade: How Stubborn are Nations in Global Integration?" NBER Working Paper 5531, National Bureau of Economic Research, Cambridge, MA.

White, H., 1980. "A Heteroskedasticity-Consistent Covariance Matrix Estimator and a Direct Test for Heteroskedasticity." *Econometrica* 48 (4): 817–38.

World Bank. Various years. *World Development Indicators*. Washington, DC: World Bank.

Yi, K.-M. 2003. "Can Vertical Specialization Explain the Growth of World Trade?" *Journal of Political Economy* 111 (2): 52–105.

3

The Growth of China and India in World Trade: Opportunity or Threat for Latin America and the Caribbean?

Daniel Lederman,
Marcelo Olarreaga, and Isidro Soloaga*

Introduction

Although the rise of China and India in the global economy cannot be ignored, the impact of those two countries on the development prospects of other developing countries is difficult to identify. The emergence of these Asian economies in world markets is seen as an opportunity by some analysts and as a threat by others. This chapter studies the relationship between the rapid growth of China and India in world trade and Latin American and Caribbean (LAC) commercial flows from two perspectives: first, from the viewpoint of China and India as fast-growing export markets and as sources of imports for LAC, and second, with regard to their potential effects on LAC trade flows with other markets.

The economic accomplishments of these Asian economies have been extraordinary. Between 1985 and 2005, their joint share of global gross domestic product (GDP) went from 3 percent to 7 percent—China is currently the sixth- and India the tenth-largest world economy as measured

* The authors are grateful to Caroline Freund, Gordon Hanson, and Guillermo Perry for discussions and suggestions. Javier Cravino provided useful comments on the econometric program.

by GDP. The growth of China and India was accompanied by their rapid integration into world markets. China is currently the third-largest trading economy in the world (behind the United States and Germany), while India ranks twenty-fifth.

These trends can be seen as an opportunity for other developing countries. For example, China and India together became the LAC region's third largest trading partner, and with their demand growing at an annual rate of close to 9 percent since 1990, the future potential appears large. The importance of China and India as destinations for LAC exports increased fourfold since 1990, when they represented about 1 percent of LAC exports. Furthermore, during 2000 to 2004, LAC nonfuel merchandise exports to China grew at an average annual rate of over 40 percent (in current U.S. dollars), while exports to India grew by 25 percent.[1] These rates of export growth signal significant opportunities, even though the levels remain low, representing less than 10 percent of total exports for most LAC economies (see figure 3.1). Similarly, the share of China and India in total LAC imports increased significantly over this period (see figure 3.2).

The emergence of China and India in world markets might have benefited LAC commercial flows through less direct channels. The most obvious is that China's and India's imports of commodities have contributed to the recent boom in commodity prices that has benefited many LAC exporters. Today, China is the largest world consumer of aluminum, copper, petroleum, soy, tin, and zinc (Hale 2005). Even when LAC exporters

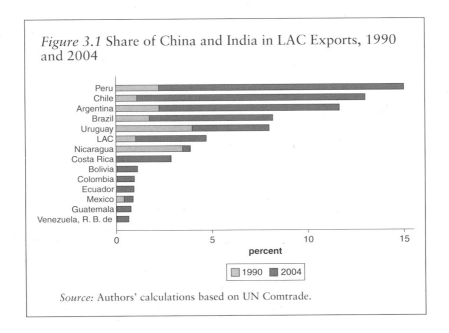

Figure 3.1 Share of China and India in LAC Exports, 1990 and 2004

Source: Authors' calculations based on UN Comtrade.

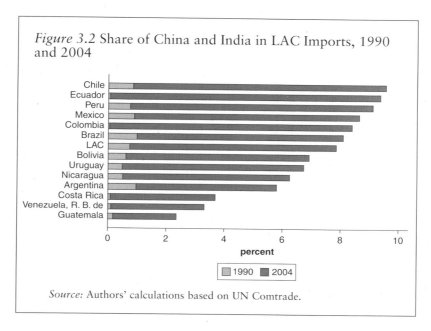

Figure 3.2 Share of China and India in LAC Imports, 1990 and 2004

Source: Authors' calculations based on UN Comtrade.

are not directly selling commodities to China and India, or when the two Asian economies only represent a small share of total exports (for example, from Bolivia, Colombia, and Ecuador), LAC economies have benefited from rising commodity prices associated with the growth of China and India (Calderón 2006; Lederman, Olarreaga, and Rubiano 2006). Manufacturing and other industries in LAC might also have benefited indirectly from the growth of China and India through international production networks. For instance, it is possible that rising exports from China and India to third markets have been associated with increases in demand for LAC products in third markets as retailers in those markets experience rising profits and rely on exports from some LAC countries to satisfy demand for just-in-time deliveries. Also, rising profits of multinational enterprises with operations in China might allow them to expand their operations in LAC. Furthermore, LAC imports from these Asian economies might allow LAC producers to reduce input costs, thus enhancing their competitiveness in third markets.

The threat that China's and India's growth may represent for LAC is associated with their growing presence in world markets that may be displacing LAC exports. China's and India's manufacturing exports increased by about 15 percent per year since 1995. China, for example, replaced Mexico as the second largest source of U.S. imports. Some analysts suggest that the Mexican *maquiladoras* have lost about 250,000 employees since the early 2000s because of the relocation of production to Asia

(Hale 2005). Similarly, Lall, Weiss, and Oikawa (2004) estimate that in 2002 about 40 percent of LAC exports to the world were under direct or partial threat from Chinese exports.[2] More recently, Hanson and Robertson (2006) explored the impact of China's increased supply capacity on LAC exports of the top manufacturing industries in Argentina, Brazil, Chile, and Mexico (metals, machinery, electronics, transport, and industrial equipment). They found that without the increase in Chinese supply of these products, export growth in these products could have been 1 percentage point higher in Argentina and Brazil, 2 percentage points higher in Chile, and 3 percentage points higher in Mexico. Freund and Özden (2006) undertook a similar exercise, but encompassing all goods, and without disentangling between supply shocks and demand shocks. They found that export growth from China is hurting LAC exports to third markets but only in some industries, namely textiles, electronics and electrical appliances, and telecommunications equipment, which were the industries studied by Hanson and Robertson.

Hence, there seems to be sufficient uncertainty about the aggregate trade effects of the rise of China and India to merit further analysis, especially because the aforementioned econometric studies (Freund and Özden 2006; Hanson and Robertson 2006) focused on intra-industry effects and ignored the potential for interindustry effects. For example, the existing studies on the threats posed by these Asian economies do not consider the *direct* effects of rising import demand in China and India as a potential boost for LAC exports. Also, none of the cited studies explore all the potential *indirect* effects mentioned above. This chapter addresses these issues by examining the potential for complementarities and substitutability between LAC and Chinese exports to third markets at the aggregate level, allowing, therefore, for both intra-industry and interindustry effects.

As mentioned, the objectives of this chapter are twofold. First, it focuses on the opportunities offered to LAC exports by the growth of Chinese and Indian demand. Second, it examines whether the growing presence of China and India in third markets should be seen as a threat or an opportunity for LAC exporters and importers.

The analysis addresses both questions using the gravity model of trade, whereby bilateral imports and exports of LAC countries are explained by the GDPs of the importer and the exporter (their economic size), their bilateral distance (as a proxy for transport costs), and country and year effects to control for time-invariant characteristics of trading partners and global conditions. Importer and exporter fixed effects are theoretically justified because they capture the influence of each economy's time-invariant trade frictions (that is, trade policies and transport costs) with the rest of the world (Anderson and Van Wincoop 2003; Feenstra 2002). Because the direct and indirect effects of the emergence of China and India undoubtedly can be different across countries with different factor endowments or production structures, the econometric specifications of the gravity model allow the relevant parameters to vary across four broad LAC subregions: Andean countries (Bolivia, Colombia, Ecuador, Peru, and República Bolivariana de Venezuela); Caribbean countries (the Dominican Republic, Haiti, Jamaica, and Trinidad and Tobago); Central America (Belize, Costa Rica, Guatemala, Honduras, Nicaragua, and Panama) and Mexico; and the Southern Cone (Argentina, Brazil, Chile, Paraguay, and Uruguay).

Overall, the results suggest that the growth of China and India in world markets is an opportunity for LAC exporters and importers. A quick calculation based on the estimates of the import-demand elasticity of China and India with respect to LAC exports suggests that the growth of China and India during 2000 to 2004 could account for up to 8 percent of LAC exports in 2004, mainly driven by China (India accounts for less than 0.5 percentage points of this 8 percent). However, this remains an untapped opportunity that has not been fully exploited, especially by exporters in the Southern Cone and among Andean countries whose exports are well below potential. Furthermore, the analysis found no robust evidence of substitution between China's trade flows and LAC exports to third markets. In fact, most of the statistically significant indirect elasticities tend to be positive for both Chinese and Indian trade flows.

The remainder of the chapter is organized as follows: The next section describes the empirical methodology and is followed by a section that presents the results. The final section concludes, and the annex describes data sources and variable construction.

Empirical Models

The methodology relies on the gravity model of trade that explains bilateral imports as a function of the GDPs of the importer and the exporter, bilateral distance between trading partners, and fixed effects to control for unobservable variables such as policy-induced and other trade frictions affecting each country's trade potential with the rest of the world (Anderson and Van Wincoop 2003; Feenstra 2002). Because the question of interest here is the impact of the growth of China's and India's demand on LAC exports, as well as the impact of China's and India's trade flows with LAC and the rest of the world on LAC exports to third markets, these two questions need to be addressed with different samples and with different augmented specifications of the gravity model. In addition, the models discussed below were estimated with data covering all LAC countries' trade flows with the world, but the models do not include data for trade among countries of the rest of the world. Hence, the models and the resulting econometric estimates need to be interpreted as applying to LAC countries only.[3]

The Growth of Chinese and Indian Bilateral Trade with LAC

The basic gravity framework in the existing literature is given by

$$M_{ijt} = \alpha Y_{it}^{\alpha} Y_{jt}^{\beta} D_{ij}^{\delta} B_{ij}^{\phi} \ell_{ij}^{\varphi} Linder_{ijt}^{\sigma} e^{\theta_i d_i + \theta_j d_j + \theta_t d_t}, \tag{3.1}$$

where M_{ijt} are imports of country i from country j at time t. The right-hand side of equation (3.1) includes the standard explanatory variables plus a minor extension. Y_{it} is the GDP of the importer at time t, Y_{jt} is the GDP of the exporter at time t, D_{ij} is the bilateral distance, B_{ij} is a dummy that takes the value 1 if the exporter and the importer share a border, and ℓ_{ij} is a dummy that takes the value 1 if the exporter and the importer share a common language. In a modest departure from the standard gravity model found in the literature, $Linder_{ijt}$ is the absolute value of the difference of GDP per capita between the importer and the exporter at time t.[4] Following Anderson and Van Wincoop (2003) as well as Feenstra (2002), d_i are importing country dummies, d_j are exporting country dummies, and d_t are time dummies.

Thus, the average impact of an importer's growing GDP on exports is captured by the parameter α. To capture the impact associated with growing demand in China (or India), the model in equation (3.1) is augmented by including the interaction of a dummy variable that takes the value 1 when China (or India) is the importer with the GDP of the importer, Y_{it}. Also, because economic and factor endowment differences can be important within LAC, this variable is also interacted with four dummy variables that take the value 1 when the exporter belongs to one of the four subregions considered (Andean countries, Caribbean countries, Central America and Mexico, and the Southern Cone). The same logic applies for the GDP of the exporter to measure the differential impact of the growth of different LAC subregions on exports to China (or India), as well as with the Linder effect.[5] The final specification that captures the impact on bilateral imports is

$$M_{ijt} = \alpha Y_{it}^{\alpha} \prod_R \left(d_{i=China} d_{j\in R} Y_{it} \right)^{\alpha_R} Y_{jt}^{\beta} \prod_R \left(d_{i=China} d_{j\in R} Y_{jt} \right)^{\beta_R} D_{ij}^{\delta} B_{ij}^{\phi} \ell_{ij}^{\varphi}$$

$$Linder_{ijt}^{\sigma} \prod_R \left(d_{i=China} d_{j\in R} Lindert_{ijt} \right)^{\sigma_R} e^{\theta_i d_i + \theta_j d_j + \theta_t d_t}, \tag{3.2}$$

where $\alpha + \alpha_R$ captures the impact of the growth of China on exports of subregion R to China, and $\beta + \beta_R$ captures the impact of growth of subregion R on exports to China.

Some caution is warranted for the interpretation of these elasticities. On the import-demand side, the estimates can capture two distinct effects. One concerns the marginal propensity to import goods exported by LAC; the other concerns substitution or relative-price effects that could be driven by the increase in demand from these countries or other global factors. Hence, the coefficients need not equal 1 as predicted by some theories underpinning the gravity model of trade (see, for example, Eaton and Kortum [2002] and Feenstra [2004], among others). Furthermore, it is noteworthy that recent contributions to the estimation (Santos Silva and Tenreyro 2006) and theory of the gravity model (Dalgin, Trindade, and Mitra 2006) have also examined the possibility that import-demand elasticities can vary across countries depending on factors such as the level of development, the size of GDP, and domestic inequality. Finally, some estimates of LAC export-supply elasticities might be negative for the same reasons, but also because of macroeconomic crises experienced by some countries (for example, Argentina and Uruguay) during 2000 to 2004, when exports grew quickly in some years while GDP contracted, thus inducing a negative correlation (or a downward bias in the correlation) between exporters' GDP and nonfuel exports to China or India.

Multiplying each of the region-specific elasticities discussed above by the change in either China's GDP or LAC's GDP provides an estimate of the change in import demand associated with either the growth of China (demand effect) or the growth of LAC (supply effect) on bilateral imports. The magnitude of the change in GDP during the period under study multiplied by the estimated elasticity provides an indication of what would have happened to LAC trade flows if, for example, China's GDP had not grown between 2000 and 2004. Of course, this is a rather discretionary counterfactual, and many others can be calculated. Perhaps more important, the validity of any counterfactual will depend on the consistency of the estimated elasticities.

One concern with the existing literature on the estimation of the gravity model is the application of ordinary least squares (OLS) or other linear estimators to model (3.2). It is now known that linear estimators can yield inconsistent coefficient estimates as a result of the correlation between the expected value of bilateral trade flows among country pairs and the variance of their regression errors.[6] This systematic heteroskedasticity produces log-linear estimates that are driven by the disproportionate influence of observations with high expected bilateral trade flows, which leads to biased estimates. Indeed, Monte Carlo simulations suggest that the application of log-linear estimators to this type of data-generation process tends to produce substantial biases in the coefficients compared with the Poisson estimator, which controls for a constant correlation between the conditional mean of each observation and its regression-error variance (see Santos Silva and Tenreyro [2006]).

Furthermore, if the data-generation process is characterized by over-dispersion (a rising ratio of variance over conditional mean), then the negative binomial estimator is preferable because it down weights even more the observations with large conditional means. Santos Silva and Tenreyro

(2006) argue that the negative binomial estimator might not be desirable if the trade data of country pairs with little bilateral trade are more prone to measurement error than the observations with greater bilateral trade. They further argue that this may be the case in a sample of both developed and developing countries because data from larger countries (measured by GDP) are less likely to be subject to measurement error. However, in the sample composed of LAC exporters and importers, there is no reason to believe that trade flows associated with small countries such as Uruguay are more likely to be subject to measurement error than the trade flows of large countries such as República Bolivariana de Venezuela.[7] The analysis, therefore, presents results from the negative binomial estimator along with OLS and Poisson estimates of equation (3.2). Because the negative binomial estimator does not fully account for the heteroskedasticity in the model, we use the Eicker-White correction by reporter to obtain a robust covariance matrix.

The Effect of China's and India's Trade Flows on LAC Exports to Third Markets

There are four potential channels through which Chinese and Indian trade could affect LAC exports to third countries: Chinese (or Indian) exports to the rest of the world, Chinese (or Indian) imports from the rest of the world, Chinese (or Indian) exports to LAC, and Chinese (or Indian) imports from LAC. Thus, in a sample of Latin American importers and exporters to all countries except China (or India), these four variables are added to the specification of model (3.1).

To account for potential differences in the relevant elasticities across the LAC subregions, the analysis also includes the products of these four variables with dummy variables that take a value of 1 when region R is an exporter.[8] The final specification for China, for example, is given by

$$M_{ijt} = \alpha Y_{it}^{\alpha} Y_{jt}^{\beta} D_{ij}^{\delta} B_{ij}^{\phi} \ell_{ij}^{\varphi} Linder_{ijt}^{\sigma} e^{\theta_i d_i + \theta_j d_j + \theta_t d_t} X_{China,z,t}^{\pi} M_{China,z,t}^{\psi} X_{China,j,t}^{\xi} M_{China,j,t}^{\eta}$$

$$\prod_R d_{j \in R} X_{China,z,t}^{\pi_R} \prod_R d_{j \in R} M_{China,z,t}^{\psi_R} \prod_R d_{j \in R} X_{China,j,t}^{\xi_R} \prod_R d_{j \in R} M_{China,j,t}^{\eta_R}.$$

$$(3.3)$$

This same specification applies to the estimation of the relevant elasticities for the case of India.

Results

The following paragraphs discuss the econometric estimates of the relevant demand and supply elasticities of model (3.2) and of the complementarity or substitution elasticities in model (3.3). The discussion focuses first on the effect that the growth of China's and India's demand (as well as LAC's GDP growth) may have had on exports of LAC to these Asian economies, as in model (3.2), using data on aggregate nonfuel merchandise exports. The section then turns to the impact of China's and India's trade flows on LAC exports to (and imports from) third markets through the four channels indicated in equation (3.3). For ease of exposition, this chapter does not report or discuss the resulting estimates of the other explanatory variables, but the estimates of the standard gravity model variable coefficients have the expected signs and all are significant, except for the *Linder* variable capturing the similarity in GDP per capita between LAC economies and their trading partners, which is generally insignificant.[9] Bilateral distance between trading partners and sharing of a border are always negative and significant; the dummy for common language is also always positive and significant.[10]

Demand and Supply Elasticities of LAC Trade with China and India

Results for the estimation of model (3.2) using nonfuel bilateral trade flows for the sample of LAC exporters and importers are reported in tables 3.1 and 3.2 for China and India, respectively. The first column of each table reports the estimated elasticity of the effect that China's, India's, or LAC's GDP has on bilateral exports of each LAC subregion to either China or India. The second column reports the p-values of the null hypotheses that the elasticities are equal to zero. In all exercises, the study cannot reject the possibility that the data suffer from over-dispersion because the estimated p-values of the null hypothesis that there is no over-dispersion were zero (not reported in the table), thus justifying the use of the negative binomial estimator. Note, however, that results using OLS or Poisson estimators, which are the most commonly used estimators in the gravity-model literature, are qualitatively similar. In particular, the results also imply a much larger impact of China's demand (China's GDP) on bilateral exports from LAC than the one obtained for the impact of LAC's supply (LAC's GDP) on LAC's exports to China.

The estimated import-demand elasticities reported in table 3.1 suggest that China's demand growth offered opportunities for LAC exporters. The highest elasticities, which exceed 4 for all LAC groups, correspond to the negative binomial estimator. The OLS estimates are all greater than 3, whereas the Poisson estimates hover around 3. The estimates for the Southern Cone are higher than those of the other country groups; the lowest estimates are those of the Central America and Mexico group. The Andean and Caribbean estimates fall in between the aforementioned groups, depending on the econometric methodology. More important, China's elasticities of demand for imports from LAC countries are significantly larger than the

Table 3.1 Trade Demand and Supply Elasticities of GDP for
LAC-China Trade: Non-Fuel Merchandise Trade Data

	OLS		Poisson		Negative binomial	
	Estimated coefficient	p-value	Estimated coefficient	p-value	Estimated coefficient	p-value
Andean countries						
Own supply	0.51	0.00	0.28	0.14	0.38	0.19
China demand	3.40	0.00	3.01	0.00	4.42	0.00
Caribbean countries						
Own supply	0.15	0.19	−0.11	0.52	−0.81	0.24
China demand	3.32	0.00	3.04	0.00	4.49	0.00
Central America and Mexico						
Own supply	−0.03	0.89	−0.97	0.01	−2.10	0.00
China demand	3.20	0.00	2.95	0.00	4.25	0.00
Southern Cone						
Own supply	0.28	0.01	−0.03	0.70	−0.09	0.58
China demand	3.59	0.00	3.19	0.00	4.69	0.00
Observations	21,480		21,480		21,480	

Source: Authors.

Note: "China demand" shows the effect of China's GDP growth on LAC exports. "Own supply" captures the effect of LAC's or the subregion's GDP growth on LAC or subregion exports to China. The reported coefficients come from the econometric estimation of the gravity model of trade, augmented by the interaction of country and country-group dummy variables. The estimated coefficients from the other variables in the empirical model are not reported, but all the gravity variables had the expected magnitudes and signs. The over-dispersion test, which corresponds to the null hypothesis that there is no over-dispersion of the errors with respect to the expected trade flows among country pairs, is not reported but was significant at the 1 percent level. Exporter, importer, and year dummies are not reported either. See text for details.

estimated supply elasticities of the four groups of LAC countries. Indeed, only two estimated supply elasticities are positive and statistically different from zero. Furthermore, the economic magnitude of the estimated Chinese demand elasticities for imports from LAC countries is large. A straightforward calculation of the magnitude of the China demand effect—the product of the demand elasticities multiplied by the change in China's GDP between 2000 and 2004—suggests that if LAC exports to China had fully exploited the increased demand from China between 2000 and 2004, they would have accounted for 8 percent of LAC exports in 2004. As mentioned, this calculation is based on a particular counterfactual analysis, the comparison of Chinese imports from LAC in 2000 and 2004 under the

Table 3.2 Trade Demand and Supply Elasticities of GDP for
LAC-India Trade: Non-Fuel Merchandise Trade Data

	OLS		Poisson		Negative binomial	
	Estimated coefficient	*p-value*	*Estimated coefficient*	*p-value*	*Estimated coefficient*	*p-value*
Andean countries						
Own supply	0.29	0.35	0.28	0.25	−0.27	0.56
India demand	1.84	0.00	1.62	0.00	2.99	0.00
Caribbean countries						
Own supply	−0.26	0.02	−0.21	0.21	−1.47	0.04
India demand	1.87	0.00	1.55	0.00	2.78	0.00
Central America and Mexico						
Own supply	−0.34	0.08	−1.40	0.00	−2.47	0.00
India demand	1.76	0.00	1.74	0.00	2.72	0.00
Southern Cone						
Own supply	0.39	0.00	−0.08	0.21	−0.09	0.50
India demand	1.78	0.00	1.88	0.00	2.90	0.00
Observations	21,480		21,480		21,480	

Source: Authors.
Note: See note to table 3.1.

assumption that these trade flows would have remained at their 2000 level if China's GDP had not grown. Of course, other counterfactuals could be chosen. For example, a low-growth scenario for China could be assumed as the base case, instead of zero growth, and the resulting estimate of the magnitude of China's demand effect on LAC exports would be smaller than 8 percent.[11] The point is that China's LAC-imports-demand elasticities are large, whereas LAC's export-supply elasticities with respect to the Chinese market are negligible. That is, even if LAC's GDP growth had matched China's during 2000 to 2004, there would have been unsatisfied Chinese demand for LAC exports. Hence, this evidence is interpreted as suggesting that LAC economies missed out on handsome export opportunities offered by the Chinese market.[12]

Table 3.2 lists the estimates of India's demand elasticities as well as LAC's supply elasticities for the Indian market. As was the case for Chinese-LAC trade, the results presented in table 3.2 suggest that India's demand elasticities were positive, large, and statistically significant for all four LAC subregions. However, table 3.2 also suggests that there were no significant differences in the magnitudes of India's demand elasticities for imports from the four LAC subregions, and the rankings across the four groups depends on the estimators. A comparison of the results in table 3.1 for China with table 3.2 for India indicates that China's demand elasticities for LAC imports (table 3.1) are significantly higher than the corresponding elasticities for India (table 3.2). Regarding LAC supply elasticities with respect to the Indian market, there is no evidence that LAC's supply response was significantly positive. Indeed, of the 12 estimates, only the OLS estimate of the Southern Cone is positive and significant.

In sum, the econometric evidence suggests that the growth of the two Asian economies during 2000 to 2004 represented a large opportunity for LAC exporters from all four subregions. There is also evidence of missed opportunities for all LAC regions in those two markets because the demand elasticities of both China and India for imports from LAC countries were dramatically larger than LAC's supply elasticities. The gap between the estimated supply and demand elasticities was significantly larger for LAC-China trade than for LAC-India trade, however.

Elasticities of LAC's Trade with Third Markets with Respect to China's and India's Trade Flows

Results for the estimation of model (3.3) using nonfuel bilateral trade flows for the sample of LAC exporters are reported in table 3.3 for China and table 3.4 for India. To clarify, the impact on LAC exports to third markets is decomposed into four trade flows: exports of either China or India to third markets, China's or India's imports from third markets, China's or India's exports to LAC, and China's or India's imports from LAC. The importance of controlling for these four trade flows to estimate consistent elasticities for each cannot be overstated, because Chinese and Indian trade with all countries grew during the period under investigation. The disadvantage of this approach is that the correlation across trade flows can itself produce imprecise and volatile estimates. The large number of observations, however, should reduce this problem. In any case, if substitution effects are large, the estimations should clearly identify them.

Table 3.3 shows the estimates from OLS, Poisson, and negative binomial regressions. Again, the tests of over-dispersion (not reported) significantly rejected the null of no over-dispersion with a p-value of zero. The results suggest that there is no robust evidence of substitution effects in third markets. In fact, of the 48 estimates, only 3 are negative and significant, and no estimate maintains its sign across the three estimators. Of interest is that the estimated elasticities of substitution between Chinese exports and LAC exports to third markets (first row under each subregion heading) are all positive except the OLS estimate for the Caribbean. The latter changes sign with the Poisson estimator.

Table 3.4 contains the estimated elasticities for India. There are seven statistically significant (at the 10 percent level) and negative estimates, but none of these are robust across the three estimators. Focusing on the signs

Table 3.3 Impact of China's Trade Flows on LAC Non-Fuel
Exports to Third Countries

	OLS		Poisson		Negative binomial	
	Estimated coefficient	*p-value*	*Estimated coefficient*	*p-value*	*Estimated coefficient*	*p-value*
Andean countries						
China's exports to third countries	0.06	0.10	0.11	0.38	0.14	0.15
China's imports from third countries	0.01	0.65	0.10	0.30	0.06	0.38
China's exports to Andean countries	−0.07	0.25	0.21	0.25	0.03	0.83
China's imports from Andean countries	−0.05	0.10	0.21	0.00	0.03	0.64
Caribbean countries						
China's exports to third countries	−0.14	0.00	0.14	0.31	−0.06	0.74
China's imports from third countries	−0.04	0.27	0.08	0.33	0.04	0.76
China's exports to Caribbean countries	−0.04	0.66	0.27	0.29	0.15	0.67
China's imports from Caribbean countries	0.00	0.82	0.02	0.46	0.09	0.03
Central America and Mexico						
China's exports to third countries	0.00	0.91	0.85	0.00	0.16	0.19
China's imports from third countries	−0.04	0.15	−0.25	0.00	0.00	0.98
China's exports to Central America and Mexico	−0.03	0.31	−0.04	0.71	0.01	0.93
China's imports from Central America and Mexico	0.03	0.10	0.06	0.40	0.10	0.08

(continued)

Table 3.3 Impact of China's Trade Flows on LAC Non-Fuel
Exports to Third Countries *(continued)*

	OLS		Poisson		Negative binomial	
	Estimated coefficient	p-value	Estimated coefficient	p-value	Estimated coefficient	p-value
Southern Cone						
China's exports to third countries	0.21	0.00	0.02	0.87	0.14	0.14
China's imports from third countries	0.02	0.51	0.19	0.05	0.06	0.33
China's exports to Southern Cone	0.05	0.56	0.05	0.72	0.30	0.08
China's imports from Southern Cone	0.02	0.64	0.45	0.00	0.21	0.09
Observations	15,440		15,440		15,440	

Source: Authors.

Note: The reported coefficients come from the econometric estimation of the gravity model of trade, augmented by the interaction of country and country-group dummy variables. The estimated coefficients from the other variables in the empirical model are not reported, but all the gravity variables had the expected magnitudes and signs. The over-dispersion test, which corresponds to the null hypothesis that there is no over-dispersion of the errors with respect to the expected trade flows among country pairs, is not reported but was significant at the 1 percent level. Exporter, importer, and year dummies are not reported either. See text for details.

of the estimates only, there are two sets of elasticities that are consistently negative. These are associated with Central America and Mexico. One concerns Indian imports from third countries, and the other concerns Indian exports to Central America and Mexico. In contrast, all estimates of the effects of Indian exports to third markets on LAC exports are positive, with one exception: the OLS estimate for the Caribbean. The latter becomes positive with the Poisson and negative binomial estimators.

Overall, the estimates of the effects of China's and India's trade on LAC exports to third markets show little evidence of strong substitution effects between the Asian economies' growing presence in world markets and LAC exports to third markets. Nonetheless, care must be exercised to avoid interpreting the estimated elasticities as evidence of causal effects, because omitted variables may be affecting these correlations. For example, the estimations do not control for bilateral terms of trade. Also, although exporter and importer dummies are included, no controls are in place for any trade policy changes that might have affected bilateral and global trade

Table 3.4 Impact of India's Trade Flows on LAC Non-Fuel Exports to Third Countries

	OLS		Poisson		Negative binomial	
	Estimated coefficient	*p-value*	*Estimated coefficient*	*p-value*	*Estimated coefficient*	*p-value*
Andean countries						
India's exports to third countries	0.10	0.13	0.36	0.04	0.20	0.22
India's imports from third countries	−0.02	0.49	0.16	0.13	−0.15	0.07
India's exports to Andean countries	−0.19	0.00	0.13	0.48	−0.04	0.71
India's imports from Andean countries	0.00	0.80	0.03	0.35	−0.02	0.47
Caribbean countries						
India's exports to third countries	−0.09	0.22	0.15	0.46	0.05	0.82
India's imports from third countries	−0.07	0.08	0.30	0.12	−0.16	0.23
India's exports to Caribbean countries	−0.08	0.12	−0.18	0.56	0.30	0.06
India's imports from Caribbean countries	−0.03	0.06	0.03	0.35	0.01	0.87
Central America and Mexico						
India's exports to third countries	0.00	0.99	1.02	0.00	0.11	0.52
India's imports from third countries	−0.02	0.36	−0.15	0.22	−0.11	0.21
India's exports to Central America and Mexico	−0.08	0.08	−0.37	0.01	−0.16	0.14
India's imports from Central America and Mexico	−0.01	0.32	0.08	0.16	0.01	0.74

(continued)

Table 3.4 Impact of India's Trade Flows on LAC Non-Fuel
Exports to Third Countries *(continued)*

	OLS		Poisson		Negative binomial	
	Estimated coefficient	p-value	Estimated coefficient	p-value	Estimated coefficient	p-value
Southern Cone						
India's exports to third countries	0.21	0.01	0.34	0.10	0.25	0.10
India's imports from third countries	0.04	0.13	0.24	0.01	−0.10	0.10
India's exports to Southern Cone	−0.12	0.19	−0.03	0.90	0.37	0.07
India's imports from Southern Cone	0.03	0.14	0.17	0.00	0.07	0.07
Observations	14,592		14,592		14,592	

Source: Authors.

Note: The reported coefficients come from the econometric estimation of the gravity model of trade, augmented by the interaction of country and country-group dummy variables. The estimated coefficients from the other variables in the empirical model are not reported, but all the gravity variables had the expected magnitudes and signs. The over-dispersion test, which corresponds to the null hypothesis that there is no over-dispersion of the errors with respect to the expected trade flows among country pairs, is not reported but was significant at the 1 percent level. Exporter, importer, and year dummies are not reported either. See text for details.

flows during any year in the period 2000 to 2004. Furthermore, exports to third markets by LAC countries could be causing increases in exports from LAC to China or India, rather than the reverse. Still, at first sight, there is little evidence consistent with dramatic negative impacts of China's growing exports to third markets on LAC exports. On the contrary, LAC exports were positively correlated with the growth of Chinese and Indian exports to third countries. These results are at odds with industry-level studies cited in the introduction, but can be explained by interindustry effects captured by the aggregate merchandise trade data, which could be the result of increasing production sharing around the world. More important, the few negative elasticities pale in comparison with the large Chinese and Indian demand elasticities for LAC exports, which were presented in tables 3.1 and 3.2. Therefore, the preponderance of the evidence makes it difficult to conclude that the threats posed by the growth of China and India in world markets have outweighed the opportunities offered to LAC exporters.

Conclusion

China's and India's rapid economic growth since the 1990s is viewed with envy by many observers. The growth of their internal markets is undoubtedly an opportunity for exporters from throughout the world, but their accompanying growing presence in world markets can be either a threat or an opportunity. It can be a threat because it may have displaced exporters from third markets. It can be an opportunity because the availability of a growing variety of Chinese and Indian products at cheaper prices in world markets open production possibilities for exporters in third markets through different channels, linked to (a) the availability of cheaper imported inputs at home that increase the efficiency of home exporters, (b) the increased presence of production networks, and (c) the learning by exporting for firms selling to the growing Chinese and Indian markets.

This chapter assessed the importance of the opportunity that the growth of China's and India's markets represented for LAC exporters during 2000 to 2004. It also explored the extent to which China's and India's growing presence in world markets affected LAC exports to third markets, aiming at disentangling the net impact through four different channels that are associated with the two Asian economies' exports to third markets, their imports from third markets, and their bilateral imports and exports with LAC countries. The preponderance of evidence suggests that the opportunities offered by the growth of China and India easily outweigh any potential threats. In other words, the growth of these Asian giants is not a zero-sum game for LAC exporters.

The analysis found that the growth of the two Asian economies represented a significant opportunity for LAC exporters. The corresponding elasticities for India were smaller than for China. But in both cases, LAC's supply elasticities were significantly smaller than the demand elasticities of the two Asian economies. Hence, even if LAC countries had experienced GDP growth similar to that of China or India during 2000 to 2004, their exports would not have matched the increase in Chinese and Indian demand for LAC exports. More active promotion policies and a better understanding of the functioning of the two Asian economies' markets may help LAC take full advantage of the growing opportunities.

No robust evidence supports the contention that China's growing presence in world markets represented a threat for LAC exporters. On the contrary, the relevant point estimates suggest that LAC exporters could have benefited from complementarities with China's exports to third markets, and perhaps from imports from China. These results thus signal the growing importance of international production networks, the impact that imports of intermediate inputs have on LAC's competitiveness, and the learning by exporting for LAC exports to China. The results for India were similar in that there is little robust evidence of substitution effects against

LAC exports to third markets through any channel. Indeed, the results for India could also be interpreted as suggesting that the effect of India's exports to third markets had positive effects on LAC exports to third markets.

In sum, the results suggest that the growth of the two Asian markets produced large opportunities for LAC exporters, which nevertheless have not been fully exploited. Also, the growth of China and India in world markets tended to complement LAC exports to third markets. These findings need to be weighed against the caveats discussed earlier in the chapter, which related to the inferences that can be made with the econometric estimations of the gravity model of trade. In general, however, China's, and to a large extent India's, growing presence in world trade has been good news for LAC, but some of the potential benefits remain unexploited.

Annex

Data Sources

Data on bilateral imports, both at the aggregate level and for commodities only, for the period 2000–04 come from the United Nation's Comtrade database accessed through the World Integrated Trade Statistics (WITS) software. Data on GDP and GDP per capita come from the World Bank's *World Development Indicators* (WDI) database. All data are deflated using the U.S. producer price index from the WDI, but all estimations included year dummies. The bilateral distance, common language, and common border variables come from Soloaga and Winters (2001).

Data for mainland China were added to Hong Kong data. Hong Kong has been a part of China since 1997 and therefore should be considered part of the Chinese economy for the period under investigation. Moreover, some observers have argued that China's and Hong Kong's trade data should be combined to approximate the trade flows coming from the China mainland because of transshipments of merchandise through Hong Kong (Fernald, Edison, and Loungani 1998). Hong Kong makes a significant contribution to the marketing and distribution of Chinese exports, thus making it difficult to differentiate the value added in each economy.

Notes

1. The rate of growth of nonfuel merchandise exports to China and India was calculated with data from WITS/UN Comtrade data in current US dollars covering the following sample of countries during 2000 to 2004: Argentina, Barbados, Belize, Bolivia, Brazil, Chile, Colombia, Costa Rica, Dominica, Ecuador, Guatemala, Guyana, Honduras, Mexico, Nicaragua, Panama, Paraguay, Peru, St. Lucia, Trinidad and Tobago, Uruguay, and República Bolivariana de Venezuela.

2. These authors identified products under threat from China as those where LAC has lost market share while China increased its market share. They also identified products under a partial threat as products for which China is gaining market share more rapidly than LAC. From an economic viewpoint, these definitions are rather loose, because even declining market shares do not necessarily reflect a direct substitution effect whereby Chinese exports would be displacing LAC exports.

3. In econometric terms, these estimations with the LAC data can be interpreted as providing estimates of the relevant parameter for LAC in models with data from the whole world, but allowing for strict heterogeneity between the LAC coefficients and those from the rest of the world.

4. The Linder variable is often used in gravity specifications to capture the effect of similarities between importers and exporters in their levels of development on bilateral trade (see, for example, Thursby and Thursby [1987]). However, this captures intra-industry trade effects, whereas most of the trade between LAC and China and India is interindustry. In 2005, LAC's trade deficit in manufactured products with China represented 277 percent of LAC exports to China, while LAC's trade surplus for agriculture and mining was 92 percent of exports. The numbers for trade with India are 108 percent and 46 percent, respectively. We nevertheless follow the traditional specification and include it as a control variable. In practice, the inclusion of this variable does not affect the parameters of interest for this chapter.

5. We also examined the differential effects on LAC imports from China and India, but we omit them from the presentation here for ease of exposition.

6. The expected variance falls with the expected level of bilateral trade.

7. República Bolivariana de Venezuela's trade flows are approximately 10 times larger than those of Uruguay.

8. As in the estimation described by equation (3.1), we also allow for heterogeneity across regions on the import side, but we do not include them in equation (3.3) for ease of exposition.

9. This is a common result in the literature when gravity models focus on developing countries. See the discussion in Arnon and Weinblatt (1998).

10. The full regression results are available from the authors upon request.

11. To be precise, it would be around 2 percent of 2004 exports, when the counterfactual is that China grows at the same rate as the rest of the world.

12. A similar conclusion is observed when comparing the predicted export growth associated with China's GDP growth with the observed export growth during the period. Export growth of LAC to China could have been 20 percent larger had it followed the increase in Chinese demand for LAC exports.

References

Anderson, James, and Eric van Wincoop. 2003. "Gravity with Gravitas: A Solution to the Border Puzzle." *American Economic Review* 93 (1): 170–92.

Arnon, A., and Jimmy Weinblatt. 1998. "Linder's Hypothesis Revisited: Income Similarity Effects for Low Income Countries." *Applied Economic Letters* 5 (10): 607–11.

Calderón, César. 2006. "Trade, Specialization and Cycle Synchronization: Explaining Output Co-movement between Latin America, China, and India." Office of the Chief Economist for Latin America and the Caribbean, World Bank, Washington, DC. http://www.worldbank.org/lac.

Dalgin, Muhammed, Vitor Trindade, and Devashish Mitra. 2006. "Inequality, Nonhomethetic Preferences, and Trade: A Gravity Approach." Unpublished, Syracuse University, New York.

Eaton, Jonathan, and Samuel Kortum. 2002. "Technology, Geography and Trade." *Econometrica* 70 (5): 1741–80.

Feenstra, Robert C. 2002. "Border Effects and the Gravity Equation: Consistent Methods for Estimation." *Scottish Journal of Political Economy* 49 (5): 491–506.

———. 2004. *Advanced International Trade.* Princeton, NJ: Princeton University Press.

Fernald, John, Hali Edison, and Prakash Loungani. 1998. "Was China the First Domino? Assessing Links between China and the Rest of Emerging Asia." Board of Governors of the Federal Reserve System, International Finance Discussion Paper 604, Washington, DC.

Freund, Caroline, and Çağlar Özden. 2006. "The Effect of China's Exports on Latin American Trade with the World." Office of the Chief Economist for Latin America and the Caribbean, World Bank, Washington, DC. http://www .worldbank.org/lac.

Hale, David. 2005. "China y América Latina." *Revista Poder*, June 11, 2005.

Hanson, Gordon, and Raymond Robertson. 2006. "China and the Recent Evolution of Latin America's Manufacturing Exports." Office of the Chief Economist for Latin America and the Caribbean, World Bank, Washington, DC. http:// www.worldbank.org/lac.

Lall, Sanjaya, John Weiss, and Hiroshi Oikawa. 2004. "People's Republic of China's Competitive Threat to Latin America: An Analysis for 1990–2002." ADB Discussion Paper 14, Asian Development Bank Institute, Tokyo.

Lederman, Daniel, Marcelo Olarreaga, and Eliana Rubiano. 2006. "Latin America's Trade Specialization and China and India's Growth." Office of the Chief Economist for Latin America and the Caribbean, World Bank, Washington, DC. http://www.worldbank.org/lac.

Santos Silva, J. M. C., and Silvana Tenreyro. 2006. "The Log of Gravity." *Review of Economics and Statistics* 88 (4): 641–58.

Soloaga, Isidro, and L. Alan Winters. 2001. "Regionalism in the Nineties. What Effect on Trade?" *North American Journal of Finance and Economics* 12 (1): 1–29.

Thursby, Jerry, and Marie Thursby. 1987. "Bilateral Trade Flows, the Linder Hypothesis, and Exchange Risk." *Review of Economics and Statistics* 69 (3): 488–95.

4

Foreign Direct Investment in Latin America during the Emergence of China and India: Stylized Facts

Javier Cravino, Daniel Lederman, and Marcelo Olarreaga[*]

Introduction

Foreign direct investment (FDI) has been increasing at an extraordinary speed. In the second half of the 1990s, world inflows grew at an annual rate of almost 40 percent, reaching US$648 billion in 2004 (UNCTAD 2005). Foreign capital stocks (FCS) increased by a factor of five between 1990 and 2004, rising from almost US$1.8 trillion in 1990 to almost US$9 trillion in 2004.[1] An even larger increase was reported in developing countries, where FCS grew from US$364 billion to more than US$2,230 billion over the same period.

In particular, FDI inflows to the Latin America and the Caribbean (LAC) region continuously grew during the 1990s, to almost half of total inflows into developing economies in 1999. In that year, FDI accounted for 25 percent of LAC's gross fixed capital formation (UNCTAD 2004, 2005). Although there was a slowdown in these inflows at the beginning of the twenty-first century, by 2004 aggregate stocks in LAC reached US$600 billion, about six times more than in 1990.[2]

[*] The authors are grateful to Pravin Krishna for helpful discussions and comments. Financial support from the World Bank's Latin American and Caribbean Regional Studies Program is gratefully acknowledged.

Concern is increasing that the growth in China and India may present a challenge to other developing countries. The low wages and large populations of these countries may entice multinational enterprises to relocate their production facilities there. In fact, FCS in China grew at an amazing speed, from US$20 billion in 1990 to US$245 billion in 2004, the largest FCS in the developing world. At the same time, stocks in India increased from US$1.6 billion to almost US$40 billion over the same period.

This chapter examines the evolution of foreign capital in Latin American economies by comparing them with China and India. In particular, it studies total inward stocks into each country, inward stocks from major Organisation for Economic Co-operation and Development (OECD) countries, inward stocks from the United States, and inward stocks from the United States into the manufacturing sector.

Although China appears to be the developing economy with the largest FCS, its stocks from OECD sources and especially from the United States are smaller than those of the major Latin American countries. In fact, FCS in China are still smaller than in Latin America, controlling for country size. However, Hong Kong (China) and mainland China together accumulated larger stocks from OECD investments than any LAC country. FCS in India, conversely, are still small compared with those in the major LAC countries.

The chapter then analyzes the evolution of relative FCS by looking at how they changed between 1990 and 1997, and between 1997 and 2003, because the data suggest that time trends of Chinese FCS changed after 1997. The analysis finds that China accumulated larger FCS than Latin America between 1990 and 1997, but not since 1997. This change in direction in 1997 did not apply to U.S. capital in the manufacturing sectors of host countries, where FCS in China grew faster than in most LAC countries between 1997 and 2003. This growth, however, is far from impressive, and is mainly explained by faster gross domestic product (GDP) growth. In contrast, Indian FCS grew faster than in LAC countries during the whole period 1990–2003, but this growth was slower than in China during the entire period according to both U.S. and OECD data.

Finally, the chapter analyzes the evolution of OECD FCS in Latin America relative to OECD FCS in China and India, after controlling for shocks affecting the source countries as well as geographic distance between source and host countries. This evidence suggests that OECD capital stocks in LAC economies relative to China changed between 1990 and 1997, but not between 1997 and 2003. At the same time, the analysis did not find any statistically significant change in the FCS relative to China including Hong Kong and India during this period, thus implying that China including Hong Kong and India receive FDI from different sources than do LAC economies. Nevertheless, these stylized facts do not reveal much about whether FDI flows to China, China including Hong Kong, or India since 1990 have come at the expense of FDI to LAC countries. Further econometric analysis is required to address this question (see, for example,

Chantasasawat et al. 2005; Cravino, Lederman, and Olarreaga forthcoming; Eichengreen and Tong 2005; and Garcia Herrero and Santabárbara 2005). However, we present some evidence from our forthcoming paper in annex table 4A.1 from the estimation of the knowledge-capital model of multinational enterprises, which also suggests that there is no robust evidence of substitution effects (see Cravino, Lederman, and Olarreaga forthcoming).

The rest of this chapter is organized as follows: The next section describes the data and is followed by a section that compares FCS levels in Latin America, China, China including Hong Kong, and India. The next two sections analyze the evolution of these stocks. The following section studies the conditional relative stocks, and the final section provides concluding remarks.

Data Description

The analyses in this chapter use data on aggregate inward FCS, outward stocks from some OECD countries, outward stocks from the United States, and outward stocks from the United States into the manufacturing sectors of China, China including Hong Kong, India, and LAC countries. Data on aggregate stocks were collected from the United Nations Conference on Trade and Development (UNCTAD) and are available from its Web site (http://www.unctad.org). UNCTAD reports aggregate FCS at book value or at historical cost in millions of U.S. dollars. The aggregate inward data is attractive because it draws a general picture of the relative evolution of FCS. One drawback of this data set is that the agencies that collected the original data vary from one host country to another. This makes comparisons between different host countries difficult to interpret. Moreover, these aggregate data do not provide information on FCS by source-host country pairs. Because the major sources of FCS for China are different from those of LAC countries, it is prudent to focus on source countries that are important for Latin America (IADB 2006).

To address these issues, the analysis also uses data on bilateral outward stocks from major OECD countries. These data were taken from OECD statistics and UNCTAD for the period 1990–2003.[3] The OECD reports the bilateral FCS of 29 OECD countries into 235 host economies in millions of U.S. dollars from 1982 to 2003. One shortcoming of this data set is that observations for most Latin American countries are missing for some source countries. Therefore, this data set was expanded using data from UNCTAD for 29 source countries into 190 host countries. For those countries for which the UNCTAD data is reported in national currency, the figures were transformed into U.S. dollars using the end-of-period exchange rate, which was taken from the OECD. The OECD data set is then used unless the observations are missing.[4] Even after including the observations from UNCTAD, some country pairs are still missing several observations. For this reason, the analysis in the next three sections of this chapter is restricted to major source countries that have most of the observations for the Latin American countries. The selected source countries are Canada, France, Germany, Japan, the Netherlands, Spain, Switzerland, the United Kingdom, and the United States.[5] Together, these countries accounted for more than 68 percent of total FCS in the major LAC countries as of 2002 (UNCTAD 2004).[6] The complete data set was used in the regression analysis of the "Conditional Relative Stocks" section, where the data were also deflated by the U.S. producer price index.[7] Although the agencies that collected the information in the OECD and UNCTAD databases vary from one source country to another, the collecting agencies remain the same within the host countries, which facilitates international comparisons, especially in econometric analyses that control for source-country effects, as follows.

Data for total outward stocks from the United States were taken from the Bureau of Economic Analysis (BEA; http://www.bea.gov). These stocks are reported on a historical cost basis in millions of U.S. dollars. These data are of particular interest for the purposes of this chapter because of the visible presence of U.S. multinational corporations in LAC countries as well as in China, Hong Kong (China), and India. An advantage of these data is that they were collected by the same agency. Finally, the U.S. stocks in the manufacturing sectors of the host countries were also taken from the BEA. Again, these data are of special interest because companies in this sector seem to be potentially more inclined to relocate production to China or India as they search for reductions in labor costs.

To make the analysis more tractable, and because of data availability on bilateral stocks from the OECD, the analysis focuses on nine Latin American countries. The major countries are included (Argentina, Brazil, Chile, Colombia, Mexico, and República Bolivarian de Venezuela) as are some Central American countries that may be of particular interest (Costa Rica, El Salvador, and Guatemala) given their dependence on manufacturing exports that compete with Chinese exports in the U.S. market. Together, these countries accounted for 86 percent of Latin America's FCS in 2003.

Relative Stocks in 2003

This section analyzes the FCS levels in LAC countries relative to those in China, China including Hong Kong, and India. Table 4.1 reports these ratios for the world total, the OECD, the United States, and U.S. manufacturing.

The first column shows how important China has become as a destination for FDI: by 2003, total FCS in China were bigger than in any LAC country. Brazil and Mexico, with the largest FCS of the region, had only 58 percent and 73 percent, respectively, of China's stock. At the same time, Argentina, Chile, and República Bolivariana de Venezuela reported less than a quarter of China's FCS, and the remaining countries, even less.

Table 4.1 FCS in Latin America Relative to China, China including Hong Kong, and India, 2003 (FCS in LAC country divided by FCS in China, China including Hong Kong, and India)

Host economy	China				China including Hong Kong				India			
	Total	OECD	United States	U.S. manufacturing	Total	OECD	United States	U.S. manufacturing	Total	OECD	United States	U.S. manufacturing
Argentina	0.22	0.84	0.95	0.31	0.08	0.34	0.22	0.20	1.60	2.95	2.27	1.36
Brazil	0.58	1.76	2.75	1.78	0.22	0.70	0.65	1.16	4.31	6.14	6.57	7.81
Chile	0.24	0.54	0.80	0.32	0.09	0.22	0.19	0.21	1.75	1.88	1.91	1.41
Colombia	0.09	0.24	0.26	0.19	0.03	0.10	0.06	0.12	0.66	0.83	0.61	0.83
Costa Rica	0.02	0.03	0.07	0.12	0.01	0.01	0.02	0.08	0.14	0.11	0.18	0.53
El Salvador	0.01	0.02	0.06	n.a.	0.01	0.01	0.01	n.a.	0.10	0.05	0.13	n.a.
Guatemala	0.02	0.01	0.03	0.03	0.01	0.00	0.01	0.02	0.14	0.04	0.06	0.15
Mexico	0.73	1.96	5.12	3.00	0.27	0.78	1.20	1.97	5.38	6.84	12.23	13.20
Venezuela, R. B. de	0.18	0.28	0.79	0.54	0.07	0.11	0.19	0.35	1.36	0.98	1.89	2.37
Reference: Total stocks in 2003[a] (US$ millions)	228,371	47,142	11,541	5,910	609,713	117,845	49,108	9,027	30,827	13,509	4,831	1,345

Source: Authors' calculations, based on UNCTAD, OECD, and BEA.

Note: n.a.= not available. OECD refers to the set of countries listed in the data description. Switzerland's stocks in Costa Rica, Guatemala, and El Salvador were not included because of data availability.

a. Figures refer to China, China including Hong Kong, and India.

Nonetheless, OECD FCS in China were significantly smaller than in two of the major LAC countries. In particular, Mexico had almost twice as much capital from the OECD as China had. This disparity is more noticeable in disaggregated data from the United States. The third column of table 4.1 shows that the relative stocks from the United States were bigger than both the aggregate and the OECD relative stocks. This reflects the fact that the United States is a relatively more important source of FDI for Latin American countries than for China (without Hong Kong). In 2003, U.S. FCS in China were only US$11.5 billion, quite small compared to the US$59 billion in Mexico or the US$37 billion in Brazil. These data show that when it comes to OECD and U.S. stocks, China is still far from being a major host of FCS.

The fourth column in table 4.1 reports the relative stocks from the United States in the manufacturing sector. Again, China does not appear as a major host of FCS, with one-third as much capital accumulated as in Mexico. However, in this sector Chinese stocks are larger than those of Argentina, Chile, and República Bolivariana de Venezuela, suggesting that China has been relatively more attractive to capital in the manufacturing sector.

China including Hong Kong had accumulated FCS of almost US$188 billion, more from the OECD than any Latin American country, by 2003. China and Hong Kong (China) are important hosts of U.S. FCS, with more than every country in Latin America except Mexico.

India, however, is a long way from reaching the FCS levels of the major LAC countries. By 2003, total FCS in Mexico alone were more than five times that in India. The OECD data show that this gap is bigger for the largest countries, but it is smaller for Costa Rica, El Salvador, and Guatemala.

The last two columns of the table reveal that India is not a major destination for U.S. capital. Except for Argentina and Chile, the difference between Latin American and Indian stocks is larger in the manufacturing sector.

Differences in FCS in Latin American countries and China and India may only reflect differences in country sizes. Thus, the analysis proceeds to normalize FCS by each country's GDP and recalculate the relative stocks. The U.S. FCS in the manufacturing sector were normalized with the manufacturing value added in each country.[8] The resulting ratios are reported in table 4.2. After controlling for country size, China had less FCS than any Latin American country in 2003. This is true for the different indicators of FCS. Most LAC countries also have more FCS from the OECD and the United States relative to their size than China including Hong Kong. The last panel shows that FCS in India are even more irrelevant once the analysis controls for country size.

In brief, the general view of China and India as major destinations for foreign capital can be deceptive. When looking at FCS, India is still far below the major LAC economies. China, however, has a larger level of FCS than these LAC economies, although this is not the case when the

Table 4.2 Normalized FCS in Latin America Relative to China, China including Hong Kong, and India, 2003 (normalized FCS in LAC country divided by normalized FCS in China, China including Hong Kong, and India)

Host economy	China				China including Hong Kong				India			
	Total	OECD	United States	U.S. manufacturing	Total	OECD	United States	U.S. manufacturing	Total	OECD	United States	U.S. manufacturing
Argentina	2.37	9.24	10.37	1.17	0.98	4.10	2.70	0.81	7.43	13.67	10.50	3.99
Brazil	1.63	4.93	7.70	3.68	0.68	2.19	2.01	2.54	5.12	7.29	7.80	12.58
Chile	4.62	10.55	15.63	2.67	1.92	4.68	4.07	1.85	14.52	15.61	15.83	9.14
Colombia	1.58	4.23	4.54	1.99	0.66	1.88	1.18	1.38	4.97	6.26	4.60	6.80
Costa Rica	1.49	2.60	6.06	3.96	0.62	1.15	1.58	2.74	4.68	3.85	6.14	13.53
El Salvador	1.34	1.47	5.30	n.a.	0.56	0.65	1.38	n.a.	4.20	2.17	5.37	n.a.
Guatemala	1.08	0.71	1.51	1.20	0.45	0.32	0.39	0.83	3.38	1.06	1.53	4.09
Mexico	1.61	4.34	11.35	3.17	0.67	1.93	2.96	2.19	5.06	6.43	11.49	10.84
Venezuela, R. B. de	3.12	4.77	13.42	4.15	1.29	2.12	3.50	2.87	9.79	7.06	13.59	14.20
Reference: Total stocks over GDP[a]	0.16	0.03	0.01	0.05	0.39	0.07	0.03	0.08	0.05	0.02	0.01	0.02

Source: Authors' calculations, based on UNCTAD, OECD, BEA, WDI, and *China Statistical Yearbook 2003.*

Note: n.a.= not available. Total, OECD, and U.S. stocks were normalized by GDP. Manufacturing U.S. stocks were normalized by the value added in manufacturing. Because of data availability, U.S. manufacturing stocks in China in 2003 were normalized by the value added in the manufacturing sector in 2002. OECD refers to the set of countries listed in the data description. Switzerland's stocks in El Salvador and Spain's stocks in Costa Rica, Guatemala, and El Salvador were not included because of data availability.

a. Figures refer to China, China including Hong Kong, and India.

source countries are restricted to the OECD or the United States. In fact, Latin American countries have greater FCS than China and India relative to their size. Finally, stocks in China are particularly large in the manufacturing sector, whereas stocks in India are relatively smaller in the manufacturing sector. However, the snapshot of the relative FCS position in 2003 hides important trends over time, as discussed in the next section.

Evolution of FCS between 1990 and 2003

This section analyzes the evolution of FCS in Latin America relative to those in China, China including Hong Kong, and India. These relative stocks are calculated as

$$\frac{FCS^{03}_i}{FCS^{03}_j} \Bigg/ \frac{FCS^{90}_i}{FCS^{90}_j}$$

where i stands for the Latin American countries, and j stands for China, China including Hong Kong, or India. When this ratio is less than 1, the relative position of country i with respect to country j was lower in 2003 than in 1990. The results of the corresponding calculations are reported in table 4.3.

The first column of table 4.3 reports that aggregate stocks in China have grown significantly faster than in Latin America during this period. Between 1990 and 2003, stocks in China grew two times faster than in Argentina, Chile, and Colombia; three times faster than in Brazil and Costa Rica; and four times faster than in Guatemala. OECD stocks in China also grew faster than in Latin American countries.

The third column shows that the fall in relative FCS is more dramatic in the U.S. data. For most countries, relative stocks in 2003 were less than 20 percent of the 1990 levels. In Brazil, Colombia, and Guatemala, the ratios are below 0.1. This reveals that U.S. stocks in China caught up with those in LAC countries. The relative decline was particularly remarkable in the manufacturing sector. Relative stocks in this sector in the major countries declined the most: stocks in Argentina, Brazil, Colombia, and Mexico, were at 5 percent or less of the 1990 levels. Again, this reflects that China is relatively more attractive to capital in the manufacturing sector.

The second column grouping in table 4.3 displays the changes in the stocks relative to those in China including Hong Kong. The fifth column shows that aggregate relative stocks in China including Hong Kong grew faster than in most Latin American countries. However, this pattern is reversed when focusing on FCS from OECD. Most LAC countries accumulated more stocks from the OECD than China including Hong Kong during this period. In fact, only in Brazil and Guatemala did the relative stocks from the OECD turn out to be smaller in 2003 than in 1990.

Table 4.3 Ratio of Relative FCS in 2003 versus 1990

Host economy	China				China including Hong Kong				India			
	Total	OECD	United States	U.S. manufacturing	Total	OECD	United States	U.S. manufacturing	Total	OECD	United States	U.S. manufacturing
Argentina	0.51	0.54	0.13	0.03	0.61	1.49	0.56	0.29	0.30	0.81	0.33	0.22
Brazil	0.32	0.20	0.07	0.02	0.38	0.56	0.29	0.19	0.19	0.31	0.17	0.15
Chile	0.49	0.50	0.15	0.20	0.58	1.40	0.63	1.76	0.29	0.76	0.37	1.37
Colombia	0.53	0.43	0.05	0.04	0.63	1.19	0.23	0.39	0.31	0.65	0.14	0.31
Costa Rica	0.29	0.46	0.11	0.10	0.35	1.27	0.45	0.94	0.17	0.69	0.26	0.73
El Salvador	1.38	0.61	0.22	n.a.	1.64	1.71	0.94	n.a.	0.82	0.93	0.55	n.a.
Guatemala	0.22	0.33	0.07	0.08	0.27	0.92	0.31	0.70	0.13	0.50	0.18	0.55
Mexico	0.67	0.45	0.18	0.05	0.80	1.25	0.75	0.48	0.40	0.68	0.44	0.37
Venezuela, R. B. de	0.98	0.66	0.26	0.11	1.17	1.85	1.09	0.99	0.58	1.00	0.65	0.77
Reference: Total stocks in 1990[a] (US$ millions)	20,691	3,565	354	138	65,763	24,837	6,409	1,894	1,657	1,546	372	220

Source: Authors' calculations, based on UNCTAD, OECD, and BEA.

Note: n.a. = not available. OECD refers to the set of countries listed in the data description. Switzerland's stocks in El Salvador and Spain's stocks in Costa Rica, Guatemala, and El Salvador were not included because of data availability. Total stocks in Costa Rica and Guatemala in 1990 were only available for Canada, Switzerland, and the United States. The United Kingdom's stocks in China were not available in 1990, and the United Kingdom's and France's stocks in Colombia were missing in 1990.

a. Figures refer to China, China including Hong Kong, and India.

The seventh column shows results for the U.S. data. Again, stocks in China including Hong Kong grew faster than in most Latin American countries. In the manufacturing sector, the ratios for most countries are significantly smaller than in China alone, suggesting that most of the growth in the manufacturing stocks in China including Hong Kong was due to FDI in mainland China rather than Hong Kong.

Finally, the last column grouping of table 4.3 reports the results relative to India. Not one of the Latin American countries accumulated more FCS than India during the period. Indeed, Latin American total stocks relative to India fell even more than those relative to China. Unlike those of China, however, these ratios are significantly larger when the exercise is repeated with the stocks from the OECD.

U.S. stocks in India also grew faster than in Latin American countries. Contrary to what happened with China, this growth was less pronounced in the manufacturing sector. The most remarkable example is Chile, where total stocks relative to India in 2003 were about one-third of those in 1990 but were 37 percent larger in the manufacturing sector.

It is interesting to estimate the share of these variations explained by GDP growth, which can be done by normalizing the FCS by the GDP and value added in manufacturing before calculating the ratios of the relative stocks between 2003 and 1990. The results of this exercise are reported in table 4.4. The first panel of the table shows the results for China. FCS in China grew more than in Latin America even after controlling for GDP growth. Although some ratios are still less than 1, they are significantly higher than those in table 4.3, reflecting that GDP growth was faster in China than in Latin American countries. FCS in India also grew more than in Latin America, even after normalizing by GDP growth.

In summary, Latin American FCS relative to those of China and India were smaller in 2003 than in 1990, even after controlling for GDP growth. This is less true when China including Hong Kong is considered as one economy. Nevertheless, there are significant differences among source and host countries: whereas in China stocks from the United States and the OECD grew relatively faster, aggregate stocks grew faster in India. Another interesting aspect when comparing the growth of FCS in China and India is that U.S. stocks in China grew more in the manufacturing sector, whereas U.S. stocks in India grew more in the aggregate.

Evolution of Relative FCS between 1997 and 2003

To get a clearer picture of the evolution of the relative stocks over time, the analysis repeats the exercise using 1997 as a benchmark year. Table 4.5 reports the ratios of the relative stocks in 2003 divided by those in 1997.

The results are quite surprising. The first column of table 4.5 shows that aggregate stocks in most Latin American countries grew faster than in

Table 4.4 Ratio of Relative FCS in 2003 versus 1990, with FCS Normalized

Host economy	China				China including Hong Kong				India			
	Total	OECD	United States	U.S. manufacturing	Total	OECD	United States	U.S. manufacturing	Total	OECD	United States	U.S. manufacturing
Argentina	2.22	2.33	0.58	0.17	2.42	5.95	2.25	1.10	0.63	1.68	0.69	0.51
Brazil	1.18	0.74	0.25	0.15	1.28	1.88	0.96	0.95	0.33	0.53	0.29	0.44
Chile	0.81	0.84	0.25	0.34	0.88	2.14	0.97	2.20	0.23	0.60	0.30	1.02
Colombia	1.06	0.86	0.11	0.14	1.16	2.19	0.42	0.89	0.30	0.62	0.13	0.42
Costa Rica	0.38	0.59	0.14	0.14	0.41	1.52	0.54	0.91	0.11	0.43	0.16	0.42
El Salvador	1.77	0.79	0.28	n.a.	1.93	2.01	1.10	n.a.	0.50	0.57	0.34	n.a.
Guatemala	0.28	0.41	0.09	0.12	0.30	1.04	0.35	0.76	0.08	0.29	0.11	0.35
Mexico	1.09	0.73	0.29	0.10	1.19	1.87	1.12	0.68	0.31	0.53	0.34	0.31
Venezuela, R. B. de	2.29	1.55	0.60	0.22	2.49	3.94	2.33	1.41	0.64	1.11	0.71	0.66
Reference: Total stocks over GDP[a]	0.06	0.01	0.00	0.01	0.15	0.06	0.01	0.05	0.01	0.00	0.00	0.00

Source: Authors' calculations, based on UNCTAD, OECD, BEA, WDI, and *China Statistical Yearbook*, various issues.

Note: n.a. = not available. Total, OECD, and U.S. stocks were normalized by the GDP. Manufacturing U.S. stocks were normalized by value added in manufacturing.

OECD refers to the set of countries listed in the data description. Switzerland's stocks in El Salvador and Spain's stocks in Costa Rica, Guatemala, and El Salvador were not included because of data availability.

Total stocks in Costa Rica and Guatemala in 1990 were only available for Canada, Switzerland, and the United States.

The United Kingdom's stocks in China were not available in 1990, and the United Kingdom's and France's stocks in Colombia were missing in 1990.

a. Figures refer to China, China including Hong Kong, and India.

Table 4.5 Ratio of Relative FCS in 2003 versus 1997

Host economy	China				China including Hong Kong				India			
	Total	OECD	United States	U.S. manufacturing	Total	OECD	United States	U.S. manufacturing	Total	OECD	United States	U.S. manufacturing
Argentina	0.79	1.21	0.44	0.23	0.78	1.07	0.46	0.33	0.41	0.68	0.32	0.13
Brazil	1.37	0.86	0.40	0.22	1.34	0.76	0.41	0.31	0.70	0.49	0.29	0.13
Chile	1.05	1.02	0.45	1.16	1.03	0.90	0.46	1.62	0.54	0.58	0.33	0.67
Colombia	0.70	0.84	0.32	0.43	0.69	0.74	0.33	0.61	0.36	0.47	0.23	0.25
Costa Rica	2.32	0.61	0.25	0.94	2.27	0.54	0.26	1.31	1.19	0.35	0.18	0.54
El Salvador	4.52	1.89	1.31	n.a.	4.44	1.67	1.35	n.a.	2.31	1.07	0.95	n.a.
Guatemala	1.22	0.77	0.38	0.58	1.20	0.68	0.39	0.81	0.63	0.44	0.28	0.34
Mexico	2.00	1.82	1.10	0.59	1.97	1.61	1.12	0.83	1.03	1.03	0.79	0.34
Venezuela, R. B. de	1.14	0.98	0.76	0.81	1.12	0.87	0.78	1.14	0.59	0.55	0.55	0.47
Reference: Total stocks in 1997[a] (million current US$)	153,995	32,967	5,150	2,737	403,355	72,784	22,465	5,854	10,630	5,341	1,563	359

Source: Authors' calculations, based on UNCTAD, OECD, and BEA.

Note: n.a. = not available. OECD refers to the set of countries listed in the data description. Switzerland's stocks in El Salvador and Spain's stocks in Costa Rica, Guatemala, and El Salvador were not included because of data availability. Netherlands's stocks in Guatemala, Costa Rica, and El Salvador were missing for 1997.

a. Figures refer to China, China including Hong Kong, and India.

China: only Argentina and Colombia accumulated fewer FCS during this period. Perhaps more unexpected is that the major winners were Central American countries: between 1997 and 2003, FDI stocks grew four times faster in El Salvador than in China, and about two times faster in Mexico and Costa Rica. FCS in Brazil, Chile, Guatemala, and República Bolivariana de Venezuela also increased more than in China during this period.

Chinese FCS from the OECD did not grow faster than those in Latin American countries. The second column shows that in general, stocks in China and Latin America have grown at similar rates since 1997. Argentina, Chile, El Salvador, and Mexico actually have accumulated more FCS from OECD than China since 1997.

FCS from the United States in China increased more rapidly than that in Latin America except for Mexico and El Salvador, each of which, once again, grew faster than China. This seems to be at odds with the perception that foreign investment in Mexico and Central America is receding because firms are increasingly moving their production facilities to China.

The fourth column reports the ratios in the manufacturing sector and shows that stocks in China continued to outgrow those in Latin America for the period 1997–2003. In particular, FCS in the manufacturing sector in Mexico relative to China were only 60 percent of the 1997 level. At the same time, relative stocks in Argentina and Brazil were less than one-fourth of their 1997 levels. It is, however, important to acknowledge that even in the manufacturing sector, the growth of Chinese FCS was not spectacular: during the same period, stocks grew faster in Chile than in China, and at about the same rate as China in Costa Rica.

The second panel exhibits the evolution of FCS relative to China including Hong Kong. The ratios for total FCS are very similar to those in China, thus indicating that FCS in Hong Kong (China) and in the mainland grew at similar rates during the period. Again, aggregate FCS in most Latin American countries have grown faster than in China including Hong Kong since 1997. The results using the major OECD countries and the United States as the only sources of FCS in Latin America are also quite similar to those in China alone. Differences appear in manufacturing-sector FCS. In this case, growth in FCS in China including Hong Kong was smaller than in Chile, Costa Rica, and República Bolivariana de Venezuela.

Regarding India, the first column of the last panel of table 4.5 shows that for the aggregate, FCS grew less than in Costa Rica, El Salvador, and Mexico. However, total FCS in India did grow faster than in the other Latin American countries, especially Argentina, Chile, and Colombia. This was also the case for OECD stocks. For the OECD, stocks in India increased more rapidly than in every country in the sample with the exception of El Salvador and Mexico.

Even more than OECD FCS, U.S. FCS in India continued to grow faster than those in Latin America between 1997 and 2003. In this period, India accumulated about three times more FCS from the United States than did Argentina, Brazil, Chile, or Guatemala, and about five times more than Colombia or Costa Rica. Even Mexican relative FCS were only 79 percent of the 1997 level. Only FCS in El Salvador grew at the same rate as those in India. Finally, the manufacturing sector stocks in India increased more than in any of the LAC countries during this period.

Table 4.6 repeats the exercise after normalizing FCS. Again, part of the relative growth in China FCS can be attributed to faster GDP growth. The ratios here are much higher than those in table 4.5. Total and OECD FCS in Latin American countries grew more than in China relative to their GDP. U.S. FCS in the manufacturing sector grew more in China than in Latin America during this period, although this growth was less than in Chile, Costa Rica, and República Bolivariana de Venezuela. Conversely, FCS in India grew faster, in general, than in LAC during this period.

In short, aggregate and OECD FCS in China did not outgrow that in Latin America between 1997 and 2003. Even for U.S. stocks, we find that some countries—Argentina, El Salvador, Mexico, and República Bolivariana de Venezuela—accumulated more FCS than China since 1997. Only in the manufacturing sector did China accumulate more capital than most Latin American countries, although these FCS were significantly smaller than those reported for the period beginning in 1990. Latin American countries have in general performed better than China despite their lack of relative GDP growth. India, in contrast, continued to accumulate FCS faster than most countries in the sample of LAC economies between 1997 and 2003.

Conditional Relative Stocks

As noted above, relative FCS trends differ across source countries, thus suggesting that bilateral characteristics may be important in determining the allocation of FDI. Consequently, this section analyzes trends in FCS while controlling for distance and source-country characteristics. To deal with these issues, the analysis uses the OECD and UNCTAD data to estimate cross-sectional regressions for each year with source and host country dummies and the bilateral distance between source and host countries.[9] Each regression excludes the dummy for China as a host country, which means the dummy-variable coefficients of the other host countries can be interpreted as the effect of each host country relative to China. The exercise is then repeated, excluding the dummies for China including Hong Kong, and then excluding the dummies for India. This econometric approach is consistent with existing literature on the determinants of FDI in developed and developing countries, which suggests that host- and source-country characteristics, as well as their bilateral characteristics, affect the investment decisions of investor firms (see, for example, Carr, Markusen, and Maskus 2001, and Blonigen, Davies, and Head 2003).

Table 4.7 reports the coefficients and the confidence intervals of the dummies for the regressions in the years 1990, 1997, and 2003. The first

Table 4.6 Ratio of Relative FCS in 2003 versus 1997, with FCS Normalized

Host economy	China				China including Hong Kong				India			
	Total	OECD	United States	U.S. manufacturing	Total	OECD	United States	U.S. manufacturing	Total	OECD	United States	U.S. manufacturing
Argentina	2.83	4.31	1.59	0.78	2.58	3.54	1.51	0.98	1.34	2.26	1.07	0.34
Brazil	3.44	2.17	1.00	1.02	3.14	1.78	0.95	1.28	1.64	1.14	0.67	0.44
Chile	1.73	1.67	0.74	2.32	1.58	1.37	0.70	2.92	0.82	0.88	0.50	1.00
Colombia	1.47	1.76	0.68	1.11	1.34	1.45	0.65	1.40	0.70	0.93	0.46	0.48
Costa Rica	2.68	0.71	0.29	1.33	2.45	0.58	0.28	1.67	1.28	0.37	0.20	0.57
El Salvador	5.32	2.22	1.54	n.a.	4.85	1.82	1.47	n.a.	2.53	1.17	1.04	n.a.
Guatemala	1.39	0.88	0.43	0.83	1.27	0.72	0.41	1.04	0.66	0.46	0.29	0.36
Mexico	1.99	1.81	1.09	0.80	1.81	1.48	1.03	1.01	0.94	0.95	0.73	0.35
Venezuela, R. B. de	1.92	1.64	1.28	1.89	1.75	1.35	1.22	2.37	0.91	0.86	0.86	0.82
Reference: Total stocks over GDP[a]	0.17	0.04	0.01	0.05	0.38	0.07	0.02	0.08	0.03	0.01	0.00	0.01

Source: Authors' calculations, based on UNCTAD, OECD, BEA, WDI, and China Statistical Yearbook, various issues.

Note: n.a. = not available. Total, OECD, and U.S. stocks were normalized by GDP. Manufacturing U.S. stocks were normalized by the value added in manufacturing.

OECD refers to the set of countries listed in the data description. Switzerland's stocks in El Salvador and Spain's stocks in Costa Rica, Guatemala, and El Salvador were not included due to data availability. Netherlands's stocks in Guatemala, Costa Rica, and El Salvador were missing in 1997.

a. Figures refer to China, China including Hong Kong, and India.

Table 4.7 Conditional Relative Means, 1990, 1997, and 2003

Country	China			China including Hong Kong			India		
	1990	1997	2003	1990	1997	2003	1990	1997	2003
Argentina	2.3	0.0	0.5	0.2	0.1	-0.2	2.3	2.3	2.4
	[1.495 to 3.150]**	[-1.125 to 1.224]	[-0.583 to 1.531]	[-0.557 to 1.045]	[-0.548 to 0.702]	[-1.073 to 0.759]	[1.371 to 3.271]**	[1.530 to 3.036]**	[1.559 to 3.325]**
Brazil	3.1	1.6	1.6	1.0	1.6	1.0	3.1	3.8	3.6
	[2.393 to 3.843]**	[0.204 to 2.926]*	[0.334 to 2.894]*	[0.379 to 1.703]**	[0.664 to 2.533]**	[-0.181 to 2.164]	[2.283 to 3.951]**	[2.776 to 4.820]**	[2.442 to 4.722]**
Chile	1.6	-0.5	-0.4	-0.5	-0.5	-1.1	1.6	1.7	1.5
	[0.926 to 2.260]**	[-1.649 to 0.646]	[-1.416 to 0.526]	[-1.122 to 0.150]	[-1.048 to 0.088]	[-1.891 to -0.268]**	[0.776 to 2.408]**	[1.030 to 2.433]**	[0.746 to 2.301]**
Colombia	0.1	-1.5	-1.9	-2.0	-1.5	-2.5	0.1	0.7	0.1
	[-0.589 to 0.723]	[-2.960 to -0.109]*	[-2.937 to -0.900]**	[-2.635 to -1.369]**	[-2.524 to -0.520]**	[-3.413 to -1.675]**	[-0.742 to 0.874]	[-0.400 to 1.798]	[-0.787 to 0.887]
Costa Rica	-3.2	-4.0	-2.9	-5.3	-4.0	-3.5	-3.2	-1.8	-0.9
	[-4.388 to -2.054]**	[-5.436 to -2.618]**	[-4.501 to -1.267]**	[-6.440 to -4.157]**	[-5.004 to -2.985]**	[-5.038 to -1.949]**	[-4.476 to -1.968]**	[-2.874 to -0.713]**	[-2.422 to 0.591]
El Salvador	-5.3	-5.0	-5.0	-7.4	-5.0	-5.6	-5.3	-2.8	-3.0
	[-6.583 to -4.104]**	[-6.859 to -3.236]**	[-6.426 to -3.584]**	[-8.627 to -6.209]**	[-6.552 to -3.480]**	[-6.947 to -4.284]**	[-6.657 to -4.033]**	[-4.390 to -1.238]**	[-4.342 to -1.732]**

(continued)

Table 4.7 Conditional Relative Means, 1990, 1997, and 2003 (continued)

Country	China			China including Hong Kong			India		
	1990	1997	2003	1990	1997	2003	1990	1997	2003
Guatemala	-3.3	-4.2	-4.2	-5.3	-4.2	-4.8	-3.3	-2.0	-2.3
	[-4.019 to -2.518]**	[-5.691 to -2.770]**	[-5.326 to -3.120]**	[-6.027 to -4.666]**	[-5.277 to -3.112]**	[-5.810 to -3.862]**	[-4.124 to -2.415]**	[-3.146 to -0.848]**	[-3.198 to -1.312]**
Mexico	1.4	-0.4	-0.4	-0.6	-0.4	-1.0	1.4	1.8	1.6
	[0.614 to 2.264]**	[-1.634 to 0.747]	[-1.266 to 0.559]	[-1.433 to 0.170]	[-1.080 to 0.244]	[-1.733 to -0.240]**	[0.483 to 2.393]**	[1.013 to 2.566]**	[0.907 to 2.322]**
Venezuela, R. B. de	-0.2	-1.8	-1.5	-2.3	-1.7	-2.2	-0.2	0.5	0.4
	[-0.886 to 0.496]	[-2.949 to -0.550]**	[-2.740 to -0.321]*	[-2.920 to -1.622]**	[-2.410 to -1.072]**	[-3.248 to -1.083]**	[-1.024 to 0.632]	[-0.307 to 1.275]	[-0.621 to 1.497]

Source: Authors.
Note: Robust 95 percent confidence intervals are in brackets.
* Significant at 5 percent level.
** Significant at 1 percent level.

panel shows the results when the dummy for China is excluded. After controlling for source-country fixed effects and distance, Mexico no longer appears to be the major destination for OECD stocks. Instead, Brazil comes out as the major recipient in Latin America. After conditioning on distance and source-country fixed effects, the dummies in 1997 decreased relative to those in 1990. However, the relative-FCS coefficients from 1997 and 2003 are not significantly different. This finding confirms that China has not become relatively more attractive for OECD capital than Latin American countries since 1997. In contrast, the relative-FCS coefficients with respect to China including Hong Kong and India do not vary significantly over time. All the coefficients for 2003 are within the confidence intervals of the 1990 coefficients.

Conclusion

In sum, India is still far from the aggregate levels of FCS found in the major Latin American economies, while China including Hong Kong as a whole has had higher FCS since 1990. Regarding China alone, when the source countries are limited to the OECD or the United States, FCS in China have grown significantly faster than in Latin America between 1990 and 2003, especially those originating in the United States and destined for the manufacturing sectors of host countries. Nevertheless, this relative growth has been less evident since 1997. From 1997 on, China accumulated more FCS than Latin American countries only in the manufacturing sector. Even in this sector, U.S. stocks in China did not grow faster than in Chile or Costa Rica. At the same time, stocks in India increased more than in Latin America in both periods. This was true for stocks originating both in the OECD and in the United States, but their growth was less significant than those in China between 1990 and 1997.

After controlling for shocks emanating from source countries and for bilateral distance between source and host countries, the OECD data suggest that the significant change in Latin America's FCS relative to China occurred between 1990 and 1997. However, even this econometric analysis is silent with respect to any substitution effects that might have affected Latin America's FCS positions. That is, further econometric analyses are needed to directly test the hypothesis that changes in Chinese or Indian FCS positions were associated with changes in Latin American FCS levels, as has been attempted by Eichengreen and Tong (2005) and Cravino, Lederman, and Olarreaga (forthcoming), among others. It is worth noting here that the model-driven estimations presented in the forthcoming article by the authors of this chapter suggest that there is no robust evidence of substitution effects, even for Central America and Mexico (see table 4A.1). In any case, the data and the findings of this chapter suggest that the threat from China and India with regard to FDI might be the dog that did not bark.

Annex

Table 4A.1 Results from the Estimation of the Knowledge-Capital Model of Multinational Enterprises: Little Evidence of Substitution Effects

| | China's and India's effects across LAC subregions | | | | | | | | |
| | Aggregate data | | | U.S. data | | | U.S. data: Manufacturing | | |
	OLS	Poisson	Negative binomial	OLS	Poisson	Negative binomial	OLS	Poisson	Negative binomial
China's effect on Central American countries	0.45 [0.00]**	0.22 [0.06]*	0.13 [0.02]**	0.02 [0.47]	0.20 [0.31]	0.05 [0.14]	-0.33 [0.03]**	0.27 [0.29]	-0.06 [0.56]
India's effect on Central American countries	0.34 [0.01]**	0.18 [0.45]	0.02 [0.70]	0.01 [0.64]	-0.01 [0.83]	0.01 [0.83]	0.86 [0.00]**	-0.10 [0.89]	0.16 [0.46]
China's effect on Andean countries	0.48 [0.00]**	0.29 [0.02]**	0.18 [0.00]**	0.03 [0.40]	0.11 [0.15]	0.13 [0.02]**	0.07 [0.73]	0.37 [0.59]	-0.01 [0.94]
India's effect on Andean countries	0.35 [0.00]**	0.19 [0.06]*	0.04 [0.58]	-0.02 [0.77]	-0.01 [0.78]	0.00 [0.97]	-0.03 [0.94]	-0.35 [0.26]	0.17 [0.60]
China's effect on Southern Cone countries	0.24 [0.02]**	0.20 [0.01]**	0.15 [0.00]**	0.08 [0.00]**	0.09 [0.02]**	0.09 [0.03]**	0.24 [0.12]	0.43 [0.01]**	0.09 [0.63]

(continued)

Table 4A.1 Results from the Estimation of the Knowledge-Capital Model of Multinational Enterprises: Little Evidence of Substitution Effects *(continued)*

| | China's and India's effects across LAC subregions | | | | | | | | |
| | Aggregate data | | | U.S. data | | | U.S. data: Manufacturing | | |
	OLS	Poisson	Negative binomial	OLS	Poisson	Negative binomial	OLS	Poisson	Negative binomial
India's effect on Southern Cone countries	0.59 [0.00]**	0.28 [0.02]**	0.15 [0.00]**	-0.02 [0.60]	0.01 [0.90]	0.07 [0.17]	-0.37 [0.13]	-0.58 [0.05]*	0.07 [0.78]
Observations	9,782	9,295	9,295	6,690	4,971	4,971	6,690	4,971	4,971
Number of groups	1,311	1,055	1,055	873	603	603	873	603	603

Source: Cravino, Lederman, and Olarreaga, forthcoming.

Note: OLS = ordinary least squares. p-values in brackets correspond to the F-test of the null hypothesis that the effect = 0. All estimates come from estimations of the fully specified knowledge-capital model, but other parameter estimates are not reported.

* Significant at 5 percent level.

** Significant at 1 percent level.

Notes

1. Throughout the chapter, stocks of FDI are referred to as foreign capital stocks (FCS).

2. These figures were taken from the UNCTAD FDI database. We do not include Bermuda, the Cayman Islands, and the Virgin Islands in the Latin American figures as part of LAC.

3. The OECD data is available from http://puck.sourceoecd.org.

4. Data for Australia for the period 1990–2000 were also taken from UNCTAD because OECD reports data for the fiscal year.

5. Stocks from Spain were calculated by accumulating the flows, which were taken from the OECD. Japan does not report stocks in 1995 for any country. It does not report stocks in any year for Colombia, Costa Rica, Guatemala, República Bolivariana de Venezuela, and in Argentina and Chile since 1996.

6. This figure does not include stocks into Mexico. However, FDI flows from these countries comprised more than 90 percent of Mexican FDI inflows in 2002.

7. The PPI was taken from the International Monetary Fund's *International Financial Statistics* database.

8. GDP and value added in manufacturing in current U.S. dollars were taken from the World Bank's *World Development Indicators*. Manufacturing value added for China in yuan was taken from China's State Statistical Bureau of the People's Republic of China, *China Statistical Yearbook* (various years), and transformed into dollars using the period average exchange rate from the International Monetary Fund's *International Financial Statistics*.

9. Because we are controlling for source-country fixed effects, we include all source and host countries that are available in the data set, but exclude host countries with populations less than 500,000 people. The bilateral distance is measured in miles and was taken from Rose (2004).

References

Blonigen, Bruce, Ronald B. Davies, and Keith Head. 2003. "Estimating the Knowledge-Capital Model of the Multinational Enterprise: Comment." *American Economic Review* 93 (3): 980–94.

Carr, David L., James R. Markusen, and Keith E. Maskus. 2001. "Estimating the Knowledge-Capital Model of the Multinational Enterprise." *American Economic Review* 91 (3): 693–708.

Chantasasawat, B., K. C. Fung, H. Lizaka, and A. Siu. 2005. "FDI Flows to Latin America, East and Southeast Asia and China: Substitutes or Complements?" Working Paper 595, Department of Economics, University of California, Santa Cruz.

Cravino, Javier, Daniel Lederman, and Marcelo Olarreaga. Forthcoming. "Substitution between Foreign Capital in China, India, the Rest of the World, and Latin America: Much Ado about Nothing?" *Journal of Economic Integration.*

Eichengreen, Barry, and Hui Tong. 2005. "Is China FDI Coming at the Expense of Other Countries?" NBER Working Paper 11335, National Bureau of Economic Research, Cambridge, MA.

Garcia-Herrero, Alicia, and Daniel Santabárbara. 2005. "Does China Have an Impact on Foreign Direct Investment to Latin America?" Working Paper 0517, Bank of Spain, Madrid.

IADB (Inter-American Development Bank). 2006. *The Emergence of China: Opportunities and Challenges for Latin America and the Caribbean*. Washington, DC: The Inter-American Development Bank.

Rose, Andrew K. 2004. "Does the WTO Make Trade More Stable?" NBER Working Paper 10207, National Bureau of Economic Research, Cambridge, MA.

State Statistical Bureau of the People's Republic of China. Various years. *China Statistical Yearbook*. Hong Kong, China: State Statistical Bureau of the People's Republic of China.

UNCTAD (United Nations Conference on Trade and Development). 2004. *World Investment Directory*. Geneva and New York: United Nations.

———. 2005. *World Investment Report*. Geneva and New York: United Nations.

Part III

The Negative Impact of Chinese and Indian Competition in Some Industries and Some Regions

5

China and the Recent Evolution of Latin America's Manufacturing Exports

Gordon H. Hanson and
*Raymond Robertson**

Introduction

In the 1980s and 1990s, international trade became the engine of growth for economies in the Latin America and the Caribbean (LAC) region. The implementation of the Common Market of the Southern Cone and the North American Free Trade Agreement, aggressive unilateral reforms, and a sustained economic expansion in the United States all contributed to a surge in Latin America's manufacturing exports.

This chapter decomposes Latin America's export performance into components associated with export-supply capabilities and import-demand conditions. It focuses on Latin America's four largest manufacturing exporters: Argentina, Brazil, Chile, and Mexico. One component of export growth is changes in demand in countries that are an exporter's primary markets. If Latin America's main destination markets expand, the country's exports will tend to grow. A second component is changes in a country's capacity to export (relative to other countries), which is determined by its production costs and the size of its industrial base.

* The authors thank David Hummels, Pravin Krishna, Ernesto Lopez-Cordoba, Marcelo Olarreaga, Guillermo Perry, Christian Volpe, and seminar participants at the Brookings Institution, George Washington University, the Inter-American Development Bank, University of California Davis, and the World Bank for comments.

A third component is changes in the export-supply capabilities of the specific countries that also trade with a country's main trading partners. If the countries with the largest expansion in export capacity are those that trade heavily with the United States—Latin America's largest trading partner—Latin American exports may be squeezed out of foreign markets. Naturally, the relative importance of demand and supply factors is likely to vary across industries, countries, and time. The framework of this analysis, which extends the gravity model of trade in Anderson and van Wincoop (2004), provides an industry-by-industry decomposition of national export growth.

The next section uses a standard monopolistic competition model of trade to develop an estimation framework. The specification is a regression of bilateral sectoral exports on importer country dummies, exporter-country dummies, and factors that affect trade costs (bilateral distance, sharing a land border, sharing a common language, belonging to a free trade area [FTA], and import tariffs). When these importer and exporter dummies are allowed to vary by sector and by year, they can be interpreted as functions of structural parameters and of country-specific prices and income levels that determine a country's export supply and import demand. The analysis decomposes manufacturing export growth for Argentina, Brazil, Chile, and Mexico into four components: (a) changes in sectoral export-supply capacity, (b) changes in import-demand conditions in a country's trading partners, (c) changes in trade costs, and (d) residual factors. Changes in import-demand conditions can, in turn, be decomposed into two parts, one that captures changes in income levels in import markets and another that captures changes in sectoral import price indexes for those markets; and the import price indexes themselves are a function of other countries' export-supply capacities.

The third section reports estimates based on this framework. The data for the analysis come from the UN Comtrade database and cover the period 1995–2004. The analysis begins by reporting estimated sectoral exporter dummy variables for the four Latin American economies with respect to China and the United States. The results describe how Latin America's export-supply capacities in different industries evolve over time. Latin America's export capabilities tend to be relatively strong in the same industries in which China's export capabilities are also strong, suggesting the LAC region is relatively vulnerable to export-supply shocks in China. Since 1994, China's export capabilities have improved relative to most of Latin America's large export manufacturing industries.

The analysis then decomposes changes in Latin American exports into components associated with changes in Latin America's export-supply capacities, changes in import-demand conditions, changes in trade costs, and changes in residual factors. Although changes in Latin America's export-supply capacities have contributed to growth in exports, changes in Latin America's import-demand conditions have not, at least since 2000. To explore why import-demand conditions have not been more favorable, two sources of negative import-demand shocks are examined: China's growth in export supply, which may have lowered import prices in destination markets and diverted import demand away from Latin America; and the slowdown in the growth of the U.S. economy, which may have reduced growth in demand for the LAC region's exports. The results suggest that had China's export-supply capacity remained constant after 1995, exports for the four Latin American countries would have been 0.5 to 1.2 percentage points higher during the 1995–2000 period and 1.1 to 3.1 percentage points higher during the 2000–04 period. Had U.S. gross domestic product (GDP) growth been the same over the 2000–04 period as it was over the 1995–2000 period, Latin American exports would have been 0.2 to 1.4 percentage points higher.

The results hold at least three important lessons for policy makers. First, part of the fluctuation in Latin America's manufacturing exports appears to be associated with fluctuations in the U.S. economy. If the U.S. economy continues to recuperate, so too will demand for Latin American goods on the world market. Because part of Latin America's export sluggishness is due to cyclical fluctuations, it is likely to be temporary. However, this consideration matters more for Mexico than for other countries in the region. Second, the growth in Latin America's export-supply capacities has slowed considerably since the late 1990s. Part of the stagnation in the growth in Latin American manufacturing exports is attributable to an inability on Latin America's part to expand the factors of production that generate export growth. Third, for the time being, export growth in China is likely to have adverse consequences on the demand for Latin American manufacturing exports. For better or worse, Latin America's most important export industries (and particularly those of Mexico) are also those in which China appears to have relatively strong export capabilities. Given that patterns of national export specialization tend to change slowly over time, Latin America's vulnerability to China appears unlikely to diminish in the near term.

An important caveat to the results of this analysis is that it focuses exclusively on manufacturing exports. In some countries, notably Argentina, Brazil, and Chile, the growth of China's economy has increased demand for commodity exports. The impact of China on Latin America's commodity exports does not enter this analysis, making the results partial equilibrium in nature. The gravity model developed here, which is based on a monopolistic competition model of trade, would not be appropriate for examining agriculture, mining, or other sectors that produce primary commodities. Thus, these results do not constitute an analysis of the aggregate impact of China on Latin American exports.

Empirical Specification

This section uses the gravity model to derive an empirical specification.

Theory

Consider a standard monopolistic model of international trade, as in Anderson and van Wincoop (2004) or Feenstra (2003). Let there be J countries and N manufacturing sectors, where each sector consists of many product varieties. All consumers have identical Cobb-Douglas preferences over constant-elasticity-of-substitution sectoral composites of product varieties, where in each sector n there are I_n varieties of n produced with country h producing I_{nh} of these varieties. There are increasing returns to scale in the production of each variety. In equilibrium, each variety is produced by a single monopolistically competitive firm and I_n is large, such that the price for each variety is a constant markup over marginal cost. Free entry drives profits to zero, equating price with average cost.

Consider the variation in product prices across countries. We allow for iceberg transport costs in shipping goods between countries and for import tariffs. The cost, insurance, and freight price of variety i in sector n produced by country j and sold in country k is then

$$P_{injk} = \left(\frac{\sigma_n}{\sigma_n - 1} \right) w_{nj} t_{nk} (d_{jk})^{\gamma_n}, \tag{5.1}$$

where P_{injk} is the free on board price of product i in sector n manufactured in country j; σ_n is the constant elasticity of substitution between any pair of varieties in sector n; w_{nj} is unit production cost in sector n for exporter j; t_{nk} is 1 plus the ad valorem tariff in importer k on imports of n (assumed to be constant across exporters that do not belong to an FTA with importer k); d_{jk} is distance between exporter j and importer k; and γ_n is the elasticity of transportation costs with respect to distance.

Given the elements of the model, total exports of goods in sector n by exporter j to importer k can be written as

$$X_{njk} = \mu_n Y_k I_{nj} P_{njk}^{1-\sigma_n} G_{nk}^{\sigma_n - 1}, \tag{5.2}$$

where μ_n is the expenditure share on sector n and G_{nk} is the price index for goods in sector n in importer k. Equation (5.2) reduces to

$$X_{njk} = \frac{\mu_n Y_k I_{nj} \left(w_{nj} \tau_{nk}^{-1|jk|} (d_{jk})^{\gamma_n} \right)^{1-\sigma_n}}{\sum_{b=1}^{H} I_{nb} \left[w_{nb} \tau_{nk}^{-1|bk|} (d_{bk})^{\gamma_n} \right]^{1-\sigma_n}}, \tag{5.3}$$

where $1[jk]$ is an indicator variable that takes a value of 1 if countries j and k belong to an FTA and zero otherwise.

Taking logs and regrouping terms in (5.3), we obtain

$$\ln X_{njk} = \theta_n + m_{nk} + s_{nj} + \beta_{1n} \ln d_{jk} + \beta_{2n} 1[jk]$$
$$+ \beta_{3n} 1[jk] \ln \tau_{jk} + \varepsilon_{njk}. \tag{5.4}$$

Equation (5.4) contains four sets of factors that affect country j's exports to country k in sector n. The first term (θ_n) captures preference shifters specific to sector n; the second term (m_{nk}) captures demand shifters exporter j faces in sector n and importer k (which are a function of importer k's income and supply shifters for other countries that also export to importer k); the third term (s_{nj}) captures supply shifters in sector n for exporter j (which reflect exporter j's production costs and its industrial capacity in the sector); the fourth through sixth terms (d_{jk}, $1[jk]$, τ_{jk}) capture gravity variables exporter j and importer k, belonging to an FTA, and import tariffs; and the seventh term is the error term.

Exporter j's shipments to importer k would expand if importer k's income increases, production costs increase in other countries that supply importer k, exporter j's supply capability expands (as a result of lower production costs or an expanded industrial base), or trade costs between the two countries decrease.

An alternative approach to estimating equation (5.4) would be to incorporate nonlinear expressions on prices, incomes, and trade costs directly into the estimation, creating a structural version of the gravity model. While this approach is attractive, it would present two problems. One is that price data needed for the estimation are very difficult to obtain. Another is that the right-hand side variables would be endogenous to trade shocks. In the absence of valid instruments for prices and trade barriers, ordinary least squares (OLS) estimation would be inconsistent. The analysis opts to use equation (5.4) as a way of avoiding these estimation problems.

Decomposing Export Growth

Using annual data on bilateral trade by sector for a large cross-section of countries, the analysis estimates the parameters in equation (5.4). Data on the components of m_{nk} or s_{nj} are not needed. By estimating equation (5.4) sector by sector and year by year, we identify the m_{nk} terms by including importer-specific dummy variables as regressors and the s_{nj} terms by including exporter-specific dummy variables as regressors.

Because equation (5.4) includes a constant term (θ_n), the estimated coefficients can be interpreted as deviations from mean industry export or import values. Thus, m_{nk} is the deviation from sector n mean import demand for importer k, and s_{nj} is the deviation from sector n mean supply for exporter j. As a practical matter, the analysis does not observe a country's exports to itself. Consequently, the country treated as the excluded category in equation (5.4), off which the constant term is estimated, must be excluded from both the set of export dummies *and* the set of import dummies. The interpretation of the constant term is, thus, the mean trade value (rather than the mean export or import value) for the excluded country, which in all regressions is designated as the United States.

The specification in equation (5.4) is quite general. Restrictions arise only when an attempt is made to interpret the importer and exporter dummies. For instance, it has been assumed that within sectors, product varieties are identical between countries. Quality may be an important dimension along which varieties differ, especially between higher-wage and lower-wage exporters (Hummels and Klenow 2005; Schott 2004). Thus, the s_{nj} terms may also embody cross-country differences in the quality of product varieties. When evaluating how these terms change over time, we need to be mindful that improving quality is an additional means through which countries can expand their export capabilities. To identify exporter and sector-specific product quality parameters, import quantities (which are unreported for many countries) *and* the value of σ_n for each sector need to be known.

For year t, let the OLS estimates of equation (5.4) be given by $\tilde{\theta}_{nt}, \tilde{m}_{nkt}, \tilde{s}_{njt}, \tilde{\beta}_{nt}$, and $\tilde{\varepsilon}_{njkt}$. For exposition simplicity, all variables associated with trade costs are subsumed into a single term, denoted by the distance variable. Shipments by exporter j to importer k in sector n and year t equal

$$X_{njkt} = e^{\tilde{\theta}_{nt}+\tilde{s}_{njt}+\tilde{m}_{nkt}+\tilde{\varepsilon}_{njkt}} d_{jk}^{\tilde{\beta}_{nt}}, \tag{5.5}$$

and total exports by exporter j in sector n and year t equal

$$X_{njt} = e^{\tilde{\theta}_{nt}+\tilde{s}_{njt}} \sum_{K=1}^{H} e^{\tilde{m}_{nkt}+\tilde{\varepsilon}_{njkt}} d_{jk}^{\tilde{\beta}_{nt}}. \tag{5.6}$$

Equations (5.5) and (5.6) allow the isolation of the sources of export growth by country and sector. The distance term is written compactly as though it were a single variable, whereas in truth trade costs are modeled as a function of bilateral distance, sharing of a common language, sharing of a land border, membership in an FTA, and import tariffs.

One source of export growth is improvement in the supply capability of exporter j in sector n, relative to the average for all other countries, which is captured by the sectoral exporter dummy, s_{njt}. The exporter dummy captures in part exporter j's average comparative advantage in sector n. A second source of export growth is change in import demand, which is a function of national income in an importer country and product prices of the importer, which are, in turn, functions of the production costs and industrial capacities of the exporting countries that supply the importer.

To decompose changes in exports into component parts associated with changes in export capabilities and changes in demand conditions, rewrite equation (5.6) as

$$X_{njkt} = e^{\tilde{\theta}_{nt}} e^{\tilde{s}_{njt}} e^{\tilde{m}_{nkt}} d_{jk}^{\tilde{\beta}_{nt}} e^{\tilde{\varepsilon}_{njkt}} \equiv \Theta_{nt} S_{njt} M_{nkt} D_{njkt} E_{njkt}. \tag{5.7}$$

For years t and $t+v$, define $\Delta Z \equiv Z_{t+v} - Z_t$ and $\bar{Z} \equiv 0.5 \times (Z_{t+v} + Z_t)$. Because X_{njkt} is the product of five terms, there are 60 (derived by $5!/2 = 60$) unique ways to decompose ΔX_{njkt}. For any individual component (Θ, S, M, D, or E), take the mean across the possible decomposition terms. Changes in exports for exporter-importer pair jk in sector n are

$$\Delta X_{njkt} = \Delta \Theta_{njt} \overline{SMDE}_{njk} + \Delta S_{njt} \overline{\Theta MDE}_{njk} + \Delta M_{nkt} \overline{\Theta SDE}_{njk}$$
$$+ \Delta D_{njkt} \overline{\Theta SME}_{njk} + \Delta E_{njkt} \overline{\Theta SMD}_{njk}, \tag{5.8}$$

where $\overline{\Theta MDE}_{njk}$ is the mean across the 60 possible orderings of the 5 elements that compose trade values in equation (5.8) and so forth. For exporter j, the change in total exports can be written by summing across sectors (n) and importers (k) in equation (5.8)

$$\Delta X_{jt} = \sum_n \sum_k \Delta X_{njkt} = \sum_n \sum_k (\Delta \Theta_{njt} \overline{SMDE}_{njk} + \Delta S_{njt} \overline{\Theta MDE}_{njk}$$
$$+ \Delta M_{nkt} \overline{\Theta SDE}_{njk} + \Delta D_{njkt} \overline{\Theta SME}_{njk} + E_{njkt} \overline{\Theta SMD}_{njk}). \tag{5.9}$$

The first term in the parentheses on the right-hand side of equation (5.9) is the change in exports for exporter j associated with changes in mean sectoral trade (designated to be that for the United States), the second term is the change in exports associated with changes in exporter j's supply capabilities, the third term is the change in exports associated with demand conditions in countries that import from exporter j, the fourth term is the change in exports associated with innovations in trade costs (or trade-cost elasticities), and the fifth term is residual sources of change in j's exports. Equation (5.9) is the basis for our decomposition results.

Decomposing Changes in Import-Demand Conditions

Returning to equation (5.3), it is apparent that a further decomposition of import-demand conditions facing country j is possible. In theory,

$$m_{nk} = \ln Y_k - \ln \left(\sum_{b=1}^{H} I_{nb} w_{nb}^{1-\sigma_n} \tau_{nb}^{-1|bk|(1-\sigma_n)} d_{bk}^{\beta_n} \right). \tag{5.10}$$

Thus, exporter j faces import-demand shocks resulting from changes in income and import prices in its trading partners, where import prices are a function of export-supply conditions in the countries that also export to country j's trading partners. One might consider estimating equation (5.4) subject to the constraint in equation (5.10). However, there are practical difficulties in imposing such a constraint. As is well known, there is zero trade at the sectoral level between many country pairs, especially in pairs involving a developing country. Santos Silva and Tenreyro (2006) propose a Poisson pseudo-maximum likelihood estimator to deal with zero observations in the gravity model. In the present application, this approach is subject to an incidental-parameters problem (Wooldridge 2002). Although in a Poisson model it is straightforward to control for the presence of unobserved fixed effects, it is difficult in this and many other nonlinear settings to obtain consistent estimates of these effects. Because, at the sectoral level, most exporters trade with no more than a few dozen countries, pseudo-maximum likelihood estimates of exporter and importer country dummies may be inconsistent.

The present approach is to estimate equation (5.4) using OLS for a set of medium-to-large exporters (OECD countries plus large developing countries, which account for approximately 90 percent of world manufacturing exports) and large importers (countries that account for approximately 90 percent of world manufacturing imports). For bilateral trade between large countries, there are relatively few zero trade values. However, because we do not account explicitly for zero bilateral trade in the data, we are left with unresolved concerns about the consistency of the parameter estimates.[1]

Using equation (5.10), the analysis modifies equation (5.9) to decompose demand shifters that are specific to importer k (for example, the United States) into (a) a component associated with the gross domestic product (GDP) in country k (for example, U.S. business cycle conditions) and (b) a component associated with the import-price index in importer k, which is, in turn, a function of trade-cost-weighted export-supply shifters among the countries that export to importer k. In this framework, the analysis can identify the contribution of changes in, for example, China's export capacity to changes in other countries' demand for imports. Counterfactual decompositions of export growth for Latin American countries (or other countries) can also be performed, which assess how export growth in the country would have been different if China's export dummies had remained unchanged (which then would have increased global demand for other countries' goods) or if U.S. GDP growth had remained unchanged (which would have affected U.S. import demand).

These counterfactual decompositions are not general equilibrium in nature. Altering China's growth in export supply would affect the export supply of all other countries, not just Latin America. Thus, the counterfactual decompositions constructed here are likely to overestimate the impact of export growth in China on Latin American manufacturing exports. These results are perhaps best seen as upper bounds of the possible impact of China on Latin America's manufacturing sector. Similar qualifications apply to the counterfactual decomposition in which U.S. GDP growth is constrained to be constant.

Empirical Results

The data for the analysis come from the UN Comtrade database and cover manufacturing imports over the period 1995–2004. The analysis examines bilateral trade at the four-digit harmonized system (HS) level. The sample is limited to the top 40 export industries in Brazil and Mexico and the top 20 export industries in Argentina and Chile. This sample of industries accounts for over 85 percent of manufacturing exports in each of the four countries. The gravity equation in (5.4) is estimated on a year-by-year basis, allowing coefficients on exporter-country dummies, importer-country dummies, and distance to vary by sector and year. The output from the regression exercise is for each sector a panel of exporter- and importer-country dummy variables, trade-cost coefficients, intercepts, and residuals. The country dummies are the deviation from the U.S. sectoral mean trade by year. For these coefficients to be comparable across time, the conditioning set for a given sector (that is, the set of comparison countries) must be constant across time. For each sector, the sample is limited to bilateral trading partners that have positive trade in every year during the sample period. (By including only consistent trading partners in the sample, another potential source of selection bias is introduced into the estimation.)

Estimates of Sectoral Export-Supply Capacities

The regression results for equation (5.4) involve a large amount of output. In each year, the analysis estimates more than 10,000 country-sector exporter coefficients, more than 5,000 country-sector importer coefficients, and more than 90 trade-cost coefficients. To summarize exporter and importer dummies compactly, figures 5.1a and 5.1b, respectively, plot kernel densities for the sector-country exporter and importer coefficients (where the densities are weighted by sector-country exports or imports). Figure 5.1a shows that most exporter coefficients are negative, consistent with sectoral exports for most countries being below exports from the United States. Over the sample period, the distribution of exporter coefficients shifts to the right, suggesting other countries are catching up to the United States. The figure indicates by vertical lines weighted mean values for Mexico's exporter coefficients in (left to right) 1994 (equal to –3.9), 2000 (equal to –2.6), and 2004 (equal to –2.1), which rise in value over time relative to the overall distribution of exporter coefficients, suggesting Mexico's export-supply capacity improves relative to other countries over the sample period. Mean exporter coefficients fall over time for Argentina (–0.21 in 1994 and –1.26 in 2004), Brazil (–0.12 in 1994 and –0.68 in 2004), and Chile (0.29 in 1994 and –0.34 in 2004). Thus, among the four Latin American countries, only Mexico shows consistent average improvement in its

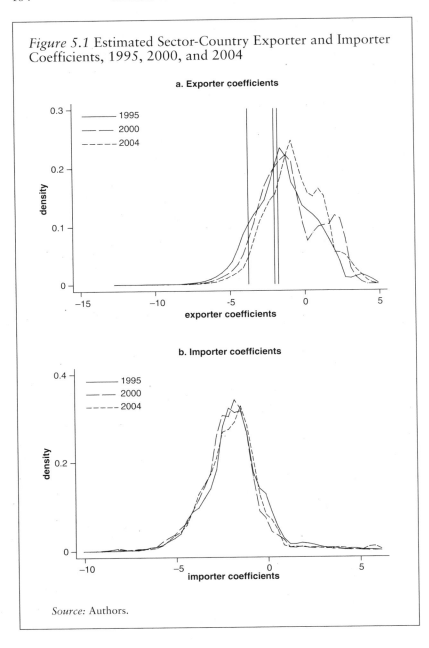

Figure 5.1 Estimated Sector-Country Exporter and Importer Coefficients, 1995, 2000, and 2004

Source: Authors.

manufacturing export capacity. This could reflect the importance of commodity exports for the countries other than Mexico. A commodity export boom could diminish manufacturing export capacity by driving up the price of immobile factors of production, such as labor and land. In figure 5.1b, most importer coefficients are also negative, again indicating that sectoral trade values for most countries are below those for the United States.

To provide further detail on the coefficient estimates, tables 5A.1 and 5A.2, respectively, in the annex report mean exporter and importer coefficients by country (across sectors and years) and the fraction of coefficient estimates that are statistically significant.[2] For the large majority of countries, exporter and importer coefficients are precisely estimated. Further detail on the coefficient estimates is available in table 5.1, which reports average parameter estimates on the trade-cost variables. For the most part, the results align with previous literature (see Anderson and van Wincoop 2004). While coefficients on distance and being in an FTA fluctuate mildly over the period, common language and adjacency show uneven downward trends. The coefficient on the tariff-FTA interaction increases markedly after 2000. Because 2000 is the dividing point between a period of global economic expansion and a period of global economic stagnation, the results may indicate that business cycles may affect substitution elasticities (or at least gravity model estimates of these elasticities).

Table 5.1 Average Coefficient Estimates on Trade Cost Variables, 1995–2004

	Coefficients				
Year	ln(distance)	Common language	Adjacency	FTA	FTA*ln(1 + tariff)
1995	−1.118	0.652	0.519	0.045	7.964
1996	−1.121	0.640	0.402	0.121	5.757
1997	−1.115	0.531	0.370	0.065	7.112
1998	−1.076	0.573	0.461	0.016	7.490
1999	−1.076	0.542	0.382	0.028	8.540
2000	−1.111	0.532	0.255	−0.074	11.396
2001	−1.086	0.493	0.239	0.001	16.854
2002	−1.049	0.545	0.348	0.165	20.709
2003	−1.063	0.479	0.299	0.184	22.771
2004	−1.118	0.497	0.207	0.128	13.804

Source: Authors.
Note: Coefficient estimates are expressed as trade-value-weighted means for manufacturing industries.
* interacted with.

Of primary interest is how Latin America's export-supply capacities compare with those of China and with import-demand conditions in the United States. Figures 5.2a through 5.2d plot exporter coefficients for the four Latin American countries against the constant terms in the regressions, which represent mean sectoral trade values for the United States. Observations are weighted by each country's sectoral shares of annual manufacturing exports. The figures show a negative relation for all countries except Chile (−0.11 for Argentina, −0.64 for Brazil, 0.27 for Chile, and −0.28 for Mexico, all of which are statistically significant), suggesting that most Latin American countries tend to have stronger exports in sectors in which the United States has *lower* levels of trade. Figures 5.3a through 5.3d plot annual changes in Latin America's exporter coefficients against annual changes in the constant terms, which are changes in mean U.S. sectoral trade. Again, for each country except Chile, there is a negative correlation between the two sets of coefficients (−0.29 for Argentina, −0.43 for Brazil, 0.11 for Chile, and -0.69 for Mexico, all statistically significant). Sectors in which Latin America shows most improvement in export-supply capacity tend to be those in which the United States shows weaker increases in trade.

Figures 5.4a through 5.4d plot exporter coefficients for the four countries against China over the sample period (again using each country's sectoral shares of annual manufacturing exports as weights). For all countries, there is a positive correlation between the two sets of exporter coefficients (0.34 for Argentina, 0.35 for Brazil, 0.49 for Chile, and 0.32 for Mexico, all statistically significant). Sectors in which Latin America has a relatively strong export-supply capacity tend to be those in which China's export capacity is also strong. Because exporter coefficients are expressed as deviations from U.S. sectoral means, the positive correlation between exporter coefficients for Latin America and China is not simply a statistical artifact of the data (as would be the case, for instance, if the analysis were comparing mean sectoral exports in Latin America and China). Figures 5.4a through 5.4d show that, conditional on sectoral trade values for the United States, China tends to have higher exports in Latin America's larger manufacturing export industries.

Figures 5.5a through 5.5d plot annual changes in exporter coefficients for Latin America against those for China (weighted by each country's annual industry export shares). For all countries except Chile, the correlation is positive (0.51 for Argentina, 0.22 for Brazil, −0.04 for Chile, and 0.74 for Mexico; all except Chile are statistically significant). This suggests that industries in which China's export-supply capacities are strengthening also tend to be those in which Latin America's export capacities are strengthening. Because the plotted values are changes in deviations from U.S. industry means (and not changes in the means themselves), the correlations are not an artifact of the data.

To compare the export capabilities of Latin America and China for individual sectors, figures 5B.1 through 5B.4 in the annex plot exporter

Figure 5.2 Sectoral Exporter Coefficients for Four Latin American Countries and U.S. Sectoral Trade
(deviations from U.S. industry means)

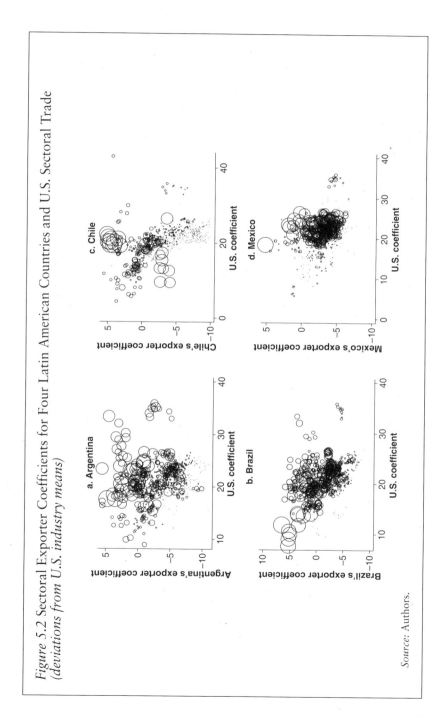

Source: Authors.

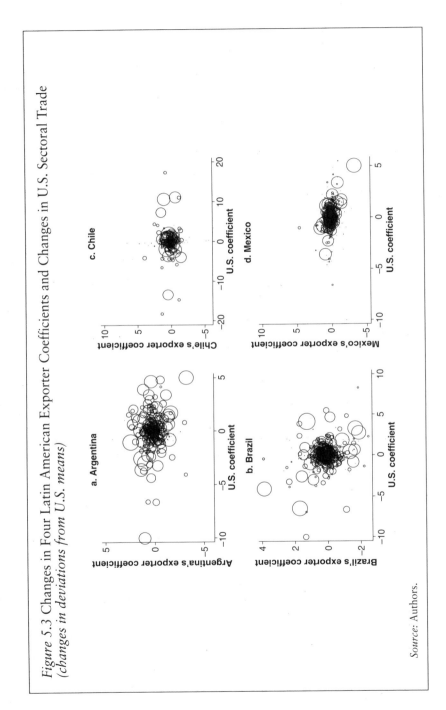

Figure 5.3 Changes in Four Latin American Exporter Coefficients and Changes in U.S. Sectoral Trade *(changes in deviations from U.S. means)*

Source: Authors.

Figure 5.4 Sectoral Exporter Coefficients, China and Four Latin American Countries
(deviations from U.S. industry means)

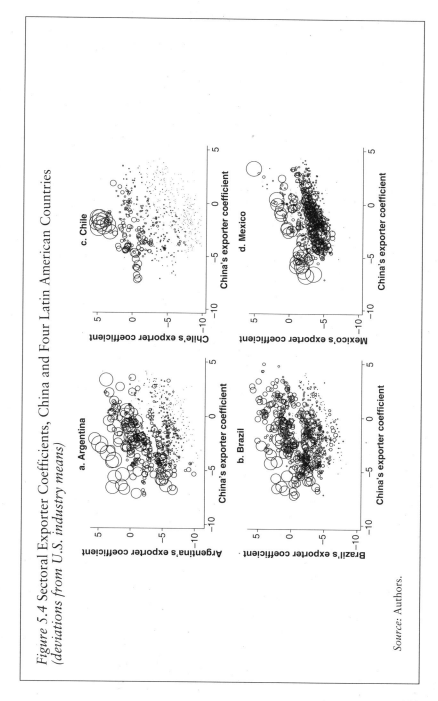

Source: Authors.

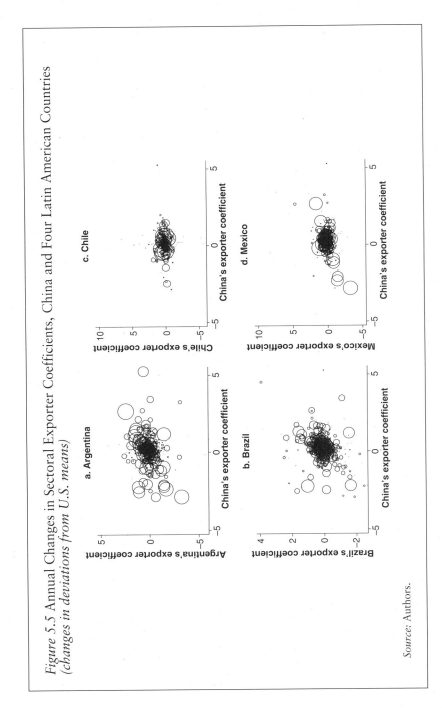

Figure 5.5 Annual Changes in Sectoral Exporter Coefficients, China and Four Latin American Countries (*changes in deviations from U.S. means*)

Source: Authors.

coefficients in China against the 16 largest manufacturing export sectors in each Latin American country (which, over the sample period, account for 85 percent of Argentina's manufacturing exports, 70 percent of Brazil's manufacturing exports, 90 percent of Chile's manufacturing exports, and 75 percent of Mexico's manufacturing exports) (see table 5B.1 for the HS industry code descriptions of the export sectors). Note first that the identities of the industries vary considerably across countries, indicating that there is variation across Latin American countries in the sectors in which national exports are concentrated. This fact makes the positive correlations between China's and Latin America's export-supply capacities in figures 5.4 and 5.5 all the more remarkable. Despite the diversity of industries represented, China tends to be strong in many or most of the larger export industries accounted for by Argentina, Brazil, and Mexico. For Argentina, China's export-supply capacities show relative improvement in 7 of the 14 industries for which estimates are available for China.[3] For Brazil, China's export-supply capacities show relative improvement in 10 of the 15 industries for which estimates are available for China. For Chile, China's export-supply capacities show relative improvement in 5 of the 13 industries for which estimates are available for China. And for Mexico, China's export-supply capacities show relative improvement in 12 of the 16 industries. The evidence in the figures in annex B suggests that among the four countries, Chile is least exposed and Mexico is most exposed to export-supply shocks from China. Results reported next will be consistent with this finding.

Decomposing Manufacturing Export Growth

The next exercise involves the decomposition of export growth for the four Latin American countries into changes in export-supply capacities, changes in import-demand conditions, and changes in other components, as proposed in equation (5.9). Table 5.2 reports the total change in manufacturing exports for Argentina, Brazil, Chile, and Mexico over two time periods, 1995–2000 and 2000–04. The reported change in trade is the total change in trade values (divided by the number of years in the subperiod), normalized by the average of trade values in the beginning and end period. Thus, for instance, table 5.2 shows that manufacturing exports in Mexico grew by an annual average of 16.5 percent over 1995–2000 and 2.4 percent over 2000–04.

The results in table 5.2 are for a restricted set of industries. When the full sample of manufacturing industries are included, implausibly large values for individual decomposition terms are obtained in food products, mineral processing, or other industries associated with the processing of primary commodities for Brazil and Chile (but not for Argentina or Mexico). As a crude way to address this problem, the results reported in this chapter are limited to those for HS two-digit industries 80 to 99, none of which are intensive in natural resources or primary commodities.

Table 5.2 Decomposing Export Growth for Four Latin American Countries, 1995–2004

Country and period	Growth in manufacturing exports	Components of growth				
		Exporter coefficients	Importer coefficients	Mean U.S. sectoral trade	Trade-cost coefficients	Residual factors
Argentina						
1995–2000	0.081	0.820	-1.249	0.247	0.692	-0.428
2000–04	-0.045	0.098	-0.088	0.075	-0.072	-0.057
Brazil						
1995–2000	0.130	20.162	-0.111	50.305	-70.172	-0.054
2000–04	0.111	1.787	-0.042	-4.587	2.924	0.029
Chile						
1995–2000	0.071	0.402	-0.007	-0.091	0.323	-0.556
2000–04	0.053	0.146	-0.016	-0.099	0.005	0.017
Mexico						
1995–2000	0.165	0.475	-0.018	0.213	-0.184	-0.322
2000–04	0.024	0.227	0.007	-0.189	0.154	-0.175

Source: Authors.

Note: This table uses equation (5.9) to decompose annual average growth in a country's manufacturing exports into components associated with changes in sectoral importer coefficients in a country's trading partners, changes in a country's sectoral exporter coefficients, changes in mean U.S. sectoral trade, changes in trade costs (log distance, common language, adjacency, FTAs, and tariffs), and changes in residual factors. These preliminary results are limited to four-digit industries in HS two-digit industries 80 to 99 (tin and articles thereof, base metals and articles thereof, tools, miscellaneous articles of base metal, boilers and machinery, electrical and electronic equipment, railway equipment, motor vehicles, aircraft, ships, miscellaneous articles of base metal, boilers and machinery, electrical and electronic equipment, railway equipment, motor vehicles, aircraft, ships, optical equipment, clocks and watches, musical instruments, arms and ammunition, furniture, toys and games, miscellaneous manufactured articles, works of art, and other commodities).

(See note to table 5.2 for a list.) Even with this sample restriction, the decomposition terms for Brazil are too large to be credible.

The first column of table 5.2 shows that in all countries, manufacturing export growth was slower after 2000 than before, with Argentina exhibiting the largest decline (during a period that followed the country's abandonment of its currency board and ensuing economic turmoil) and Mexico showing the next largest decline.

Two other patterns in table 5.2 are worthy of note. One is that in the second column, for all countries the contribution of the exporter coefficients to export growth is larger before 2000 than after. This suggests that in Latin America, a slowdown in the growth of manufacturing-export-supply capacity contributed to the slowdown in manufacturing export growth. While the decomposition does not isolate the source of the slowing in Latin America's export-supply capacity, one obvious source would be constraints on manufacturing growth. These constraints are likely to vary by country. In Brazil and Chile, which have enjoyed export-driven booms in commodity production, constraints on manufacturing growth may have come from other sectors of the economy benefiting from relative price increases and as a result, expanding more rapidly, absorbing resources that would have otherwise gone into manufacturing. In Mexico, which has not enjoyed a similar commodity boom, domestic factors may be the primary obstacles to growth. These may include relatively high energy prices, poor telecommunications infrastructure, and slow growth in the supply of skilled labor, among other possible factors.

A second notable pattern in table 5.2 is that mean U.S. sectoral trade contributes much less to export growth in Latin America after 2000 than before. There are several possible explanations for this. One is that the slowing of the U.S. economy after 2000 resulted in slower growth in U.S. demand for imports, thereby contributing to slower export growth in Latin America. If the sluggishness of the U.S. economy was the primary source of the slowing in U.S. demand for Latin America's exports, this shock is likely to be temporary. As the U.S. economy continues to recuperate, demand for Latin America's exports will likely grow. A second possibility is that China's continued export expansion lowered relative prices for manufacturing goods and displaced exports from other countries, including those from Latin America, in the U.S. market. A China-related negative demand shock for Latin American manufacturing exports would be of greater concern than a negative demand shock associated with slow growth in the U.S. economy, for China's export strength in manufacturing is likely to persist. The next section explores these two options in more detail.

Counterfactual Decompositions

The results in table 5.2 provide a summary of how Latin American exports have grown, but they do not reveal why they have grown. To explore this issue, the analysis applies insights derived from equation (5.10). Table 5.3 explores how Latin America's export growth might have differed had the U.S. economy not slowed down after 2000. The assumption is made that average annual U.S. GDP growth over 2000 to 2004 (actually 2.6 percent) was the same as that over 1995 to 2000 (3.2 percent). Returning to equation (5.9), we perform the following counterfactual calculation:

$$X_{njkt} = e^{\tilde{\theta}_{nt}} e^{\tilde{s}_{njt}} e^{\tilde{m}_{nkt} + \pi_{nkt}} e^{\tilde{\varepsilon}_{njkt}} d_{jk}^{\tilde{\beta}_{nt}} \equiv \Theta_{nt} S_{njt} \hat{M}_{nkt} E_{njkt} D_{njkt}, \tag{5.11}$$

in which we set π_{nkt} equal to 0.024 (4 × 0.006) if k equals the United States and t equals 2004, and zero otherwise. This has the effect of inflating the import-demand coefficient for the United States in 2004 to what it would have been had the U.S. economy grown by the same rate after 2000 as it had before (and no other changes occurred in the global economy). The analysis then uses equation (5.11) to estimate counterfactual export growth

Table 5.3 Counterfactual Decompositions of Export Growth for Four Latin American Countries

Country and period	Counterfactual growth in manufacturing exports		
	Actual growth in manufacturing exports	Exporter coefficients in China, constant over time	U.S. GDP growth 2000–04 = 1995–2000
Argentina			
1995–2000	0.081	0.085	n.a.
2000–04	−0.045	−0.034	−0.043
Brazil			
1995–2000	0.130	0.137	n.a.
2000–04	0.111	0.125	0.119
Chile			
1995–2000	0.071	0.079	n.a.
2000–04	0.053	0.076	0.060
Mexico			
1995–2000	0.165	0.177	n.a.
2000–04	0.024	0.055	0.038

Source: Authors.

Note: n.a. = not applicable. This table reports actual and counterfactual export growth in four Latin American countries based on two scenarios: U.S. GDP growth over 2000–04 equals that for 1995–2000, and China's export-supply capacity remains constant over the sample period (1995–2004) at levels equal to 1995 values.

in the four Latin American countries during the period 2000–04, and ΔM_{nkt} is replaced with $\Delta \hat{M}_{nkt}$.

It is important to recognize that the counterfactual estimation of Latin American export growth in table 5.3 is not a general-equilibrium exercise. Because the United States is a large country, stronger U.S. economic growth (resulting from, for example, higher levels of Hicks-neutral technological change) would have likely affected the global demand for goods and therefore global factor demands, generating changes in factor prices in U.S. trading partners, including Latin America. The counterfactual calculations reported here assume away such feedback effects from import demand into factor prices. Because higher demand for Latin American exports would have likely increased production costs in the country and the relative price of Latin American exports, the counterfactual export growth reported here likely overstates what would have actually occurred.

The results in table 5.3 suggest that had U.S. GDP growth not decelerated after 2000, over 2000–04 Argentine exports would have grown by 0.2 percentage point more, Brazilian exports would have grown by 0.8 percentage point more, Chilean exports would have grown by 0.7 percentage point more, and Mexican exports would have grown by 1.4 percentage points more. This exercise imposes the unitary coefficients on the variables on the right-hand side of equation (5.10). The results suggest that had the U.S. economy not slowed down in the early 2000s, only in Mexico would export growth have been more than nominally higher than it was. That the U.S. slowdown matters more for Mexico is not surprising. The United States is a much larger trading partner for Mexico than for the countries of South America. What perhaps is surprising is that changes in U.S. GDP appear to matter so little for Latin American exports overall.

To evaluate the impact of China's export growth on Latin America, equation (5.10) is again used. The analysis imposes the assumption that China's exporter coefficients remain unchanged from 1995 forward. Following equation (5.10), this would have the effect of raising the import-price index in importing countries, leading to an overall increase in their importer coefficients. For country k, the change in importer coefficient in equation (5.11) is redefined to be

$$\pi_{nkt} = ln\left(\sum_{b \neq c} e^{\tilde{s}_{nbt}} d_{bk}^{\tilde{\beta}_{nt}} + e^{\tilde{s}_{nc0}} d_{bk}^{\tilde{\beta}_{nt}} \right) - ln\left(\sum_{b \neq c} e^{\tilde{s}_{nbt}} d_{bk}^{\tilde{\beta}_{nt}} + e^{\tilde{s}_{nct}} d_{bk}^{\tilde{\beta}_{nt}} \right), \qquad (5.12)$$

where $b = c$ indicates China and $\tilde{s}_{nc0}$ indicates China's exporter coefficient in sector n in the initial period. Thus, equation (5.12) shows how the importer coefficient for country k would have differed in year t had China's exporter coefficients remained unchanged from the initial year. Again, it is important to recognize that this is not a general-equilibrium exercise.

The results in table 5.3 suggest that had China's export-supply capacity not changed over the sample period, (a) Argentina's annual average export growth would have been 0.4 percentage points higher over 1995–2000 and 1.1 percentage points higher over 2000–04, (b) Brazil's annual average export growth would have been 0.7 percentage points higher over 1995–2000 and 1.4 percentage points higher over 2000–04, (c) Chile's annual average export growth would have been 0.8 percentage points higher over 1995–2000 and 2.3 percentage points higher over 2000–04, and (d) Mexico's annual average export growth would have been 1.2 percentage points higher over 1995–2000 and 3.1 percentage points higher over 2000–04. Naturally, the effects are larger in the latter time period, because the impact of holding China's export-supply capacities constant accumulates over time. Consistent with figures 5.4, 5.5, and the figures in annex B, of the four countries, Mexico appears to be the most exposed to export competition from China. This exposure results from the fact that China's strong export industries overlap more with Mexico than with the other countries of Latin America.

Of interest, the impact on Latin American exports of China's export-capacity growth is two to five times as large as the impact of the U.S. economic slowdown. Although it may be reasonable to view sluggish U.S. growth as a temporary shock, the same does not hold for China's export growth. Thus, only a small part of the recent slowdown in Latin American export growth appears associated with transitory business cycle factors.

Comparing the results in tables 5.2 and 5.3, the estimated impact of China's growth on Latin America is small relative to the impact of changes in the countries' export-supply capacities, distance coefficients, or residual factors. Although China's performance clearly seems to affect Latin America, other factors matter more.

Discussion

This chapter uses the gravity model of trade to decompose Latin America's export growth into components associated with export-supply capacity, import-demand conditions, and other factors. The analysis applies the framework to Argentina, Brazil, Chile, and Mexico. There are three main findings. First, since the mid-1990s, export-supply capacities in Mexico, but not the other countries, have improved relative to the rest of the world. Commodity booms in Brazil and Chile and economic crisis in Argentina may account for the apparent decrease in those countries' manufacturing-export-supply capabilities. Second, Argentina, Brazil, and Mexico are relatively exposed to export-supply shocks from China, with Mexico being the most exposed. Industries in which Mexico has strong export capabilities are also those in which China's capabilities are strong, and in most industries, China's capabilities improve over time relative to those of Mexico. Had China's export-supply capacities remained constant from 1994 onward, Latin America's annual export growth rate would have been up to 0.4 to 1.4 percentage points higher during the late 1990s and 1.1 to 3.1 percentage points higher during the early 2000s. Third, although changes in Latin America's export-supply capacities have contributed positively to the region's export growth, changes in U.S. import demand in Latin America's key export industries have not. Latin America's exports are concentrated in sectors in which the United States has shown relatively weak growth in trade. Had U.S. GDP grown at the same rate from 2000 to 2004 as it had in the late 1990s, Latin America's annual export growth rate would have been up to 0.2 to 1.4 percentage points higher.

Several important caveats must accompany these results. The framework and analysis are confined to manufacturing industries and the decomposition of export growth is confined to a subset of manufacturing industries (mainly industrial machinery, electronics, and transportation equipment). There may be important consequences of Chinese or U.S. business cycles for Latin America's commodity trade that are not captured here. The reported counterfactual decompositions of export growth do not account for general-equilibrium effects. There could be feedback effects from a slowdown in China's export growth or an increase in U.S. GDP growth that would cause the growth consequences of such shocks for Latin America to be overstated. There are also concerns about the consistency of the coefficient estimates because the analysis does not account for zero trade between some countries.

The results have a number of important lessons for policy makers. Of the four countries, Mexico appears to be the most exposed to import-demand shocks associated with U.S. aggregate demand and competition from China. Given that patterns of industrial specialization tend to change slowly, Mexico's exposure to China is unlikely to change in the short to medium run. Yet, although negative, the effects of China's growth on Latin America's manufacturing exports are not as large as many appear to believe. Domestic constraints on manufacturing appear to be a more important factor limiting export growth in all four of the countries examined.

Annex A

Table 5A.1 Average Exporter Coefficients
(for countries that do not appear as importers)

Country	Mean exporter coefficient	Percentage significant
Angola	0.776	62.50
Bangladesh	0.900	70.17
Bulgaria	−3.292	99.40
Cameroon	−0.009	60.00
Côte d'Ivoire	0.939	89.12
Dominican Republic	−4.061	91.46
Gabon	−0.268	70.00
Honduras	−2.187	100.00
Iran, Islamic Rep. of	0.935	87.26
Kuwait	0.884	83.28
Nigeria	0.955	67.45
Pakistan	−1.363	87.49
Philippines	−2.544	97.75
Qatar	0.682	76.47
Saudi Arabia	1.599	85.67
Sri Lanka	−1.621	88.38
Taiwan (China)	−1.200	92.65
Thailand	−2.481	84.52
Trinidad and Tobago	−2.842	96.40
United Arab Emirates	1.135	98.70

Source: Authors.

Table 5A.2 Average Country Importer and Exporter Coefficients *(for countries that appear as exporters and importers)*

Country	Importer coefficient	Percentage significant	Exporter coefficient	Percentage significant
Algeria	−5.204	100.00	−0.790	75.00
Argentina	−3.121	97.94	−2.466	98.60
Australia	−1.925	96.59	−2.380	98.22
Austria	−4.104	100.00	−3.935	100.00
Brazil	−2.173	98.67	−1.662	99.47
Canada	−2.148	99.06	−2.291	99.77
Chile	−3.222	98.19	−4.654	98.46
China	−1.440	93.59	0.367	83.13
Colombia	−3.949	99.88	0.211	98.84
Costa Rica	−5.670	100.00	−3.446	99.94
Czech Republic	−4.522	99.98	−3.767	99.12
Denmark	−4.165	100.00	−3.090	99.22
Ecuador	−4.565	99.98	−0.536	89.43
Egypt, Arab Rep. of	−4.871	100.00	−1.173	97.94
El Salvador	−5.676	100.00	−1.877	95.65
Finland	−4.024	100.00	−2.836	98.88
France	−2.306	99.52	−1.539	91.75
Germany	−1.554	93.57	−0.196	68.49
Greece	−4.026	100.00	−3.368	97.11
Guatemala	−5.376	100.00	−1.883	99.63
Hong Kong (China)	−1.829	94.40	−1.385	93.18
Hungary	−4.096	100.00	−3.835	98.22
Iceland	−6.030	100.00	−8.117	100.00
India	−3.559	99.97	−1.906	90.43
Indonesia	−3.252	99.06	−0.835	78.45
Ireland	−3.674	100.00	−3.349	98.63
Israel	−3.420	99.35	−3.679	100.00
Italy	−2.482	99.45	−1.220	83.48

(continued)

Table 5A.2 Average Country Importer and
Exporter Coefficients *(continued)*
(for countries that appear as exporters and importers)

Country	Importer coefficient	Percentage significant	Exporter coefficient	Percentage significant
Japan	−1.351	95.95	0.332	78.57
Korea, Rep. of	−1.840	99.14	−1.135	82.87
Malaysia	−1.860	98.59	−1.599	91.67
Mexico	−2.592	99.92	−2.129	95.85
Morocco	−4.878	100.00	−2.615	94.57
Netherlands	−2.413	99.85	−3.027	97.12
New Zealand	−3.012	99.02	−3.921	99.40
Norway	−3.908	99.51	0.533	98.99
Oman	−4.489	100.00	0.628	79.77
Peru	−4.377	100.00	−1.022	99.59
Poland	−3.677	99.78	−2.933	98.41
Portugal	−4.197	99.84	−3.368	93.01
Romania	−4.885	100.00	−2.402	92.13
Singapore	−1.392	97.32	−1.679	93.96
South Africa	−2.897	99.52	−3.531	99.84
Spain	−2.886	99.38	−2.052	96.06
Sweden	−3.366	100.00	−2.349	99.53
Switzerland	−3.924	99.81	−3.835	99.72
Tunisia	−6.049	100.00	−2.583	93.98
Turkey	−3.510	99.31	−1.092	91.70
United Kingdom	−1.688	94.94	−1.679	96.64
Venezuela, R. B. de	−3.924	99.48	−0.254	86.11

Source: Author.

Annex B: Exporter Coefficients by Sector

Table 5B.1 Harmonized System Industry Code Descriptions

4-digit HS	Description
0901	Coffee; Coffee Husks, etc.; Substitutes with Coffee
2203	Beer Made from Malt
2709	Crude Oil from Petroleum and Bituminous Minerals
2710	Oil (Not Crude) from Petrol and Bitum Mineral, etc.
6109	T-Shirts, Singlets, Tank Tops, etc., Knit or Crocheted
6110	Sweaters, Pullovers, Vests, etc., Knit or Crocheted
6203	Women's or Girls' Overcoats, etc., Not Knit or Crocheted
6204	Men's or Boys' Suits, Ensembles, etc., Not Knit, etc.
8407	Spark-Ignition Recip or Rotary Int Comb Piston Eng
8409	Parts for Engines of Heading 8407 or 8408
8414	Air or Vac Pumps, Compr and Fans; Hoods and Fans; Parts
8415	Air Conditioning Machines (Temperature and Humidity Change), Parts
8418	Refrigerators, Freezers, etc.; Heat Pumps Nesoi, Parts
8471	Automatic Data Process Machines; Magn Reader, etc.
8473	Parts, etc. for Typewriters and Other Office Machines
8481	Taps, Cocks, Valves etc. for Pipes, Tanks, etc., Parts
8501	Electric Motors and Generators (No Sets)
8504	Electric Trans, Static Conv and Induct, Adp Power Supp, Parts
8512	Electric Light, etc., Equip; Windshield Wipers, etc., Parts
8516	Electric Water, Space and Soil Heaters; Hair, etc. Dry, Parts
8517	Electric Apparatus for Line Telephony, etc., Parts
8518	Microphones; Loudspeakers; Sound Amplifier, etc., Parts
8525	Trans Appar for Radiotele, etc.; TV Camera and Rec
8527	Reception Apparatus for Radiotelephony, etc.
8528	TV Receivers, Including Video Monitors and Projectors
8529	Parts for Television, Radio and Radar Apparatus
8536	Electrical Apparatus for Switching, etc., Nov 1000 V

(continued)

Table 5B.1 Harmonized System Industry Code Descriptions (*continued*)

4-digit HS	Description
8537	Boards, Panels, etc., Electric Switch and N/C Apparatus, etc.
8541	Semiconductor Devices; Light-Emit Diodes, etc., Parts
8542	Electronic Integrated Circuits and Microassemblies, Parts
8544	Insulated Wire, Cable, etc.; Optical Sheath Fiber Cables
8703	Motor Cars and Vehicles for Transporting Persons
8704	Motor Vehicles for Transport of Goods
8708	Parts and Access for Motor Vehicles (Head 8701–8705)
9018	Medical, Surgical, Dental or Vet Inst, No Elec, Parts
9029	Revolution and Production Count, Taximeters, etc., Parts
9032	Automatic Regulating or Control Instruments; Parts
9401	Seats (Except Barber, Dental, etc.), and Parts
9403	Furniture Nesoi and Parts Thereof
9405	Lamps and Lighting Fittings and Parts, etc. Nesoi

Source: http://comtrade.un.org/.
Note: Nesoi = not elsewhere specified or included.

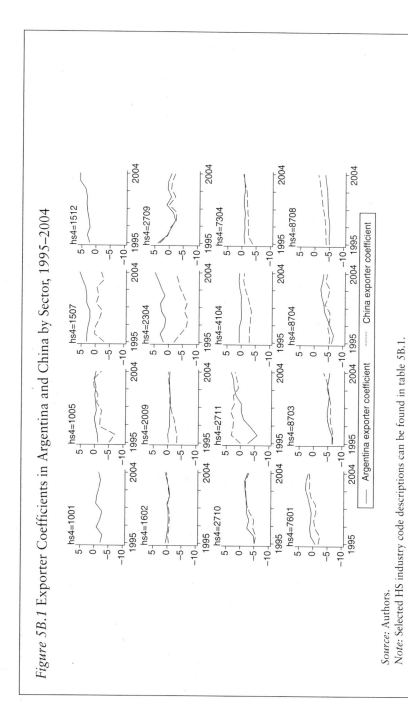

Figure 5B.1 Exporter Coefficients in Argentina and China by Sector, 1995–2004

Source: Authors.

Note: Selected HS industry code descriptions can be found in table 5B.1.

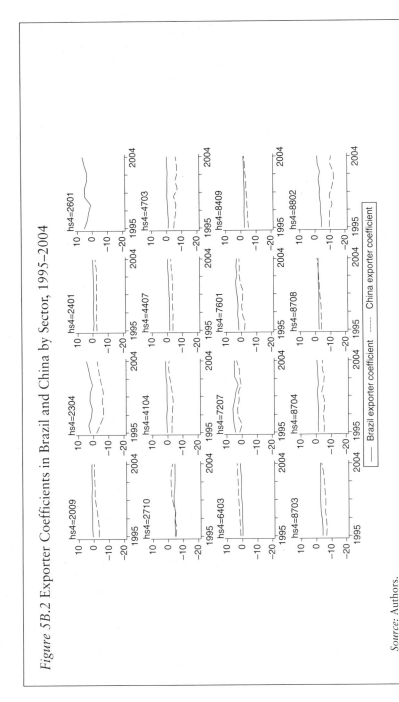

Figure 5B.2 Exporter Coefficients in Brazil and China by Sector, 1995–2004

Source: Authors.

Note: Selected HS industry code descriptions can be found in table 5B.1.

Figure 5B.3 Exporter Coefficients in Chile and China by Sector, 1995–2004

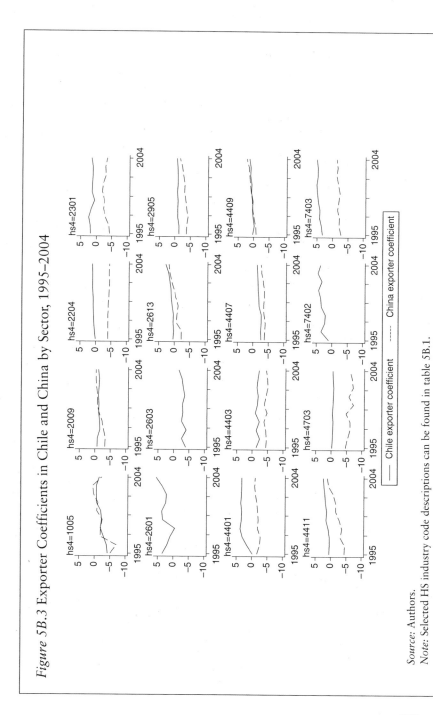

Source: Authors.
Note: Selected HS industry code descriptions can be found in table 5B.1.

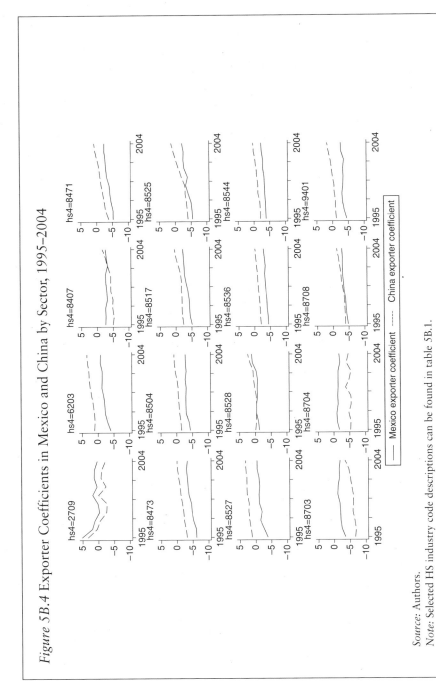

Figure 5B.4 Exporter Coefficients in Mexico and China by Sector, 1995–2004

Source: Authors.

Note: Selected HS industry code descriptions can be found in table 5B.1.

Notes

1. Choosing large countries may subject the specification to selection bias. See Helpman, Melitz, and Rubinstein (2008).

2. The tables give results for 40 of the 90 industries in the sample.

3. Sectors for which we do not have estimates of export-supply capacities for China are those in which China does not export to at least one country in all years covered in the sample (1995–2004).

Bibliography

Anderson, James E., and Eric van Wincoop. 2003. "Gravity with Gravitas: A Solution to the Border Puzzle." *American Economic Review* 93 (1): 170–92.

———. 2004. "Trade Costs." *Journal of Economic Literature* 42 (3): 691–751.

Devlin, Robert, Antoni Estevadeordal, and Andres Rodriguez. 2005. *The Emergence of China: Opportunities and Challenges for Latin America and the Caribbean.* Washington, DC: Inter-American Development Bank.

Eichengreen, Barry, and Hui Tong. 2005. "Is China's FDI Coming at the Expense of Other Countries?" NBER Working Paper 11335, National Bureau of Economic Research, Cambridge, MA.

Feenstra, Robert C. 2003. *Advanced International Trade: Theory and Evidence.* Princeton: Princeton University Press.

Feenstra, Robert C., Robert Lipsey, and Charles Bowen. 1997. "World Trade Flows, 1970–1992, with Production and Tariff Data." NBER Working Paper 5910, National Bureau of Economic Research, Cambridge, MA.

Feenstra, Robert C., Robert Lipsey, Haiyan Deng, Alyson C. Ma, and Hengyong Mo. 2005. "World Trade Flows: 1962–2000." NBER Working Paper 11040, National Bureau of Economic Research, Cambridge, MA.

Fujita, Masahisa, Paul Krugman, and Anthony Venables. 1999. *The Spatial Economy: Cities, Regions, and International Trade.* Cambridge, MA: MIT Press.

Hanson, Gordon, and Chong Xiang. 2004. "The Home-Market Effect and Bilateral Trade Patterns." *American Economic Review* 94 (4): 1108–29.

Harrigan, James. 1995. "Factor Endowments and the International Location of Production: Econometric Evidence for the OECD, 1970–1985." *Journal of International Economics* 39 (1–2): 123–41.

———. 1997. "Technology, Factor Supplies, and International Specialization: Estimating the Neoclassical Model." *American Economic Review* 87 (4): 475–94.

Head, Keith, and Theiry Mayer. 2004. "The Empirics of Agglomeration and Trade." In *Handbook of Regional and Urban Economics,* ed. J. Vernon Henderson and Jacque Thisse. Amsterdam: North Holland.

Head, Keith, and John Ries. 2001. "Increasing Returns versus National Product Differentiation as an Explanation for the Pattern of US-Canada Trade." *American Economic Review* 91(4): 858–76.

Helpman, Elhanan, Marc J. Melitz, and Yona Rubinstein. 2008. "Estimating Trade Flows: Trading Partners and Trading Volumes." *Quarterly Journal of Economics* 123 (2): 441–88.

Hummels, David. 1999. "Towards a Geography of Trade Costs." Unpublished, University of Chicago.

Hummels, David, and Peter Klenow. 2005. "The Variety and Quality of a Nation's Exports." *American Economic Review* 95 (93): 704–23.

Leamer, Edward E. 1984. *Sources of International Comparative Advantage: Theory and Evidence*. Cambridge, MA: MIT Press.

Lopez-Cordoba, Ernesto, Alejandro Micco, and Danielken Molina. 2005. "How Sensitive are Latin American Exports to Chinese Competition in the U.S. Market?" Unpublished, Inter-American Development Bank, Washington, DC.

Redding, Stephen, and Anthony J. Venables. 2003. "Geography and Export Performance: External Market Access and Internal Supply Capacity." NBER Working Paper 9637, National Bureau of Economic Research, Cambridge, MA.

————. 2004. "Economic Geography and International Inequality." *Journal of International Economics* 62 (1): 53–82.

Santos Silva, J. M. C., and Silvana Tenreyro. 2006. "The Log of Gravity." *The Review of Economics and Statistics* 88 (4): 641–58.

Schott, Peter. 2004. "Across Product versus Within Product Specialization in International Trade." *Quarterly Journal of Economics* 119 (2): 647–78.

Wooldridge, Jeffrey M. 2002. *Econometric Analysis of Cross Section and Panel Data*. Cambridge, MA: MIT Press.

6

The Effect of China's Exports on Latin American Trade with the World

*Caroline Freund and Çağlar Özden**

Introduction

Latin American merchandise exports have increased nearly fivefold since 1985.[1] Chinese exports have increased more than 20 times in this same period, and now exceed exports from Latin America by about 15 percent. The aim of this chapter is to assess the impact of China's rapid export expansion on Latin American and Caribbean trade with the rest of the world. The analysis determines which countries in the Latin America and the Caribbean (LAC) region have been most negatively affected by Chinese export growth and the industries that have been hardest hit. It also evaluates how LAC trade is evolving—whether it is expanding into high- or low-wage industries.

Using bilateral trade data at the four-digit Standard International Trade Classification (SITC) level from 1985 through 2004, the study finds that China's export expansion has had a significant negative effect on Latin American exports. The effect is concentrated primarily in industrial exports from Mexico to North America since 1995. In addition, China is displacing LAC in relatively high-wage export sectors. Thus, China's export surge has limited LAC's ability to move up the export ladder.

*The authors are grateful to Cristina Neagu Constantinescu for excellent research assistance.

In response to concerns raised by several LAC countries about China's export surge, a number of recent studies have examined these issues. A paper by Lall and Weiss (2005) is the most closely related to the present topic. They used trade data at the 3-digit level and focused on overlapping industrial structure and correlations in the change in market share from 1990 to 2002 for LAC and China to the world and to the United States. They found that in 1990, 30 percent of trade was in industries where China was gaining and LAC was losing market share, which the authors referred to as industries under "direct threat" from China. In contrast, in 2002, the share of LAC trade under direct threat was only 11 percent. They concluded that LAC's trade structure is now relatively complementary to China's.

Devlin, Estevadeordal, and Rodríguez (2006) examined the export similarity between China and Latin America and discussed textiles and apparel in detail. Using data on exports to the United States at the 10-digit level of disaggregation, they found that export similarity has increased significantly since 1972, and was greatest for Mexico and the Dominican Republic. They also argued that China has displaced LAC exports of textiles in products in which trade preferences are small or nonexistent—though they did not provide an empirical analysis.

A number of studies focused on the specific effect of China on Mexico in the U.S. market. Quintin (2004) found that displacement by China over the period 1999–2003 was segregated to only a handful of industries and argued that Mexico's stagnating exports in this period were mainly a result of slow growth in the United States. Hanson and Robertson (2006) found that Mexico's sluggish performance in the late 1990s was due to a slow-down in the United States and the surge in China's exports. A U.S. General Accounting Office (GAO) report (2003) looked at the period 1995–2002 and found that Mexico lost market share in 47 of its 152 main export industries. Of these 47, China gained market share in 35, or about three-fourths. In addition, over one-half of *maquiladoras* surveyed mentioned China as playing an important role in their decline (U.S. GAO 2003, 26). Dussel Peters (2005) also found that Mexico had lost substantial ground to China in the U.S. market, especially in recent years, and that both countries increasingly specialized in electronics and auto parts.

This chapter builds on the previous work in several ways. First, using bilateral trade data at the four-digit SITC level over 20 years, this analysis can more carefully assess China's threat. The main goal is to evaluate whether LAC exports to a given market declined or grew more slowly in the four-digit products in which Chinese exports increased, controlling for country demand. If China and LAC countries are competing in different markets or different four-digit products, then the threat may be smaller than previously indicated. Second, rather than relying on changes in market shares alone, this study uses empirical analysis, controlling for exporter-supply and importer-demand effects, to more carefully gauge the magnitude of the threat. Third, this study evaluates the type of products—high wage or low wage—in which China is displacing LAC exports.

The chapter proceeds as follows: The next section describes the methodology for evaluating whether Chinese exports are substitutes for LAC exports in third-country markets. The third section presents the results and is followed by a section that evaluates whether LAC exporters are moving to high-wage or low-wage industries in response to the entry of China into global markets. The final section concludes.

Chinese Exports as Substitutes: Methodology

The aim of this section is to determine which Latin American countries and industries have been affected by competition from Chinese exports. This issue has received much attention, as Chinese exports have rapidly increased their share in the global market since 1990. Most other studies use changes in market shares in relatively aggregate export categories, which introduces two problems. First, it is possible that China is increasing its market share at the expense of domestic producers but *not* displacing other exporters. As a result, the export market shares of other exporters will decline, by definition, but they will not necessarily suffer an economic loss. Second, using a relatively aggregate export category may overstate displacement if exports are actually in very different subcategories. For example, assume China sells primarily overcoats and LAC sells mainly suits. At the three-digit level, these products will appear to be competing, but it is unlikely that an increase in overcoat exports from China displaces suit exports from LAC. The results section briefly discusses changes in market shares, but relies on different measures of export performance to more accurately assess the China effect.

This empirical analysis essentially tests whether Chinese exports to a particular country, for example, the United States, in a given category are affecting LAC exports to a greater extent than exports from third countries, such as Germany, while controlling for overall exporter-supply growth. Thus, if Chinese export growth is primarily displacing domestic producers, or is not competing with LAC for some other reason, that issue will not be picked up. Although, even in the present case, Chinese exports might not be pushing out LAC exports—it could be that China is entering because LAC is exiting—this is less likely because the analysis is controlling for exporter-supply growth. Moreover, given China's meteoric rise in exports and the ensuing rhetoric in LAC countries, LAC's exit seems unlikely.

To motivate the empirical work, the analysis starts with two export equations by industry, one general and one for China, respectively:

$$exports_{ijt} = \gamma_{ij}\gamma_{it}\gamma_{jt} \quad \text{and} \tag{6.1}$$

$$China_{jt} = \gamma_{chj}\gamma_{cht}\gamma_{jt},$$ (6.2)

where, $exports_{ijt}$ ($China_{jt}$) is the natural log of exports from country i (China) to country j at time t; γ_{ij} (γ_{chj}) is a country-pair fixed effect that will pick up fixed country-pair characteristics (or characteristics that change slowly), such as distance, size, comparative advantage, and multilateral resistance between country i (China) and country j; γ_{it} is an exporter-year idiosyncratic effect that will pick up positive or negative shocks to the sector; γ_{jt} is the importer-year variable that reflects time-varying importer characteristics such as demand conditions in the industry in year t. Finally, γ_{cht} is a special shock to China.

This implies that total imports to country j from all countries other than China can be written as

$$imports_{jt} = \gamma_{jt}\left(\sum_i \gamma_{it}\gamma_{ij}\right).$$ (6.3)

Assume the exporter-specific variables grow at rate g with a multiplicative error that is independent and identically $\gamma_{it} = (1+g)^t(1+\varepsilon_{it})$, then the total import equation can be rewritten as

$$E(imports_{jt}) = \gamma_{jt}(1+g)^t\,\bar{\gamma}_{ij}.$$ (6.4)

Equation (6.4) says that the expected value of imports in country j in year t is equal to the average bilateral imports multiplied by average exporter growth and importer demand.

Writing equations (6.1) and (6.4) in log first differences yields

$$d(exports)_{ijt} = \alpha_{it} + \alpha_{jt}$$ (6.5)

$$d(imports)_{jt} = \alpha_{jt} + \ln(1+g).$$ (6.6)

Substituting equation (6.6) into equation (6.5), export growth can be rewritten as

$$d(exports)_{ijt} = \alpha_{it} + d(imports)_{jt} - g$$ (6.7)

where g is a constant representing average import growth. Assuming this is the correct specification, the coefficient on imports should be close to 1; that is, on average, a 1 percent increase in total imports is correlated with a 1 percent increase in a given country's exports, after controlling for overall export supply growth.

Now assume that in some products there is a negative effect on country i's exports to country j, as a result of increased exports from China to country j. Equation (6.1) can be rewritten as

$$exports_{ijt} = \gamma_{ij}\gamma_{it}\gamma_{jt}\,/\,K_{jt}China_{jt}.$$ (6.8)

This implies that an increase in Chinese exports reduces country i's exports by a factor $1/K$. Now, export growth is

$$d(exports)_{ijt} = \alpha_{it} + d(imports)_{jt} - d(China)_{jt} + \varepsilon_{ijt}. \qquad (6.9)$$

The objective is to estimate whether Chinese exports have displaced Latin American exports. To the extent that China's export growth does not impact LAC exporters specifically, the coefficient on China should be zero. If Chinese imports are driving LAC imports out of the market to a greater extent than third countries' imports, the coefficient should be negative. If Chinese imports complement LAC imports, the coefficient on China should be positive. Note that this is essentially a test of whether China is affecting LAC countries more than other exporting countries (such as Germany) are affecting LAC countries in the U.S. market. If China has roughly the same effect on all exporting countries, then the coefficient on imports will be close to 1 and the coefficient on China will be zero.

The regression is run with both China's export growth and China's export growth weighted by the lagged share of Chinese exports in country j's imports. Results are reported below using weighted Chinese export growth because the fit was much better—though results are qualitatively similar for both specifications. The intuition for weighting export growth by lagged trade share is that China's export growth will only matter if China is a significant supplier—that is, equation (6.8) is only relevant when China is an important exporter. For example, export growth of 100 percent by China if China's exports are 0.00001 percent of the market is probably meaningless. With regard to the framework above, the intuition is that K is dependent on Chinese market share. Thus, the final equation estimated is

$$d(exports)_{ijt} = \alpha_{it} + \beta_0 d(imports)_{jt} + \beta_1 d(China)_{jt} + \varepsilon_{ijt}. \qquad (6.10)$$

Recall that $imports_{jt}$ is imports from all (non-LAC) countries other than China. The variable of interest is $d(China)_{jt}$, which is growth of China in country j and sector k multiplied by China's lagged market share in that sector and market. A negative coefficient on China (β_1) indicates that Chinese export growth is correlated with a decline in Latin American export growth in a given industry.[2]

This equation is estimated using data from 1985 through 2004. The advantage of this specification is that it exploits both cross-section and time-series variation to estimate how LAC exports are affected by China. There is variation across markets in a given product in Chinese import penetration and in growth of Chinese imports over time. In addition, the data are readily available and the coefficient is easy to understand.

Chinese Exports as Substitutes: Results

The analysis uses bilateral trade data at the four-digit SITC level. The data were collected as import data, which are reported more accurately than export data, and then converted to export data. As an initial pass at the data, figure 6.1 presents a scatter plot of the change in world market

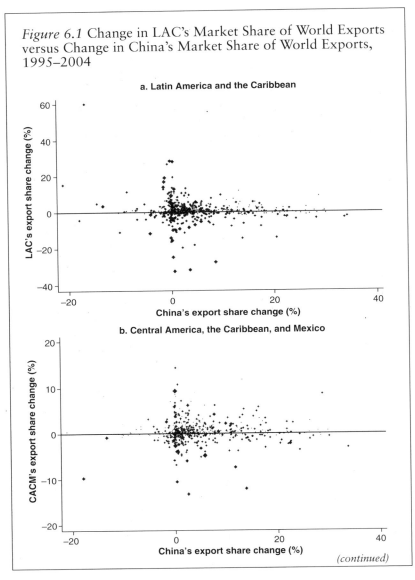

Figure 6.1 Change in LAC's Market Share of World Exports versus Change in China's Market Share of World Exports, 1995–2004

(continued)

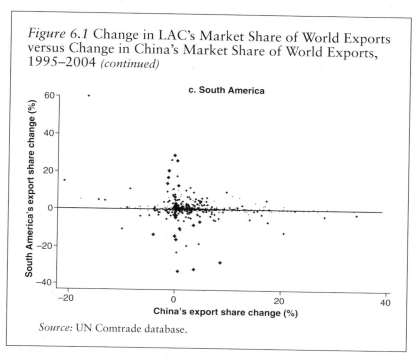

Figure 6.1 Change in LAC's Market Share of World Exports versus Change in China's Market Share of World Exports, 1995–2004 *(continued)*

c. South America

Source: UN Comtrade database.

share from 1995 to 2004 for LAC exports and Chinese exports, weighted by LAC exports at the beginning of the period. Points in the lower right quadrant reflect products where LAC market share has fallen and China's market share has risen. Figure 6.1 shows the change in LAC market share; in market share of Central America, the Caribbean, and Mexico (CACM); and in South American market share, respectively. Figure 6.2 is similar, except it reports exports as shares of North American imports.

The scatter plots indicate that there are some significant industries where LAC has lost and China has gained. This is especially true for CACM exports to North America (figure 6.2b).

Table 6.1 reports the results of estimating equation (6.10) on all industries, and on nonindustrial and industrial products separately. Industrial products are defined as those with SITC codes above 6000; these include manufactured products such as steel, electronics, and textiles and apparel. Nonindustrial products are those with SITC codes below 6000 and include agricultural products, minerals, and raw materials.

The first three columns of table 6.1 report the results on all exports with exporter-year fixed effects, exporter-two-digit-product fixed effects, and exporter-four-digit-product fixed effects, respectively. Thus, the third column estimates rely entirely on cross-country variation. The coefficient on ln(*imports*)—dlnimp in table—is greater than one, implying that LAC

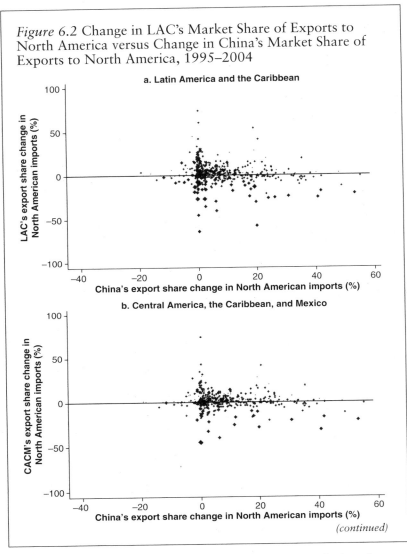

Figure 6.2 Change in LAC's Market Share of Exports to North America versus Change in China's Market Share of Exports to North America, 1995–2004

a. Latin America and the Caribbean

b. Central America, the Caribbean, and Mexico

(continued)

export growth has been above non-China import growth, but that, on average, export growth is low when Chinese exports are large and growing. Looking at nonindustrial products (fourth through sixth columns) versus industrial products (seventh through ninth columns), the effect on industrials is more robust. The remaining tables report results using exporter-two-digit-product-year fixed effects in all regressions.

The coefficient of about –0.3 on dlnChina implies that in a product with the average Chinese market share of 10 percent and Chinese export growth

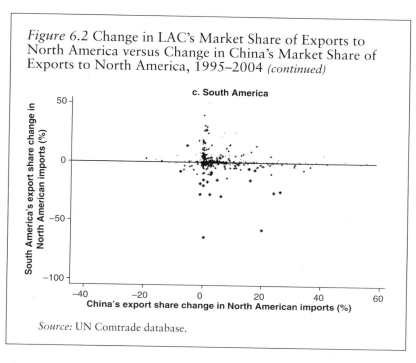

Figure 6.2 Change in LAC's Market Share of Exports to North America versus Change in China's Market Share of Exports to North America, 1995–2004 *(continued)*

c. South America

Source: UN Comtrade database.

of 20 percent, LAC export growth would be reduced by 0.6 percentage points (0.3 × 0.1 × 20). Note that although the coefficient on Chinese export growth is large, the magnitude of the effect depends on the market share of Chinese products. Thus, the overall effect is much smaller.

Table 6.2 disaggregates the China effect by the income level or region of the importer. In the first column, both variables are interacted with a dummy that is 1 if the importer is a developing country. The negative coefficient on dlnCHN_dev implies that the negative impact of China has been at least as strong in developing countries. The second column reports the results for interactions of the variables with dummies for North America (NA), LAC, and other developing countries (devnoLAC). OECD countries aside from those in North America are omitted from the table. The negative impact of China is strongest in North America and developing countries other than those in LAC. The impact in North America is especially strong in industrial goods. The coefficient of 0.95 (sixth column) implies that in a product with 10 percent Chinese market share and growth of 20 percent, LAC exports would be reduced by nearly 2 percent.[3]

Table 6.3 looks at the effect over time, disaggregating it into four periods, 1986–89, 1990–94, 1995–99, and 2000–04. The negative effect of China on LAC exports is only evident since 1995. It is especially strong and robust on CACM exporters and in industrial products. This is not

Table 6.1 Determinants of LAC Export Growth

	All exporters								
	All products			Nonindustrial products			Industrial products		
	dlntrade expyrdum	dlntrade expprod2yrdum	dlntrade expprodydum	dlntrade expyrdum	dlntrade expprod2yrdum	dlntrade expprodydum	dlntrade expyrdum	dlntrade expprod2yrdum	dlntrade expprodydum
dlnimp	1.178***	1.225***	1.318***	1.062***	1.079***	1.127***	1.252***	1.278***	1.390***
	[14.01]	[13.74]	[9.74]	[31.07]	[36.44]	[31.83]	[10.06]	[10.69]	[7.60]
dlnChina	−0.243*	−0.326***	−0.302***	−0.300	−0.395***	−0.456**	−0.359***	−0.358***	−0.315***
	[1.75]	[3.96]	[2.88]	[1.23]	[2.77]	[2.33]	[2.73]	[3.47]	[2.82]
Observations	786,110	786,110	786,110	223,901	223,901	223,901	562,209	562,209	562,209
R-squared	0.21	0.39	0.58	0.23	0.4	0.58	0.24	0.39	0.58
Number of dummies	757	29,936	148,731	746	13,217	49,020	757	16,719	99,711

Source: Authors.

Note: Robust t-statistics are in brackets. For weighted least squares, weights equal trade value.

* Significant at 10 percent.

** Significant at 5 percent.

*** Significant at 1 percent.

Table 6.2 Determinants of LAC Export Growth: Isolating Markets

	All exporters					
	All products		Nonindustrial products		Industrial products	
	dlntrade	dlntrade	dlntrade	dlntrade	dlntrade	dlntrade
dlnimp	1.273***	1.589***	1.045***	1.101***	1.382***	1.958***
	[8.20]	[6.23]	[28.83]	[23.81]	[6.33]	[4.93]
dlnChina	−0.241**	0.164	−0.08	−0.138	−0.446***	0.027
	[2.43]	[1.14]	[0.51]	[0.76]	[2.99]	[0.10]
dlnimp_dev	−0.100		0.077		−0.202	
	[0.69]		[1.36]		[0.98]	
dlnCHN_dev	−0.212		−0.574**		0.169	
	[1.35]		[2.33]		[0.77]	
dlnimp_NA		−0.575***		−0.150**		−0.947***
		[2.62]		[2.25]		[2.59]
dlnimp_LAC		−0.491**		−0.046		−0.850**
		[1.99]		[0.72]		[2.19]
dlnimp_ devnoLAC		−0.182		0.121		−0.454
		[0.75]		[1.13]		[1.20]
dlnCHN_NA		−0.971***		0.569*		−0.957***
		[4.62]		[1.84]		[2.81]
dlnCHN_LAC		−0.271		0.263		−0.186
		[1.57]		[1.02]		[0.65]
dlnCHN_ devnoLAC		−0.701***		−0.576**		−0.512
		[3.13]		[2.06]		[1.15]
Observations	786,110	786,110	223,901	223,901	562,209	562,209
R-squared	0.39	0.40	0.40	0.41	0.39	0.40
Number of dummies	29,936	29,936	13,217	13,217	16,719	16,719

Source: Authors.
Note: Robust t-statistics are in brackets. Exporter-two-digit product-year fixed effects are included in all regressions. For weighted least squares, weights equal trade value.
* Significant at 10 percent.
** Significant at 5 percent.
*** Significant at 1 percent.

Table 6.3 Determinants of LAC Export Growth: Isolating Periods and Exporters

	All exporters			South American exporters			CACM exporters		
	All products	Nonindustrial products	Industrial products	All products	Nonindustrial products	Industrial products	All products	Nonindustrial products	Industrial products
	dlntrade	dlntrade	dlntrade	dlntrade	dlntrade	dlntrade	dlntrade	dlntrade	dlntrade
dlnimports_8689	1.078***	1.023***	1.105***	1.247***	1.186***	1.284***	0.891***	0.747***	0.948***
	[15.12]	[11.59]	[11.50]	[18.30]	[10.32]	[15.46]	[6.51]	[6.14]	[5.36]
dlnimports_9094	1.178***	1.255***	1.146***	1.247***	1.355***	1.199***	1.018***	0.958***	1.035***
	[22.48]	[15.80]	[17.65]	[20.13]	[14.14]	[15.27]	[12.34]	[8.65]	[10.27]
dlnimports_9599	1.101***	1.161***	1.078***	1.104***	1.187***	1.053***	1.097***	1.057***	1.106***
	[22.27]	[22.59]	[16.14]	[27.87]	[23.31]	[19.14]	[9.35]	[6.75]	[8.15]
dlnimports_0004	1.337***	0.978***	1.455***	1.073***	0.992***	1.100***	1.684***	0.948***	1.796***
	[7.62]	[22.01]	[6.47]	[26.17]	[19.07]	[19.69]	[4.69]	[12.16]	[4.54]
dlnCHN_8689	-0.252	-0.272	-0.242	-0.157	-0.279	0.062	-0.448	-0.188	-0.785*
	[1.36]	[1.21]	[0.75]	[0.71]	[1.19]	[0.16]	[1.25]	[0.35]	[1.75]
dlnCHN_9094	-0.228	-0.742	0.087	-0.304	-0.779	0.081	0.056	0.043	0.063
	[0.86]	[1.19]	[0.58]	[0.95]	[1.16]	[0.62]	[0.15]	[0.12]	[0.15]
dlnCHN_9599	-0.405***	-0.303	-0.445**	-0.250**	-0.312	-0.155	-0.769**	-0.18	-0.863**
	[2.87]	[1.60]	[2.29]	[2.12]	[1.51]	[1.13]	[2.15]	[0.56]	[2.19]

(continued)

Table 6.3 Determinants of LAC Export Growth: Isolating Periods and Exporters (continued)

	All exporters			South American exporters			CACM exporters		
	All products	Nonindustrial products	Industrial products	All products	Nonindustrial products	Industrial products	All products	Nonindustrial products	Industrial products
	dlntrade	dlntrade	dlntrade	dlntrade	dlntrade	dlntrade	dlntrade	dlntrade	dlntrade
dlnCHN_0004	-0.274**	-0.453**	-0.454***	-0.172	-0.407*	0.01	-0.829***	-0.885	-0.855***
	[2.18]	[2.08]	[2.87]	[1.19]	[1.79]	[0.09]	[3.48]	[1.35]	[3.30]
Observations	786,110	223,901	562,209	468,336	138,194	330,142	317,573	85,596	231,977
R-squared	0.39	0.40	0.39	0.35	0.39	0.32	0.44	0.43	0.45
Number of dummies	29,936	13,217	16,719	11,693	5,611	6,082	18,241	7,604	10,637

Source: Authors.

Note: Robust t-statistics are in brackets. Exporter-two-digit product-year fixed effects are included in all regressions. For weighted least squares, weights equal trade value.

* Significant at 10 percent.
** Significant at 5 percent.
*** Significant at 1 percent.

too surprising, given that rhetoric has been greatest in Mexico and other studies have also found some effects on Mexico.[4]

Table 6.4 combines this information to examine different importers in different periods. The table shows robust negative effects on CACM exporters to North America and to other LAC countries from 1995 through 2004, as well as for South American exporters to non-LAC developing countries for all types of products during the period 1995–2004. The sign and magnitude of the coefficient for CACM exporters implies that they are also negatively affected in exports of industrial products to other developing countries in this period, but their trade is not large enough for the results to be significant.

Table 6.5 further disaggregates the effect by source of exports in the Caribbean, Central America, and Mexico. The results are the strongest in Mexico because of strong effects in industrial products in the most recent period. In Central America, there were strong effects in 1990–99, but they have died out in the most recent period. In individual countries, there are significant negative effects in Costa Rica and El Salvador in 1990–94 and in Panama in 1995–99 (not shown in table 6.5). In the Caribbean, there are also strong effects in the recent period. The Caribbean effect is driven primarily by The Bahamas. When The Bahamas are excluded, the effect is no longer robust. Aside from The Bahamas, only Cuba shows a robust negative effect in the recent period in industrials.

The coefficient of –0.759 and an average market share of 13 percent in industrial products implies that Chinese export growth of 20 percent has limited Mexican export growth by about 2 percentage points.

Tables 6A.1 and 6A.2 in the annex to this chapter report the results for each two-digit category separately for all years (table 6A.1) and for the first period and the second period separately (table 6A.2). Of the almost 70 categories, 15 show significant negative impacts of Chinese exports in the second period (three show positive and significant impacts: dyeing, tanning, and coloring materials; arms of war and ammunition; and road vehicles, including air cushion vehicles). The 14 categories with negative impacts are reported in table 6.6. Many of these products are electronics, consistent with earlier work by Dussel Peters (2005) and U.S. GAO (2003) for Mexico.

Of interest, while the coefficient on textiles is negative in both periods, and significant in the second period, the coefficient on apparel is negative and significant only in the first period. It is positive and not significant in the second period, implying that China did not have a significant role in displacing LAC apparel exports. The coefficient on overall imports (excluding China) of apparel is 0.85, implying that LAC exports were not growing as fast as exports from other countries (excluding China) in the latter period. Thus, LAC exporters were losing market share in apparel from 1995 through 2004, but mainly to other exporters. This supports the argument that, for the most part, China and LAC do not compete in

Table 6.4 Determinants of LAC Exports: Isolating Year, Market, and Exporter Effects

	All exporters			South American exporters			CACM exporters		
	All products	Nonindustrial products	Industrial products	All products	Nonindustrial products	Industrial products	All products	Nonindustrial products	Industrial products
	dlntrade	dlntrade	dlntrade	dlntrade	dlntrade	dlntrade	dlntrade	dlntrade	dlntrade
dlnimp_8694NA	1.013***	1.036***	1.002***	1.114***	1.171***	1.075***	0.928***	0.796***	0.969***
	[14.34]	[11.55]	[10.58]	[12.80]	[8.59]	[9.52]	[8.86]	[8.99]	[7.30]
dlnimp_9504NA	1.007***	0.896***	1.018***	1.043***	1.041***	1.059***	0.960***	0.637***	0.955***
	[14.70]	[14.13]	[13.97]	[17.44]	[12.63]	[12.27]	[12.36]	[6.26]	[12.88]
dlnimp_8694OECD	1.130***	1.077***	1.195***	1.284***	1.217***	1.356***	0.796***	0.726***	0.826***
	[17.31]	[13.42]	[12.13]	[20.12]	[17.19]	[12.88]	[6.27]	[4.40]	[4.62]
dlnimp_9504OECD	1.779***	1.117***	2.234***	1.174***	1.116***	1.251***	2.599***	1.155***	2.887***
	[5.26]	[20.47]	[4.58]	[21.26]	[21.22]	[11.16]	[4.54]	[6.70]	[4.86]
dlnimp_8694LAC	1.057***	1.293***	1.008***	1.028***	1.292***	0.977***	1.204***	1.313***	1.176***
	[30.93]	[10.73]	[31.17]	[27.41]	[9.36]	[27.49]	[15.24]	[5.60]	[15.35]
dlnimp_9504LAC	1.109***	1.013***	1.131***	1.023***	0.968***	1.036***	1.309***	1.125***	1.347***
	[26.34]	[19.62]	[23.01]	[24.04]	[14.68]	[20.84]	[16.00]	[17.18]	[13.80]
dlnimp_8694DEV	1.591***	1.650***	1.555***	1.619***	1.758***	1.570***	1.450***	1.123***	1.618***
	[16.64]	[7.09]	[15.28]	[16.55]	[6.73]	[15.17]	[6.38]	[5.21]	[4.80]
dlnimp_9504DEV	1.308***	1.126***	1.453***	1.196***	1.118***	1.267***	1.546***	1.147***	1.651***
	[14.06]	[10.48]	[9.64]	[13.26]	[9.46]	[8.32]	[6.37]	[7.97]	[5.64]
dlnCHN_8694NA	-0.219	0.579	-0.435	0.27	0.634	0.104	-0.523	0.308	-0.689
	[0.72]	[1.51]	[1.16]	[0.78]	[1.22]	[0.23]	[1.18]	[0.61]	[1.34]

(continued)

Table 6.4 Determinants of LAC Exports: Isolating Year, Market, and Exporter Effects *(continued)*

	All exporters			South American exporters			CACM exporters		
	All products	Nonindustrial products	Industrial products	All products	Nonindustrial products	Industrial products	All products	Nonindustrial products	Industrial products
	dlntrade	dlntrade	dlntrade	dlntrade	dlntrade	dlntrade	dlntrade	dlntrade	dlntrade
dlnCHN_9504NA	-0.884***	0.405	-0.988***	-0.307	0.518	-0.781*	-0.962***	0	-0.949***
	[5.06]	[1.26]	[5.17]	[1.05]	[1.25]	[1.94]	[4.73]	[0.00]	[4.51]
dlnCHN_8694OECD	-0.028	-0.233	0.259	-0.087	-0.203	0.091	0.354	-0.162	0.717
	[0.17]	[1.29]	[1.26]	[0.50]	[1.07]	[0.37]	[0.91]	[0.32]	[1.53]
dlnCHN_9504OECD	0.22	-0.057	-0.293	0.073	0.021	0.018	0.113	-1.334	0.319
	[1.04]	[0.23]	[0.72]	[0.45]	[0.09]	[0.09]	[0.17]	[1.25]	[0.38]
dlnCHN_8694LAC	-0.152	0.247	-0.197	0.038	0.216	0.026	-0.907	0.469	-1.247*
	[0.94]	[0.39]	[1.21]	[0.28]	[0.24]	[0.25]	[1.57]	[1.16]	[1.75]
dlnCHN_9504LAC	-0.095	0.108	-0.147	0.09	0.227	0.039	-0.701**	-0.419	-0.758**
	[0.91]	[0.56]	[1.21]	[1.03]	[1.00]	[0.41]	[2.22]	[1.35]	[2.04]
dlnCHN_8694DEV	-0.704	-1.497	0.165	-0.768	-1.431	0.04	0.854	-1.194*	1.913***
	[1.16]	[1.46]	[0.71]	[1.23]	[1.39]	[0.17]	[1.14]	[1.65]	[2.71]
dlnCHN_9504DEV	-0.565***	-0.648***	-0.709	-0.565***	-0.671***	-0.488**	-0.906	-0.149	-1.161
	[3.10]	[3.10]	[1.50]	[3.47]	[3.05]	[2.34]	[1.10]	[0.31]	[1.28]
Observations	786,110	223,901	562,209	468,336	138,194	330,142	317,573	85,596	231,977
R-squared	0.40	0.41	0.41	0.36	0.40	0.32	0.46	0.43	0.48
Number of dummies	29,936	13,217	16,719	11,693	5,611	6,082	18,241	7,604	10,637

Source: Authors.
Note: Robust t-statistics are in brackets. Exporter-two-digit product-year fixed effects are included in all regressions. For weighted least squares, weights equal trade value.
* Significant at 10 percent.
** Significant at 5 percent.
*** Significant at 1 percent.

Table 6.5 China's Effects on Exports from Mexico, Central America, and the Caribbean

	Mexican exporters			Central American exporters			Caribbean exporters			Caribbean exporters, without The Bahamas		
	All products	Non-industrial products	Industrial products	All products	Non-industrial products	Industrial products	All products	Non-industrial products	Industrial products	All products	Non-industrial products	Industrial products
	difhtrade	difhtrade	difhtrade	difhtrade	difhtrade	difhtrade	difhtrade	difhtrade	difhtrade	difhtrade	difhtrade	difhtrade
dlngen_8689	0.922***	0.707***	0.985***	0.884***	1.104***	0.719***	0.620***	0.370**	0.774***	0.643***	0.421**	0.763***
	[5.57]	[4.35]	[4.86]	[8.71]	[6.31]	[6.90]	[6.11]	[2.09]	[5.89]	[6.08]	[2.14]	[5.83]
dlngen_9094	1.104***	0.769***	1.207***	0.812***	0.774***	0.821***	1.156***	1.711***	0.790**	1.240***	1.399***	1.115***
	[10.52]	[5.64]	[9.29]	[6.43]	[5.85]	[5.75]	[4.30]	[5.85]	[2.04]	[6.17]	[5.09]	[3.83]
dlngen_9599	1.019***	1.141***	1.000***	1.289***	0.961***	1.341**	1.160***	0.847***	1.341***	0.971***	0.846***	1.068***
	[12.09]	[5.12]	[11.01]	[2.73]	[9.25]	[2.47]	[6.33]	[3.93]	[5.75]	[6.14]	[3.82]	[5.06]
dlngen_0004	1.166***	0.963***	1.193***	2.800***	1.133***	3.069***	0.924***	0.185	1.236***	0.848***	0.698***	0.924***
	[14.33]	[10.06]	[13.18]	[4.16]	[13.57]	[4.66]	[4.01]	[0.40]	[4.96]	[5.05]	[2.63]	[4.41]
dlnCHN_8689	-0.346	-0.237	-0.618	-0.569	0.828	-1.103*	-0.591	-1.262	-0.718	-0.611	-1.19	-0.709
	[0.72]	[0.41]	[0.78]	[1.22]	[1.50]	[1.70]	[1.03]	[0.34]	[1.37]	[1.07]	[0.29]	[1.35]
dlnCHN_9094	0.576	0.219	0.704	-1.287**	-0.106	-1.497**	0.051	-1.597	0.806	-0.13	-1.919	0.335
	[1.38]	[0.57]	[1.47]	[2.02]	[0.16]	[1.98]	[0.07]	[0.98]	[1.03]	[0.20]	[1.32]	[0.49]

(continued)

195

Table 6.5 Mexico, Central America, and the Caribbean (continued)

	Mexican exporters			Central American exporters			Caribbean exporters			Caribbean exporters, without The Bahamas		
	All products	Non-industrial products	Industrial products	All products	Non-industrial products	Industrial products	All products	Non-industrial products	Industrial products	All products	Non-industrial products	Industrial products
	dif|ntrade	dif|ntrade	dif|ntrade	dif|ntrade	dif|ntrade	dif|ntrade	dif|ntrade	dif|ntrade	dif|ntrade	dif|ntrade	dif|ntrade	dif|ntrade
dlnCHN_9599	-0.355*	-0.145	-0.383	-2.067***	-0.647	-2.156***	0.837	0.599	0.838	0.726	0.652	0.72
	[1.69]	[0.40]	[1.63]	[3.17]	[1.28]	[3.32]	[1.52]	[0.54]	[1.33]	[1.32]	[0.58]	[1.14]
dlnCHN_0004	-0.699***	-0.105	-0.759***	-0.392	0.034	-0.464	-2.954**	-10.106	-1.935*	-0.811	0.402	-1.013
	[2.63]	[0.36]	[2.65]	[1.09]	[0.11]	[1.09]	[2.08]	[1.34]	[1.73]	[1.12]	[0.58]	[1.23]
Constant	0.078***	0.052***	0.086***	0.163***	0.116***	0.196***	0.170***	0.205***	0.166***	0.151***	0.151***	0.155***
	[14.52]	[5.56]	[13.92]	[8.03]	[17.82]	[7.80]	[9.56]	[4.83]	[10.75]	[13.07]	[6.74]	[11.04]
Observations	123,324	31,103	92,221	115,452	29,255	86,197	78,856	25,271	53,585	75,273	23,612	51,661
R-squared	0.26	0.34	0.24	0.61	0.43	0.64	0.63	0.54	0.7	0.67	0.6	0.71

Source: Authors.
Note: Robust t-statistics are in brackets. For weighted least squares, weights equal trade value.
* Significant at 10 percent.
** Significant at 5 percent.
*** Significant at 1 percent.

Table 6.6 Industries for Which China's Export Growth Is Significantly Correlated with Lower LAC Growth

Two-digit code	Industry name	PRODY
04	Cereals and cereal preparations	7,683
11	Beverages	10,442
61	Leather, leather manufactures, n.e.s., and dressed furskins	6,264
62	Rubber manufactures, n.e.s.	11,775
64	Paper, paperboard, articles of paper, paper-pulp/board	13,564
65	Textile yarn, fabrics, made-up articles, related products	8,477
67	Iron and steel	10,121
69	Manufactures of metal, n.e.s.	11,907
71	Power-generating machinery and equipment	14,324
74	General industrial machinery and equipment, and parts	12,952
76	Telecommunications and sound recording apparatus	12,936
77	Electrical machinery, apparatus, and appliances, n.e.s	11,225
79	Other transport equipment	5,028
82	Furniture and parts thereof	9,478
	All imports	11,208

Source: Authors.

Note: n.e.s. = not elsewhere specified; PRODY = an index that ranks traded goods by their implied productivity.

the same categories of apparel. This may have changed since the complete removal of apparel quotas began in 2005.

In sum, this study examines how LAC exports were affected by Chinese export growth and finds that Mexican producers were the main victims, with some negative effects on countries in Central America and the Caribbean. The study also finds that effects are largely confined to the western hemisphere and the past 10 years, and that industrial products, especially electronics, have been affected most.

Is LAC Moving into High-Wage or Low-Wage Industries?

This section evaluates how LAC has fared with respect to the types of industries in which trade growth has been above or below world averages, and which industries China has affected. Industries are evaluated according to the average real per capita income of countries that export in a given industry, that is, countries that have revealed comparative advantage. The analysis interprets the average income level associated with each product as representative of the productivity or average real wage associated with the product. It then examines whether LAC is moving into or out of industries associated with a relatively high or low average wage. The analysis also examines the industries in which China is negatively affecting LAC, according to these criteria.

To determine which exports are growing at above-average rates, the regression is run without a special China effect and then examined for categories where the coefficient on overall import growth (including China) is significantly greater than 1.[5] These are categories in which export growth from LAC significantly exceeds import demand from the rest of the world, on average. Thus, these are categories in which LAC exports are growing the fastest relative to the rest of the world. There are 19 growth products at the two-digit level, reported in table 6.7. Chinese growth is significantly associated with a slowdown in LAC growth for 3 of these 19 products. These are electrical machinery, iron and steel, and leather and leather manufactures.

The analysis also examines categories for which the coefficient on import growth is significantly less than 1. This occurs in only five categories. LAC is not keeping pace with other exporters in these categories; they are reported in table 6.8. Of these five, two are products for which Chinese growth is significantly associated with slower LAC export growth. These are cereals and cereal preparations, and manufactures of metal.

To characterize the industries, the analysis follows Hausman, Hwang, and Rodrik (2005) and creates an index of the average real wage (as measured by per capita gross domestic product [GDP] at purchasing power parity) associated with exporters in a given industry. The index is created at the world level and is defined as follows:

$$PRODY_k = \sum_j \frac{(exports_{jk}/EXPORTS_j)}{\sum_j (exports_{jk}/EXPORTS_j)} GDPPC_j, \qquad (6.11)$$

where k denotes the industry and j denotes the country. $GDPPC$ is per capita GDP at purchasing power parity. The term $exports_{jk}$ is exports of country j in industry k, and $EXPORTS_j$ is total exports of country j. Thus, the weight on $GDPPC$ is a country's share of its export basket in a product over the sum of the export shares of all countries. The reason for using revealed comparative advantage as a weight is that using export weights alone would place too much weight on large exporters of k for whom k might still be a small portion of overall exports. The analysis

Table 6.7 Relatively High-Growth LAC Industries

Two-digit code	Industry name	PRODY
02	Dairy products and birds' eggs	16,041
03	Fish, crustaceans, mollusk, preparations thereof	4,060
23	Crude rubber (including synthetic and reclaimed)	10,564
24	Cork and wood	8,763
26	Textile fibers (except wool tops) and their wastes	5,103
27	Crude fertilizers and crude materials (excluding coal)	7,267
33	Petroleum, petroleum products, and related materials	5,180
42	Fixed vegetable oils and fats	5,227
53	Dyeing, tanning, and coloring materials	11,418
61	Leather, leather manufactures, n.e.s. and dressed furskins	6,264
66	Non-metallic mineral manufactures, n.e.s.	11,588
67	Iron and steel	10,121
72	Machinery specialized for particular industries	12,573
75	Office machines and automatic data processing equipment	14,739
77	Electrical machinery, apparatus and appliances, n.e.s	11,225
78	Road vehicles (including air cushion vehicles)	15,639
85	Footwear	7,713
89	Miscellaneous manufactured articles, n.e.s.	11,880
93	United Nations Special Code	7,464
	All imports	9,977

Source: Authors.

Note: n.e.s. = not elsewhere specified; PRODY = index that ranks traded goods by their implied productivity.

calculates PRODY for each four-digit SITC industry using average bilateral trade and average GDPPC data from 2000 through 2004.

The idea behind PRODY is that some traded goods are associated with higher productivity levels than others. The PRODY index is a quantitative index that ranks traded goods by their implied productivity. The country-level PRODY is the income level of a country's exports. It is meant to capture the notion that countries that export higher productivity goods will perform better. That is, if the PRODY level of the export basket is above

Table 6.8 Relatively Low-Growth LAC Industries

Two-digit code	Industry name	PRODY
04	Cereals and cereal preparations	7,683
21	Hides, skins, and furskins, raw	4,353
52	Inorganic chemicals	7,813
69	Manufactures of metal, n.e.s.	11,907
84	Articles of apparel and clothing accessories	4,962
	All imports	6,609

Source: Authors.
Note: n.e.s. = Not elsewhere specified; PRODY = index that ranks traded goods by their implied productivity.

a country's per capita income, the country will likely grow relatively fast. This has certainly been the case for China.

Some potential problems are that even a four-digit disaggregation may not correctly capture the type of good being produced. In addition, it should really be a measure of value added of exports as opposed to total exports.

Using this measure, the top two panels of table 6.9 report the five products associated with the lowest and highest PRODY at the four-digit level. Sisal and similar fibers is the lowest with an average PRODY of $886 and sheet piling of iron and steel is the highest with a level of $35,599. Both of these are among the categories Hausman, Hwang, and Rodrik (2005) also find using Harmonized System six-digit data. The lower two panels of table 6.9 report the two-digit categories that are associated with the highest and lowest levels of exporter income, where each four-digit PRODY is weighted by LAC's share of trade in that category. Thus, these are the two-digit categories where LAC is primarily competing with low-income or high-income exporters.

Overall, LAC exports in the period 2000–04 are characterized using this index. The analysis creates a trade-weighted average of the index by LAC exports. For 2000–04, LAC exports have an average PRODY of $9,128, which implies that LAC's exports on average are representative of exporters with a per capita real income of $9,128. The average per capita income in LAC, weighted by exports, is $8,143, indicating that LAC exports are somewhat above LAC's income level.[6] How the level of their exports has changed over time can also be examined. Holding values of PRODY constant and weighting those values by LAC trade shares in 1990–94, the average PRODY is $8,007—about 14 percent lower—indicating that LAC has moved toward relatively high-wage products in the past 10 years (table 6.9).[7]

Table 6.9 Low-Income and High-Income Industries

Product code	Product name	PRODY
Low-income four-digit products		
2654	Sisal, agave fibers, raw or processed but not spun, and waste	886
2713	Natural calcium phosphates, natural aluminium, etc	1,018
6642	Optical glass and elements of optical glass (unworked)	1,131
12	Sheep and goats, live	1,137
2922	Natural gums, resins, lacs, and balsams	1,145
High income four-digit products		
7913	Mechanically propelled railway, tramway, trolleys, etc.	24,738
113	Pig meat fresh, chilled, or frozen	25,223
6647	Safety glass consisting of toughened or laminated glass, cut or not	25,300
6572	Bonded fiber fabrics, etc., whether or not impregnated or coated	29,638
6733	Angles, shapes, sections, and sheet piling, of iron or steel	35,599
Low-income and high-income two-digit products (four-digit weighted by LAC share of trade)		
Low-income two-digit products		
7	Coffee, tea, cocoa, spices, manufactures thereof	2,732
12	Tobacco and tobacco manufactures	3,445
94	Animals, live, zoo animals, dogs, cats, etc.	2,252
95	Arms, of war and ammunition thereof	2,196
96	Coin (other than gold), not being legal tender	3,364
High-income two-digit products		
2	Dairy products and birds' eggs	16,041
54	Medicinal and pharmaceutical products	19,654
71	Power-generating machinery and equipment	14,324
75	Office machines and automatic data processing equipment	14,739
78	Road vehicles (including air cushion vehicles)	15,639

Source: Authors.

Table 6.10 also reports the real wage level of China's exports. It is slightly above that of LAC, and growing somewhat faster, increasing by nearly 20 percent between the 1990–94 period and the 2000–04 period. Most interesting is that the PRODY level of China's exports is more than double China's real income level in 2000–04. Rodrik (2006) argues that the structure of China's exports, heavily geared to relatively high-wage, high-productivity products, helps to explain China's success, and is at least partly a result of industrial policy.

Examining the LAC subregions in more detail reveals a much higher value of PRODY for Mexico, in part explaining that country's more intense competition with China. The two countries are producing the same types of goods. Of interest, the Caribbean shows a slight decline in PRODY, implying that that subregion is not moving up the value chain. This result could also reflect relatively faster trade growth among the low-income countries in the Caribbean. In any case, there is no evidence that the Caribbean is moving into high productivity goods.[8]

Next, the analysis looks at the LAC trade-weighted average PRODY of the three groups of products defined above: (a) the products in which China is displacing LAC, (b) the products in which LAC is expanding, and (c) the products in which LAC is contracting. The results for the products where China is displacing LAC are reported in table 6.6. These products tend to be products that are high wage. Of the 15, 11 are products with PRODY above LAC average PRODY. Specifically, the trade-weighted average PRODY of this group of products is $11,208, well above LAC's average PRODY of $9,128. This implies that competition from China is mainly in the relatively high-wage products that LAC exports.[9]

Table 6.10 The Average PRODY of Exports (US$)

Region or country	1990–94	2000–04
LAC	8,143	9,128
South America	7,312	7,764
Central America	6,169	7,302
Caribbean	6,661	6,574
Mexico	10,451	11,389
China	8,308	9,963
World	10,679	11,108

Source: Authors' calculations.
Note: Averages were calculated using the PRODY index in 2000–04 weighted by the region's or country's average industrial trade share over the period.

Table 6.7 reports the values of the PRODY index for the group (b) products, where LAC exports are expanding more rapidly than the rest of the world. In 10 of the 19 products, the average PRODY is above the average for LAC. The trade-weighted average is nearly $10,000, slightly above the overall average for LAC, though not as high as the products threatened by China.

Table 6.8 reports the values of PRODY for group (c), the low-growth LAC products. All but one—manufactures of metal (also a China threat product)—are products that are below LAC's average. Weighted by LAC's trade, the average value of PRODY is $6,609, well below LAC's average PRODY.

Overall, the results indicate that LAC is moving to high-wage products, though at a slow rate, especially when compared with China. There is some evidence that China is depressing LAC's upward movement because China is displacing LAC in relatively high-wage industries.

Conclusion

China's tremendous trade growth in recent years has had a large effect on the global economy. This chapter has explored the effect of China on the exports of LAC countries. The main findings are (a) China's export growth has had only small effects on overall LAC exports, (b) China's export growth is primarily affecting Mexican export growth in industrial goods in Western Hemisphere markets, and (c) China's export growth is negatively affecting LAC exports of relatively high-wage goods.

Annex

Table 6A.1 Determinants of LAC Exports: Two-Digit Industry Effects

		dlnimports	t-stat	dlnCHN	t-stat	Observations	R-squared
code01	Meat and meat preparations	0.838***	[3.79]	−0.654	[1.30]	2,124	0.32
code02	Dairy products and birds' eggs	0.211	[1.48]	−9.775	[1.47]	178	0.75
code03	Fish, crustaceans, mollusk, preparations thereof	1.291***	[16.16]	0.095	[0.31]	14,348	0.25
code04	Cereals and cereal preparations	0.876***	[5.95]	−0.897***	[3.22]	4,519	0.57
code05	Vegetables and fruit	1.068***	[15.22]	0.155	[0.93]	29,922	0.25
code06	Sugar, sugar preparations, and honey	1.061***	[12.43]	0.338	[0.91]	5,352	0.41
code07	Coffee, tea, cocoa, spices, manufactures thereof	1.032***	[14.27]	0.232	[0.55]	10,426	0.55
code08	Feeding stuff for animals, not including unmil. cereals	1.303***	[6.98]	−0.383	[0.93]	2,666	0.30
code09	Miscellaneous edible products and preparations	1.016***	[8.32]	−2.263	[1.13]	5,194	0.42
code11	Beverages	1.339***	[6.42]	−94.670***	[2.99]	7,332	0.59
code12	Tobacco and tobacco manufactures	0.989***	[13.85]	−0.343	[0.97]	2,631	0.40
code21	Hides, skins, and furskins, raw	0.781***	[4.41]	−0.209	[0.34]	1,122	0.50
code22	Oil seeds and oleaginous fruit	1.369***	[6.88]	−1.185	[0.94]	2,999	0.35
code23	Crude rubber (including synthetic and reclaimed)	1.993***	[4.94]	−0.754	[0.35]	844	0.39
code24	Cork and wood	1.338***	[4.91]	−0.883	[0.76]	4,408	0.36
code25	Pulp and waste paper	1.044***	[4.47]	−1.640	[0.56]	349	0.71
code26	Textile fibers (except wool tops) and their wastes	0.971***	[7.03]	−0.605**	[2.14]	5,088	0.46

(continued)

Table 6A.1 Determinants of LAC Exports: Two-Digit Industry Effects (continued)

		dlnimports	t-stat	dlnCHN	t-stat	Observations	R-squared
code27	Crude fertilizers and crude materials (excluding coal)	1.275***	[9.42]	0.164	[0.85]	5,467	0.30
code28	Metalliferous ores and metal scrap	0.817***	[6.21]	0.245	[0.55]	4,307	0.36
code29	Crude animal and vegetable materials, n.e.s.	0.783***	[12.83]	0.454	[1.41]	15,957	0.20
code32	Coal, coke, and briquettes	1.374***	[6.30]	0.129	[0.14]	348	0.43
code33	Petroleum, petroleum products, and related materials	0.877***	[4.09]	0.278	[0.35]	2,178	0.71
code34	Gas, natural and manufactured	2.626	[0.76]	−1,975.76	[0.25]	51	0.94
code41	Animal oils and fats	1.282***	[4.00]	−3.944	[1.14]	238	0.77
code42	Fixed vegetable oils and fats	1.041***	[10.14]	0.237	[1.53]	1,370	0.60
code43	Animal–vegetable oils–fats, processed, and waxes	0.983***	[6.02]	0.192	[0.54]	781	0.40
code51	Organic chemicals	1.136***	[7.86]	0.282	[0.34]	20,621	0.19
code52	Inorganic chemicals	0.764***	[5.46]	0.230	[0.70]	12,181	0.20
code53	Dyeing, tanning, and coloring materials	1.355***	[5.76]	0.556**	[2.42]	9,069	0.25
code54	Medicinal and pharmaceutical products	1.074***	[24.04]	0.590	[1.19]	12,326	0.48
code55	Essential oils and perfume materials; toilet–cleansing materials	0.984***	[8.16]	0.200	[0.60]	11,875	0.25
code56	Fertilizers, manufactured	0.617	[0.96]	−0.713	[0.69]	692	0.31
code57	Explosives and pyrotechnic products	0.935***	[3.28]	0.321	[1.28]	359	0.47
code58	Artificial resins, plastic materials, cellulose esters/ethers	1.130***	[14.90]	0.175	[0.40]	14,626	0.21
code59	Chemical materials and products, n.e.s.	1.080***	[11.75]	0.058	[0.21]	11,947	0.20

(continued)

Table 6A.1 Determinants of LAC Exports: Two-Digit Industry Effects (continued)

		dlnimports	t-stat	dlnCHN	t-stat	Observations	R-squared
code61	Leather, leather manufactures, n.e.s. and dressed furskins	1.626***	[7.05]	−0.678*	[1.93]	9,711	0.35
code62	Rubber manufactures, n.e.s.	1.109***	[16.28]	−0.931**	[2.07]	13,565	0.23
code63	Cork and wood manufactures (excluding furniture)	1.118***	[11.16]	−0.038	[0.08]	11,230	0.31
code64	Paper, paperboard, articles of paper, paper-pulp/board	1.319***	[8.04]	−0.896*	[1.69]	14,675	0.28
code65	Textile yarn, fabrics, made-up articles, related products	1.072***	[26.33]	−0.474***	[3.10]	44,382	0.25
code66	Nonmetallic mineral manufactures, n.e.s.	1.125***	[16.17]	0.547*	[1.86]	33,826	0.26
code67	Iron and steel	1.253***	[11.86]	−0.100	[0.61]	12,457	0.25
code68	Nonferrous metals	1.088***	[13.84]	−0.046	[0.22]	6,863	0.35
code69	Manufactures of metal, n.e.s.	0.969***	[15.05]	−0.400***	[2.60]	45,687	0.18
code71	Power-generating machinery and equipment	0.681***	[8.02]	−1.100	[1.59]	11,553	0.45
code72	Machinery specialized for particular industries	1.057***	[10.41]	−0.022	[0.10]	19,186	0.26
code73	Metalworking machinery	1.544***	[4.52]	−1.431	[1.17]	5,592	0.19
code74	General industrial machinery and equipment, and parts	1.087***	[14.92]	−1.085**	[2.55]	39,228	0.24
code75	Office machines and automatic data processing equipment	1.371***	[6.48]	−0.718	[0.87]	16,580	0.51
code76	Telecommunications and sound recording apparatus	1.077***	[9.10]	−1.052**	[2.22]	16,360	0.35
code77	Electrical machinery, apparatus, and appliances, n.e.s	2.346***	[3.53]	−0.874*	[1.69]	44,119	0.52
code78	Road vehicles (including air cushion vehicles)	1.167***	[14.49]	0.762*	[1.77]	11,360	0.34

(continued)

Table 6A.1 Determinants of LAC Exports: Two-Digit Industry Effects *(continued)*

		dlnimports	t-stat	dlnCHN	t-stat	Observations	R-squared
code79	Other transport equipment	1.159***	[3.24]	−2.372***	[3.30]	2,456	0.45
code81	Sanitary, plumbing, heating, and lighting fixtures	0.885***	[7.34]	0.214	[0.73]	4,106	0.34
code82	Furniture and parts thereof	1.479***	[3.17]	−2.066**	[2.32]	10,504	0.37
code83	Travel goods, handbags, and similar containers	1.088***	[8.08]	0.543	[0.95]	5,462	0.47
code84	Articles of apparel and clothing accessories	0.994***	[24.82]	0.027	[0.25]	67,619	0.30
code85	Footwear	1.190***	[21.47]	0.055	[0.24]	5,373	0.51
code87	Professional, scientific, and controlling instruments	1.087***	[7.27]	−1.630	[1.25]	20,883	0.29
code88	Photographic apparatus, optical goods, watches	1.227***	[7.15]	0.283	[0.81]	10,608	0.22
code89	Miscellaneous manufactured articles, n.e.s.	0.928***	[10.51]	−0.286	[0.97]	69,587	0.33
code91	United Nations Special Code	1.418	[1.57]	−120.444	[0.90]	355	0.86
code93	United Nations Special Code	1.318***	[6.64]	−3.303	[0.96]	6,066	0.75
code94	Animals, live, zoo animals, dogs, cats, etc.	0.733***	[2.88]	−0.374	[0.38]	1,778	0.57
code95	Arms, of war and ammunition thereof	0.821***	[3.26]	0.563	[1.49]	497	0.63
code96	Coin (other than gold), not being legal tender	−0.153	[0.08]	−5.500	[0.16]	147	0.97
code97	Gold, nonmonetary except ore	−0.547	[0.47]	36.267	[0.35]	394	0.85

Source: Authors.

Note: n.e.s. = not elsewhere specified. Exporter-two-digit product-year fixed effects are included in all regressions. For weighted least squares, weights equal trade value.

* Significant at 10 percent.
** Significant at 5 percent.
*** Significant at 1 percent.

Table 6A.2 Determinants of LAC Exports: Two-Digit and Period Effects

		dlnimp_8694	t-stat	dlnimp_9504	t-stat	dlnCHN_8694	t-stat	dlnCHN_9504	t-stat	Observations	R-squared
code01	Meat and meat preparations	0.905***	[8.52]	0.822***	[3.01]	0.200	[0.72]	−0.877	[1.45]	2,124	0.32
code02	Dairy products and birds' eggs	3.147	[0.79]	0.187	[1.34]	12.138	[0.23]	−10.646	[1.59]	178	0.77
code03	Fish, crustaceans, mollusk, preparations thereof	1.506***	[9.20]	1.152***	[17.23]	0.519	[0.75]	0.140	[0.41]	14,348	0.26
code04	Cereals and cereal preparations	1.062***	[4.51]	0.852***	[5.05]	−1.227	[1.25]	−0.929***	[3.09]	4,519	0.57
code05	Vegetables and fruit	1.283***	[7.50]	0.939***	[21.35]	0.332	[0.59]	0.084	[0.50]	29,922	0.25
code06	Sugar, sugar preparations, and honey	1.093***	[8.12]	1.070***	[10.54]	−0.406	[0.68]	0.587	[1.27]	5,352	0.41
code07	Coffee, tea, cocoa, spices, manufactures thereof	1.017***	[8.21]	1.048***	[12.72]	1.311	[0.99]	0.030	[0.07]	10,426	0.55
code08	Feeding stuff for animals, not including unmil. cereals	1.638***	[4.62]	1.103***	[5.69]	−0.820	[1.55]	0.037	[0.08]	2,666	0.31
code09	Miscellaneous edible products and preparations	0.950***	[6.31]	1.036***	[7.44]	−0.136	[0.07]	−6.954	[1.42]	5,194	0.42
code11	Beverages	1.346***	[5.26]	1.271***	[5.11]	19.658**	[2.12]	−97.164***	[3.08]	7,332	0.59
code12	Tobacco and tobacco manufactures	0.827***	[6.31]	1.023***	[12.31]	−0.097	[0.09]	−0.336	[0.91]	2,631	0.40
code21	Hides, skins, and furskins, raw	0.721**	[2.09]	0.771***	[3.96]	−0.577	[0.81]	2.406	[1.22]	1,122	0.50

(continued)

Table 6A.2 Determinants of LAC Exports: Two-Digit and Period Effects *(continued)*

		dlnimp_8694	t-stat	dlnimp_9504	t-stat	dlnCHN_8694	t-stat	dlnCHN_9504	t-stat	Observations	R-squared
code22	Oil seeds and oleaginous fruit	2.333***	[5.61]	1.040***	[5.69]	-1.355	[0.79]	0.017	[0.04]	2,999	0.37
code23	Crude rubber (including synthetic and reclaimed)	1.949***	[2.85]	1.999***	[4.54]	63.532**	[2.43]	-1.390	[0.57]	844	0.40
code24	Cork and wood	0.621*	[1.90]	1.450***	[4.63]	14.965	[1.47]	-1.186	[0.95]	4,408	0.37
code25	Pulp and waste paper	1.450**	[2.00]	0.977***	[4.05]	-4.199	[1.43]	-0.800	[0.18]	349	0.71
code26	Textile fibers (except wool tops) and their wastes	0.817***	[4.78]	1.229***	[6.11]	-0.345*	[1.75]	-1.098	[1.36]	5,088	0.46
code27	Crude fertilizers and crude materials (excluding coal)	0.869***	[4.91]	1.452***	[8.64]	0.427**	[2.21]	-0.139	[0.43]	5,467	0.31
code28	Metalliferous ores and metal scrap	0.833***	[4.92]	0.806***	[4.67]	-0.943	[0.88]	0.388	[0.81]	4,307	0.36
code29	Crude animal and vegetable materials, n.e.s.	0.809***	[9.33]	0.770***	[9.42]	1.058	[1.20]	0.274	[0.84]	15,957	0.20
code32	Coal, coke, and briquettes	1.954***	[3.41]	1.333***	[5.93]	5.865**	[2.11]	0.028	[0.03]	348	0.44
code33	Petroleum, petroleum products, and related materials	0.570*	[1.93]	1.177***	[3.95]	-0.578	[0.21]	0.475	[1.03]	2,178	0.71
code34	Gas, natural and manufactured	0.000	[.]	2.626	[0.76]	0.000	[.]	-1,975.760	[0.25]	51	0.94
code41	Animal oils and fats	0.000	[.]	1.282***	[4.00]	0.000	[.]	-3.944	[1.14]	238	0.77

(continued)

209

Table 6A.2 Determinants of LAC Exports: Two-Digit and Period Effects (*continued*)

		dlnimp_8694	t-stat	dlnimp_9504	t-stat	dlnCHN_8694	t-stat	dlnCHN_9504	t-stat	Observations	R-squared
code42	Fixed vegetable oils and fats	0.903***	[5.81]	1.142***	[9.08]	0.303**	[2.15]	−0.229	[0.72]	1,370	0.60
code43	Animal–vegetable oils–fats, processed, and waxes	1.241***	[6.29]	0.871***	[4.04]	0.244	[0.39]	0.136	[0.31]	781	0.40
code51	Organic chemicals	1.271***	[9.14]	1.066***	[5.08]	−1.422	[0.90]	0.418	[0.46]	20,621	0.19
code52	Inorganic chemicals	1.068***	[6.48]	0.663***	[4.01]	0.237	[0.39]	0.206	[0.55]	12,181	0.20
code53	Dyeing, tanning, and coloring materials	0.671***	[4.27]	1.721***	[5.14]	4.737**	[1.96]	0.594***	[2.77]	9,069	0.26
code54	Medicinal and pharmaceutical products	1.151***	[7.49]	1.055***	[22.17]	0.031	[0.08]	1.615	[1.37]	12,326	0.48
code55	Essential oils and perfume materials; toilet–cleansing materials	1.306***	[8.85]	0.930***	[7.02]	0.312	[0.71]	−0.045	[0.10]	11,875	0.26
code56	Fertilizers, manufactured	−0.128	[0.28]	0.659	[0.99]	98.505***	[2.76]	−0.725	[0.70]	692	0.31
code57	Explosives and pyrotechnic products	−0.188	[0.55]	1.036***	[3.27]	1.556	[1.53]	0.317	[1.24]	359	0.48
code58	Artificial resins, plastic materials, cellulose esters/ethers	1.201***	[6.67]	1.111***	[13.47]	−1.206	[0.71]	0.392	[0.83]	14,626	0.21
code59	Chemical materials and products, n.e.s.	0.975***	[4.85]	1.099***	[11.05]	1.160**	[2.02]	−0.240	[0.80]	11,947	0.20
code61	Leather, leather manufactures, n.e.s., and dressed furskins	1.328***	[10.37]	1.776***	[5.52]	0.024	[5.52]	−1.004**	[2.19]	9,711	0.35

(*continued*)

Table 6A.2 Determinants of LAC Exports: Two-Digit and Period Effects (continued)

	dlnimp_8694	t-stat	dlnimp_9504	t-stat	dlnCHN_8694	t-stat	dlnCHN_9504	t-stat	Observations	R-squared
code62 Rubber manufactures, n.e.s.	1.230***	[8.94]	1.069***	[14.68]	-0.223	[0.17]	-0.874*	[1.84]	13,565	0.23
code63 Cork and wood manufactures (excluding furniture)	1.055***	[7.60]	1.157***	[8.31]	2.523**	[2.55]	-0.218	[0.44]	11,230	0.31
code64 Paper, paperboard, articles of paper, paper-pulp/board	1.629***	[3.78]	1.161***	[9.34]	0.630	[0.49]	-1.061*	[1.90]	14,675	0.28
code65 Textile yarn, fabrics, made-up articles, related products	1.264***	[15.62]	0.953***	[25.48]	-0.218	[0.72]	-0.579***	[3.42]	44,382	0.25
code66 Nonmetallic mineral manufactures, n.e.s.	1.134***	[6.46]	1.123***	[16.52]	0.818**	[2.49]	0.504	[1.50]	33,826	0.26
code67 Iron and steel	1.245***	[8.14]	1.268***	[9.65]	0.323*	[1.67]	-0.315*	[1.67]	12,457	0.25
code68 Nonferrous metals	1.286***	[10.73]	1.012***	[10.40]	0.074	[0.16]	-0.046	[0.21]	6,863	0.35
code69 Manufactures of metal, n.e.s.	1.236***	[9.94]	0.875***	[12.44]	-0.234	[0.42]	-0.391**	[2.41]	45,687	0.19
code71 Power-generating machinery and equipment	0.605***	[5.00]	0.712***	[6.46]	5.249*	[1.82]	-1.384*	[1.71]	11,553	0.45
code72 Machinery specialized for particular industries	1.149***	[8.63]	1.021***	[7.91]	0.079	[0.95]	-0.052	[0.20]	19,186	0.26
code73 Metalworking machinery	1.820***	[2.93]	1.402***	[3.67]	-1.811	[0.38]	-1.404	[1.12]	5,592	0.20
code74 General industrial machinery and equipment, and parts	1.350***	[8.15]	0.952***	[13.52]	-2.362**	[2.52]	-0.929**	[2.06]	39,228	0.24
code75 Office machines and automatic data processing equipment	0.385	[1.25]	1.527***	[6.42]	-3.943**	[1.68]	-0.695	[0.80]	16,580	0.51

(continued)

Table 6A.2 Determinants of LAC Exports: Two-Digit and Period Effects *(continued)*

		dlnimp_8694	t-stat	dlnimp_9504	t-stat	dlnCHN_8694	t-stat	dlnCHN_9504	t-stat	Observations	R-squared
code76	Telecommunications and sound recording apparatus	1.285***	[3.43]	1.032***	[8.78]	0.572	[0.31]	−1.233***	[2.64]	16,360	0.35
code77	Electrical machinery, apparatus, and appliances, n.e.s	0.830***	[6.52]	2.543***	[3.70]	−0.191	[0.36]	−1.115*	[1.85]	44,119	0.54
code78	Road vehicles (including air cushion vehicles)	1.049***	[9.96]	1.189***	[12.62]	0.312	[0.53]	0.770*	[1.71]	11,360	0.34
code79	Other transport equipment	0.408*	[1.95]	1.480***	[3.14]	−0.608	[0.35]	−2.383***	[3.65]	2,456	0.47
code81	Sanitary, plumbing, heating, and lighting fixtures	1.153***	[3.52]	0.854***	[7.30]	1.248**	[2.24]	0.145	[0.46]	4,106	0.34
code82	Furniture and parts thereof	1.050***	[5.90]	1.628***	[2.80]	−1.871*	[1.66]	−2.063**	[2.28]	10,504	0.37
code83	Travel goods, handbags, and similar containers	1.435***	[5.90]	0.974***	[5.96]	−1.868	[1.08]	0.982*	[1.70]	5,462	0.48
code84	Articles of apparel and clothing accessories	1.219***	[14.67]	0.854***	[25.60]	−0.551*	[1.88]	0.175	[1.62]	67,619	0.31
code85	Footwear	1.259***	[9.17]	1.167***	[21.14]	0.283	[0.58]	−0.012	[0.05]	5,373	0.51
code87	Professional, scientific, and controlling instruments	1.034***	[4.97]	1.066***	[5.58]	−6.165**	[2.17]	−0.770	[0.61]	20,883	0.30
code88	Photographic apparatus, optical goods, watches	2.322***	[3.78]	0.991***	[7.03]	0.228	[0.99]	0.666	[1.03]	10,608	0.23
code89	Miscellaneous manufactured articles, n.e.s.	0.710***	[4.36]	1.079***	[12.57]	−0.952**	[2.14]	−0.006	[0.01]	69,587	0.34

(continued)

Table 6A.2 Determinants of LAC Exports: Two-Digit and Period Effects (continued)

	dlnimp_8694	t-stat	dlnimp_9504	t-stat	dlnCHN_8694	t-stat	dlnCHN_9504	t-stat	Observations	R-squared
code91 United Nations Special Code	1.418	[1.57]	0.000	[.]	−120.444	[0.90]	0.000	[.]	355	0.86
code93 United Nations Special Code	1.634***	[9.95]	0.978***	[5.18]	2.273	[0.46]	−2.348	[0.59]	6,066	0.75
code94 Animals, live, zoo animals, dogs, cats, etc.	0.828***	[2.84]	0.782**	[1.96]	−2.946	[1.43]	0.071	[0.07]	1,778	0.57
code95 Arms, of war and ammunition thereof	0.311	[0.97]	1.066***	[3.52]	0.603	[0.13]	0.642*	[1.91]	497	0.63
code96 Coin (other than gold), not being legal tender	1.231	[0.33]	−0.049	[0.03]	−49.217	[1.25]	12.295	[0.41]	147	0.98
code97 Gold, nonmonetary except ore	−14.216	[0.83]	−0.118	[0.12†]	57.985	[0.24]	104.934	[0.73]	394	0.88

Source: Authors.

Note: n.e.s. = not elsewhere specified. Exporter-two-digit product-year fixed effects are included in all regressions. For weighted least squares, weights equal trade value.

* Significant at 10 percent.

** Significant at 5 percent.

*** Significant at 1 percent.

Notes

1. Measured using balance-of-payments data in current U.S. dollars, Latin American exports increased by 470 percent.

2. There is potential concern resulting from the possibility that China may be exporting more because LAC exports are declining or that China's exports and LAC exports are responding to a third factor. Given the surge of China's exports over the period, the former is unlikely to be a major issue. On the second issue our hope is that including imports from other countries (non-LAC, non-China) will control for these other factors. Ideally, we would like to use instruments representing the increased supply of China; unfortunately, we do not have them at the necessary level of disaggregation. Eichengreen, Rhee, and Tong (2007) use a distance measure (and a time-varying distance measure) as an instrument, though that does not quite serve our purpose, given the disaggregation and the set of fixed effects we include.

3. The sum of the coefficients on dlnChina and dlnCHN_NA is significantly different from zero. Because the coefficient on dlnChina is close to zero, the effect in North America is roughly 0.95.

4. See U.S. GAO (2003) and Dussel Peters (2005).

5. Import growth in this specification is import growth from the world.

6. Using the same data, this is calculated as the sum over the LAC countries in the sample of (share of LAC total exports) × (GDPPC at purchasing power parity).

7. We hold PRODY constant because otherwise it would not be clear if changes in a region's export structure over time are actually due to changes in the region's export structure or to changes in the classification of the industries. Although the rank of the industries is largely constant over time, the wage associated with most industries has fallen as a result of more trade by China and other low-income countries.

8. Using world export shares, the average value of PRODY over this period increased from $10,679 to $11,108, only a 4 percent rise. In part, this is due to the large increase in exports by poor countries that compete primarily in low PRODY products.

9. Lall and Weiss (2005) make a related point—that China's expansion into high-tech products may have limited the scope for Latin American expansion in these types of products.

References

Devlin, Robert, Antoni Estevadeordal, and Andres Rodríguez, eds. 2006. *The Emergence of China: Opportunities and Challenges for Latin America and the Caribbean.* Washington, DC: Inter-American Development Bank.

Dussel Peters, E. 2005. "The Implications of China's Entry into the WTO for Mexico." Global Issues Papers 24, Heinrich Böll Foundation, Berlin.

Eichengreen, B., Y. Rhee, and H. Tong. 2007. "China and the Exports of Other Asian Countries." *Review of World Economics/Weltwirtschaftliches Archiv* 143 (2): 201–26.

Hanson, Gordon, and Raymond Robertson. 2006. "China and the Recent Evolution of Mexico's Manufacturing Exports." Unpublished, University of California at San Diego and National Bureau of Economic Research.

Hausman, R., J. Hwang, and D. Rodrik. 2005. "What You Export Matters." NBER Working Paper 11905, National Bureau of Economic Research, Cambridge, MA.

Lall, S., and John Weiss. 2005. "China's Competitive Threat to Latin America: An Analysis for 1990–2002." QEH Working Paper 120, Queen Elizabeth House, Oxford University, UK.

Quintin, E. 2004. "Mexico's Export Woes Not All China-Induced." *The Southwest Economy* 2004 (Nov): 9–10.

Rodrik, D. 2006. "What's So Special About China's Exports?" NBER Working Paper 11947, National Bureau of Economic Research, Cambridge, MA.

U.S. GAO (United States General Accounting Office). 2003. "Mexico's Maquiladora Decline Affects U.S. Mexico Border Communities and Trade; Recovery Depends in Part on Mexico's Actions." Report to Congressional Requestors 03-891, Washington, DC.

7
_____

Effects on Services Trade with the United States

Caroline Freund

Introduction

The goal of this analysis is to see how services exports of Latin America and the Caribbean (LAC) compete with those from China and India. Because consistent bilateral time-series data are available for only the United States, trade in the U.S. market is the focus of this chapter. Although this means that the conclusions are specific to trade with the United States, the U.S. market is probably the most important market for LAC services providers. The analysis uses data on U.S. bilateral trade in services from 1986 through 2004. The data include imports and exports from China, India, Argentina, Bermuda, Brazil, Chile, Mexico, República Bolivariana de Venezuela, and other LAC countries (combined), as well about 30 other nations and regions.[1]

First, some simple summary statistics on services are calculated, including export growth, import growth, composition of services exports and imports, and share of intrafirm trade. These statistics show that South America, Central America, and Mexico lag behind China and India in services export and import growth. The only area in which LAC has performed well is travel, which comprises mainly tourism. In contrast, the Caribbean subregion has performed on par with China and India, though this is primarily due to large and growing services trade between the United States and offshore financial centers.

Second, an index of overall similarity in services imports and exports is calculated, based on the distribution of imports and exports across five broad categories of services trade and 16 classes of nontransport unaffiliated services trade.[2] The export index shows to what extent LAC countries are competing in the same sectors as China and India (at least, in the U.S. market). The import index provides information on whether China, India, and LAC are outsourcing services to the same extent. Among the broad categories, the structure of exports between LAC and both India and China appears to be similar and roughly stable. However, when a more detailed breakdown, available only for India, is examined, a sharp decline in export similarity with LAC countries is found.

Finally, the analysis examines the extent to which India and China have displaced LAC services exports to the United States. Some evidence is found of displacement by India in business services.

Data

Data on international services trade is from the U.S. Department of Commerce, Bureau of Economic Analysis, Balance of Payments Division. Services trade data are collected through quarterly surveys of large firms that trade in services. Services trade by small firms is estimated. Services trade is inherently different from goods trade in that it is measured as value added. Services data do not contain information on wholesale trade and retail trade industries that provide distributive services because these services are embedded in the value of goods sold. Table 7.1 defines the main services industries for which data are available.

Data on other private services are divided into two categories: affiliated and unaffiliated trade. Affiliated trade refers to trade between U.S. parents and their foreign affiliates and between U.S. affiliates and their foreign parents. For example, U.S. imports of computer-related services could be from unaffiliated foreigners or an affiliated firm (parent or subsidiary) located in a foreign country. Trade disaggregated beyond the five broad categories, however, is not broken down by country for affiliated firms. Therefore, when imports and exports of more detailed classifications are discussed, the focus is on trade between unaffiliated entities.

Unlike in manufactures, in which there has been a notable increase in intrafirm trade, U.S. services trade statistics do not record any strong trend. Affiliated exports made up one-third of total services exports in both 1994 and 2004; affiliated imports were nearly 40 percent over the same period (table 7.2). Trade in services with LAC remains predominantly between unrelated parties, though intrafirm trade with South America, Central America, and Mexico (SCM) is increasing (table 7.2). U.S. intrafirm imports from SCM have increased over the past 10 years from about 9 percent to 29 percent. Intrafirm trade has also increased for both China and India. In 2004, more than half of U.S. imports from China and 30 percent of imports from India were intrafirm. In contrast, the share that is intrafirm between the United States and the Caribbean (shown in the table as other Western Hemisphere Economies), largely the off-shore financial centers, has declined.

Table 7.1 Main Services Industries

Broad industry	Description
Travel	This includes purchases of goods and services by foreign residents.
Passenger fares	These include fares paid to one country by airline and vessel operators that reside in another country.
Other transportation	This includes payments for the transportation of goods by ocean, air, land (truck and rail), pipeline, and inland waterway carriers.
Royalties and license fees	These include payments for transactions with nonresidents that involve patented and unpatented techniques, processes, formulas, and other intangible assets and proprietary rights used in the production of goods; transactions involving trademarks, copyrights, franchises, broadcast rights, and other intangible rights; and the rights to distribute, use, and reproduce general-use computer software.
Other private services	These accounts consist of other affiliated and unaffiliated services. The unaffiliated services consist of six major categories: education; financial services; insurance; telecommunications; business, professional, and technical services; and "other unaffiliated services."
Unaffiliated sectors	
Education	This includes expenditures for tuition and living expenses of foreign students.
Financial services	These include payments for funds management, credit card services, explicit fees and commissions on transactions in securities, fees on credit-related activities, and other financial services. Implicit fees paid and received on bond trading are also covered.

(continued)

Table 7.1 Main Services Industries (*continued*)

Broad industry	Description
Insurance	This includes the portion of premiums earned or incurred for primary insurance and for reinsurance for the provision of services.
Telecommunications	This includes receipts and payments between U.S. and foreign communications companies for the transmission of messages between the United States and other countries; channel easing; telex, telegram, and other jointly provided basic services; value added services, such as electronic mail, video conferencing, and online access services (including Internet backbone services, router services, and broadband access services); and telecommunications support services.
Business, professional, and technical services	These include a variety of services, such as legal, accounting, advertising, and computer. See tables 7.4 and 7.5.
Other private services	U.S. receipts include expenditures (other than employee compensation) by foreign governments in the United States for services such as maintaining embassies and consulates; noncompensation-related expenditures by international organizations headquartered in the United States; expenditures of foreign residents employed temporarily in the United States; and receipts from unaffiliated foreigners for the display, reproduction, or distribution of motion pictures and television programs. Payments consist primarily of payments to unaffiliated foreign residents for the display, reproduction, or distribution of foreign motion pictures and television programs.

Source: Borga and Mann 2002.

Table 7.2 Share of Trade between Affiliated Firms, 1994 and 2004

	U.S. exports		U.S. imports	
	1994	2004	1994	2004
LAC and other Western Hemisphere economies	0.13	0.14	0.13	0.12
South America, Central America, and Mexico	0.10	0.13	0.09	0.29
Argentina	0.09	0.16	0.08	0.28
Brazil	0.15	0.18	0.17	0.38
Chile	0.08	0.09	0.02	..
Mexico	0.09	0.14	0.09	0.41
Venezuela, R. B. de	0.13	0.12	0.12	0.33
Other Western Hemisphere economies	0.24	0.15	0.18	0.08
Bermuda	0.40	0.17	0.19	0.04
China	0.04	0.15	0.15	0.56
India	0.00	0.05	0.06	0.30
All countries	0.33	0.33	0.39	0.38

Source: U.S. Department of Commerce.
Note: .. = negligible.

Basic Trends in Services Growth

Figure 7.1 shows U.S. imports and exports of total private services for the Caribbean, China, India, and SCM. Figure 7.2 shows import and export growth for these economies and the world. While the Caribbean, India, and China have outpaced world growth, SCM has lagged behind.

Total private services trade can be disaggregated into the following categories: travel, passenger fares, other transportation, royalties and license fees, and other private services. Figures 7.3 through 7.7 show U.S. import and export growth in these categories. SCM lags behind the world and other regions in all areas except for travel services. This indicates that SCM has grown faster than the rest of the world as a tourist destination for U.S. residents.

Unaffiliated trade in other services between the United States and its partner countries (not transport and not royalties and license fees) can be further broken down into 16 categories. This means that the analysis that involves trade by industry will exclude affiliated trade. An additional concern is that sometimes entries are left blank in the statistics to avoid disclosing individual company data.

Figure 7.8 shows total trade growth and growth of unaffiliated trade by region and country from 1994 to 2004. For most countries and

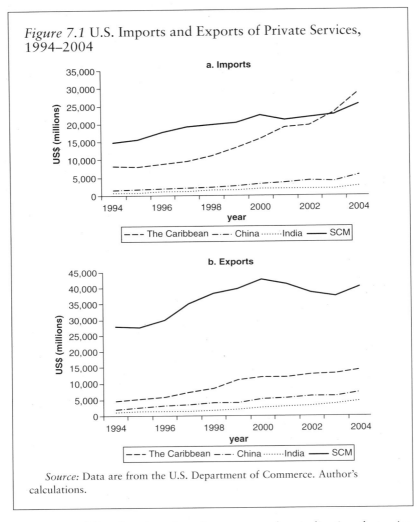

Figure 7.1 U.S. Imports and Exports of Private Services, 1994–2004

Source: Data are from the U.S. Department of Commerce. Author's calculations.

regions, unaffiliated and total trade move together, indicating that using unaffiliated trade to measure trends is not a bad approximation. However, Chinese and Mexican exports to the United States are an exception—total trade has grown, but there has been no growth in unaffiliated trade in services. In addition, unaffiliated U.S. exports to Chile have grown much more than total exports (which actually decreased over the period). This implies that the results drawn from unaffiliated trade must be viewed with some caution because a breakdown of trade in services by country and industry is only available for unaffiliated trade.

Figure 7.8 also highlights the rapid growth in the category entitled "other private services." U.S. imports of services have nearly tripled

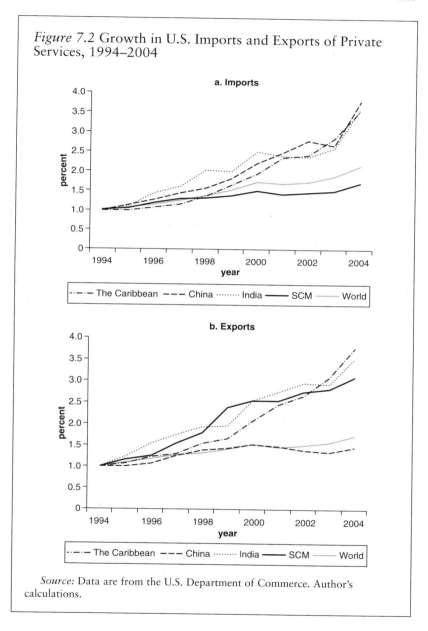

Figure 7.2 Growth in U.S. Imports and Exports of Private Services, 1994–2004

Source: Data are from the U.S. Department of Commerce. Author's calculations.

(growth of nearly 200 percent), and U.S. exports of services have more than doubled over the past 10 years. Growth in services imports from India has been exceptional, while growth in imports from LAC (and China) has been lower than overall services import growth.

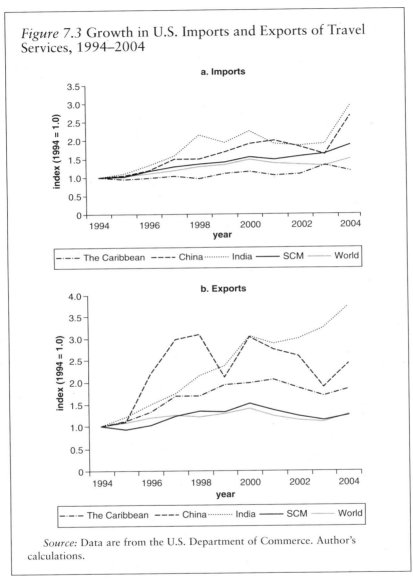

Figure 7.3 Growth in U.S. Imports and Exports of Travel Services, 1994–2004

a. Imports

b. Exports

Source: Data are from the U.S. Department of Commerce. Author's calculations.

Within "other private services," unaffiliated bilateral trade data can be disaggregated into data on education; financial services; insurance; tele-communications; business, professional, and technical services; and other services. Finally, "business, professional, and technical services" (BPT) can be broken down into advertising; computer and data processing services; database and other information services; research, development, and testing

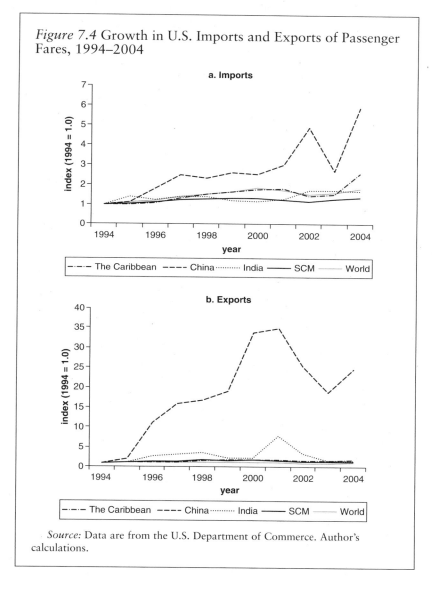

Figure 7.4 Growth in U.S. Imports and Exports of Passenger Fares, 1994–2004

a. Imports

b. Exports

Source: Data are from the U.S. Department of Commerce. Author's calculations.

services; management, consulting, and public relations services; legal services; construction, architectural, and engineering services; industrial engineering; installation, maintenance, and repair of equipment; operational leasing; and other BPT services.

Growth in trade in BPT services with India has been especially high, largely as a result of improved telecommunications and the expansion in

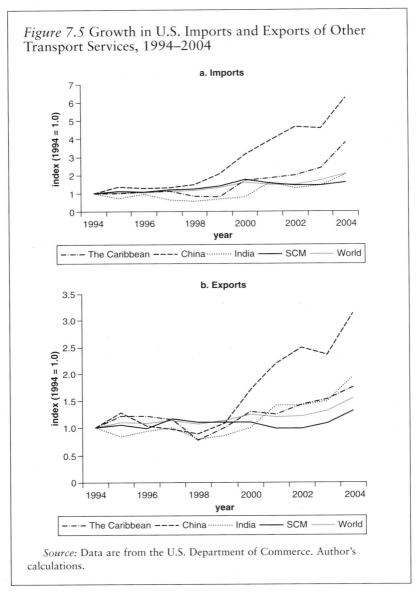

Figure 7.5 Growth in U.S. Imports and Exports of Other Transport Services, 1994–2004

a. Imports

b. Exports

Source: Data are from the U.S. Department of Commerce. Author's calculations.

new technologies, such as the Internet, which allow services to be provided from a distance (see Freund and Weinhold 2002). Figure 7.9 shows growth in BPT services imports and exports between 1994 and 2004. U.S. BPT services imports from India expanded by a factor of 25 since

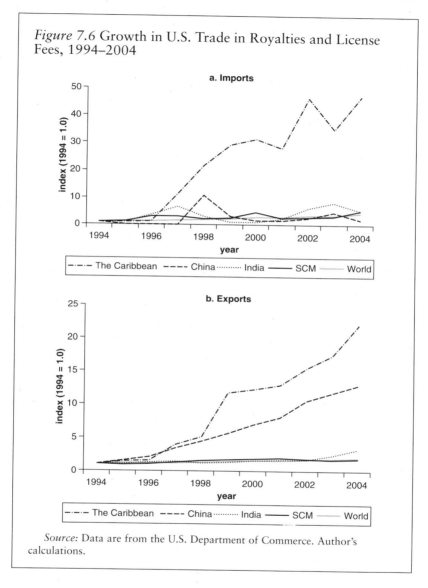

Figure 7.6 Growth in U.S. Trade in Royalties and License Fees, 1994–2004

a. Imports

index (1994 = 1.0)

year

--·-- The Caribbean ---- China ·········· India —— SCM —— World

b. Exports

index (1994 = 1.0)

year

--·-- The Caribbean ---- China ·········· India —— SCM —— World

Source: Data are from the U.S. Department of Commerce. Author's calculations.

1994, while import growth from LAC kept pace with world growth, at just above 200 percent. In 1994, Argentina and India both exported roughly US$20 million in BPT services to the United States. By 2004, India exported US$528 million in BPT services to the United States, or more than 50 percent of LAC's combined BPT services exports.

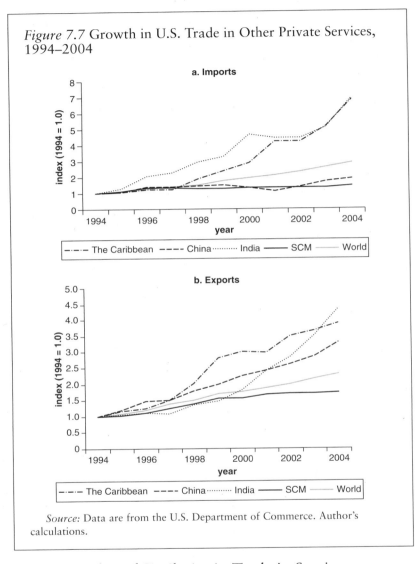

Figure 7.7 Growth in U.S. Trade in Other Private Services, 1994–2004

a. Imports

b. Exports

Source: Data are from the U.S. Department of Commerce. Author's calculations.

Index of Similarity in Trade in Services

This analysis uses the Finger and Kreinin (1979) index, as in the Devlin, Estevadeordal, and Rodríguez (2006) report on China and LAC. The index ranges from 0 to 100, where 0 represents no overlap in services trade and 100 indicates industry-country market shares are identical.[3]

First, an index is created of similarity for the five broad categories of overall trade. Figures 7.10 and 7.11 display the indexes for India and China,

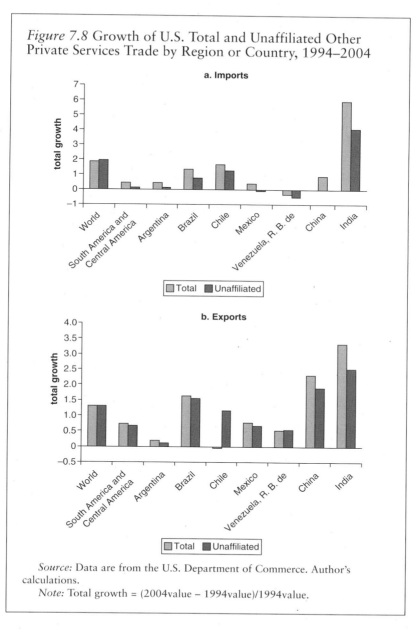

Figure 7.8 Growth of U.S. Total and Unaffiliated Other Private Services Trade by Region or Country, 1994–2004

a. Imports

b. Exports

Source: Data are from the U.S. Department of Commerce. Author's calculations.

Note: Total growth = (2004value − 1994value)/1994value.

respectively. Similarity in U.S. imports from SCM, from the Caribbean, and from both India and China in general declined from 1994 through 2004. LAC as a region shows an increase, but this is due to compositional effects between the Caribbean and SCM. As importers, however, despite

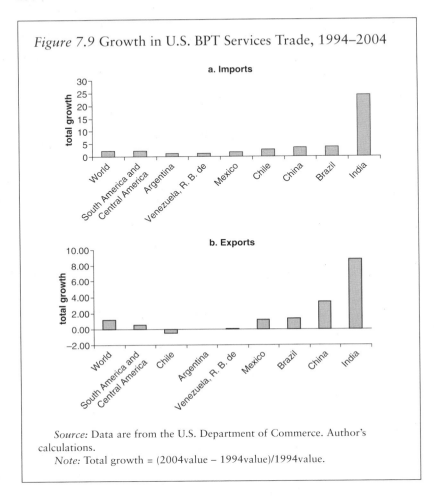

Figure 7.9 Growth in U.S. BPT Services Trade, 1994–2004

a. Imports

b. Exports

Source: Data are from the U.S. Department of Commerce. Author's calculations.
Note: Total growth = (2004value − 1994value)/1994value.

a recent decrease, the LAC regions have become more similar to China and India over the period. The increase is largely due to an increase in the "other private services" share of LAC imports.

The problem with these indexes is that only four categories of services were included. Next, the analysis looks at similarity in other private services (OPS), excluding affiliated company trade. Only trade with India is examined because missing data from China for many years and categories makes it impossible to provide an accurate comparison. Because most of Chinese trade in services with the United States is in transport, comparing similarities in trade in OPS is not very meaningful.

Figure 7.12 shows the indexes of similarity in OPS with India. Similarity in exports from LAC and India (U.S. imports) has declined markedly since

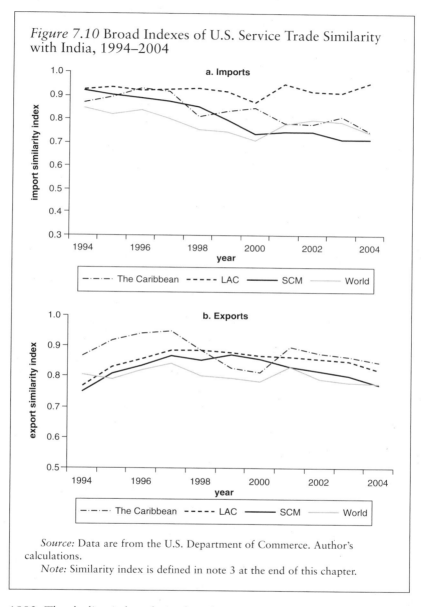

Figure 7.10 Broad Indexes of U.S. Service Trade Similarity with India, 1994–2004

Source: Data are from the U.S. Department of Commerce. Author's calculations.

Note: Similarity index is defined in note 3 at the end of this chapter.

1993. The decline is largely in the telecom sector and may be a result of privatization and the large decline in prices (and, hence, the value of trade) over this period. U.S. exports to LAC and India are not very similar and did not change much between 1993 and 2003.

Figure 7.13 shows similarity in BPT services since 1993. Again, a sharp decline is observed in similarity between LAC exports and

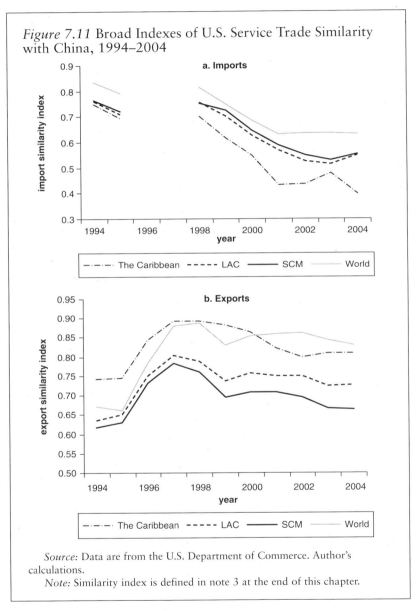

Figure 7.11 Broad Indexes of U.S. Service Trade Similarity with China, 1994–2004

Source: Data are from the U.S. Department of Commerce. Author's calculations.

Note: Similarity index is defined in note 3 at the end of this chapter.

exports from India (U.S. imports). This is largely due to the category "other private BPT services," which did not grow as rapidly in LAC countries as other service categories.

Figure 7.13 also shows that regarding importers of BPT services (U.S. exports), there is little change over the period in the similarity between LAC and India.

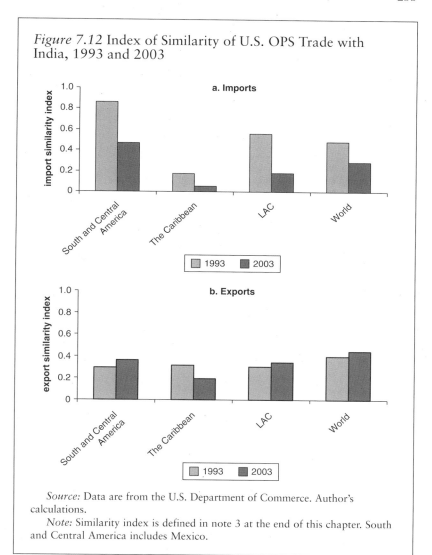

Figure 7.12 Index of Similarity of U.S. OPS Trade with India, 1993 and 2003

Source: Data are from the U.S. Department of Commerce. Author's calculations.

Note: Similarity index is defined in note 3 at the end of this chapter. South and Central America includes Mexico.

Regression Analysis—Is India Displacing Latin America?

The estimating equation follows from chapter 6 in this volume. It regresses bilateral export growth in an industry on importer, exporter, and year fixed effects, as well as on overall import growth and import growth from India. Specifically,

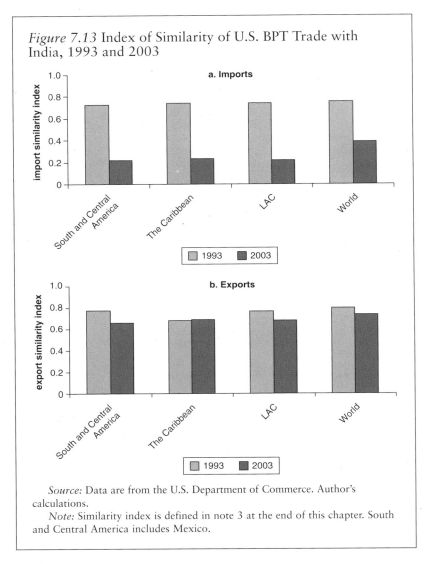

Figure 7.13 Index of Similarity of U.S. BPT Trade with India, 1993 and 2003

Source: Data are from the U.S. Department of Commerce. Author's calculations.

Note: Similarity index is defined in note 3 at the end of this chapter. South and Central America includes Mexico.

$$\text{d}\ln\exp_{ijt} = \gamma_i + \gamma_j + \gamma_t + \beta_1\text{d}\ln US_{jt} + \beta_2\text{d}\ln India_{jt} + \varepsilon_{ijt}, \qquad (7.1)$$

where d ln $\exp_{ijt}$ is the first difference of the natural log of exports from LAC country i in industry j to the United States at time t; γ_i is an exporter fixed effect that will pick up fixed country characteristics (or characteristics that change slowly), such as comparative advantage, geography, and remoteness; γ_j is an industry fixed effect that controls for high growth sectors, γ_t is a time fixed effect that will pick up overall export growth in a given year; d ln US_{jt} is import growth in the United States from countries other than India; d ln $India_{jt}$ is growth in Indian exports to the United States; and ε is an error term that is assumed to be independent and identically distributed. Alternative fixed effects are also tried.

A negative coefficient on d ln *India* indicates that Indian export growth is negatively correlated with LAC export growth, after controlling for growth from the rest of the world. This implies that Indian exports are displacing LAC exports to a greater extent than they are displacing exports from other countries. In particular, it is an elasticity, representing how a 1 percent increase in Indian exports is related to LAC exports, in percentages.

Because an increase in exports to India is likely to have a larger effect on LAC trade if India is a large exporter, the analysis also tries an alternative specification with Indian export growth weighted by India's lagged share of exports in the category. The regression equation is

$$d\ln\exp_{ijt} = \gamma_i + \gamma_j + \gamma_t + \beta_1 d\ln US_{jt} + \beta_2 dw\ln India_{jt} + \varepsilon_{ijt}. \qquad (7.2)$$

These equations are estimated using data from 1990 through 2003. The advantage of this specification is that it exploits both cross-section and time-series variation to estimate how LAC exports are affected by India. In addition, the data are readily available and the coefficients are easy to understand.

Results of using panel data on BPT services are reported in tables 7.3a and 7.3b for equations (7.1) and (7.2), respectively. Although the coefficients on Indian export growth are negative for exports, they are not significant. Thus, there is no evidence that Indian exports have significantly displaced LAC exports across all industries (columns (4)–(6) in tables 7.3a and 7.3b).

Tables 7.4a and 7.4b report the results on U.S. imports for each BPT services industry separately. In only one industry, "Other" BPT services, is there robust evidence of displacement. The coefficient of –.28 in table 7.4a implies that a 1 percent increase in export growth from India leads to a 0.3 percent decline in export growth from LAC. However, this is a catchall category so it is difficult to pinpoint its true economic importance.[4] When weighted Indian export growth is used (table 7.4b), there are significant negative effects in the following four categories: research, development, and testing services; legal services; industrial engineering; and other business, professional, and technical services. Thus, there is some evidence that India's export growth in these business categories is having a negative impact on LAC export growth.

Tables 7.5a and 7.5b repeat the exercise for U.S. exports. There is little evidence that exports of services to India affect exports of services to LAC. Of interest, U.S. export growth in database and other information services to India is negatively correlated with U.S. export growth to LAC

Table 7.3a Growth in Latin American BPT Trade with the United States

Determinant	U.S. exports			U.S. imports		
	(1)	(2)	(3)	(4)	(5)	(6)
d ln all	0.908***	0.902***	0.882***	0.589***	0.584***	0.484***
	[5.52]	[5.28]	[4.88]	[4.47]	[4.21]	[3.40]
d ln india	0.037	0.038	0.029	−0.042	−0.044	−0.026
	[1.21]	[1.18]	[0.85]	[0.95]	[0.95]	[0.52]
Fixed effects						
Country	x			x		
Industry	x		x	x		x
Year	x	x		x	x	
Country-industry		x			x	
Country-year			x			x
Observations	820	820	820	550	550	550
R-squared	0.21	0.26	0.41	0.20	0.25	0.39

Source: Data are from the U.S. Department of Commerce. Author's calculations.
Note: Robust t-statistics are in brackets.
*** Significant at 1 percent level.

(table 7.5b). Because there is likely to be much intra-industry trade in this category, this may be of concern. One possible explanation is that India's thriving computer and database industry requires substantial inputs from the United States. And as trade in this area is being oriented toward India, it is also being steered away from LAC countries.

Policy Implications

Services export growth from LAC countries to the United States is unremarkable when compared with that from India or even from China. Previous work has shown that income, financial depth, use of the same language, and adjacency promote services exports, while distance retards exports—though to a lesser extent than it slows goods trade.[5] Exports of business, professional, and technical services are aided by telecommunications and Internet development (Freund and Weinhold 2002). This implies

Table 7.3b Growth in Latin American BPT Trade with the United States, Using Weighted Indian Export Growth

Determinant	U.S. exports			U.S. imports		
	(1)	(2)	(3)	(4)	(5)	(6)
d ln allni	0.895***	0.890***	0.859***	0.607***	0.601***	0.486***
	[5.41]	[5.18]	[4.69]	[4.61]	[4.33]	[3.50]
d ln india	5.291	5.509	6.85	−3.998	−3.858	−4.821
	[1.21]	[1.26]	[1.47]	[1.03]	[0.96]	[1.17]
Fixed effects						
Country	x			x		
Industry	x		x	x		x
Year	x	x		x	x	
Country-industry		x			x	
Country-year			x			x
Observations	820	820	820	550	550	550
R-squared	0.21	0.26	0.41	0.19	0.25	0.39

Source: Data are from the U.S. Department of Commerce. Author's calculations.
Note: Robust t-statistics are in brackets.
***Significant at 1 percent level.

that, to the extent possible, countries aiming to expand services exports will need to pursue policies that improve financial services and extend the English-speaking population. Promoting bilingual education in schools will improve potential for services exports, and will help LAC to benefit more generally from globalization. Technological development can also help expand trade in BPT services.

In addition, countries may find niche service markets—for example, computer services in India, financial services in Bermuda, port services in China. Given its climate and proximity to the United States, LAC's key markets are health and retirement. Countries should use regional agreements to push for international insurance coverage and other policies to help growth in this sector.

Tourism in LAC has performed relatively well since 2002. In part, this is because U.S. residents prefer to stay in region after the events of 9/11. This inclination will likely continue in the medium term; LAC should take advantage of this trend and improve infrastructure for tourism, roads,

Table 7.4a Determinants of U.S. Imports of BPT Services from Latin America by Industry

Determinant	All BPT services	Advertising	Computer and data processing services	Database and other information services	Research, development, and testing services	Management, consulting, and public relations services	Legal services	Construction, architectural, and engineering services	Industrial engineering	Installation, maintenance, and repair of equipment	Other
dlnall	0.786*	1.662***	-0.035	2.519*	-0.074	1.864***	0.712***	-0.141	4.180**	0.340***	0.789*
	[1.88]	[3.47]	[0.09]	[1.84]	[0.12]	[4.30]	[3.37]	[0.16]	[2.11]	[2.90]	[1.81]
dlnindia	-0.089	0.064	0.077	-0.102	-0.447	0.142	-0.096	0.262*	-0.032	-0.028	-0.279**
	[1.35]	[0.55]	[0.65]	[0.41]	[1.65]	[1.11]	[1.58]	[1.72]	[0.12]	[0.15]	[2.13]
Observations	113	59	67	45	62	83	68	43	33	46	44
R-squared	0.35	0.36	0.30	0.21	0.11	0.36	0.21	0.34	0.51	0.29	0.68

Source: Data are from the U.S. Department of Commerce. Author's calculations.
Note: Year and country fixed effects are included in all regressions. Robust t-statistics are in brackets.
* Significant at 10 percent level.
** Significant at 5 percent level.
*** Significant at 1 percent level.

Table 7.4b Determinants of U.S. Imports of BPT Services from Latin America by Industry, Using Weighted Indian Export Growth

Determinant	All BPT services	Advertising	Computer and data processing services	Database and other information services	Research, development, and testing services	Management, consulting, and public relations services	Legal services	Construction, architectural, and engineering services	Industrial engineering	Installation, maintenance, and repair of equipment	Other
dlnallni	0.762*	1.414***	-0.004	3.109**	0.333	1.715***	0.782***	-0.198	2.360***	0.341***	0.849*
	[1.85]	[4.59]	[0.01]	[2.57]	[0.52]	[4.61]	[4.04]	[0.19]	[3.99]	[3.36]	[2.01]
dlnindia	-8.535	-10.083	-1.824	-17.226	-32.362*	10.604	-30.765***	30.299**	-19.881***	46.912	-69.063**
	[1.59]	[0.32]	[0.39]	[1.44]	[1.73]	[1.16]	[3.15]	[2.28]	[4.00]	[0.48]	[2.38]
Observations	113	59	67	45	62	83	68	43	33	46	44
R-squared	0.36	0.36	0.30	0.24	0.10	0.35	0.26	0.35	0.73	0.31	0.70

Source: Data are from the U.S. Department of Commerce. Author's calculations.
Note: Robust t-statistics are in brackets.
* Significant at 10 percent level.
** Significant at 5 percent level.
*** Significant at 1 percent level.

Table 7.5a Determinants of U.S. Exports of BPT Services to Latin America by Industry

Determinant	All BPT services	Advertising	Computer and data processing services	Database and other information services	Research, development, and testing services	Management, consulting, and public relations services	Legal services	Construction, architectural, and engineering services	Industrial engineering	Installation, maintenance, and repair of equipment	Other
dlnall	1.020***	1.834*	0.298	2.048***	-0.326	0.615	1.489***	0.942***	0.881**	1.814	-1.467*
	[2.71]	[1.82]	[0.77]	[3.97]	[0.24]	[1.25]	[3.73]	[3.48]	[2.11]	[1.63]	[1.85]
dlnindia	-0.011	0.666	0.009	-0.193	-0.113	-0.033	0.06	0.04	0.238	0.517**	-0.01
	[0.12]	[1.08]	[0.11]	[1.39]	[0.38]	[0.11]	[0.67]	[0.81]	[0.71]	[2.05]	[0.17]
Observations	121	44	111	89	79	107	70	101	56	106	57
R-squared	0.10	0.17	0.14	0.24	0.29	0.32	0.18	0.16	0.49	0.21	0.62

Source: Data are from the U.S. Department of Commerce. Author's calculations.
Note: Year and country fixed effects are included in all regressions. Robust t-statistics are in brackets.

* Significant at 10 percent level.
** Significant at 5 percent level.
*** Significant at 1 percent level.

Table 7.5b Determinants of U.S. Exports of BPT Services to Latin America by Industry, Using Weighted Indian Export Growth

Determinant	All BPT services	Advertising	Computer and data processing services	Database and other information services	Research, development, and testing services	Management, consulting, and public relations services	Legal services	Construction, architectural, and engineering services	Industrial engineering	Installation, maintenance, and repair of equipment	Other
dlnallni	0.997***	2.201**	0.197	2.453***	-0.27	0.613	1.485***	0.937***	0.866**	1.789	-1.477*
	[2.62]	[2.41]	[0.51]	[6.09]	[0.21]	[1.26]	[3.76]	[3.49]	[2.55]	[1.61]	[1.79]
dwlnindia	-5.115	49.329	9.362	-34.418***	-20.865	-4.855	40.856	9.269	24.328**	109.094**	-1.979
	[0.41]	[0.28]	[1.26]	[3.56]	[0.42]	[0.12]	[0.66]	[1.19]	[2.02]	[1.99]	[0.26]
Observations	121	44	111	89	79	107	70	101	56	106	57
R-squared	0.10	0.14	0.15	0.31	0.29	0.32	0.17	0.17	0.52	0.21	0.62

Source: Data are from the U.S. Department of Commerce. Author's calculations.
Note: Robust t-statistics are in brackets.
* Significant at 10 percent level.
** Significant at 5 percent level.
*** Significant at 1 percent level.

airport customs, and so forth, and explore niche markets, such as golf, which attract high-end tourists.

Conclusion

This chapter examined services trade growth with the United States and found Latin America to be lagging behind China, India, and the rest of the world. Although exports from LAC countries exceed those from India and China, services export growth from the region, with the important exception of the Caribbean, has been well below world growth since 1999. China has benefited from rapid growth in goods trade and exports of transport services, and India has benefited from new technologies and rapid growth in exports of business services. South America, Central America, and Mexico have exceeded world growth only in exports of travel services, though even in this category, growth from India and China has outpaced Latin American growth.

Language and proximity have been shown to be important determinants of services trade (Freund and Weinhold 2002). One area where Latin America has a large advantage over India and China is geography. Tourism and provision of health services are especially attractive, owing to proximity, labor costs, and climate. If Latin America wants to seriously compete in provision of business services to the United States, LAC countries will have to expand their English-speaking populations.

Notes

1. The exact country breakdown depends on year and industry.

2. These include royalties and license fees; travel, passenger fares, and other transportation; education; insurance; financial services; telecommunications; accounting, auditing, and bookkeeping services; advertising; computer and data processing services; database and other information services; research, development, and testing services; management, consulting, and public relations; legal services; medical services; construction, engineering, architecture, and mining; industrial engineering; installation, maintenance, and repair of equipment; sports and performing arts; operational leasing; miscellaneous disbursements; other business, professional, and technical services; other private services; and other unaffiliated services.

3. $ESI_{ij} = 100 \times \Sigma_c \min(X_{ci}, X_{cj})$, where X_{ci} and X_{cj} represent the share of exports in industry c of countries i and j, respectively.

4. This category consists of agricultural services; language translation services; security services; collection services; salvage services; satellite photography and remote sensing/satellite imagery services; transcription services; waste treatment and depollution services; mailing, reproduction, and commercial art services; personnel supply services; management of health care facilities services; auction services; and other trade-related services.

5. Freund and Weinhold (2002) find an elasticity of trade to distance of −0.4 compared with −1.0 usually found for goods trade.

References

Borga, Maria, and Michael Mann. 2002. "U.S. International Services: Cross-Border Trade in 2002 and Sales Through Affiliates in 2001." *Survey of Current Business* 2002: 58–118.

Devlin, Robert, Antoni Estevadeordal, and Andres Rodríguez, eds. 2006. *The Emergence of China: Opportunities and Challenges for Latin America and the Caribbean.* Washington, DC: Inter-American Development Bank.

Finger, J. M., and M. E. Kreinin. 1979. "A Measure of 'Export Similarity' and its Possible Uses." *Economic Journal* 89 (356): 905–12.

Freund, C., and D. Weinhold. 2002. "The Internet and International Trade in Services." *American Economic Review* 92 (2): 236–40.

8

Trade Liberalization and Export Variety: A Comparison of Mexico and China

*Robert C. Feenstra and Hiau Looi Kee**

Introduction

The hallmark of the endogenous growth models (Grossman and Helpman 1991; Romer 1990) is their focus on the creation of new or higher quality products, and the effects of such innovations on productivity and economic growth. Opening a country to trade opportunities through tariff reductions will typically increase the product variety of imports available, and may also increase the variety of exports, both of which contribute to growth. Despite the microeconomic focus of these models, the link between trade and growth is usually assessed at a more aggregate level, in which case the causality between the two is unclear (Dollar and Kraay 2001; Frankel and Romer 1999; Rodriguez and Rodrik 2000). To move beyond these aggregate statistics, more detailed information is needed on the product variety of traded goods and on the link between tariff reductions and product variety.

The issue of measuring product variety has received relatively little attention because of its inherent difficulty. In the language of index numbers, an expansion in the range of inputs or outputs is a "new goods" problem: a

* Research funding from the World Bank is gratefully acknowledged. The authors thank the anonymous referees for helpful comments.

good that is newly available will have an observed price and quantity, but no corresponding price or quantity the year before. The availability of this new good will yield a welfare gain to consumers, as well as a productivity gain to firms buying the new input. This chapter shows how product variety can be measured in the case of a constant elasticity of substitution (CES) aggregator function. These results are applied to the measurement of export variety from China and Mexico to the United States.

The application to China and Mexico is motivated by the changes in trade policy facing those countries in recent years. Mexico joined the North America Free Trade Agreement (NAFTA) in 1994, which substantially lowered it tariffs to the U.S. and Canadian markets. What has happened to Mexico's export variety since that time? Kehoe and Ruhl (2002) argue that goods from Mexico that were the least traded before tariff liberalization account for a disproportionately large amount of the growth in trade following the reduction of trade barriers. This chapter also documents the expansion in export varieties from Mexico resulting from NAFTA. Similarly, although China was acccepted into the World Trade Organization (WTO) in 2000, it was implementing unilateral tariff reductions of its own before that time and benefiting from low tariffs abroad. The chapter investigates the growth in export variety from China over 1990–2001, and compares those findings to Mexico. In addition, the chapter argues that the expansion of China's export variety resulting from the decrease of U.S. tariffs has caused an adverse market competition effect on the export variety from Mexico.

This chapter is organized as follows: A literature review on the "new goods" problem is presented in the second section, and the measurement of export variety in the CES case is discussed in the third section. The following two sections discuss the empirical applications to export variety growth in Mexico and China. Regression results relating trade liberalization to industry export variety are presented in the sixth section, and conclusions are given in the final section.

Literature Review

This section reviews the theoretical results on the "new goods" problem and presents some empirical applications.

Theoretical Results

The problem of computing welfare gains for a consumer resulting from new goods is similar to evaluating productivity gains for a firm with new inputs. Hicks (1940) recommended one solution to this problem: a newly available good should be evaluated at its "reservation price" when it is not available, where demand is zero. When the new good becomes available, demand is positive and its price is lower than the reservation price. Thus, the fall in prices can be computed as the difference between the reservation and observed prices, and integrating the demand curve between these prices is a measure of the consumer welfare gain, or firm productivity gain, resulting from the new good. Examples of this approach applied empirically include Griliches and Cockburn (1994) and Berndt, Kyle, and Ling (2002) for generic drugs, and Hausman (1997, 1999) for breakfast cereals and cellular telephones.

The productivity gain from a new input for a firm is illustrated in figure 8.1. Given $y_t = \bar{y}_t$, the inputs would lie along an isoquant ACD as illustrated. If only input 1 is available, then the costs of producing $\bar{y}_t$ would be minimized at point A, with the budget line AB. But if input 2 is also available, then the costs are instead minimized at point C, with a decline in costs. This illustrates the benefits of input variety.

The difficulty with applying this solution in practice is that reservation prices are not easy to estimate, especially when there are many new goods appearing. A simpler solution is proposed by Feenstra (1994) for that case where new goods appear within a CES aggregator function (that is, a production function for firms, expenditure function for consumers, or production possibility frontier for an economy). Suppose that the elasticity of substitution between the goods is $\sigma > 1$. In that case, the reservation price for any good is infinite: the isoquants of the firm hit the axis in figure 8.1 with slope zero (at point A) and infinity (at point D). But the

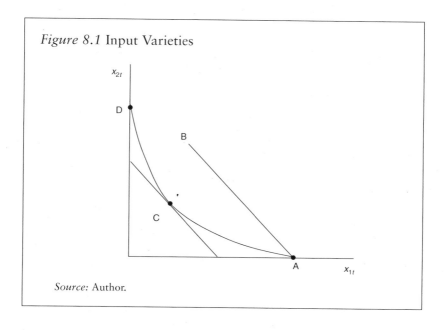

Figure 8.1 Input Varieties

Source: Author.

total reduction in costs resulting from the new input can still be computed. Suppose that the set of inputs available to the firm each period is I_t, $t = 0$, 1, with the common $I \equiv \left(I_0 \cap I_1 \right) \neq \varnothing$. Feenstra (1994) shows that costs fall as a result of the appearance of new inputs by the amount

$$\left(\frac{\lambda_1(I)}{\lambda_0(I)} \right)^{1/(\sigma-1)}, \tag{8.1}$$

where the values $\lambda_t(I)$ are constructed as

$$\lambda_t(I) \equiv \left(\frac{\sum_{i \in I} p_{it} x_{it}}{\sum_{i \in I_t} p_{it} x_{it}} \right) = 1 - \left(\frac{\sum_{i \in I_t, i \notin I} p_{it} x_{it}}{\sum_{i \in I_t} p_{it} x_{it}} \right), \quad t = 0, 1. \tag{8.2}$$

In these expressions, I_t denotes the set of inputs available in periods $t = 0$, 1, at the prices p_{it} and with cost-minimizing quantities x_{it}. New goods will be in the set I_1 but not I, whereas disappearing goods are in the set I_0 but not I. From equation (8.2), each of the terms $\lambda_t(I) \leq 1$ can be interpreted as the "period t expenditure on the goods in the set I relative to total expenditure in that period." Alternatively, this can be interpreted as "1 minus the share of period t expenditure on 'new' goods (not in the set I)." When there are more new goods in period t, the value of $\lambda_t(I)$ will be lowered. Notice that the ratio $[\lambda_1(I)/\lambda_0(I)]$ in equation (8.1) is raised to the power $1/(\sigma-1)$, so with $\sigma > 1$ a lower value of $\lambda_1(I)$ resulting from new inputs will *reduce* the ratio in equation (8.1) by an amount depending on the elasticity of substitution.

Although equation (8.1) measures the reduction in costs from the appearance of new inputs, the term $[\lambda_1(I)/\lambda_0(I)]$ itself is an inverse measure of product variety: when $[\lambda_1(I)/\lambda_0(I)] < 1$, there are more "new" than "disappearing" goods, and product variety is expanding. Simply inverting this term yields a direct measure of product variety that can be implemented using data on observed expenditures on goods. There are several applications of this method to measuring the variety of traded goods, as discussed in the next section.

Before turning to these applications, note that the formulas in equations (8.1) and (8.2) cannot be applied when $0 \leq \sigma \leq 1$, because in that case inputs are essential to the production process, and having zero of any input results in zero output. So the "new goods" problem cannot be considered in that case. However, these formulas are still relevant when $\sigma < 0$. That case applies to measuring the benefits from *output variety* for an economy. This is illustrated in figure 8.2, which shows the production possibility frontier between two output varieties x_{1t} and x_{2t}. For a given production possibility frontier, and given prices, an increase in the number of output varieties will raise revenue. For example, if only output variety 1 is available, then the economy would be producing at the corner A, with revenue shown by the line AB. Then if variety 2 becomes available,

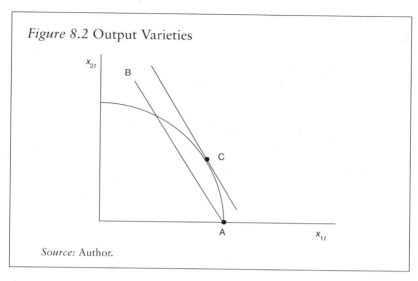

Figure 8.2 Output Varieties

Source: Author.

the new equilibrium will be at point C, with an increase in revenue. When $\sigma < 0$, then equation (8.1) measures the increase in revenue resulting from the appearance of new outputs, and the ratio $[\lambda_1 (I)/ \lambda_0 (I)]$ is an inverse measure of output variety.

Empirical Applications

Several studies measure the benefits of input or output variety in raising productivity. Feenstra et al. (1999) provide an application of this method to industry productivity growth in the Republic of Korea and Taiwan (China). The data used to measure variety are the disaggregate exports from these countries to the United States. Those authors analyzed the relationship between changes in export variety and the growth in total factor productivity across Korea and Taiwan, for 16 sectors over 1975–91. They found that changes in relative export variety (entered as either a lag or a lead) had a positive and significant effect on total factor productivity in 9 of the 16 sectors. Of these, 7 sectors were classified as secondary industries, in that they rely on, as well as produce, differentiated manufactures, and therefore seem to fit the idea of endogenous growth. Among the primary industries, which rely more heavily on natural resources, the authors found mixed evidence: the correlation between export variety and productivity can be positive, negative, or insignificant. In addition, the authors also found evidence of a positive and significant correlation between upstream export variety and productivity in six downstream sectors, five of which were secondary industries.

Funke and Ruhwedel (2001) applied the same measure of product variety to analyze economic growth across the Organisation for Economic

Co-operation and Development countries. Using a panel data set of 19 countries over 1989–96, they found that a country's export variety relative to the United States was a significant determinant of its gross domestic product (GDP) per capita. Notice that these measures of product variety, which are constructed from highly disaggregate trade data, are unlikely to suffer from the endogeneity problem that plagues aggregate trade flows (as discussed by Frankel and Romer 1999). Therefore, the construction of product variety indexes and their correlation with total factor productivity offers an alternative way to assess the importance of trade in economic growth.

Hummels and Klenow (2005) decomposed the growth of world trade into that part resulting from countries' exporting new products—what they call the "extensive margin"—and that part resulting from countries exporting more of the same products, or the "intensive margin." They found that extensive margin accounted for two-thirds of the greater exports of larger economies, and one-third of their imports. In another application, Broda and Weinstein (2006) measured the impact on welfare for the importer. For the United States, they found that the upward bias in the conventional import price index (resulting from ignoring product variety) was approximately 1.2 percent per year, implying that the welfare gains from cumulative variety growth in imports were 2.8 percent of GDP in 2001. Finally, Feenstra and Kee (2008) estimated the impact of export variety on productivity growth for a group of countries, and Broda, Greenfield, and Weinstein (2006) showed how import variety is related to country productivity.

Export Variety Measurement

The previous results are stated as changes in product variety over time. But the same results apply to a comparison of two countries at a point in time. Suppose that the set of exports from countries a and c differ, but have some product varieties in common. Denote this common set $I \equiv \left(I_t^a \cap I_t^c \right) \neq \varnothing$. If one rewrites equation (8.2), an inverse measure of export variety from country c relative to country a is

$$\frac{\lambda_t^c(I)}{\lambda_t^a(I)},$$

where

$$\lambda_t^c(I) \equiv \frac{\sum\limits_{i \in I} p_{it}^c q_{it}^c}{\sum\limits_{i \in I_{it}^c} p_{it}^c q_{it}^c}. \tag{8.3}$$

Notice that $\lambda_t^c(I) \leq 1$ in equation (8.3) because of the differing summations in the numerator and denominator. This term will be strictly less than 1 if there are goods in the set I_t^c that are not found in the common set I. In other words, if country c is selling some goods in period t that are not sold by country a, this will mean $\lambda_t^c(I) < 1$, so it is an inverse measure of country c's export variety.

The ratio $[\lambda_t^c(I)/\lambda_t^a(I)]$ is an inverse measure of export variety from country c relative to country a. Taking the reciprocal, $[\lambda_t^a(I)/\lambda_t^c(I)]$ is measured using exports of Mexico and China to the United States. While it would be preferable to use Mexico's and China's worldwide exports, the data for the United States are more disaggregated and allow for a finer measurement of "unique" products sold by one country and not another. Specifically, for 1989–2001 the analysis uses the 10-digit Harmonized System classification of imports.

To measure the $[\lambda_t^a(I)/\lambda_t^c(I)]$, a consistent comparison country is needed. For this purpose, the analysis uses worldwide exports from all countries to the United States averaging over time as the comparison. Denote this comparison country by a, so that the set $I^a \equiv \bigcup_{c,t} I_t^c$ is the total set of varieties imported by the United States over all years, and $p_i^a q_i^a$ is the average value of imports for product i (summed over all source countries and averaged across years). Aggregating across countries and over time yields a consistent comparison set of good I^a that does not itself vary over time.[1]

When comparing country c to the "aggregate" country a, the common set of goods exported $I \equiv I_t^c \cap I^a = I_t^c$, or simply, the set of goods exported by country c. Therefore, from equation (8.3) we have $\lambda_t^c(I_t^c) = 1$ and

$$Variety_t^c \equiv \frac{\lambda_t^a(I_t^c)}{\lambda_t^c(I_t^c)} = \frac{\sum_{i \in I_t^c} p_{it}^a q_{it}^a}{\sum_{i \in I^a} p_{it}^a q_{it}^a}. \tag{8.4}$$

Notice that the denominator on the right-hand side of equation (8.4) is total U.S. imports, summed over all products and countries, but using average import values over time. The numerator equals the value of imports in products that country c sells to the United States, again summed over all source countries and averaged over time. This expression for the export variety of country c, $Variety_t^c$ is therefore interpreted as the "share of total U.S. imports from products that are exported by country c." Note that this measure depends on the set of exports by country c, I_t^c, but not on the value of those exports (except insofar as they affect the value of worldwide exports). The following sections document export variety from Mexico and China to the United States, as measured by equation (8.4) over 1990–2001. The sections also discuss the ways tariffs have changed for those countries, and statistically relate the change in export variety to the change in tariffs.

Mexico's Export Variety: 1990 versus 2001

The analysis breaks down the aggregate exports of Mexico to the United States into seven major groups and constructs the export variety indexes of these seven industries according to equation (8.4). Table 8.1 presents

Table 8.1 Mexico's Trade with the United States, 1990 and 2001 (percent)

a. Mexico's Export Variety to the United States

Year and rate	Average	Agriculture	Textiles and garments	Wood and paper	Petroleum and plastics	Mining and metals	Machinery and transport	Electronics
1990	52.4	41.5	71.2	47.3	55.4	46.6	65.6	39.5
2001	66.7	50.9	82.6	63.2	72.7	56.4	75.8	65.6
Growth rate[a]	2.2	1.9	1.4	2.6	2.5	1.7	1.3	4.6

b. Mexico's Tariffs on Imports from the United States

	Overall industry	Agriculture	Textiles and garments	Wood and paper	Petroleum and plastics	Mining and metals	Machinery and transport	Electronics
1990	12.1	8.5	17.7	10.9	9.9	9.7	14.0	13.9
2001	1.1	2.1	0.5	0.6	1.5	1.3	1.1	0.6

c. U.S. Tariffs on Imports from Mexico

	Overall industry	Agriculture	Textiles and garments	Wood and paper	Petroleum and plastics	Mining and metals	Machinery and transport	Electronics
1990	4.1	4.4	13.0	2.2	0.6	2.1	2.5	4.1
2001	0.3	0.8	0.4	0.0	0.1	0.7	0.1	0.1

Sources: Export variety in panel (a) and U.S. tariffs in panel (c) are computed from the U.S. import data described in Feenstra, Romalis, and Schott 2002. Tariffs in panel (b) are computed from the World Integrated Trade Statistics database at the World Bank.

a. The growth rate in panel (a) is computed as $[\ln(\text{Variety}_{2001}) - \ln(\text{Variety}_{1990})] \times 100$.

the indexes of these industries in 1990 and 2001 to illustrate the variation across industries and years. For example, panel (a) of table 8.1 shows that in 1990 for agriculture, Mexico exported 42 percent of all the product varieties that the United States imported (from any country). That share increased to 51 percent in 2001, for an annual average growth rate of 1.9 percent. During the same period, the export variety from Mexico in the textiles and garments industry increased by 1.4 percent annually, from covering 71 percent of all varieties imported by the United States in 1990 to 83 percent in 2001.

The highest growth rate of variety is in the electronics industry, where in 1990 only 40 percent of U.S. imports were products exported by Mexico, and in 2001 that share was 66 percent. This represents an average annual growth rate of 4.6 percent. Conversely, the slowest growth of export variety is observed in the machinery and transport industry, with an annual growth rate of 1.3 percent. That industry, along with textiles and garments, already had high export variety in 1990, which limited future growth in variety. By contrast, export variety in the mining and basic metals industry is among the lowest among all nonagriculture industries in both years. Exports in that industry covered 47 percent of the varieties in U.S. imports in 1990, and increased to 56 percent in 2001.

In summary, over the decade of the 1990s, Mexico expanded its export variety across a range of different industries. Averaging over the industries, 67 percent of U.S. import varieties in 2001 are from products that Mexico exports, whereas that share was 52 percent in 1990. Could trade liberalization explain the expansion in Mexico's export variety over this sample period? Given that Mexico joined NAFTA in 1994, the average variety within each industry before 1994 can be compared with that after 1994 to identify NAFTA effect on export variety. Figure 8.3 presents the average variety indexes pre- and post-1994 in each of the seven industries. At the industry level, the increases range from 5.2 percent in the agriculture industry to 21.4 percent in the electronics industry. Overall, Mexico's export variety increased by 11.4 percent since 1994. That effect is statistically significant and robust to industry fixed effects, as confirmed in a later section.

Panel (b) of table 8.1 presents the tariff liberalizations in Mexico at the industry level in the pre- and post-1994 eras with respect to products from the United States. In 1990, the average tariff levied on U.S. products entering Mexico was 12.1 percent; by 2001 that figure dropped to 1.1 percent. The most dramatic reductions can be found in the textiles and garments industry, for which tariffs dropped from 17.7 percent to 0.5 percent. Large tariff decreases also occurred in machinery and transport and in electronics. The industry with the smallest reduction was agriculture, which still achieved a reduction from 8.5 percent to 2.1 percent over the 11-year period. Thus, Mexico went through some very dramatic declines in tariffs with respect to goods from the United States.

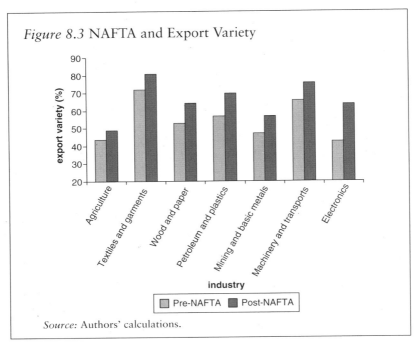

Figure 8.3 NAFTA and Export Variety

Source: Authors' calculations.

Panel (c) of table 8.1 presents the tariff liberalizations in the United States at the industry level in the pre- and post-1994 eras with respect to Mexico's exports. In 1990, the average tariff imposed by the United States on Mexico's products was 4.1 percent, and in 2001, it was 0.3 percent. Measured in absolute changes, the largest fall in tariffs was in the textiles and garments industry, where the average tariff dropped from 13.0 percent to 0.4 percent. In agriculture and electronics, the decrease in tariffs was similar to the overall average, and in other industries the drop was less. A challenge for the empirical work of this chapter is to explain the substantial increase in export variety over 1990–2001 using the relatively small (but permanent) drop in U.S. tariffs under NAFTA. The chapter returns to this task after reviewing the export variety and tariffs for China.

China's Export Variety: 1990 versus 2001

Panel (a) of table 8.2 presents China's export variety in 1990 and 2001. The product varieties imported by the United States that were also exported by China ranged from 30 percent in the agricultural industry to 79 percent in textiles and garments in 1990, while in 2001, the range was between 34 percent and 88 percent. Over the same period, the fastest growth in export product variety was in the machinery and transport equipment industry, with an average annual growth rate of 7.3 percent.

Table 8.2 China's Trade with the United States, 1990 and 2001 (percent)

Year and rate	Average	Agriculture	Textiles and garments	Wood and paper	Petroleum and plastics	Mining and metals	Machinery and transport	Electronics
a. China's Export Variety to the United States								
1990	42.1	29.6	79.4	52.2	39.2	31.1	28.1	35.2
2001	63.3	34.0	87.6	65.2	70.3	55.1	62.7	68.1
Growth rate[a]	3.7	1.3	0.9	2.0	5.3	5.2	7.3	6.0
b. China's Tariffs on Imports from the United States								
1990	22.9	14.0	52.6	15.8	17.8	17.0	33.7	18.3
2001	18.1	69.8	17.6	10.6	11.3	9.0	11.4	10.7
c. U.S. Tariffs on Imports from China								
1990	5.8	1.4	13.0	6.6	2.7	6.4	5.1	5.1
2001	3.6	1.7	10.9	1.3	3.1	4.1	3.0	1.2

Sources: Export variety in panel (a) and U.S. tariffs in panel (c) are computed from the U.S. import data described in Feenstra, Romalis, and Schott 2002. Tariffs in panel (b) are computed from the World Integrated Trade Statistics database at the World Bank.

a. The growth rate in panel (a) is computed as $[\ln(\text{Variety}_{2001}) - \ln(\text{Variety}_{1990})] \times 100$.

In 1990, China was ahead of Mexico in export variety in the textiles and garments industry (with 8.2 percent more export variety than Mexico), and wood and paper products (4.9 percent more export variety). However, Mexico was ahead in the machinery and transport equipment industry (37.5 percent more variety), petroleum and plastics (16.2 percent more), mining and basic metals (15.5 percent more), agriculture (11.9 percent more), and electronics (4.3 percent more).

By 2001, China's advantage over Mexico in textiles and garments and wood and paper products was reduced to 5 percent and 2 percent, respectively. Thus, to the extent that NAFTA caused an expansion in Mexico's export variety, the most dramatic effects are in these two industries. Despite the expansion in Mexican export variety across all industries, however, China caught up in those cases where Mexico led in 1990. In fact, for the electronics industry, China's export variety exceeded Mexico's by 2.5 percent in 2001, while the gaps in the petroleum and plastics, mining and basic metals, and machinery and transport equipment industries were reduced to 2.4 percent, 1.3 percent and 13.1 percent, respectively.

Panel (b) of table 8.2 presents the import-weighted average tariffs at the industry level for China's imports from the United States. It is evident that while Mexico was liberalizing its tariffs because of NAFTA, China was unilaterally reducing its tariffs, too. The average Chinese tariff on U.S. products dropped from 22.9 percent in 1992, the first year for which tariff data is available, to 18.1 percent in 2001. The biggest reductions were in the most protected industries, which were textiles and garments and machinery and transport equipment. For the rest of the industries, with the exception of agriculture, the tariff level was close to 10 percent in 2001.

The agriculture industry in China was protected by nontariff barriers, (NTBs) such as import licensing and quotas, in addition to the high tariffs. Figure 8.4 shows the extent of NTBs maintained by China in 1996. For rice and wheat, for example, 100 percent of imports were subject to NTBs. Under its entry to the WTO, China made substantial progress in reducing its NTBs in agriculture, which resulted in increases in import volume of goods in those products where NTBs are most restrictive. Such increases pushed up the import-weighted average tariff in agriculture from 14 percent to nearly 70 percent, as shown in panel (b) of table 8.2. This does not reflect an increase in protection, however, because the *unweighted* average tariff in this industry has dropped from 48 percent to 27 percent (see Bhattashli, Li, and Martin 2004, for a discussion).

Panel (c) of table 8.2 shows the United States' import-weighted average tariffs on China's exports at the industry level. Given that the United States does not have any trade agreement with China, these tariffs reflect the most favored nations tariffs. Overall, the average tariff on China's products was 5.8 percent in 1990, dropping to 3.6 percent by 2001. Industries with the largest reductions were wood and paper products and electronics. In most industries, however, the percentage point reduction in U.S. tariffs on China's exports was no greater than that for Mexico under NAFTA, and

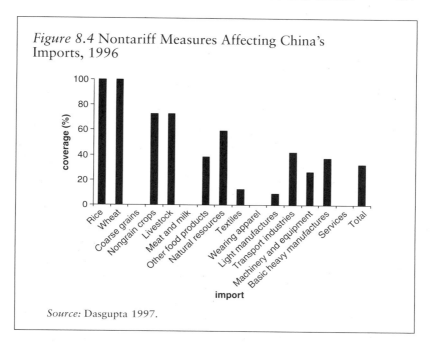

Figure 8.4 Nontariff Measures Affecting China's Imports, 1996

Source: Dasgupta 1997.

sometimes less. Average U.S. tariffs on imports from China in agriculture and in petroleum and plastic products have increased very slightly.[2]

Regression Results

To determine the effects of trade liberalization on export variety, the analysis focuses on Mexico. Table 8.3 presents the regression results. The regression pools observations across industries and years, using the full sample from 1974–2001 for the initial regressions.[3] There are seven industries and 28 years, which forms a balanced sample of 196 observations. Column (1) regresses the log of industry export variety of the industries on the NAFTA indicator variable, which is set to 1 for 1994 and later years, and 0 otherwise. Controlling for industry fixed effects, the NAFTA indicator is statistically significant, which indicates an increase in export product variety. The estimated coefficient is 0.20, which implies a 20 percent increase in export variety resulting from NAFTA.

The analysis studies the partial effects of the U.S. tariff reduction on Mexico's export variety in column (2). The NAFTA indicator variable may be picking up other factors that change over time monotonically, which will bias the estimates. Thus, in addition to the NAFTA indicator, the log value of 1 plus the U.S. tariffs on Mexican products is introduced.

Table 8.3 Dependent Variable—Log of Industry Export Variety

	(1) OLS	(2) OLS	(3) OLS	(4) IV	(5) 3SLS	(6) 3SLS
NAFTA indicator	0.198** [0.036]	0.143** [0.044]	0.043 [0.033]	-0.006 [0.034]		
ln(1+Mexico tariff)		-2.049* [0.997]	-2.109** [0.540]	-2.139** [0.460]	-4.535** [0.932]	
China's export variety			0.316** [0.046]	0.474** [0.042]	-0.508** [0.108]	
ln(1+China tariff)						-2.974* [0.897]
Mexico's export variety						0.116 [0.142]
Constant	3.520** [0.044]	3.630** [0.069]	2.669** [0.137]	2.782** [0.148]	5.70** [0.391]	3.11** [0.566]
Industry fixed effects	Yes	Yes	Yes	Yes	Yes	Yes
No. of observations	196	196	196	196	84	84
R-squared	0.50	0.51	0.78	0.71		
Chi-square					131.2	241.4

Source: Authors.

Note: OLS = ordinary least squares; IV = independent variable; 3SLS = three-stage least squares. White-robust standard errors are in brackets. Dependent variables are the log of Mexico's export variety in columns (1)–(5), and the log of China's export variety in column (6). Columns (4), (5), and (6) are estimated with instruments for export variety, which consist of that country's tariffs. Columns (5) and (6) have common industry fixed effects. Samples are from 1974 through 2001 in columns (1)–(4), and 1990 through 2001 in columns (5) and (6). Seven industries are included, as shown in tables 8.1 and 8.2.

* Significant at 5 percent level.
** Significant at 1 percent level.

Controlling for industry fixed effects, the tariff term is negative and statistically significant. The coefficient on the U.S. tariff in column (2) is interpreted as a semi-elasticity: each 1 percentage point reduction in U.S. tariffs increases export variety from Mexico by 2 percent.

This estimate of the semi-elasticity indicates that tariff cuts in the United States are important in increasing Mexico's export product variety, but the cuts cannot explain the observed increase in variety after NAFTA. Notice that the NAFTA indicator in column (2) is still estimated at 0.14, showing that the U.S. tariff cuts only explain 6 percentage points of the expansion in export variety from Mexico, with the remaining 14 percent attributable to some other NAFTA effect. Another way to arrive at this conclusion is to multiply the semi-elasticity of 2 by the average drop in U.S. tariffs, which is $4.1 - 0.3 = 3.8$ percent from panel (c) of table 8.1, arriving at a predicted increase in average export variety of 7.6 percent. This is only about one-half of the total increase in export variety reported in panel (a) of table 8.1, of $66.7 - 52.4 = 14.3$ percent.

The results in columns (1) and (2) may be biased if there are omitted variables that are correlated with the NAFTA liberalization and with the expansion of export variety. One such variable is the negative market competition effect from the expansion of other countries' export variety. To the extent that the reduction of the U.S. most favored nation tariff causes an expansion in China's export variety, Mexico's exports are expected to be crowded out and its export variety to decrease. Given that the trade liberalization of China coincided with Mexico's liberalization, omitting the competition from China may cause a downward bias on the estimated coefficient of the U.S. tariffs on Mexico.

The market competition effect from China is controlled for by including the industry export variety of China as an explanatory variable. Column (3) includes the export variety of China within the NAFTA indicator specification, along with the U.S. tariff reduction. It is clear that including China's export variety results in a substantial decrease of the NAFTA impact, to 4 percent in column (3), which is insignificantly different from zero. However, the results in column (3) could themselves be biased because of the endogeneity of Chinese export variety. As mentioned before, including China's export variety may pick up the market competition effect, which leads to a negative effect on the export variety of Mexico. But the expansion of China's export variety may also be driven by industry-specific technological progress or U.S. demand shocks that are common to the two countries within industry and year. This would have a positive effect on the export variety of Mexico. Although industry-specific technological progress is unobservable, the expansion of Chinese export variety resulting from China's tariff reductions can be used to capture the market competition effect.

The analysis studies this hypothesis by using China's industry tariffs as an instrumental variable for Chinese export variety. When the specification in column (3) is run using this instrument, the results (not reported in table 8.3) are qualitatively similar: the coefficient on Chinese export variety is still positive, so that the regression is not picking up a market competition effect. This appears to be a result of the long time span of the sample—1974 to 2001. Columns (5) and (6) use a shorter time period, from 1990 through 2001, which is the focus of this study. A system of two equations is run, one for the export variety of Mexico and another for the export variety of China. In both equations, the setup is identical to that of column (4), which includes the U.S. tariff, the export variety of the other country, and industry-specific effects that are treated as common across the equations. Export variety of the other country is endogenous, and the analysis uses the U.S. tariff on that country as an instrumental variable.

Column (5) shows the equation for Mexico's industry export variety, and (6) shows the equation for China's industry export variety. This reveals that the market competition effect of Chinese products on Mexico's exports are negative and statistically significant. Every 1 percent increase in China's export variety reduces Mexico's export variety by one-half of 1 percent, in column (5). However, an expansion of Mexico's variety does not have a significant impact on China's export variety, in column (6). Controlling for the expansion in Chinese products resulting from tariff reductions in China and the United States, the marginal effect of the U.S. tariff liberalization in column (5) is *larger* than it was before: each 1 percentage point reduction in tariffs now increases Mexican export variety by 4.5 percent. This demonstrates the substantial impact of tariff liberalization on product variety of the exporting country.

To see how much of Mexico's export variety increase the analysis is now explaining, we go through a similar calculation as before. The semi-elasticity of 4.5 is multiplied by the average drop in U.S. tariffs, which is 3.8 percent from panel (c) of table 8.1, arriving at a predicted increase in average export variety of 17.2 percent. This is slightly larger than the total increase in export variety reported in panel (a) of table 8.1, of 14.3 percent, so that the U.S. tariff cut fully explains the average increase in export variety from Mexico. However, regression (5) also predicts a fall in Mexico's export variety because of the competitive impact from China, of $0.5 \times 21.2 = 10.6$ percent.[4] So in total, the regression under-predicts the average increase in Mexico's export variety. Performing the same calculation on specific industries, regression (5) over-predicts the increase in export variety in textiles and apparel from Mexico, and under-predicts most other industries. Evidently, textiles and apparel is an outlier, with a very substantial drop in U.S. tariffs on exports from Mexico but a modest increase in export variety. The fact that this industry performs differently from the others also indicates that the regression should be run separately across industries. That is beyond the scope of the present chapter because of a lack of observations, but it would be possible in a panel data set with more countries, which is an important direction for further research (Debaere and Mostashari 2005).

Conclusion

The 1990s witnessed a significant increase in Mexico's export variety in all industries, especially since NAFTA went into effect. Overall, 67 percent of U.S. imports in 2001 were from products Mexico exported, whereas this share was 52 percent in 1990. Over the same period, China also experienced a rapid expansion in export variety, and in certain industries, China exceeded Mexico in exported varieties.

This chapter studies the effects of U.S. tariff reductions on export variety. The empirical results indicate that tariff liberalization is important in expanding export variety. In particular, statistical evidence links U.S. tariff liberalization resulting from NAFTA to increased export variety from Mexico. That effect is robust to the market competition effect of Chinese exports, and in fact, the semi-elasticity between tariff cuts and export variety is higher when competition from Chinese exports is taken into account.

Although the static gains from trade have been widely studied and documented to be relatively small, the dynamic gains from the expansion of export variety may well be more important. Broda and Weinstein (2006) documented that the expansion of import varieties in the United States has had a significant impact on lowering the "true" import price index, and therefore on raising U.S. welfare. Similarly, Feenstra and Kee (2008) argued that the growth of export varieties benefits aggregate productivity in the exporting country. This chapter shows how expansion in the variety of traded goods is linked to tariff reductions, thereby contributing to short-term and long-term gains.

Notes

1. In contrast, Feenstra and Kee (2004) measure export variety each year relative to the set of products imported into the United States that year, which can lead to inconsistent cross-year comparisons.

2. The increase in average tariffs in those industries most likely reflects a shifting import bundle in the United States toward products with slightly higher tariffs.

3. For 1974–88, we construct export variety using the 7-digit Tariff Schedule of the United States, Annotated. Because that classification differs from the Harmonized System used after 1989, the export variety indexes are inconsistent between 1988 and 1989; so we rescale the earlier indexes so that for each industry and each country, export variety in 1988 equals that in 1989. In addition, we include an indicator variable for 1989 in the regressions, to further control for the change in classification systems.

4. This amount is the elasticity of Mexico's export variety with respect to China's export variety, multiplied by the average increase in China's export variety, which is 63.3 – 42.1 = 21.2, from panel (a) of table 8.2.

References

Berndt, E. R., M. K. Kyle, and D. Ling. 2002. "The Long Shadow of Patent Expiration: Generic Entry and Rx to OTC Switches." In *Scanner Data and Price Indexes*, ed. Robert C. Feenstra and Matthew Shapiro, NBER Studies in Income and Wealth, 229–67. Chicago: University of Chicago Press.

Bhattashli, D., S. Li, and W. Martin. 2004. *China and the WTO: Accession, Policy Reform, and Poverty Reduction Strategies*. Washington, DC: World Bank.

Broda, C., J. Greenfield, and D. Weinstein. 2006. "From Groundnuts to Globalization: A Structural Estimate of Trade and Growth." NBER Working Paper 12512, National Bureau of Economic Research, Cambridge, MA.

Broda, C., and D. Weinstein. 2006. "Globalization and the Gains from Variety." *Quarterly Journal of Economics* 121 (2): 541–85.

Dasgupta, Dipak. 1997. *China 2020: China Engaged, Integration with the Global Economy*. Washington, DC: World Bank.

Debaere, Peter, and Shalah Mostashari. 2005. "Do Tariffs Matter for the Extensive Margin of International Trade? An Empirical Analysis." CEPR Discussion Paper 5260, Centre for Economic Policy Research, London.

Dollar, D., and A. Kraay. 2001. "Trade, Growth and Poverty." Policy Research Working Paper 2615, World Bank, Washington, DC.

Feenstra, R. C. 1994. "New Product Varieties and the Measurement of International Prices." *American Economic Review* 84 (A1): 157–77.

Feenstra, R. C., and H. L. Kee. 2004. "On the Measurement of Product Variety in Trade." *American Economic Review* 94 (2): 145–49.

———. 2008. "Export Variety and Country Productivity: Estimating the Monopolistic Competition Model with Endogenous Productivity." *Journal of International Economics* 74 (2): 500–18.

Feenstra, R. C., D. Madani, T. Yang, and C. Liang. 1999. "Testing Endogenous Growth in South Korea and Taiwan." *Journal of Development Economics* 60 (2): 317–41.

Feenstra, R. C., J. Romalis, and P. Schott. 2002. "U.S. Imports, Exports, and Tariff Data, 1989–2001." NBER Working Paper 9387, National Bureau of Economic Research, Cambridge, MA.

Frankel, J. A., and D. Romer. 1999. "Does Trade Cause Growth?" *American Economic Review* 89 (3): 379–99.

Funke, M., and R. Ruhwedel. 2001. "Product Variety and Economic Growth: Empirical Evidence from the OECD Countries." *IMF Staff Papers* 48 (2): 225–42.

Griliches, Z., and I. M. Cockburn. 1994. "Generics and New Goods in Pharmaceutical Price Indexes." *American Economic Review* 84 (A5): 1213–32.

Grossman, G. M., and E. Helpman. 1991. *Innovation and Growth in the Global Economy*. Cambridge, MA: MIT Press.

Hausman, J. A. 1997. "Valuation of New Goods under Perfect and Imperfect Competition." In *The Economics of New Goods*, ed. Timothy F. Bresnahan and Robert J. Gordon. NBER Studies in Income and Wealth, vol. 58, 209–37. Chicago: University of Chicago Press.

———. 1999. "Cellular Telephone, New Products, and the CPI." *Journal of Business and Economic Statistics* 17 (A2): 188–94.

Hicks, J. R. 1940. "The Valuation of Social Income." *Economica* 7: 105–24.

Hummels, D., and P. Klenow. 2005. "The Variety and Quality of a Nation's Trade." *American Economic Review* 95 (3): 704–23.

Kehoe, T. J., and K. J. Ruhl. 2002. "How Important Is the New Goods Margin in International Trade?" Federal Reserve Bank of Minneapolis, *Staff Report* No. 324.

Rodriguez, F., and D. Rodrik. 2000. "Trade Policy and Economic Growth: A Skeptic's Guide to the Cross-National Evidence." In *NBER Macroeconomics Annual 2000*, ed. Ben S. Bernanke and Kenneth Rogoff, 261–325. Cambridge, MA: MIT Press.

Romer, P. 1990. "Endogenous Technical Change." *Journal of Political Economy* 98 (5, Part 2): S71–S102.

9

The Impact of Trade with China and India on Argentina's Manufacturing Employment

*Lucio Castro, Marcelo Olarreaga, and Daniel Saslavsky**

"China and India are seen by many as two mighty giants threatening the jobs of the manufacturing industry."
La Nación Newspaper, Buenos Aires
March 2005

"[We] must not repeat the mistakes of the nineties, when an 'invasion' of Chinese products destroyed entire sectors of our industry ...."
Communiqué of CAME
(Medium Enterprises Association of Argentina)
April 6, 2004

Introduction

For many in Latin America, the increasing participation of China and India in international markets is seen as a looming shadow of two "mighty giants" on the region's industrial sector, and one of the major causes behind the significant reduction of employment in the manufacturing

* The opinions presented here are those of the authors and do not necessarily represent the official position of the institutions to which they belong. A version of this paper is part of Lucio Castro's DPhil in Economics dissertation at the University of Sussex.

industry in the 1990s. Are these claims justified? Are China and India driving the secular fall in manufacturing jobs in Latin America?

This chapter attempts to provide answers to these questions with a focus on Argentina, which experienced a 31 percent decline in industrial employment over the 1990s, while the share of imports from China and India increased sixfold. The analysis applies a dynamic econometric model where labor demand in each industry is a function of wages, capital stock, prices, and productivity. Prices and productivity are functions of import and export penetration, and allow identification of the impact that trade with China and India is having on labor demand in Argentina's manufacturing sector.

In principle, trade should affect the level of employment across and within sectors. Empirical research on the impact of trade on employment has found little evidence either way, particularly in developing countries.[1] Using plant-level data for Morocco, Currie and Harrison (1997) found only a small impact of trade liberalization on the level of employment. Revenga (1997) found no statistically significant relationship between the level of employment and tariff liberalization in the case of Mexico. Pagés-Serra and Márquez (1998) examined the relationship between trade liberalization and employment in the Latin America and the Caribbean region (LAC) and could not find any substantial effect. A comprehensive study by the Inter-American Development Bank (IADB 2004) using household survey data for 10 LAC countries did not find a statistically significant association between the two phenomena. De Ferranti et al. (2002) confirmed this result for several countries in LAC. In a similar study that also contemplated the effects of exchange rate appreciation, Haltiwanger et al. (2004) did not find robust results on the relationship between trade liberalization and changes in net employment in the region. In their paper on the impact of trade liberalization on income distribution in Colombia, Attanasio, Goldberg, and Pavcnik (2003) found no evidence of labor reallocation across sectors. Similarly, small employment effects in Latin America are reported in Levinsohn (1999) for Chile; Moreira and Najberg (2000) for Brazil; and Casacuberta, Fachola, and Gandelman (2004) for Uruguay.

For Argentina, in particular, Galiani and Sanguinetti (2003) found only a small correlation between trade liberalization and the rate of employment in the 1990s. Pessino and Andres (2005) attributed the negative effects of trade liberalization on employment to the distortions and rigidities of Argentina's labor market rather than to trade liberalization. Sánchez and Butler (2004) pointed to other factors beyond trade liberalization, such as labor costs, access to credit finance, financial and real shocks, informality, and the like.

Other studies, such as Altimir and Beccaria (1999) and Damill, Frenkel, and Maurizio (2002), pointed to the accelerated process of trade liberalization combined with exchange rate appreciation as the main culprits of the net employment loss suffered by the Argentine manufacturing sector in the 1990s. In sum, the evidence presented in these studies is not conclusive. This chapter is not concerned about which policies may have been the cause of that decline, but rather about whether imports from the two rapidly growing Asian economies can explain part of this trend.

Results suggest that increased trade with China can explain just a negligible share of the decline in manufacturing labor demand. Moreover, the increase in overall import penetration during the period could explain a relatively small share of the decline in manufacturing employment. To be more precise, a 1 percentage point increase in import penetration leads to a 0.07 percent decline in labor demand. Given that import penetration increased by 79 percent over the sample period (1991–2003), the decline in labor demand that can be attributed to the increase in import penetration is about 6 percent. Given that manufacturing employment declined by 31 percent over the sample period, the increase in import penetration can at most explain 20 percent of the observed loss in manufacturing employment. The other 80 percent resulted from other causes. The increased importance of China as a source of imports had an almost negligible marginal impact on the decline in labor demand associated with the increase in overall imports. A 1 percentage point increase in the share of imports from China leads to an additional 0.02 percent decline in the growth of Argentina's labor demand. Thus, the sixfold increase in the share of imports from China over the period (from 1 percent to 6 percent) could only explain an additional 0.1 to 0.2 percent decline in labor demand. Moreover, an increase in the share of imports from Brazil of 1 percentage point would have a marginal impact that is twice as large, which arguably is still very small, taking into account Brazil is Argentina's largest trade partner. Perhaps more worrisome, the small negative impact on employment of increased imports from China and Brazil is concentrated in unskilled-labor-intensive sectors. Results for India, the European Union (EU), and the United States suggest that increases in the share of imports from these countries do not have an impact on labor demand (beyond the overall impact of import penetration on labor demand). Increases in exports do not seem to have an impact on manufacturing employment regardless of their destination, with the exception of the Indian market.

The remainder of the chapter is organized as follows: The following section presents some stylized facts about trade liberalization in Argentina and the country's trade with China and India, as well as about the evolution of manufacturing employment. The next section presents the theoretical model and the empirical strategy, and is followed by a section presenting the results. The final section concludes.

Stylized Facts

Manufacturing employment in Argentina has continuously declined since the early 1980s (figure 9.1). Between 1991 and 2003, industrial

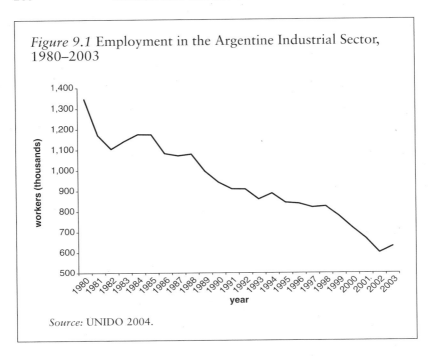

Figure 9.1 Employment in the Argentine Industrial Sector, 1980–2003

Source: UNIDO 2004.

employment declined by 31 percent.[2] Losses in industrial employment were only partially compensated for by an increase in employment in the services sector. The net change in overall employment was negative, resulting in two-digit unemployment rates over most of the period. Only from 2003 onward has manufacturing employment experienced a recovery.

During the same approximate period, the aggregate productivity of the industrial sector increased by an average of 6.8 percent for 1991–99. Productivity increased most in capital-intensive sectors such as iron and steel, electric machinery, and transport equipment and least in natural resources and labor-intensive subsectors.[3]

In parallel to these changes in the aggregate level of industrial employment, Argentina experienced a deep, fast process of trade liberalization.[4] The trade-openness coefficient (exports plus imports as a percentage of gross domestic product [GDP]) went from 6.0 percent in 1993 to 23.4 percent in 2001, falling to 21.7 percent in 2003 as a result of the economic collapse of Argentina in 2002. Imports as a percentage of GDP increased from 9 percent in 1990 to 11 percent in 2001, and fell to 8 percent in 2003. Exports as a percentage of GDP rose from 7 percent to 12 percent over the period.[5] For the manufacturing industry, in particular, import penetration increased by almost 79 percent from 1991 to 2003.

As shown in table 9.1, changes in import penetration and share in an industry's total employment varied significantly across manufacturing

Table 9.1 Total Import Penetration and Changes in Industry Share in Total Industrial Employment, 1980–2003

| ISIC | Industry description | Total import penetration (average annual percentage) | | | Year-on-year percentage change in industry share in total industrial employment, 1991–2003 |
		1980–90	1991–2000	2001–03	
311	Food products	1.0	3.8	2.7	21.79
313	Beverages	0.7	1.6	0.5	57.26
314	Tobacco	0.3	0.1	0.5	25.58
321	Textiles	1.7	12.4	11.7	−24.83
322	Wearing apparel, except footwear	1.2	6.5	4.2	−3.18
323	Leather products	0.9	12.0	11.3	26.14
324	Footwear, except rubber or plastic	0.8	10.7	6.0	60.55
331	Wood products, except furniture	8.2	16.4	12.3	−21.45
332	Furniture, except metal	0.2	11.4	18.0	6.64
341	Paper and products	8.2	19.8	15.9	22.18
342	Printing and publishing	1.9	4.2	2.8	29.20
351	Industrial chemicals	24.2	40.0	41.7	−19.20
352	Other chemicals	6.0	12.4	13.0	31.87
353	Petroleum refineries	1.7	5.4	4.9	4.55
354	Miscellaneous petroleum and coal products	5.8	25.9	28.0	−92.83

(continued)

Table 9.1 Total Import Penetration and Changes in Industry Share in Total Industrial Employment, 1980–2003 (continued)

ISIC	Industry description	Total import penetration (average annual percentage)			Year-on-year percentage change in industry share in total industrial employment, 1991–2003
		1980–90	1991–2000	2001–03	
355	Rubber products	4.3	28.8	33.5	1.69
356	Plastic products	2.6	12.5	8.2	64.30
361	Pottery, china, and earthenware	2.0	13.8	13.1	−74.63
362	Glass and products	5.0	18.5	15.5	−8.14
369	Other non-metallic mineral products	3.9	5.3	3.3	−54.09
371	Iron and steel	14.5	16.2	29.7	−35.58
372	Non-ferrous metals	19.7	29.5	33.1	−16.16
381	Fabricated metal products	3.8	16.1	14.6	−37.68
382	Machinery, except electrical	28.8	55.3	45.7	21.46
383	Machinery, electric	23.0	49.0	48.2	5.96
384	Transport equipment	7.6	35.5	44.2	−27.54
385	Professional and scientific equipment	43.7	61.8	70.9	−4.52
390	Other manufactured products	23.8	60.3	55.3	−18.61

Source: Author's calculations based on UNIDO 2004 and UN Comtrade 2004.
Note: ISIC = International Standard Industrial Classification.

subsectors in the 1990s. However, a clear pattern does not seem to emerge by simply looking at the evolution of these two variables. For instance, sectors such as textiles, apparel, and footwear experienced similar increases in import penetration over the period, but the first two sectors saw their share of total manufacturing employment decline, whereas footwear experienced an above-average increase in its share of manufacturing employment. More generally, while import penetration increased for all manufacturing subsectors in 1991–2003 relative to 1980–90, only half of these subsectors experienced a contraction in their share in total industrial employment.[6] This evidence suggests that disentangling the impact of imports on employment may not be straightforward.

The growing importance of China and India as trading partners is a relatively new phenomenon for Argentina. Figure 9.2 shows that imports from China, and to a lesser extent India, did not begin to represent a nonnegligible share of Argentina's imports until the mid-1990s. Though the share of China in Argentina's total imports remained relatively low, it increased almost sixfold between 1990 and 2003. Likewise, India's share increased almost sevenfold. Figure 9.3 reports the same information for Argentina's main trading partners: Brazil, EU, and the United States.[7]

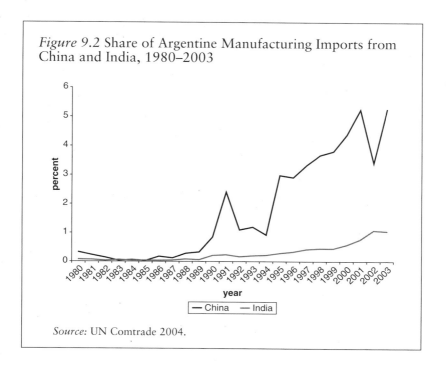

Figure 9.2 Share of Argentine Manufacturing Imports from China and India, 1980–2003

Source: UN Comtrade 2004.

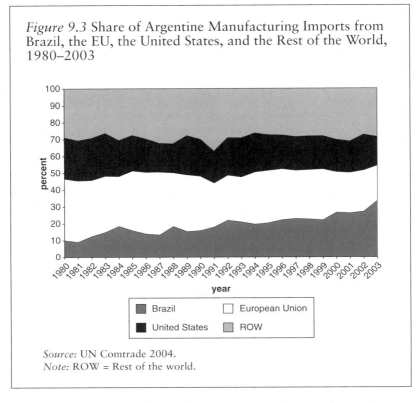

Figure 9.3 Share of Argentine Manufacturing Imports from Brazil, the EU, the United States, and the Rest of the World, 1980–2003

Source: UN Comtrade 2004.
Note: ROW = Rest of the world.

The already small share of imports from China in total imports declined severely during Argentina's economic collapse in 2002 and began to recover after 2003. Imports from India were not an important share of total imports at any time during the entire period. Imports from India amounted to more than 1 percent of total imports only after 2002.

Nevertheless, trade with China and India is mostly interindustry (that is, trade of goods between different industry classifications), highlighted by very low intra-industry trade indicators.[8] At the same time, both imports from and exports to these markets are extremely concentrated in a few products (Tramutola, Castro, and Monat 2005). This suggests that the potential for intersector reallocation of labor could be important even when Argentine trade with these Asian economies is relatively small.

Thus, it is important to capture these trends at the industry level. Table 9.2 shows information on China's import penetration into Argentina for 28 manufacturing industries between 1980 and 2003. In the 1990s, China's import penetration was concentrated in a few, mostly capital-intensive, sectors, such as electric and nonelectric machinery, scientific and professional

Table 9.2 Argentine Import Penetration from China, 1980–2003

ISIC	Industry description	Import penetration from China (average annual percentage over the period)		
		1980–90	*1991–2000*	*2001–03*
311	Food products	0.00	0.02	0.02
313	Beverages	0.00	0.00	0.00
314	Tobacco	0.00	0.00	0.00
321	Textiles	0.07	0.65	0.36
322	Wearing apparel, except footwear	0.02	**1.25**	0.82
323	Leather products	0.01	**4.77**	**5.30**
324	Footwear, except rubber or plastic	0.01	**1.85**	0.56
331	Wood products, except furniture	0.00	0.22	0.23
332	Furniture, except metal	0.00	0.36	**1.13**
341	Paper and products	0.00	0.02	0.03
342	Printing and publishing	0.00	0.09	0.08
351	Industrial chemicals	0.05	0.63	**1.50**
352	Other chemicals	0.01	0.15	0.14
353	Petroleum refineries	0.00	0.00	0.01
354	Miscellaneous petroleum and coal products	0.00	0.00	0.01
355	Rubber products	0.00	0.45	0.97
356	Plastic products	0.01	0.98	0.71
361	Pottery, china, and earthenware	0.06	**3.13**	**2.95**
362	Glass and products	0.00	0.44	0.76
369	Other non-metallic mineral products	0.00	0.05	0.10
371	Iron and steel	0.00	0.14	0.93
372	Non-ferrous metals	0.00	0.15	0.57
381	Fabricated metal products	0.02	0.86	**1.19**
382	Machinery, except electrical	0.01	**1.17**	**2.94**
383	Machinery, electric	0.02	**2.21**	**4.75**
384	Transport equipment	0.02	0.31	0.64
385	Professional and scientific equipment	0.14	**2.10**	**3.64**
390	Other manufactured products	0.56	**10.51**	**13.88**

Source: Authors' calculations based on UNIDO 2004 and UN Comtrade 2005.

Note: ISIC = International Standard Industrial Classification. Import penetration coefficients higher than 1 percent are in bold.

instruments, and other manufactures. These subsectors are facing more competition from imports from all sources, not only from China. Some labor-intensive sectors such as leather and furniture also faced relatively higher import competition from China.

Likewise, table 9.3 describes import competition from India. Although import competition from India increased slightly in the 1990s compared with previous decades, it remained at very low levels. In fact, with the exception of industrial chemicals, imports from India represented less than 1 percent of Argentina's output.

Table 9.3 Argentine Import Penetration from India, 1980–2003

ISIC	Industry description	Import penetration from India (average annual percentage over the period)		
		1980–90	1991–2000	2001–03
311	Food products	0.0	0.0	0.0
313	Beverages	0.0	0.0	0.0
314	Tobacco	0.0	0.0	0.0
321	Textiles	0.0	0.2	0.2
322	Wearing apparel, except footwear	0.0	0.2	0.2
323	Leather products	0.0	0.1	0.1
324	Footwear, except rubber or plastic	0.0	0.0	0.0
331	Wood products, except furniture	0.0	0.0	0.0
332	Furniture, except metal	0.0	0.0	0.0
341	Paper and products	0.0	0.0	0.0
342	Printing and publishing	0.0	0.0	0.0
351	Industrial chemicals	0.0	0.4	1.3
352	Other chemicals	0.0	0.1	0.1
353	Petroleum refineries	0.0	0.0	0.1
354	Miscellaneous petroleum and coal products	0.0	0.0	0.0
355	Rubber products	0.0	0.2	0.3
356	Plastic products	0.0	0.0	0.0

(continued)

Table 9.3 Argentine Import Penetration from India, 1980–2003 (*continued*)

ISIC	Industry description	Import penetration from India (average annual percentage over the period)		
		1980–90	*1991–2000*	*2001–03*
361	Pottery, china, and earthenware	0.0	0.0	0.0
362	Glass and products	0.0	0.0	0.0
369	Other non-metallic mineral products	0.0	0.0	0.0
371	Iron and steel	0.0	0.0	0.2
372	Non-ferrous metals	0.0	0.0	0.0
381	Fabricated metal products	0.0	0.1	**0.1**
382	Machinery, except electrical	0.0	**0.0**	**0.0**
383	Machinery, electric	0.0	**0.0**	**0.0**
384	Transport equipment	0.0	0.2	0.1
385	Professional and scientific equipment	0.0	0.1	0.1
390	Other manufactured products	0.0	0.1	0.2

Source: Authors' calculations based on UNIDO 2004 and UN Comtrade 2005.
Note: ISIC = International Standard Industrial Classification. Import penetration coefficients higher than 1 percent are in bold.

To summarize, the surface evidence regarding the impact of increases in import penetration on employment in Argentina is mixed. Moreover, the rapid growth in imports from China and India is even less likely to have had a significant impact given that they still represent a small share of Argentina's imports. However, this quick look at the data does not obviously imply causality, and can be misleading. It would be misleading if, for example, there is correlation of the evolution of import penetration and import shares from China and India with other forces that had a significant impact on manufacturing employment in Argentina. It would also be misleading in the presence of reverse causality: import penetration might be increasing because employment is declining. To try to identify the role played by trade and the growth of Argentina's trade with China and India, the chapter now turns to a more formal empirical model that will help address these issues.

The Model and the Empirical Strategy

The model and empirical strategy are as follows.

The Model

To estimate the impact of changes on import penetration on labor demand, the analysis follows Greenaway, Hine, and Wright (1999) and assumes a Cobb-Douglas production function across industry and time:

$$q_{it} = A_{it} k_{it}^{\alpha} l_{it}^{\beta}, \tag{9.1}$$

where q is real output, k is capital stock, l is units of labor employed, and A is a Hicks-neutral productivity term; α and β are the share of each factor used in total output. The analysis further assumes that labor markets are perfectly competitive so that the wage bill equals the value of output multiplied by the labor share in output. Solving the first-order condition for labor yields

$$l_{it} = \frac{\beta p_{it} q_{it}}{w_{it}}, \tag{9.2}$$

where p is the domestic price of the good i and w is the labor wage. By substituting equation (9.1) into equation (9.2) and rearranging, the equation yields the following expression:

$$l_{it} = \beta p_{it} \frac{\left[A k_{it}^{\alpha} l^{\beta} \right]}{w_{it}}. \tag{9.3}$$

Then equation (9.3) is solved for labor demand of industry i at time t:

$$l_{it} = \left\{ \frac{\left[\left(p_{it} \beta A k_{it}^{\alpha} \right) \right]}{w_{it}} \right\}^{(1/1-\beta)}. \tag{9.4}$$

In contrast to Greenaway, Hine, and Wright's (1999) output-constrained model, equation (9.4) conditions labor demand not on output but on the capital stock. Thus, output is allowed to vary according to changes in domestic prices associated with changes in trade liberalization. This may be an important channel through which trade affects the level of employment at the industry level. One would expect the impact of import penetration on labor demand to be larger when conditioning on capital rather than on output because the former allows for the adjustment of output as import penetration changes. By conditioning labor demand on output, the only channel left for changes in import penetration to affect employment is through its impact on total factor productivity. This is likely to be positive because it reduces x-inefficiencies when less efficient firms exit and more efficient firms become more prominent in the industry.[9] By conditioning on capital, the analysis allows imports to affect employment through changes in both total factor productivity and domestic prices leading to changes in output.[10]

More formally, the analysis assumes that Ap_{it} is a function of import and export penetration:

$$Ap_{it} = e_{it}^{(\lambda_0 T_i)} M_{it}^{\left(\lambda_1 + \left(1/\eta^M\right)\right)} X_{it}^{\left(\lambda_2 + \left(1/\eta^X\right)\right)}, \quad \lambda_0, \lambda_1, \lambda_2 > 0 \tag{9.5}$$

where T is a time trend, M is a measure of import penetration, X is a measure of export penetration, η^M the import-demand elasticity, and η^X is the export-supply elasticity.

While η^M is negative and, therefore, an increase in imports will decrease p_{it} (and thus employment) through this channel, η^X positive and, therefore, an increase in exports will increase p_{it} (and consequently employment) through this conduit.

Substituting equation (9.5) into equation (9.4) and taking logs yields

$$\ln l_{it} = \alpha_0 + \alpha_1 \ln K_{it} + \alpha_2 \ln w_{it} + \alpha_3 \ln M_{it} + \alpha_4 \ln X_{it} + \alpha_5 T + \alpha_6 I + \varepsilon \tag{9.6}$$

Equation (9.6) is the basis for this chapter's empirical model using both industry and time dummies. Time dummies (T) capture not only the time trend of the productivity parameter, but also any general liberalization program that may have occurred (such as an overall 10 percent cut in tariffs) or increase in tariffs, as well as the impact of changes in the exchange rate or any other macroeconomic shock, such as the 2001 crisis. Industry dummies (I) capture industry particularities, such as the fact that some of the industries (for example, petroleum products) were subject to significant privatization during the 1990s. So the estimates refer to the within-industry impact of trade liberalization on industry employment, controlling for macroeconomic shocks and the general equilibrium effects of general trade liberalization with year dummies.

Because the point of interest is the impact that Argentina's trade with China and India had on manufacturing employment, the study also adds to equation (9.6) the Chinese and Indian shares on total imports and exports, as well as the import and export share of Argentina's three main trading partners (Brazil, the European Union, and the United States) to capture the marginal impact associated with trade with different partners. Finally, the analysis also examines whether unskilled labor tends to be relatively more affected, by interacting unskilled and skilled labor dummies with the trade shares.

Empirical Strategy

Two problems with the estimation of equation (9.6) can bias the estimates. First, labor demand is likely to show inertia, which may lead to first-order serial correlation in the errors. Second, wages and capital stocks are potentially endogenous variables (although theoretically they have been treated as exogenous).

The potential serial correlation of the error term is addressed by including lagged employment as an explanatory variable, and testing for first- and second-order correlation of the error term after introducing the lagged dependent variable. This also provides long-run elasticity estimates. However, as shown in the mainstream literature (see Kiviet 1995), the inclusion of a lagged dependent variable in a panel setting also leads to biased and inconsistent estimates when using ordinary least squares.

The second problem is addressed by using the first, second, and third lagged values of wage and capital as instruments for wages and capital stocks, and using the first, second, and third lagged values of our additional instruments—a proxy for transportation costs, sector value added, and the share of low-skilled labor in each industry.[11]

Results

Table 9.4 reports the estimates of equation (9.6) using not only the system generalized method of moments (GMM) estimator, but also the output-constrained model as in Greenaway, Hine, and Wright (1999). The capital-constrained model results reported in the first column of table 9.4 have the expected signs; wages and capital are statistically significant at 1 percent, as is the lagged dependent variable.[12] Capital seems to have a complementary effect on employment, as indicated by the positive sign of its coefficient.[13] Import penetration is significant at the 5 percent level. According to these results, a 1 percentage point increase in import penetration tends to reduce employment by 0.084 percent in the short run and 0.15 percent in the long run. Export penetration has a positive, but statistically insignificant, coefficient.

The second column reports the results of the model in which estimates are conditional on output. Again, all coefficients have the expected signs. Of interest, the estimated coefficient on import penetration is 60 percent smaller than in the case of the model conditional on capital. They are not, however, statistically different from each other.

The null hypothesis of no second-order serial correlation of the error term cannot be rejected in both regressions, and the null hypothesis of no over-identification is rejected. This suggests that there is no evidence that these estimates are biased because of either serial correlation of the error term or lack of identification in the regressions.

Table 9.4 Regression Results from Base Model

Dependent variable: Employment	(1) Capital constrained	(2) Output constrained
Employment (t-1)	0.456***	0.187***
	[0.052]	[0.037]
Wage	−0.279***	−0.280***
	[0.040]	[0.024]
Capital or output	0.222***	0.624***
	[0.039]	[0.059]
Total import penetration	−0.084**	−0.050**
	[0.033]	[0.022]
Total export penetration	0.007	0.029**
	[0.019]	[0.013]
Constant	3.397**	1.424
	[1.390]	[1.051]
Hansen J-Statistic/Sargan	0.00	0.07
2nd-order auto-correlation (AC) test (p-value)	0.63	0.80

Source: Authors.

Note: Time and sector dummies are included in all regressions but are not reported. Robust standard error is in brackets. System GMM corresponds to one-step estimation. All continuous variables are expressed in logs.

**Significant at 5 percent level.
***Significant at 1 percent level.

Table 9.5 reports the system GMM estimations only for the capital-constrained specification, but including trade shares by partner, to assess the marginal impact of imports and exports with different trading partners. The coefficients on lagged employment, wage, and capital stock show the expected signs and are highly significant and stable across specifications. The total import penetration coefficient is always negative and significant around the 1 to 5 percent threshold. As shown, an increase of 1 percentage point in total import penetration generates a job loss of around 0.07 percent. Given that import penetration increased by 79 percent over the sample period (1991–2003), the decline in labor demand that can be attributed to the increase in import penetration is around 6 percent in the short run and 10 percent in the long run. Given that manufacturing employment declined by 31 percent over the sample period (1991–2003), the increase in import penetration can at most explain 32 percent of the observed loss in

Table 9.5 Regression Results from Augmented Model, 1991–2003

Dependent variable: Employment	(1)	(2)	(3)	(4)
Employment (−1)	0.493*** [0.054]	0.459*** [0.056]	0.453*** [0.051]	0.457*** [0.049]
Wage	−0.276*** [0.039]	−0.276*** [0.039]	−0.281*** [0.045]	−0.296*** [0.047]
Capital	0.238*** [0.041]	0.218*** [0.036]	0.230*** [0.042]	0.256*** [0.047]
Import penetration		−0.082** [0.032]	−0.072** [0.033]	−0.068** [0.033]
Share of imports from China			−0.018* [0.010]	−0.017** [0.008]
Share of imports from Brazil			−0.040*** [0.012]	−0.039** [0.014]
Share of imports from EU + United States			−0.048 [0.028]	−0.047 [0.034]
Share of imports from India			0.004 [0.008]	0.002 [0.007]
Export penetration				0.027 [0.023]
Share of exports to China				0.001 [0.003]
Share of exports to Brazil				0.009 [0.011]
Share of exports to EU + United States				0.006 [0.006]
Share of exports to India				0.017** [0.008]
Constant	2.687* [1.496]	3.469*** [1.198]	3.064** [1.245]	2.465* [1.440]
Year dummy 1991	−0.141*** [0.049]	−0.070* [0.035]	−0.124*** [0.039]	−0.107** [0.045]
Year dummy 1992	−0.188*** [0.047]	−0.078** [0.038]	−0.129** [0.050]	−0.103 [0.064]
Year dummy 1993	0.105* [0.054]	0.228*** [0.047]	0.177*** [0.040]	0.203*** [0.040]
Year dummy 1994	0.121*** [0.029]	0.252*** [0.029]	0.204*** [0.033]	0.225*** [0.038]

(continued)

Table 9.5 Regression Results from Augmented Model, 1991–2003 (*continued*)

Dependent variable: Employment	(1)	(2)	(3)	(4)
Year dummy 1995	0.082** [0.032]	0.216*** [0.033]	0.186*** [0.031]	0.193*** [0.034]
Year dummy 1996	0.098*** [0.031]	0.237*** [0.031]	0.210*** [0.033]	0.216*** [0.036]
Year dummy 1997	−0.022 [0.035]	0.134*** [0.037]	0.102** [0.038]	0.101** [0.039]
Year dummy 1998	0.046* [0.024]	0.206*** [0.029]	0.175*** [0.035]	0.187*** [0.038]
Year dummy 1999	0.022 [0.018]	0.177*** [0.027]	0.157*** [0.028]	0.168*** [0.030]
Year dummy 2000	0.016 [0.013]	0.166*** [0.027]	0.150*** [0.025]	0.159*** [0.027]
Year dummy 2001		0.149*** [0.027]	0.131*** [0.027]	0.128*** [0.026]
Year dummy 2002	−0.080*** [0.012]			
Year dummy 2003	0.006 [0.016]	0.100*** [0.016]	0.093*** [0.019]	0.097*** [0.019]
Hansen J-Statistic/ Sargan	0.02	0.01	0.00	0.00
2nd order auto-correlation (AC)	0.78	0.66	0.77	0.54
Observations: 364				

Source: Authors.

Note: Sector dummies are included in all regressions but are not reported. Robust standard error is in brackets. System GMM corresponds to one-step estimation. All continuous variables are expressed in logs.

* Significant at 10 percent level.
** Significant at 5 percent level.
*** Significant at 1 percent level.

manufacturing employment. The coefficient on total exports/consumption (or "exports penetration") shows the expected sign, but it is not statistically significant, thus supporting the specification of the models.

The last two columns explore the marginal impact on employment of imports and exports with China, India, and Argentina's three main trading partners. For China, the coefficient on imports is negative and significant at the 5 percent level in both columns. This implies that, other things being equal, an increase of 1 percentage point in the share of Chinese imports generates a decrease in labor demand of around 0.02 percent (and around 0.04 percent in the long run). Thus, the sixfold increase in the share of imports from China over the period (from 1 percent to 6 percent) could explain an almost negligible 0.1 to 0.2 percent additional decline in labor demand. Of interest, an increase in the share of imports from Brazil of 1 percentage point would have an impact twice as large, which arguably is still very small. Imports from India, or the European Union and the United States do not appear to have any additional impact on employment levels. Exports to different trading partners do not seem to have any additional impact on employment, except for exports to India, but its economic significance is negligible.

Finally, year dummies reported in table 9.5 indicate that unobserved effects had negative and significant effects on sectoral employment, as in 1991 and 1992. In fact, those years marked the beginning of a sweeping and profound structural reform package implemented in Argentina. Among other things, these measures included privatization and downsizing of state-owned companies in the services and manufacturing sectors, and an aggressive unilateral tariff-cut program.[14] The other coefficient found to be negative was reported for 2002, when the financial and currency crisis was taking place. Again, all four regressions in table 9.5 cannot reject the null hypothesis of no second-order serial correlation in the error term and reject the null hypothesis of no over-identification.

Table 9.6 reports the results for the third column in table 9.5, but exploring for heterogeneity across industries' labor-skill intensity. Results suggest that the marginal (and small) additional impact of imports from both China and Brazil is concentrated in low-skill-intensive industries. In the case of China, an increase of 1 percentage point in its import share leads to a decline in the employment of unskilled-intensive sectors of around 0.02 percent. The effect is again twice as large for Brazil. In contrast, high-skill-intensive sectors seem not to be affected by imports sourced from either China or Brazil. Again, the over-identification and the second-order serial correlation tests do not suggest that there are problems with this regression.

Conclusion

Over the decade of the 1990s, import penetration in Argentina's manufacturing sector increased by 79 percent, while imports from China and India increased sixfold, and manufacturing employment declined by 33 percent. Many believed that the sharp decline in employment was mainly due to rapidly growing imports from the two Asian economies. A more careful look suggests that the evidence is mixed at best. Total import competition increased significantly across sectors but manufacturing employment (measured as a share of total employment in the industry) declined for

Table 9.6 Regression Results from Augmented Model, 1991–2003

Dependent variable: Employment	(1)	(2)	(3)
Employment (−1)	0.461*** [0.062]	0.463*** [0.062]	0.494*** [0.078]
Wage	−0.279*** [0.043]	−0.277*** [0.042]	−0.282*** [0.043]
Capital	0.230*** [0.040]	0.228*** [0.039]	0.251*** [0.045]
Low skill dummy		0.070 [0.117]	0.133 [0.123]
Import penetration	−0.071** [0.033]	−0.073** [0.033]	−0.077** [0.032]
Share of imports from China * low skill dummy	−0.018* [0.011]	−0.017* [0.011]	−0.017* [0.012]
Share of imports from China * high skill dummy	−0.016 [0.011]	−0.019 [0.012]	−0.025* [0.013]
Share of imports from Brazil * low skill dummy	−0.038*** [0.012]	−0.038*** [0.012]	−0.033** [0.016]
Share of imports from Brazil * high skill dummy	−0.030 [0.035]	−0.042 [0.041]	−0.079* [0.040]
Share of imports from EU + United States * low skill dummy	−0.044 [0.028]	−0.044 [0.028]	−0.051 [0.033]
Share of imports from EU + United States * high skill dummy	−0.049 [0.045]	−0.074 [0.070]	−0.171** [0.082]
Share of imports from India * low skill dummy	0.005 [0.006]	0.005 [0.007]	0.005 [0.007]
Share of imports from India * high skill dummy	0.005 [0.013]	0.004 [0.013]	0.003 [0.013]
Export penetration			0.035 [0.025]
Share of exports to China * low skill dummy			−0.001 [0.005]
Share of exports to China * high skill dummy			0.003 [0.006]
Share of exports to Brazil * low skill dummy			0.001 [0.008]
Share of exports to Brazil * high skill dummy			0.052*** [0.016]

(continued)

Table 9.6 Regression Results from Augmented Model, 1991–2003 *(continued)*

Dependent variable: Employment	(1)	(2)	(3)
Share of exports to EU + United States * low skill dummy			0.007 [0.006]
Share of exports to EU + United States * high skill dummy			0.002 [0.022]
Share of exports to India * low skill dummy			0.021 [0.012]
Share of exports to India * high skill dummy			0.021** [0.008]
Constant	3.013** [1.246]	2.973** [1.261]	1.752 [1.656]
Hansen J Statistic/Sargan	0.0	0.0	0.0
2nd order auto-correlation (AC)	0.83	0.77	0.95
Observations: 364			

Source: Authors.

Note: Sector dummies are included in all regressions but are not reported. Robust standard error is in brackets. System GMM corresponds to one-step estimation. All continuous variables are expressed in logs.

* Significant at 10 percent level.
** Significant at 5 percent level.
*** Significant at 1 percent level.

some subsectors and increased for others. With the exception of apparel and footwear, employment did not decline in sectors in which China and India had significant and growing shares of Argentina's imports. Moreover, the two Asian economies still account for less than 6 percent of Argentina's import bundle.

To take a more careful look at whether imports from China and India are responsible for the decline in manufacturing employment in Argentina, this analysis develops a dynamic econometric model, in which import penetration and export penetration can affect the level of employment through their impacts on domestic prices and productivity, while controlling for industry and time effects.

Results suggest that the rapid increase in import penetration in Argentina's manufacturing employment can only explain a small fraction (20 percent) of the large decline in manufacturing employment observed during the period. Imports from China had a slightly larger impact on manufacturing employment than imports from the rest of the world, probably because China is a relatively labor-abundant country. However, the marginal impact of imports from Brazil is twice as large as imports from China, although economically still insignificant. Imports from India or Argentina's other two main trading partners (the European Union and the United States) do not seem to have any additional marginal impact (beyond the impact of import penetration) on manufacturing employment.

Imports from both China and India tend to impose larger declines on the level of employment in unskilled-intensive sectors, although, again, the marginal effect on unskilled employment of imports from Brazil is twice as large as the effect of imports from China. Again, imports from other sources do not have a statistically significant impact when exploring the heterogeneity across skilled- and unskilled-intensive industries.

Perhaps a surprise, exports do not seem to contribute to manufacturing employment. The coefficient on export penetration is always positive, but never statistically so. Moreover, even if such coefficients were statistically significant, the magnitude of the impact is small, given the estimated coefficients. This result holds regardless of the export destination, with the exception of India, but again the magnitude is negligible, suggesting that increases in exports are not accompanied by increases in manufacturing employment.

To conclude, the decline in Argentina's manufacturing employment can only marginally be attributed to import competition from China and India, or from any other source for that matter. The "mighty giants" that could explain this decline are to be found somewhere else.

Annex

Data Sources

Table 9A.1 summarizes the data sources used in this chapter. The main data source for the analysis here is the UNIDO INDSTAT Database of Industrial Statistics at the 3-digit, ISIC Revision 2 nomenclature (UNIDO 2004). It comprises output, wages, employment, and value added data for 28 manufacturing sectors, covering the years 1980–2003. The database was used as an instrument in our estimations. All variables (except for the number of employed people) were converted to 1976 constant dollars using a GDP deflator retrieved from the U.S. Bureau of Economic Analysis.

In addition, we computed an initial capital stock using the ECLAC-PADI database, adjusted later using (scarce) gross fixed investment data found in the UNIDO database, applying the permanent inventory method. Trade data were gathered from UN Comtrade and then converted to

Table 9A.1 Summary of Data: Available Years and Sources

Variable	Years	Sources
Output Employment Wages Value added	1980–2003	UNIDO INDSTAT database
Capital stock	1980–2003	ECLAC-PADI / UNIDO INDSTAT
Transport cost	1991–2003	US ITC (International Trade Commission), BLS (Bureau of Labor Statistics), CEPII distance database, UN Comtrade
Imports and exports	1980–2003	UN Comtrade
Share of low-skill workers	1980, 1982, 1985, 1987, 1988, 1990–2003	INDEC (National Institute of Statistics and Census), permanent household surveys of Greater Buenos Aires

Source: Authors.

1976 constant U.S. dollars, except for transport costs, later used as an additional instrument in our econometric estimations. We calculated freight costs per mile using U.S. imports data from Argentina, gathered from U.S. International Trade Commission and Bureau of Labor Statistics sources. Then we computed total freight costs, multiplying freight costs per mile by each trading partner's distance to Argentina using the French Research Center in International Economics distance database. Finally, we applied a simple average to avoid collinearity issues with other explanatory variables.

Another variable of interest used as an instrument in our estimations is the share of unskilled workers by industrial sector. This was gathered from Argentina's INDEC (National Institute of Statistics and Census), using all permanent household surveys available for Greater Buenos Aires. Any person with unfinished secondary education or less was considered low skilled throughout the whole sample. Because we found some gaps in the data, missing years were filled with the averages of immediate past and future observations, because it is highly unlikely that sudden structural changes in the skill intensity of each industry would be encountered from one year to another.

Variable Construction

1. *Total import penetration* for sector i in year t is defined by the ratio between imports (M) from a specific partner p (in this case, the world) and apparent consumption, calculated as

$$Penetration^p_{it} = \frac{M^p_{it}}{Q_{it} - X_{it} + M_{it}},\qquad(9A.1)$$

where consumption is the expression found in the denominator. Accordingly, consumption equals output (Q) plus total imports (M) minus total exports (X) for each manufacturing sector i and year t.

2. The *total exports/consumption* ratio for sector i in year t is defined by the ratio between exports (X) from a specific partner p (in this case, the world) and consumption:

$$\frac{Export}{Consumption^p_{it}} = \frac{X^p_{it}}{Q_{it} - X_{it} + M_{it}}.\qquad(9A.2)$$

3. *Share of imports by trading partner* is the ratio of imports M from partner p and total imports for each manufacturing sector i and year t:

$$S^{I,p}_{it} = \frac{M^p_{it}}{\sum_p M^p_{it}}.\qquad(9A.3)$$

4. *Share of exports by trading partner* is the ratio of exports X to partner p and total exports for each manufacturing sector i and year t:

$$S^{X,p}_{it} = \frac{X^p_{it}}{\sum_p X^p_{it}}.\qquad(9A.4)$$

Low (high) skill is a dichotomous variable that takes a value of 1 when a particular sector i in year t has a lower (higher) share of low (high) skilled workers compared with the industry average.

Notes

1. See Hoekman and Winters (2006) for a comprehensive survey on the recent empirical evidence on the effects of trade on employment.

2. More dramatic, the manufacturing employment level in 2003 was only 47 percent of its level in 1980.

3. For a comprehensive analysis of the changes in Argentine industrial employment, see Altimir and Beccaria (1999), and Beccaria, Altimir, and Gonzalez Rozada (2003). Dussel Peters (2004) offers a comparative analysis with Mexico and Brazil.

4. See Berlinski (2004) for a detailed account of the Argentine trade liberalization process in the 1990s.

5. These indicators were calculated with data retrieved from ECLAC (2005).

6. In some sectors (miscellaneous petroleum products and fabricated metal
products) the employment contraction is mostly explained by the radical process
of privatization of Argentina's public sector in the 1990s.

7. These three economies accounted for almost 70 percent of Argentina's
imports during the period 1980–2003.

8. For instance, Tramutola, Castro, and Monat (2005) report a Grubel-Lloyd
(GL) coefficient of 0.01 for Argentina-China trade in 2003 (and similar or lower
figures for previous years). India displays similar values. The GL coefficient is
a statistical indicator of the extent of intra-industry trade with the world or a
partner within a sector or the whole manufacturing industry. The GL coefficient
ranges from 1 to 0. A GL coefficient equal to 1 means that all trade in that trade
flow is of an intra-industry nature; a GL equal to 0 means that trade is purely
interindustry. See Fontagne and Freudenberg (1997) for a complete explanation of
the GL coefficient and its variants.

9. See Leibenstein (1966) for the classical explanation of the concept of
x-efficiency.

10. A more refined version of this model can be found in Castro (forthcoming), featuring imperfect competition and explicit adjustment cost effects on
labor demand.

11. See the annex for a description of the methodology and statistical information
used for the construction of each variable.

12. Our estimates for wages and lagged employment are within the range of
estimates obtained for other countries in the region using similar specifications.
Hamermesh (2004) provides a summary of the results of the existing econometric
studies on trade and changes in the derived static and dynamic labor demand in
Latin America.

13. See Hamermesh (1993).

14. Even though it is out of this chapter's reach, we must highlight that
a new Currency Board scheme was implemented in 1991, causing the real
exchange rate to appreciate greatly, as in 1991 and 1992, thanks to lagging
inflationary pressures.

References

Altimir, O., and L. Beccaria. 1999. "El Mercado de trabajo bajo el nuevo régimen
económico en Argentina." Serie Reformas Económicas 28, CEPAL (Comisión
Económica Para América Latina y el Caribe), Buenos Aires.

Attanasio, O., P. Goldberg, and N. Pavcnik. 2003. "Trade Reforms and Wage
Inequality in Colombia." CEPR Discussion Paper 4023, Centre for Economic
Policy Research, London.

Beccaria, L., O. Altimir, and M. Gonzalez Rozada. 2003. Economia Laboral y
politicas de empleo. CEPAL (Comisión Económica Para América Latina y el
Caribe), Buenos Aires.

Berlinski, J. 2004. Los Impactos de la Política Comercial: Argentina y Brasil,
1988–1997. Buenos Aires: Siglo Veintiuno de Argentina Editores.

Casacuberta, C., G. Fachola, and N. Gandelman. 2004. "The Impact of Trade Liberalization on Employment, Capital and Productivity Dynamics: Evidence from the
Uruguayan Manufacturing Sector." Journal of Policy Reform 7 (4): 225–48.

Castro, L. (Forthcoming). "The Impacts of Trade with China and India in Argentina's Manufacturing Employment: The Role of Imperfect Competition and Adjustment Costs." Chapter 1 in *Essays on the Economic Impacts of China on Developing Countries*, DPhil in Economics dissertation, University of Sussex, Department of Economics, Falmer, U.K.

Currie, Janet, and Ann Harrison. 1997. "Sharing the Costs: The Impact of Trade Reform on Capital and Labor in Morocco." *Journal of Labor Economics* 15 (3): S44–S72.

Damill, M., R. Frenkel, and R. Maurizio. 2002. "Argentina: A Decade of Currency Board. An Analysis of Growth, Employment and Income Distribution." Employment Paper 2002/42, Employment Sector, International Labor Office, Geneva.

De Ferranti, D., G. Perry, D. Lederman, and W. Maloney. 2002. *From Natural Resources to the Knowledge Economy: Trade and Job Quality*. Washington, DC: World Bank.

Dussel Peters, E. 2004. "Efectos de la apertura comercial en el empleo y el mercado laboral de México y sus diferencias con Argentina y Brasil (1990–2003)." Documentos de Estrategias de Empleo 2004/10, Unidad de Análisis e Investigación sobre el Empleo, Departamento de Estrategias de Empleo, Oficina Internacional del Trabajo, Ginebra.

ECLAC (Economic Commission for Latin America and the Caribbean). 2005. *Statistical Yearbook for Latin America and the Caribbean 2004*. Statistics and Economic Projections Division. http://www.eclac.cl/badestat/anuario_2004/eng.htm.

Fontagne, L., and M. Freudenberg. 1997. "Intra-Industry Trade: Methodological Issues Reconsidered." CEPII Working Paper 1997-01, Centre D'Etudes Prospectives et D'Informations Internationales, Paris.

Galiani, S., and P. Sanguinetti. 2003. "The Impact of Trade Liberalization on Wage Inequality: Evidence from Argentina." *Journal of Development Economics* 72 (2): 497–513.

Greenaway, D., R. C. Hine, and P. Wright. 1999. "An Empirical Assessment of the Impact of Trade on Employment in the United Kingdom." *European Journal of Political Economy* 15 (3): 485–500.

Haltiwanger, J., A. Kugler, M. Kugler, A. Micco, and C. Pages. 2004. "Effects of Tariffs and Real Exchange Rates on Job Reallocation: Evidence from Latin America." *Policy Reform* 7 (4): 201–18.

Hamermesh, D. H. 1993. *Labor Demand*. Princeton, NJ: Princeton University Press.

———. 2004. "Labor Demand in Latin America and the Caribbean: What Does It Tell Us?" In *Law and Employment: Lessons from Latin America and the Caribbean*, ed. J. J. Heckman and C. Pagés. Chicago: The University of Chicago Press.

Hoekman, B., and L. A. Winters. 2006. "Trade and Employment: Stylized Facts and Research Findings." Policy Research Working Paper 3676, World Bank, Washington, DC.

IADB (Inter-American Development Bank). 2004. "IPES 2004: Se buscan buenos empleos: los mercados laborales de América Latina." Departamento de Investigaciones, Banco Interamericano de Desarrollo, Washington, DC.

Kiviet, J. 1995. "On Bias, Inconsistency, and Efficiency of Various Estimators in Dynamic Panel Data Models." *Journal of Econometrics* 68 (1): 53–78.

Leibenstein, H. 1966. "Allocative Efficiency and X-Efficiency." *The American Economic Review* 56 (3): 392–415.

Levinsohn, J. R. 1999. "Employment Response to International Liberalization in Chile." *Journal of International Economics* 47 (2): 321–44.

Moreira, M. M., and S. Najberg. 2000. "Trade Liberalization in Brazil: Creating or Exporting Jobs?" *Journal of Development Studies* 36 (3): 78–99.

Pagés-Serra, C., and G. Márquez. 1998. "Trade and Employment: Evidence from Latin America and the Caribbean." Working Paper 366, Inter-American Development Bank, Washington, DC.

Pessino, C., and L. Andres. 2005. "Creación y destrucción de empleos en Argentina." In *Para bien o para mal? Debate sobre el impacto de la globalización en los mercados de trabajo de América Latina,* ed. G. Márquez, Inter-American Development Bank, Washington, DC.

Revenga, A. 1997. "Employment and Wage Effects of Trade Liberalization: The Case of Mexican Manufacturing." *Journal of Labor Economics* 15 (3): S20–43.

Sánchez, G., and I. Butler. 2004. "Market Institutions, Labor Market Dynamics and Productivity in Argentina During the 1990s." *Journal of Policy Reform* 7 (4): 249–78.

Tramutola, C., L. Castro, and P. Monat. 2005. *China: Como puede la Argentina aprovechar la gran oportunidad.* Buenos Aires: Edhasa Editorial.

UN (United Nations) Comtrade. 2004. UN Comtrade Database. UNCTAD. http://comtrade.un.org/db/.

UNIDO (United Nations Industrial Development Organization). 2004. UNIDO INDSTAT3 2004. Industrial Statistics Database at the 3-digit Level of ISIC (Rev. 2), UNIDO. http://www.unido.org/index.php?id=o3531.

10

Factor Adjustment and Imports from China and India: Evidence from Uruguayan Manufacturing

*Carlos Casacuberta and Néstor Gandelman**

Introduction

Between 1984 and 2004, exports from China and India grew three times faster than world trade. Chinese and Indian exports represented 2.0 percent of world trade in 1984, 3.6 percent in 1994, and 7.6 percent by 2004. While the overall importance of these exports is still relatively small,[1] there are hardly any signs that this trend toward increased world trade is slowing. Moreover, in some industries their joint shares in world markets can be much higher. For example, Chinese and Indian exports account for 24 percent of world trade in textiles, apparel, and footwear (International Standard Industrial Classification [ISIC] 32).

The importance of China and India as a share of Uruguay's imports has grown even faster. Although the two countries jointly represented

*The authors are grateful to Marcelo Olarreaga and Guido Porto for very helpful comments on an earlier version, and Caroline Freund and Guillermo Perry for their suggestions at a World Bank seminar. The authors also gratefully acknowledge Gabriela Fachola for her work with the database and in particular for the construction of the capital series and her valuable comments. All errors are the responsibility of the authors.

less than 0.9 percent of Uruguayan imports in 1984, their share of Uruguayan imports in 2004 reached 6.3 percent (see figure 10.1).[2] And again, in some industries the share of China and India in Uruguay's imports is much higher: 17.2 percent for textiles, apparel, and footwear (ISIC 32) and 27.6 percent for manufacturing industries not elsewhere classified (ISIC 39) in 2004; see table 10.1.

The rapid growth of imports from these two unskilled-labor-abundant countries (China and India) is likely to impose factor adjustments in the Uruguayan manufacturing industry, especially for unskilled workers, but also for skilled workers and capital. The extent of these factor adjustments will depend on the size of adjustment costs, which will, in turn, determine the impact of China's and India's rapid growth on factor unemployment, and more important, economic efficiency.

The objective of this chapter is to assess the impact of growing competition from China and India on Uruguayan manufacturing firms and on their factor adjustments of unskilled labor, skilled labor, and capital. Are sectors more exposed to competition from China and India subject to larger adjustment costs? Are adjustment costs more important in the presence of surpluses, when firms need to reduce current employment levels, or in the presence of shortages, when firms need to increase their current employment levels? How does the impact of the growing presence of China and India differ for the adjustment of skilled workers, unskilled workers, and capital? The answers to these questions will shed some light on whether more attention needs to be paid to facilitating factor adjustment as exposure to Chinese and Indian competition increases, and

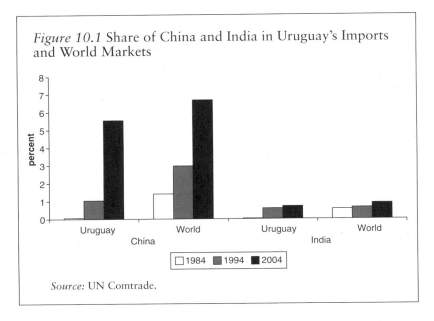

Figure 10.1 Share of China and India in Uruguay's Imports and World Markets

Source: UN Comtrade.

Table 10.1 Share of Imports from China and India by Industry, 1984, 1994, and 2004
(percent)

ISIC	Industry description	1984	1994	2004
31	Food and beverage	0.1	0.0	1.1
32	Textiles and apparel	0.9	5.8	17.2
33	Wood and furniture	0.0	0.7	4.6
34	Paper and products	0.0	0.1	0.6
35	Chemicals	0.0	0.6	7.4
36	Nonmetallic minerals	0.1	0.6	5.5
37	Basic metal industries	0.0	0.0	1.2
38	Machinery	0.2	2.0	9.8
39	Other manufactures	1.9	6.9	27.6

Source: UN Comtrade.

whether the focus should be on hiring versus firing costs, capital versus labor, skilled versus unskilled workers, and so forth.

The literature on trade and adjustment costs generally focuses on social adjustment costs measured by the impact of trade reforms on factor unemployment. Baldwin, Mutti, and Richardson (1980) and Magee (1972) measured the number of workers falling in unemployment after a trade reform in the United States, as well as the duration of their unemployment, to provide estimates of the adjustment costs associated with the unemployment spell. Their estimates suggest that social adjustment costs represented only 4 percent to 12 percent of the welfare gains associated with the reforms. Matusz and Tarr (1999) in a review of the literature confirmed that the measured net labor employment effect of trade reforms is generally small.

It is tempting to extrapolate these conclusions to the Uruguayan manufacturing sector as it faces rising competition from China and India, but there are two problems with this approach. First, most of the existing literature reviewed by Matusz and Tarr (1999) focuses on adjustment costs in the labor markets of developed countries. Regulation of factor markets in Uruguay can be significantly more stringent than in the average Organisation for Economic Co-operation and Development country. According to the World

Bank (2006), Uruguay ranks 111th out of 155 countries for ease of starting a business, and 85th for overall business climate.[3] Second, and more important, by focusing on the impact on unemployment (or employment levels) to capture factor adjustment costs, the literature assumes that firms are always at their desired levels of employment. If this is not the case, the small measured impact of trade opening on unemployment does not necessarily imply that adjustment costs are small, but rather that firms may be reluctant to fire or hire when subject to trade shocks, precisely because of the presence of very large factor-adjustment costs faced by firms (hiring and firing costs, training, loss of firm-specific human or physical capital, and the like). Putting it differently, one should expect trade reforms to have little impact on unemployment levels in the presence of large factor-adjustment costs faced by firms (or private adjustment costs in Matusz and Tarr [1999] terminology). In the extreme case, in which adjustment costs are infinite, trade would have no impact on employment, and the earlier literature would have concluded that there are no (social) adjustment costs. This may be true, but there are very large opportunity costs in production efficiency (and probably employment) from the fact that firms face infinite factor-adjustment costs.

This chapter assesses the extent to which factor adjustment is prevented by the presence of adjustment costs and whether the rising importance of China and India matters for the ease of factor adjustments among Uruguayan firms. The analysis follows Caballero, Engel, and Haltiwanger's (1997) approach to the estimation of factor adjustment functions, which was recently applied by Casacuberta and Gandelman (2006) to a panel of Uruguayan manufacturing firms. The idea is simple. Without adjustment costs, the level of factor employment chosen by firms depends only on current shocks and future expectations. In the presence of adjustment costs, it also depends on past factor employment decisions and the gap between the current level of factor employment and the "desired" level. The extent of factor adjustment is measured by the extent to which the gap between actual and desired levels gets closed. In the absence of adjustment costs, the gap would get fully closed, whereas in the presence of prohibitive adjustment costs, the gap will remain unchanged.

A key step in this methodology is the construction of this desired level of factor employment. For labor, the analysis exploits the fact that hours are easily adjustable even though the level of employment is not, and assumes that in the absence of frictions firms have optimal levels of hours per worker. This assumption has substantial empirical support and has been used by Caballero, Engel, and Haltiwanger (1997) and Casacuberta and Gandelman (2006) to estimate factor adjustment functions. For capital, it is assumed that if plants did not face capital adjustment costs, technology is such that plants would always keep the same capital-to-energy ratio (as in Casacuberta and Gandelman 2006). The optimal number of hours, energy, and materials demanded by each firm of the less flexible factors of production (skilled and unskilled workers and capital) are derived using a textbook firm maximization problem. Finally, to answer the questions raised earlier, once the adjustment functions for each factor are obtained, the analysis explores the potential heterogeneity of factor adjustment for firms exposed to different levels of import competition from China and India.

Results suggest that factor adjustment costs could be large in the Uruguayan manufacturing sector, replicating the results of Casacuberta and Gandelman (2006). Firms with a factor surplus equal to 50 percent of the firm's current level of employment would generally only cut between 10 percent and 20 percent of the shortage or surplus, depending on the factor. Similar values were obtained for firms facing a factor shortage of 100 percent. Factor adjustment also tends to show lumpiness, that is, a larger proportion of the gap between observed and desired levels of factor employment is closed in the presence of large surpluses or shortages. In the case of very large factor surpluses, adjustments are larger for skilled workers and capital, suggesting larger adjustment costs for unskilled workers. For small factor shortages and surpluses, adjustment costs faced by firms when hiring workers (search, recruiting, and training costs) are smaller than those faced when firing workers (severance payments and negative effects on the morale of other employees). Thus, low levels of volatility are desirable because they will lead to higher levels of employment. Conversely, for large shortages and surpluses, adjustment costs faced by firms when hiring workers are larger than those faced when firing workers. Thus, high levels of volatility may be costly when measured by employment.

Firms exposed to higher levels of competition from China tend to face higher adjustment costs when firing unskilled workers, but smaller adjustment costs when hiring unskilled workers. To take full advantage of the efficiency gains associated with the reallocation of workers to more productive firms, one would have to address the high costs of firing workers for firms subject to high import competition from China. For the other two factors, there is not a large difference in adjustment costs between firms exposed to Chinese competition and those that are not so exposed.

For firms exposed to high levels of competition from India, factor adjustments differ for unskilled workers, skilled workers, and capital. For skilled workers, factor adjustments are smaller when facing significant import competition from India, suggesting larger adjustment costs in both the firing and the hiring of skilled workers, at least for relatively large factor shortages. We observed for unskilled workers a pattern similar to that observed for firms subject to import competition from China (except for very large shortages or surpluses). Capital adjustment is smaller for firms subject to higher import competition from India in the presence of surpluses, suggesting higher capital adjustment costs, also.

The next section describes the empirical methodology used to estimate adjustment functions and the role played by the growing importance of China and India on factor adjustment. The third section describes the data and the fourth provides the results. The final section concludes.

Estimation of Firms' Factor Adjustment

In the traditional model without adjustment costs, firms' employment (capital) choice depends only on current shocks and future expectations.[4] In the presence of adjustment costs, the choice also depends on past employment (capital) decisions and on the gap between the actual level of employment (capital) and the *desired* level. The analysis uses the notation U^*, S^*, and K^* and U, S, and K for the desired and actual levels of unskilled labor, skilled labor, and capital, respectively.

The extent of factor adjustment is defined as the ratio of the changes in factor usage levels to the average of the factor's past and present values (which allows for entry and exit of firms), following Davis and Haltiwanger (1992), and Davis, Haltiwanger, and Schuh (1996).[5] Using the notation Δ for the rates of growth yields

$$
\begin{aligned}
\Delta U_{jt} &= \frac{U_{jt} - U_{jt-1}}{\frac{1}{2}\left(U_{jt} + U_{jt-1}\right)}, \\[2ex]
\Delta S_{jt} &= \frac{S_{jt} - S_{jt-1}}{\frac{1}{2}\left(S_{jt} + S_{jt-1}\right)}, \text{ and} \\[2ex]
\Delta K_{jt} &= \frac{K_{jt} - K_{jt-1}}{\frac{1}{2}\left(K_{jt} + K_{jt-1}\right)}.
\end{aligned}
\tag{10.1}
$$

Before a firm adjusts its factors of production, the employment (capital) shortage at time t can be defined as the difference between the desired level of employment (capital) at time t and the actual level at time $t - 1$. Paralleling the previously defined growth rates, the shortage rate is expressed as a fraction of the average of the present desired level and the past observed level. More formally, factor shortages (ZU_{jt}, ZS_{jt}, and ZK_{jt}) are given by

$$
\begin{aligned}
ZU_{jt} &= \frac{U^*_{jt} - U_{jt-1}}{\frac{1}{2}\left(U^*_{jt} + U_{jt-1}\right)}, \\[2ex]
ZS_{jt} &= \frac{S^*_{jt} - S_{jt-1}}{\frac{1}{2}\left(S^*_{jt} + S_{jt-1}\right)}, \text{ and} \\[2ex]
ZK_{jt} &= \frac{K^*_{jt} - K_{jt-1}}{\frac{1}{2}\left(K^*_{jt} + K_{jt-1}\right)}.
\end{aligned}
\tag{10.2}
$$

The adjustment function of each factor is then defined as the share of the gap that is actually closed, following Eslava et al. (2005) and Casacuberta and Gandelman (2006). Hence, adjustment functions (AU_{jt}, AS_{jt}, and AK_{jt}) are given by

$$AU_{jt} = \frac{\Delta U_{jt}}{ZU_{jt}},$$

$$AS_{jt} = \frac{\Delta S_{jt}}{ZS_{jt}}, \text{ and} \qquad (10.3)$$

$$AK_{jt} = \frac{\Delta K_{jt}}{ZK_{jt}}.$$

The next step is to characterize such adjustment functions according to the shortages in all three factors. It is relevant to consider the case in which the adjustment function in each factor is not independent of the shortages observed in the other two. The analysis follows a parametric strategy in which capital and labor shortages each are allowed to depend on their own shortage, on the other factors' shortages, and on interactive terms. The adjustment functions are not restricted to being linear and different intercepts and slopes are allowed for shortages and surpluses (or negative shortages). These variations are necessary because the causes of adjustment costs associated with creation differ from those associated with destruction. For instance, hiring new employees entails search, recruiting, and training costs while firing current employees is associated with severance payments and eventual effects on the morale of remaining employees.

Rearranging equation (10.3), and solving for the observed factor adjustment yields the basic specifications, omitting the asymmetric interactions for positive shortages. They are[6]

$$\Delta U_{jt} = ZU_{jt}\left[\lambda_0 + \lambda_1 ZS_{jt}^2 + \lambda_2 ZS_{jt}ZK_{jt} + \lambda_3 ZW_{jt}ZU_{jt} + \lambda_4 ZU_{jt}^2 \right.$$
$$\left. + \lambda_5 ZU_{jt}ZK_{jt} + \lambda_6 ZK_{jt}^2\right],$$

$$\Delta S_{jt} = ZS_{jt}\left[\nu_0 + \nu_1 ZS_{jt}^2 + \nu_2 ZS_{jt}ZK_{jt} + \nu_3 ZS_{jt}ZU_{jt} + \nu_4 ZU_{jt}^2 \right.$$
$$\left. + \nu_5 ZU_{jt}ZK_{jt} + \nu_6 ZK_{jt}^2\right], \text{ and} \qquad (10.4)$$

$$\Delta K_{jt} = ZK_{jt}\left[\kappa_0 + \kappa_1 ZS_{jt}^2 + \kappa_2 ZS_{jt}ZK_{jt} + \kappa_3 ZS_{jt}ZU_{jt} + \kappa_4 ZU_{jt}^2 \right.$$
$$\left. + \kappa_5 ZU_{jt}ZK_{jt} + \kappa_6 ZK_{jt}^2\right].$$

Casacuberta and Gandelman (2006) found that nonlinear terms and interaction terms were often significant explanatory variables for the adjustment process of Uruguayan manufacturing firms; therefore, such terms are also used here. A positive and statistically significant nonlinear coefficient would indicate that a firm with a larger gap between desired and actual factor levels adjusts more. This suggests the presence of fixed adjustment costs. These fixed costs cause the adjustment decisions to be lumpy. The significance of the interaction terms indicates that shortages of other factors are relevant to the adjustment process. A negative sign on the interaction term implies that large shortages of one factor lead to less responsiveness in the adjustment of other factors when these other factors exhibit shortages, and larger responsiveness when these other factors exhibit surpluses.

Finally, to assess whether firms subject to more import competition from China and India face different adjustment functions, the right-hand side of equation (10.4) includes an interaction of the shortage of each factor with the share of imports coming from either China or India, allowing again for different slopes for positive and negative shortages.[7] Interactions that are significant would suggest that firms subject to stronger competition from China and India face different adjustment costs. A negative sign on the coefficient suggests that the adjustment is smaller (larger adjustment costs) in the presence of shortages and larger (smaller adjustment costs) in the presence of surpluses.

To estimate equation (10.4), the analysis needs an estimation of the desired level of factor employment, that is, the level of employment in the absence of adjustment costs. These estimates are borrowed from Casacuberta and Gandelman (2006), and consist of solving the profit maximization problem faced by each firm in the absence of adjustment costs, and deriving the firm's optimal (or desired) factor demand.[8] The parameters of the production function and total factor productivity at the firm level are estimated using Levinsohn and Petrin's (2003) methodology to control for selection and simultaneity problems (that is, in a panel, the econometrician only observes surviving firms, and factor demand depends on the productivity of those firms). For a more detailed description of how desired levels of employment are obtained, see section 3 of Casacuberta and Gandelman (2006).

Data

The analysis uses annual establishment-level observations from the Manufacturing Survey conducted by the Instituto Nacional de Estadística (INE) for the period 1982–95 (INE has not made any of the surveys conducted after 1995 publicly available). The survey-sampling frame encompasses all Uruguayan manufacturing establishments with five or more employees.

The INE divided each four-digit ISIC sector into two groups. All establishments with more than 100 employees were included in the survey. The random sampling process for firms with fewer than 100 employees satisfies the criterion that the total employment of all the selected establishments must account for at least 60 percent of total employment in the sector according to the economic census (1978 or 1988).

The data for the whole period are actually obtained from two subsample sets: from 1982 until 1988, and from 1988 until 1995. In 1988, the Second National Economic Census was conducted. After that, the INE made a major methodological revision to the manufacturing survey and changed the sample of establishments. The statistical analysis in this chapter controls for the sample of origin. Firms entering the sample in 1988 behave similarly to the firms from the old sample with regard to factor adjustment.

In total, 627 different establishments are present in at least one period. There are 208 starting in 1982, of which just 185 made it to 1995. The 1988 sample is composed of 304 establishments included for the first time in that year, and 254 from the old sample, not all of which were followed in subsequent years.

To construct the establishment capital stock series, the analysis follows a methodology close to Black and Lynch (1997). The 1988 census reports information on capital stock. The analysis uses machinery capital. Overestimation of the amount of depreciation is avoided by calculating an average depreciation rate by industrial sector and year. The resulting depreciation rate is then used for all firms within each sector yearly. The value of assets sold is excluded from the measure of capital, assuming assets have been totally depreciated at that point. Thus, the equation for estimating the capital stock for years later than 1988 is

$$K_{jit} = K_{jit-1} + I_{jit} - \delta_{it}K_{jit-1},$$

(10.5)

with

$$\delta_{it}^{x} = \frac{\sum_{j} D_{jit}}{\sum_{j} K_{jit}},$$

(10.6)

where j indexes firms, i the industrial sector, and t the year. K is the capital stock, I is amount invested, δ is the depreciation rate, and D is depreciation in pesos.

For years before 1988, the equation is reversed and each year's capital is obtained by subtracting each year's investment and applying a depreciation factor. The depreciation rate before 1988 was not available and was estimated using 1988 data. A simple ordinary least squares model was run for the log of total depreciation conditional on the log of gross output, capital stock, total hours, and electricity usage. This model predicted the pre-1988 depreciation levels:

$$K_{jit-1} = \left(K_{jit} - I_{jit}\right) \times \left(\frac{1}{1-\hat{\delta}_{jit}}\right).$$

(10.7)

The share of imports from China and India were obtained at the 5-digit level of the Standard International Trade Classification from UN Comtrade, and filtered into the 4-digit level of the ISIC to match the industry description of the manufacturing survey. The evolution of the import shares is shown in table 10.1. On average, imports from China are two to eight times larger than imports from India.

Results

The results of the estimation of the adjustment functions in equation (10.4), including the interaction terms for positive shortages and the share of imports from China and India, are reported in table 10.2 for the interaction with China's import share, and table 10.3 for the interaction with India's import share.[9]

The significance and positive coefficient for the variable positive shortage for skilled and unskilled labor indicates that there are asymmetries in

Table 10.2 Estimated Parametric Adjustment Functions and China's Imports, 1982–95

Variable	Skilled labor adjustment	Unskilled labor adjustment	Capital adjustment
Constant	0.07805 [0.02292]***	0.14387 [0.02274]***	0.06312 [0.02197]***
Positive shortage[a]	0.11968 [0.03944]***	0.15604 [0.03653]***	0.03065 [0.03610]
(Shortage skilled)^2	0.18656 [0.01049]***	0.03108 [0.01208]**	−0.0037 [0.01227]
(Shortage skilled)^2 × Positive	−0.09338 [0.01721]***		
(Shortage unskilled)^2	−0.00414 [0.01430]	0.10413 [0.01209]***	−0.03261 [0.01363]**
(Shortage unskilled)^2 × Positive		−0.09534 [0.01897]***	
(Shortage capital)^2	−0.00942 [0.01102]	0.02626 [0.01001]***	0.18195 [0.00751]***
(Shortage capital)^2 × Positive			−0.14658 [0.01375]***

(continued)

Table 10.2 Estimated Parametric Adjustment Functions and
China's Imports, 1982–95 *(continued)*

Variable	Skilled labor adjustment	Unskilled labor adjustment	Capital adjustment
(Shortage skilled) × (Shortage unskilled)	−0.04244 [0.01403]***	0.01477 [0.01249]	0.02543 [0.01625]
(Shortage skilled) × (Shortage capital)	−0.02915 [0.01272]**	−0.00913 [0.01401]	−0.00383 [0.01227]
(Shortage unskilled) × (Shortage capital)	0.02288 [0.01634]	−0.05743 [0.01208]***	−0.05466 [0.01088]***
Constant × China[b]	−0.44954 [0.36462]	0.46141 [0.36578]	−0.34021 [0.46811]
Positive shortage × China	0.9443 [0.63399]	−0.06473 [0.55996]	−0.09696 [0.63970]
(Shortage skilled)^2 × China	0.16794 [0.20034]		
(Shortage skilled)^2 × Positive × China	−0.45834 [0.33521]		
(Shortage unskilled)^2 × China		−1.13997 [0.16753]***	
(Shortage unskilled)^2 × Positive × China		1.95618 [0.35506]***	
(Shortage capital)^2 × China			−0.11391 [0.30230]
(Shortage capital)^2 × Positive × China			0.84503 [0.41907]**
Observations	4,861	4,861	4,861
Number of establishments	625	625	625
R-squared	0.30	0.31	0.38

Source: Authors' calculations.

Note: Regressions include firm fixed effects. Standard errors are in brackets and are corrected for clustering within ISIC 4-digit industries.

a. Positive shortage is a dummy that takes the value 1 for all observations where there is a positive shortage.

b. China is the share of imports from China in overall imports at the ISIC 4-digit level.

*Significant at 10 percent level.

**Significant at 5 percent level.

***Significant at 1 percent level.

Table 10.3 Estimated Parametric Adjustment Functions and India's Imports, 1982–95

Variable	Skilled labor adjustment	Unskilled labor adjustment	Capital adjustment
Constant	0.08465 [0.02318]***	0.17366 [0.02346]***	0.0601 [0.02198]***
Positive shortage[a]	0.12463 [0.03971]***	0.11988 [0.03740]***	0.03279 [0.03618]
(Shortage skilled)^2	0.17895 [0.01098]***	0.03111 [0.01226]**	−0.00178 [0.01229]
(Shortage skilled)^2 × Positive	−0.09673 [0.01758]***		
(Shortage unskilled)^2	−0.00574 [0.01429]	0.06263 [0.01324]***	−0.03227 [0.01365]**
(Shortage unskilled)^2 × Positive		−0.0394 [0.01952]**	
(Shortage capital)^2	−0.01233 [0.01106]	0.02589 [0.01015]**	0.18442 [0.00748]***
(Shortage capital)^2 × Positive			−0.14435 [0.01379]***
(Shortage skilled) × (Shortage unskilled)	−0.04293 [0.01401]***	0.00781 [0.01263]	0.01954 [0.01634]
(Shortage skilled) × (Shortage capital)	−0.0263 [0.01282]**	. 0.0034 [0.01420]	0.00156 [0.01229]
(Shortage unskilled) × (Shortage capital)	0.02277 [0.01642]	−0.05985 [0.01225]***	−0.05533 [0.01086]***
Constant × India[b]	−2.00292 [1.17640]*	−2.61286 [1.18570]**	−0.05905 [1.13801]
Positive shortage × India	0.03733 [1.88626]	5.63713 [1.87061]***	−0.66106 [1.61349]
(Shortage skilled)^2 × India	2.3584 [0.96902]**		
(Shortage skilled)^2 × Positive × India	0.2264 [1.51973]		
(Shortage unskilled)^2 × India		3.43413 [0.90142]***	
(Shortage unskilled)^2 × Positive × India		−4.50428 [1.07073]***	

(continued)

Table 10.3 Estimated Parametric Adjustment Functions and India's Imports, 1982–95 *(continued)*

Variable	Skilled labor adjustment	Unskilled labor adjustment	Capital adjustment
(Shortage capital)^2 × India			−1.11407 [0.57543]*
(Shortage capital)^2 × Positive × India			1.48336 [0.78641]*
Observations	4,861	4,861	4,861
Number of establishments	625	625	625
R-squared	0.30	0.29	0.38

Source: Authors' calculations.

Note: Regressions include firm fixed effects. Standard errors are in brackets and are corrected for clustering within ISIC 4-digit industries.

a. Positive shortage is a dummy that takes the value 1 for all observations where there is a positive shortage.

b. India is the share of imports from India in overall imports at the ISIC 4-digit level.

*Significant at 10 percent level.

**Significant at 5 percent level.

***Significant at 1 percent level.

the adjustments for these two factors (for capital the coefficient is positive, but small and insignificant). The positive value for positive shortage suggests that, everything else equal, it is easier to adjust in the presence of shortages (when the desired level is larger than the actual level): hiring adjustment costs are smaller than firing costs.

However, the interaction of the dummy positive shortage with factor shortages is negative and significant, which suggests that the slope of the adjustment function is different for factor shortages than it is for surpluses. The negative coefficient suggests that the slope of the adjustment function is smaller for shortages than for surpluses. Thus, it is possible that factor adjustment is larger for very large surpluses (for example, firm exit) than for very large shortages (for example, firm entry), despite the fact that adjustment functions have a higher intercept for positive shortages (in the case of skilled and unskilled labor).

Adjustment always increases with the size of the shortage—all the coefficients on factor shortages are positive and statistically significant (except sometimes for those of other factor shortages, more on this below). This illustrates the lumpiness of the adjustment process: a larger percentage of the gap is closed in the presence of large shortages or surpluses.

Interaction terms with other factor shortages are not always significant, suggesting that other factor shortages do not necessarily affect the adjustment process. However, when they are significant, they always have a negative coefficient, suggesting that it is harder to adjust in the presence of other factor shortages (all these results are consistent with Casacuberta and Gandelman 2006).

Are Adjustment Costs Different When Facing Import Competition from China and India?

Let's start with the estimates for China in table 10.2. For skilled labor, none of the interaction terms with the import share from China are significant, suggesting that the adjustment costs associated with skilled labor for firms facing strong competition from China are not different from those of firms facing no competition from Chinese imports. The presence of China, however, is felt on the adjustment cost for unskilled workers. Both interaction terms with shortages and shortages interacted with the positive shortage dummy are significant, but they have different signs. In the case of shortages, the coefficient is negative, suggesting that the adjustment is smaller (and adjustment costs larger) for unskilled workers in the presence of surpluses. However, when interacted with the positive shortage dummy the coefficient is positive, and larger than the coefficient on shortages, suggesting that in the presence of positive shortages the adjustment is larger: it is easier to hire unskilled workers. For capital, only the interaction with the positive shortage dummy is significant. The coefficient is positive, suggesting that firms subject to strong competition from China find it easier to adjust in the presence of capital shortages.

Note that the analysis does not imply causality here because it is possible that smaller adjustment costs allow for higher import penetration from China. However, one may wonder why the adjustment costs are smaller in the presence of shortages and larger in the presence of surpluses when firms are exposed to import competition from China. One potential explanation lies in the perceived volatility of Chinese imports. If Chinese imports are perceived to be more volatile than imports from other regions (because China is a new player in world markets, is a relatively more distant trading partner, and has large cultural and business practices differences), then one would expect firms to be more reluctant to fire workers and more willing to hire workers when exposed to more import competition from China than from more established and better-understood trading partners. The data confirm this with coefficients of variation for imports from China and India that are each twice the coefficient of variation of imports from the rest of the world.

Results for India in table 10.3 suggest that the adjustment of all factors varies in the presence of stronger import competition from India. Because a number of interactions with India's import shares are significant, and have different signs, it is difficult to assess the direction of this heterogeneity by simply looking at the sign of the coefficients. More generally, the statistical significance of the coefficients does not necessarily imply that the differences in adjustment are economically meaningful.

To assess how important these differences in adjustment are in the presence of import competition from China and India, the analysis simulates the predicted adjustment using the coefficients reported in tables 10.2 and 10.3 for different levels of factor shortages and surpluses, as well as for different levels of import competition from either China or India. Because interaction terms with other factor shortages are sometimes insignificant, for the purpose of this exercise they are all set to zero. The predicted adjustment is then plotted for different levels of factor shortages in figures 10.2 through 10.4 for China and figures 10.5 through 10.7 for India.

In figures 10.2 through 10.7, negative shortages (surpluses) in the horizontal axis indicate that the past level of factor employment is above the desired level. Hence, to close this gap the firm needs to reduce the employment level of this factor (fire some of this factor). For positive shortages, past levels of factor employment are below the desired level and to close the gap the firm needs to increase the employment of this

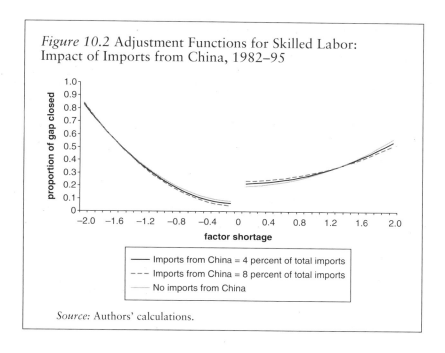

Figure 10.2 Adjustment Functions for Skilled Labor: Impact of Imports from China, 1982–95

Source: Authors' calculations.

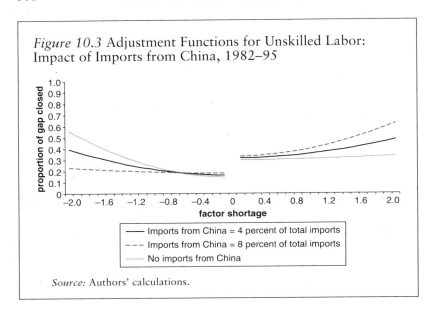

Figure 10.3 Adjustment Functions for Unskilled Labor: Impact of Imports from China, 1982–95

Source: Authors' calculations.

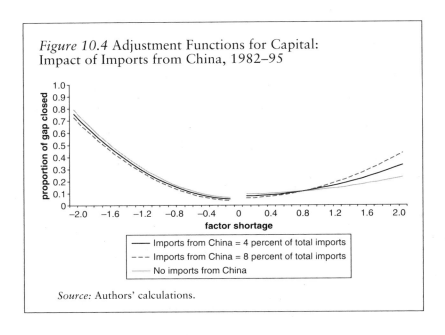

Figure 10.4 Adjustment Functions for Capital: Impact of Imports from China, 1982–95

Source: Authors' calculations.

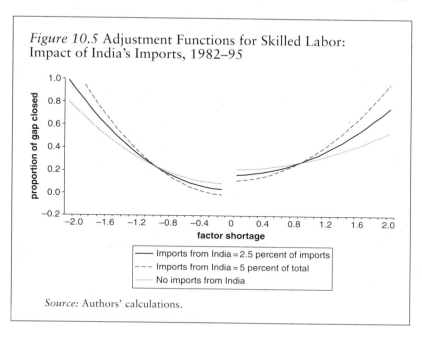

Figure 10.5 Adjustment Functions for Skilled Labor:
Impact of India's Imports, 1982–95

Source: Authors' calculations.

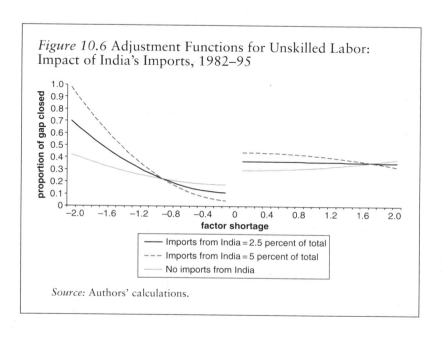

Figure 10.6 Adjustment Functions for Unskilled Labor:
Impact of India's Imports, 1982–95

Source: Authors' calculations.

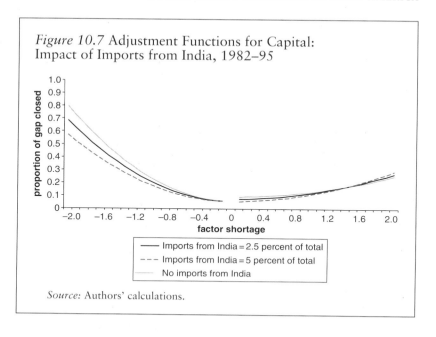

Figure 10.7 Adjustment Functions for Capital: Impact of Imports from India, 1982–95

Source: Authors' calculations.

factor (hire some of this factor). As argued when discussing equation (10.2), factor shortages vary between –2 (exit of the firm) and +2 (entry of a new firm). However, reasonable values of factor shortage or surplus are between –0.66 and 0.66. This corresponds to a factor shortage of 100 percent (the firm's desired level of factor employment is twice its current level) and a factor surplus of 50 percent (the firm's desired level of factor employment is half its current level). The vertical axis measures the proportion of the gap that was closed, and it varies between 0 and 1.

Figure 10.2 confirms that for firms subject to strong competition from China, the adjustment of skilled labor is not different from that of firms not subject to import competition from China. Figure 10.3 also confirms that the adjustment cost of unskilled workers faced by firms subject to competition from Chinese imports is larger in the presence of unskilled labor surpluses, but smaller in the presence of large unskilled labor shortages. Figure 10.4 confirms that for capital, the adjustment cost in the presence of shortages is smaller for firms subject to import competition from China.

Figures 10.5 through 10.7 confirm that there are important differences in the adjustment costs faced by firms subject to import competition from India. Figure 10.5 suggests that for relatively small shortages or surpluses (between –0.66 and 0.66) of skilled labor, the adjustment cost is larger for firms facing higher competition from India. For unskilled workers, we

observe a similar pattern (at least for relatively small shortages and surpluses) to the pattern observed for unskilled labor when firms are exposed
to import competition from China (see figures 10.3 and 10.6). For capital,
adjustment costs seem to be larger in the presence of large surpluses (see
figure 10.7).

How Large Are Factor Adjustment Costs?

The previous subsection showed that adjustment costs tend to be larger
for firms subject to import competition from China and India, except
for unskilled workers in the presence of surpluses. For other factors,
adjustment costs are either unchanged when subject to import competition
from China and India, or adjustment costs tend to be larger.

Moreover, the size of these adjustment costs can be quite large. For
example, a firm that would like to double the level of all factors (factor
shortage = 0.66; see equation [10.2]) would actually increase its level of
skilled workers by only 20 percent, its level of unskilled workers by 30
percent, and its level of capital by 10 percent (see figures 10.2 through
10.7 for values of factor shortage = 0.66). This suggests strong adjustment
costs on the hiring side for Uruguayan manufacturing firms. Similarly, a
firm that would like to cut all levels of factor employment by half (factor shortage = −0.66) would reduce its level of skilled workers by only
5 percent (10 percent of 50 percent), its level of unskilled workers by
10 percent (20 percent of 50 percent) and its level of capital by 5 percent
(10 percent of 50 percent); see figures 10.2 through 10.7 at factor shortage equal to −0.66. Again, this signals some important adjustment costs,
which would have important consequences on unemployment levels and
economic efficiency.

Finally, a quick look at figures 10.2 and 10.3 for China and 10.5 and
10.6 for India confirms, as suggested earlier, that the intercepts of adjustment functions are higher for both unskilled and skilled workers, but the
slopes tend to be smaller than in the absence of import competition from
China and India. Thus, for very small shortages and surpluses, the overall
adjustment is larger on the creation side (positive shortages), but for very
large shortages and surpluses the adjustment is smaller on the destruction
side (surpluses).

These results have some interesting implications. In the presence
of low volatility of economic activity (with a mean of zero to make
the argument simpler), the fact that adjustment costs are larger on the
destruction side (firing workers) than on the creation side (hiring workers) suggests that the overall impact of low volatility in employment
is positive. It allows more efficient firms to expand rapidly while less
efficient firms are more reluctant to fire their workers. However, in the
presence of high volatility, the opposite is true and the adjustment cost
is smaller on the destruction side (firing workers) than on the creation

side (hiring workers). The impact on employment is, therefore, likely to be negative.

With regard to policy targeting, the fact that adjustment costs are larger on the destruction side (firing workers) for small shortages and surpluses, but larger on the creation side for very large shortages and surpluses (firm entry and exit), also has some interesting implications. Policies should concentrate on reducing the adjustment costs faced by firms when firing workers (for example, severance payments and mobility of pension schemes), and on the adjustment costs faced by firms trying to enter the market. According to World Bank (2006), among other procedures, Uruguayan firms need to deposit the equivalent of 151 percent of the national income per capita to obtain a business registration number. This is six times higher than the average level in Latin America and the Caribbean, and this ranks Uruguay 116th out of 155 countries for ease of starting a business.

Conclusion

Adjustment costs faced by capital, skilled labor, and unskilled labor are nontrivial in the Uruguayan manufacturing sector; this has consequences for factor unemployment and economic efficiency. For skilled and unskilled labor, adjustment costs tend to be larger in the presence of small surpluses (when the firms need to fire workers) than in the presence of small shortages (when the firm needs to hire workers). However, for large surpluses and shortages (for example, exit and entry of firms), adjustment costs are larger on the entry side. These results suggest that to introduce more efficiency and generate more employment in the Uruguayan manufacturing sector, policy makers should focus on reducing adjustment costs for those firms that would like to fire workers (severance payments, mobility of pension schemes, and the like) and those that would like to enter the market (reduction of the number of bureaucratic procedures required, the number of days it takes, and the cost of the business registration license).

These asymmetries in adjustment costs for small versus large shortages and surpluses have some interesting implications for employment. In the presence of low levels of volatility, the economy is likely to experience reductions in unemployment, whereas for high levels of volatility the economy is likely to experience increases in unemployment. This underscores the importance of credible and stable economic policies that do not allow for high economic volatility.

The growing importance of China and India in world markets, and in the Uruguayan manufacturing sector, seems to be increasing the need for addressing the adjustment costs of all factors in the presence of factor surpluses, but in particular for unskilled labor. Adjustment costs faced by firms subject to strong Chinese and Indian competition seem to be particularly large for firms that would like to reduce their levels of unskilled labor. For firms experiencing factor shortages, however, adjustment costs seem to be smaller when subject to import competition from China and India (except perhaps for small shortages of skilled labor when subject to import competition from India).

What can explain the asymmetry between shortages and surpluses when examining the impact of the growing importance of China and India on factor adjustment costs? One potential explanation is in the perceived volatility of Chinese and Indian imports. If Chinese and Indian imports are perceived to be more volatile than imports from other regions (because China and India are new players in world markets, are relatively more distant trading partners, and have large cultural and business practices differences), then one would expect firms to be more reluctant to fire workers and more willing to hire workers when exposed to more import competition from China than from more established and better-understood trading partners. The data confirm this, with a coefficient of variation for imports from China and India that is twice the coefficient of variation of imports from the rest of the world. Addressing the causes of this volatility (which can sometimes be policy induced, for example, antidumping duties, nontariff barriers, and the like) is likely to help reduce adjustment costs in the presence of surpluses. An alternative explanation is in the degree of substitution between domestically produced goods and Chinese and Indian goods. Other studies (Facchini et al. 2007) have found that in Latin America, and the Southern Cone in particular, this elasticity tends to be higher than the elasticity of substitution between domestically produced goods and imports from the rest of the world. If this were the case, the increase in import penetration from China and India could be signaling new market opportunities, and could increase the amount of information available for domestic firms regarding domestic market potential. This information would reduce the adjustment costs for firms experiencing factor shortages. Similarly, for firms experiencing factor surpluses, the information regarding growing domestic market potential is likely to make such firms more reluctant to reduce their factor employment in the presence of adjustment costs on the destruction side.

Notes

1. Note that China's share is seven times larger than India's share.
2. This was partly helped by the reestablishment of diplomatic relationships between Uruguay and China in 1988.
3. The presence of a relatively large informal sector, which represents 50 percent of gross domestic product, suggests that these regulatory barriers may be easily overcome in the informal sector.

4. This section closely follows Casacuberta and Gandelman (2006).

5. A feature of these growth rates is that they are bound between −2 and 2. They take the value −2 when the firm exits and the value 2 when the firm enters. There is a monotonic relationship between the rates of growth so defined and the usual ones. Let $G_{jt} = (x_{jt} - x_{jt-1})/(1/2)(x_{jt} + x_{jt-1})$ and $g_{jt} = (x_{jt} - x_{jt-1})/x_{jt-1}$, and it can be shown that they are both related by $g_{jt} = 2G_{jt}/(2 - G_{jt})$.

6. Note that factor shortages are squared for interpretation purposes. For positive shortages, an increase in this variable indicates that the (positive) factor shortage is increasing, whereas for negative shortages, an increase in this variable indicates that the (negative) factor shortage is declining.

7. This is identical to the approach followed by Eslava et al. (2005) to examine the impact of Colombian deregulation on factor adjustment, and Casacuberta and Gandelman (2006) to examine the impact of trade openness on factor adjustment in Uruguay.

8. This assumes separability between the production function and the factor adjustment functions.

9. We also run it with the interaction of the joint China and India import share. Results were statistically not different from the ones reported in table 10.2 for China, probably because of the relative larger size of Chinese imports.

References and Other Resources

Baldwin, Robert E., John Mutti, and J. David Richardson. 1980. "Welfare Effects on the United States of a Significant Multilateral Tariff Reduction." *Journal of International Economics* 10 (3): 405–23.

Black, S., and L. Lynch. 1997. "How to Compete: The Impact of Workplace Practices and Information Technology on Productivity." NBER Working Paper 6120, National Bureau of Economic Research, Cambridge, MA.

Caballero, R., E. Engel, and J. Haltiwanger. 1997. "Aggregate Employment Dynamics: Building from Microeconomic Evidence." *American Economic Review* 87 (1): 115–37.

Casacuberta, Carlos, Gabriela Fachola, and Néstor Gandelman. 2004. "The Impact of Trade Liberalization on Employment, Capital and Productivity Dynamics: Evidence from the Uruguayan Manufacturing Sector." Research Department Working Paper R-479, Inter-American Development Bank, Washington, DC.

Casacuberta, Carlos, and Néstor Gandelman. 2006. "Protection, Openness and Factor Adjustment: Evidence from the Manufacturing Sector in Uruguay." Policy Research Working Paper 3891, World Bank, Washington, DC.

Davis, S., and J. Haltiwanger. 1992. "Gross Job Creation, Gross Job Destruction, and Employment Reallocation." *Quarterly Journal of Economics* 107 (3): 819–63.

Davis, S., J. Haltiwanger, and S. Schuh. 1996. *Job Creation and Destruction.* Cambridge, MA: MIT Press.

Eslava, M., J. Haltiwanger, A. Kugler, and M. Kugler. 2005. "Factor Adjustment after Deregulation: Panel Evidence from Colombian Plants." NBER Working Paper 11656, National Bureau of Economic Research, Cambridge, MA.

Facchini, Giovanni, Marcelo Olarreaga, Peri Silva, and Gerald Willmann. 2007. "Substitutability and Protectionism: Latin America's Trade Policy and Imports from China and India." CESifo Working Paper 1947, CESifo, Munich.

Levinsohn, J., and A. Petrin. 2003. "Estimating Production Functions Using Inputs to Control for Unobservables." *Review of Economic Studies* 70 (2): 317–41.

Magee, Stephen. 1972. "The Welfare Effects of Restrictions on US Trade." *Brookings Papers on Economic Activity* 3: 645–701.

Matusz, Steven, and David Tarr. 1999. "Adjusting to Trade Policy Reform." Policy Research Working Paper 2142, World Bank, Washington, DC.

World Bank. 2006. *Doing Business.* Washington, DC: World Bank.

Index

Boxes, figures, notes, and tables are denoted by b, f, n, and t.

A

agriculture
  export variety from China, 254,
    255t, 256
  export variety from Mexico,
    252t, 253
  NAFTA and export variety,
    253, 254f
  nontariff barriers (NTBs) in
    China on, 256, 257f
  tariff between U.S. and
    China, 257
  tariff reduction between U.S.
    and Mexico, 252t,
    253, 254
Altimir, O., 266
Andean countries
  See also specific countries
  intra-industry trade (IIT) with
    China and India, 55,
    56f, 66
  output correlation with China,
    83, 90–91f
  trend in trade with China, 54, 77
  trend in trade with India, 79
Anderson, James E., 146, 148
Andres, L., 266
antidumping cases against China,
    28, 33n28

apparel industry. *See* textiles and
    apparel industry
Argentina
  antidumping cases against
    China, 28
  business, professional, and
    technical services,
    growth in (1994–
    2004), 227, 230f
  Chinese growth's effect
    on commodity
    exports, 147
  competition with Argentina
    in manufacturing
    sector, 267
  Currency Board scheme and
    exchange rate, 288n14
  decomposing manufacturing
    export growth in,
    161–63, 162t
  counterfactual estimation of
    growth if U.S. economy
    had not decelerated,
    164t, 165
  economic crisis in, 166
  estimates of sectoral export-
    supply capacities in, 153
  comparison with China,
    156, 159–60f, 161,
    171–72t, 173f

315